CREDIT MANAGEMENT
PRINCIPLES AND PRACTICES

National Association of Credit Management

CREDIT MANAGEMENT
PRINCIPLES AND PRACTICES

Fourth Edition Revised

By

Dr. Charles L. Gahala, CCE, CICP
Finance Professor Emeritus
Benedictine University
Lisle, Illinois

National Association of Credit Management

© 2017 by the National Association of Credit Management.
All Rights Reserved.

First Edition: 1994
Second Edition: 1996
Third Edition: 2003
Fourth Edition: 2011
Fourth Edition Revised: 2013
Printed in the United States of America

10 9 8 7 6 5 4 3 2 1

ISBN10: 1-888505-37-0
ISBN13: 978-1888505-37-5

Library of Congress Registration Number: **TXu 1-861-722**

No part of this book may be reproduced, stored in a retrieval system or transmitted in any form or by any means, electronic. mechanical, photocopying, recording, scanning or otherwise, without prior written permission of the copyright owner. Requests to the Publisher for permission should be addressed to NACM, Publications Department, 8840 Columbia 100 Parkway, Columbia, MD 21045-2158.

This publication is designed to provide accurate and authoritative information in regard to the subject matter covered. It is sold with the understanding that the publisher is not engaged in rendering legal, accounting or other professional services. If legal advice or other expert assistance is required, the services of a competent professional person should be sought.

To my wife, Jan Gahala, who has provided the most important support for the completion of the fourth edition of this book. Her encouragement and editorial contributions have been most appreciated. And to our sons, Eric and Carl, who have grown into men that we can both be proud of.

Table of Contents

PART I: AN INTRODUCTION TO BUSINESS CREDIT MANAGEMENT

Chapter 1	**The Changing Nature of Credit Management**	**3**
	The Credit Management Profession	4
	Removing the Credit Management Mystique	7
	Additional Research Examining the Tasks Performed by Business Credit Managers	10
	National Association of Credit Management	13
	Chapter 1: Follow-Up	16
	Appendix: A List of 70 Business Credit Tasks	20
Chapter 2	**Organizing the Credit Function**	**25**
	Benchmarking	26
	Developing Job Specifications for the Credit Function	31
	Motivating Credit Personnel	34
	Business Process Outsourcing	37
	Automating Credit Activities	38
	Chapter 2: Follow-Up	41
Chapter 3	**Credit Management in a Global Marketplace**	**47**
	A Change in World Growth	48
	Risk in a Global Marketplace	49
	Foreign Company Analysis	56
	Export Letters of Credit	58
	Export Credit Insurance	60
	Foreign Exchange Risk	61
	Conclusions	66
	Chapter 3: Follow-Up	67

vii

Part II: Credit Policy and the Extension of Credit

Chapter 4	**Managing Credit Policy**	**75**
	Strategic Planning and the Role of the Credit Function	76
	Four Key Credit Department Objectives	77
	Establishing Credit Policy	80
	Signs That Indicate a Need to Review Credit Policy	81
	Receivables Portfolio Analysis	82
	Economic Value Added	83
	The Credit Department Policy Audit	85
	Policy and Procedures Used to Establish Bad Debt Reserves and Write-Offs	88
	Chapter 4: Follow-Up	90
Chapter 5	**Legislation and Regulations Pertinent to Business Credit Decision-Making**	**95**
	The Dodd-Frank Wall Street Reform and Consumer Protection Act of 2010	96
	An Overview of Antitrust Regulation	99
	The Sarbanes-Oxley Act	101
	The Red Flags Rules	102
	Consumer Credit Legislation Pertinent to Business Credit	103
	Chapter 5: Follow-Up	116
Chapter 6	**Conducting the Credit Investigation**	**123**
	The Five Cs of Credit	124
	Processing Applications for Credit	125
	Analyzing Business Credit Information	129
	An Analysis of Credit Scoring Systems	135
	Monitoring Existing Accounts	143
	Chapter 6: Follow-Up	144
	Appendix: Sample Credit Application	149
Chapter 7	**Business Credit Reporting**	**151**
	Business Credit Reporting Services	152
	Consumer Credit Reports	161
	Consumer Credit Scoring	162
	Chapter 7: Follow-Up	164

Preface

Many years have passed since I began work on the first edition of *Credit Management: Principles and Practices*. The purpose of the first edition was to bridge the gap between academic theory and credit practice. The gap between academic theory and practice needs to be addressed through a book that is devoted specifically to the focused needs of business credit managers.

This book is intended for use both in college-level finance courses in credit management and by practicing credit executives as a training tool and reference. Although the material in the text is presented sequentially, college instructors may assign almost any chapter as a self-contained unit. The book can easily be used to customize course lengths. This book includes the basic tenets of knowledge in credit management covered in earlier editions. However, with the support from leading experts in the credit profession, the book has been expanded to focus upon the significant changes that have been occurring.

The theory and practice of credit management is dynamic. The ability to cover evolving issues and problems in one text has become virtually impossible. Therefore, instructors are encouraged to supplement this text with readings. The National Association of Credit Management (NACM) Credit Learning Center can be used as an excellent resource for supplemental topics.

Each chapter in this book has been designed as a teaching-learning system. The objectives for each chapter are presented early in the chapter. An end-of-chapter recap of important concepts reinforces key material. There are review questions at the end of chapters that can be used by credit practitioners to prepare for the CBA, CBF and CCE exams in credit management. One of the most important tools in the fourth edition is the Credit Management Online section at the end of each chapter. Finally, at the close of each chapter there is a summary of related readings that can be used to delve more in-depth into a particular subject.

Part I of this textbook is designed to provide readers with an introduction to credit management. Chapter 1 introduces readers to the credit profession by examining tasks performed by credit managers and the role of NACM. Chapter 2 incorporates management skills into the credit function. Planning, organizing and evaluating the credit function are the focal points contained in Chapter 2. Chapter 3 adds an international dimension to the credit function by examining the role of credit in a global marketplace.

Part II contains four chapters that focus on credit policy and the extension of credit. Chapter 4 provides a rationale for credit policy and specific credit-related policy focal points. Chapter 5 explains the importance of credit-related government legislation and how legislation influences credit decisions. Chapter 6 identifies sources of credit information and explains how to utilize those sources. An overview of business credit reporting services is presented in Chapter 7.

Part III consists of three chapters containing information essential to collections and credit analysis. Chapter 8 provides a systemic approach to using alternative collection methods. Chapter 9 provides a primer on financial statement analysis; focal points examined include both common-size analysis and ratio analysis. Chapter 10 shows how cash flow analysis can be useful—in particular, the importance of cash flow analysis for highly leveraged transactions.

Part IV is the final section of the textbook. Two highly technical chapters develop subjects of particular interest to business credit personnel. Chapter 11 focuses on the development of secured credit arrangements. Chapter 12 discusses the topics of bankruptcy and reorganization.

Each of the 12 chapters in this text could easily be expanded into a specialized full course. Readers who have an interest in a specialized component of a chapter are encouraged to refer to the references and websites listed at the end of each chapter. The chapters provide a sound foundation in each topic. Because chapters are self-contained, rearranging the sequence for studying material should not present the reader with any particular problems.

A debt of gratitude goes out to the individuals who have assisted with the preparation of this text. In particular, the services of Caroline Zimmerman, Laura Redcay and Ainslee Sadler in the NACM Communications Department were most helpful. Likewise, Bruce Nathan, Esq., Scott Cargill, Esq. and David Banker, Esq. of Lowenstein Sandler LLP provided an incisive and generous review of Chapters 5 and 12 and Wanda Borges, Esq. of Borges & Associates who reviewed Chapter 12 in 2013.

A high degree of professionalism was exhibited by the following credit professionals and academics, who need to be recognized:

Garry Abezetian • Kurt Albright • Walter (Buddy) Baker • Lowell Belk • Thom Beaupre • Rich Bellis • Paul Bernardoni • Bruce Bialy • Wanda Borges • Paul Brunner • Tom Burke • Stacy Cashman • Linda Chernault • Rita Childers • Dr. Ron Chung • Dr. John Cicero • Norm Cowie • Dr. Jane Crabtree • Bill Dearhammer • Frank DuBrava • Dr. John Eber • Larry Engels • Doug Ernst • John Fahey • Susan Fattore • Ross Fisher • Annette Flemming • Joan Fowler • Marge Frens • Don Henschel • Dick Gamble • Dr. Sandra Gill • O.D. Glauss • Ron Gordon • Tom Gordon • Gary Grissom • Paul Grossart • Hank Haegerich • Mark Hanley • Robert Healy • Joe Jackson • John Jaeger • Dr. Dan Jennings • Vickie Jobst • Dr. Nona Jones • Jeep Joyner • Dave Judeika • Ruby Kerr • George Kokkines • John Korun • Phil Lattanzio • Bill Lovitt • Carl Lowery • Jeff Madura • Dr. Maury Margotta • Jim Meehan • Ron Mefford • Chuck Meister • Fred Morris • Bill Mowers • Bruce Nathan • Christopher Nelson • Larry O'Brien • Madeline Parisi • Dick Pearson • Nino Pellettieri • Dick Powers • Rocci Primavera • Dr. Larry Quick • Jim Rimmer • Curt Rothlisberger • Marty Scaminaci • Robin Schauseil • Henry Schmerler • Jim Schmidt • Stephan Seko • Stan Senalik • Don Slaby • Michael Snouffer • Ray Sojka • Dr. David Sonnenberger • Dave Spitler • Gordon Stagge • Rick Stevens • Ray Stober • Charles Tatelbaum • Lee Teigen • Bob Thompson • Bob Togtman • Jim Varney • Bob Vodraska • Marty Volpe • Thom Walthour • Jesse Ward • Bill Weilemann • Tom Wuich

Part I

An Introduction to Business Credit Management

Chapter 1

THE CHANGING NATURE OF CREDIT MANAGEMENT

"In the past, individuals have come into the credit field without previous preparation. Their entrance into this line was frequently not a matter of deliberate choice and planning. The specialized knowledge essential for effective credit management was learned through experience that was precluded by an attendant waste of time."[1]

Dr. Theodore N. Beckman
Ohio State University, 1924

The credit profession is both exacting and exciting. Almost 100 years have elapsed since Dr. Theodore Beckman authored the above quote in one of the earliest credit management textbooks. During this period, thousands of individuals have entered the credit field without adequate preparation. The attendant needs of today's credit professionals coupled with the rapid pace of change suggests that the need for a sound approach to learning credit-related skills is more important than ever.

The complexity of tasks that are often performed by credit managers demand a mastery of skills. Yet the skills essential to manage credit are usually acquired through on-the-job experience. This textbook will help to accelerate the mastery of skills that are essential to manage credit effectively.

Credit management activities are dynamic in nature. The role of the credit manager goes well beyond the routine task of collecting money. The complexity of tasks, combined with the wide range of required skills, make credit management one of the most challenging of all business occupations.

The **Key Learning Objective** in Chapter 1 is to provide you with an overview of credit management. After reading this chapter, you should be able to master specific additional **Learning Objectives** that include:

1. Recognize the status of the credit manager as a professional.

---

[1] Theodore N. Beckman, *Credits and Collections in Theory and Practice* (New York: McGraw-Hill Book Company Inc., 1924), vii.

2. Provide a job specification for a credit manager.
3. Identify tasks essential for initial employment and tasks essential for job advancement in the credit profession.
4. Examine current research relating to the performance of business credit tasks.
5. Consider some key changes that are shaping the credit profession.
6. Examine the role of the National Association of Credit Management in maintaining the high status of the credit profession.

THE CREDIT MANAGEMENT PROFESSION

The professional status of the credit manager has evolved over time. Accountants, attorneys, ministers and physicians each qualify as professionals. In order to qualify for the status of professional, an occupation should satisfy certain criteria that can be used to evaluate the occupation.

Estelle Popham[2] developed the specific criteria that can be used to evaluate an occupation as a profession. These criteria are effective in measuring the professional status of any occupation and are useful to recognize the status of the credit manager as a professional.

1. *A Strong Professional Association.* Accountants receive recognition through the American Institute of Certified Public Accountants; attorneys are acknowledged as professionals through their membership in the American Bar Association; doctors maintain professional status through membership in the American Medical Association. Credit managers have the commitment of the National Association of Credit Management (NACM) to advance the established goals of credit professionals. NACM provides the support of a strong professional association, which is essential to elevate the status of credit manager to professional.

2. *Code of Ethics.* NACM's "Canons of Business Credit Ethics" are listed in Table 1-1. These principles govern the activities of business credit grantors. Credit is based upon trust. The credit occupation mandates the application of high ethical standards. The attitude and conduct of credit practitioners is what distinguishes individual credit managers as professionals.

---

[2] Estelle L. Popham, Adele Frisbie Schrag, and Wanda Blockhus, *A Teaching-Learning System for Business Education* (New York: McGraw-Hill, 1975).

1: The Changing Nature of Credit Management

TABLE 1-1   NACM's Canons of Business Credit Ethics

The cornerstone of the global business economy is the extension of commercial credit. As such, business credit executives, as the guardians of commercial receivables, play the vital and critical role of ensuring the flow of commercial goods and services that support world commerce.

In fulfilling their professional duties, business credit professionals pledge to conduct their duties within the constraints of law and to not maliciously injure the reputation of others. Further, business credit professionals pledge themselves to the highest professional standards and principles and to guarding and securing, in confidence, information obtained for the sole purpose of analyzing and extending commercial credit.

Credit professionals pledge to:

- Adhere to the highest standards of integrity, trust, fairness and personal and professional behavior in all business dealings.
- Negotiate verbal or written credit agreements, contracts, assignments and/or transfers with honesty, fairness and due diligence to and for the benefit of all parties.
- Render reasonable assistance, cooperating with impartiality and without bias or prejudice, to debtors, third parties and other credit professionals.
- Exchange appropriate, historical and current factual information to support the process of independent credit decisioning.
- Exercise due diligence as required to prevent unlawful or improper disclosure to third parties.
- Disclose any potential conflict in all business dealings.

Further, credit professionals acknowledge the importance of and shall promote the benefits of continued improvement of their knowledge, skills and expertise in business credit. The pursuit of knowledge will support the strategic advancement of the commercial credit function, as it leads businesses to profitability and growth.

Source: National Association of Credit Management, Columbia, MD, 2017

---

3. *Autonomy within the Profession.* Autonomy, in a self-governing context, can be used to recognize the credit manager as a professional. A good example of the autonomous nature of the credit profession can be perceived through industry credit groups. As a member of an industry credit group, a credit executive must have factual credit and financial information available to share with other group members. Moreover, reciprocity is essential to the nature of openly sharing factual payment information with other creditors. Therefore, credit practitioners set standards for conduct within their profession. NACM members elect fellow members as officers at both the national and affiliate levels. This election process contributes to the autonomous nature of the credit profession.

4. ***Contribution to the Welfare of Society.*** When credit executives are efficient in allocating credit to customers, they benefit their employers and society. Efficient credit decisions make products more readily available to users. Moreover, product pricing can be held down when carrying costs and bad debts are under the control of credit professionals. Credit executives also help to prevent fraud through credit investigations that deny repeat abusers the privilege of obtaining new credit.

5. ***A Controlled Admission Procedure.*** The admission of an individual into a credit-related position varies widely among employers. The credit function in a particular company also can vary widely. The admission of an individual into an occupation or the use of the title "credit manager" does not elevate one to the status of credit professional. The demonstration of competency for credit-related tasks is essential in order to elevate the status of credit manager to that of professional.

    NACM has a certification program that comprises six designations used to evidence competency for credit-related skills. The CCRA^{SM}, CBA^{SM}, CBF^{SM} and CCE® designations are geared toward most credit personnel. For the international credit manager, the CICP^{SM} and ICCE^{SM} are available through NACM-FCIB. These designations will be explained later in this chapter. The designations can be useful to demonstrate evidence of competency in the credit profession. However, the lack of an NACM designation does not imply that a credit manager is not a professional.

6. ***An Existing Body of Knowledge and Career-Long Learning.*** Credit management skills unfold gradually. Most credit practitioners acknowledge that their real education in credit management came through the college of hard knocks. Over time, credit practitioners recognize the application of technical skills to particular situations. Certain situations become somewhat repetitive; these situations constitute the common body of knowledge. For example, when should a credit manager ask for collateral?

    Other situations require the credit manager to adapt to change; these situations require career-long learning. For example, on July 21, 2010, the U.S. government announced the Dodd-Frank Wall Street Reform and Consumer Protection Act which was signed into law. Dodd-Frank was enacted in response to a financial crisis. This is the most significant overhaul of financial regulation since the Great Depression. How does Dodd-Frank inpact upon credit decisions? How has the law been changed since it was first enacted? There are continuing education requirements not only for the CCE in the credit profession but also for members of virtually any profession. Count on a need for career-long learning in order to keep up with changes that include rapid advances in technology, improved communications and a globalization of world trade.

What makes a credit manager a professional? The six criteria identified by Popham provide a starting point for all credit practitioners to recognize. However, one final criterion is that the conduct of each individual credit manager should embody the highest level of professional conduct possible on an ongoing basis. In essence, a careful self-evaluation of the status of an individual credit manager as a professional should be made on a regular basis.

REMOVING THE CREDIT MANAGEMENT MYSTIQUE

There is often a mystique associated with the activities that relate to credit management. Academics have historically neglected to encourage students to enter the credit field. Most high school and college students are not aware that careers exist in business credit. Human resource managers may not know the details for qualifications essential when recruiting credit personnel. Even credit practitioners may not be fully aware of the wide range of activities that the credit department is capable of performing.

Dr. Edward K. Strong, while director of vocational interest at Stanford University, designed a test to measure vocational interest. This type of test does not measure specific abilities nor does it measure intelligence. The test is intended to measure the likelihood of enjoying a particular occupation as a career choice.

Strong analyzed 452 credit managers and determined that credit managers tend to have general business interests instead of narrow interests in a particular area of business. His research suggests that, in general, credit managers are not as interested in writing the programs to use a computer as they are interested in using the computer to make decisions. Strong determined that the interests of credit managers are most similar to the interests of operations managers, accountants and human resource managers. The interests of credit managers are least similar to the interests of mathematicians, architects, carpenters and ministers.[3]

---

[3] Edward K. Strong, *Credit Management and the Strong Vocational Interest Test* (New York: Credit Research Foundation and NACM, n.d.), 14.

TABLE 1-2   Job Specifications for Credit Managers
Based on Research by Dr. Edward K. Strong

Education: College graduate or equivalent with courses in credit and collection principles, accounting, financial statement analysis, commercial law, marketing, management, psychology and economics.

Experience: Five years or more in credit and collection work with exposure to multiple aspects of credit activities, including at least two years in a supervisory capacity in the same or similar industry.

1. Sincere interest in credit work as a career.
2. Fact finding, analysis and interpretation of the financial position of customers.
3. Supervision of the extension of credit and collection of receivables.
4. Familiarity with credit procedure and credit department administration.
5. Training of credit personnel.
6. Familiarity with accounting, order entry, sales, transportation and adjustment procedures.
7. Maintenance of satisfactory customer relations.
8. Contact with financial institutions and sources of credit information.
9. Participation in meetings of credit groups.

Special Personal Characteristics

1. Ability to communicate persuasively and effectively, and resourcefulness in eliciting confidential information.
2. Considerateness and fairness in dealing with people.
3. Emotional stability in handling unpleasant situations with tact and diplomacy.
4. Ability to analyze complex problems constructively.
5. Integrity and ethical standards that are exemplary in nature.

The research performed by Strong led to the creation of job specifications for credit managers. Table 1-2 contains an updated job specification for credit managers based on the original job specification designed by Strong. Education, experience and special personal characteristics should each become focal points for the development of credit managers.

Job specifications are essential to effectively recruit and train credit personnel. In order to hone in on the detailed tasks performed by business credit grantors, the author of this textbook surveyed 358 business credit practitioners. The focus of the study was to determine tasks performed by credit personnel. Specific tasks that are essential to initial employment in credit positions and to job advancement in business credit positions were identified.

From among 64 potential tasks, the 10 tasks that business credit managers identified as being most important to gain initial employment

1: The Changing Nature of Credit Management 9

**TABLE 1-3   Credit Tasks Necessary for Initial Employment
Identified by Business Credit Managers**

Tasks listed in order of most frequently reported as necessary for initial employment in business credit positions.

1. Contact banks and suppliers to investigate credit references.
2. Analyze requests for credit in order to extend credit.
3. Analyze financial statements on customers.
4. Extend credit to customers in accordance with established company policy.
5. Establish credit lines for individual accounts.
6. Order reports from credit reporting agencies.
7. Write personal letters to prospective or existing customers.
8. Discuss delinquent accounts with sales personnel.
9. Interpret reports generated by a computer.
10. Manage and control the receivables portfolio by direct involvement with accounts.

Source: An Identification and Analysis of Tasks Performed by Trade Credit Personnel, Charles Gahala, Doctoral Dissertation at Northern Illinois University, DeKalb, IL, 1983.

---

in a credit management position are listed in Table 1-3. These tasks suggest that someone who wants to gain initial employment in the credit field should be able to conduct a credit investigation. Moreover, training for employees new to credit could center upon the competencies necessary to complete the tasks contained in Table 1-3.

Unsurprisingly, credit managers did not select the same tasks as being "necessary for initial employment" as those tasks that were selected as being "necessary for job advancement." An overwhelming percentage of respondents identified the tasks contained in Table 1-4 as being essential for job advancement in business credit. Out of 64 possible tasks to select from, the 10 tasks that are most frequently identified as being necessary for job advancement are listed in Table 1-4.

The first task listed in Table 1-4, "attend workshops and conferences to update credit skills," reflects the dynamic nature of credit management. Most credit managers recognize the need to keep in touch with changes that affect their jobs. This suggests that credit managers have lifelong learning needs that can be partially fulfilled by attending workshops and conferences.

Each of the tasks identified as essential for job advancement requires higher-level competencies than those tasks that are essential for initial employment. Continuing education needs for experienced credit managers are centered more in the areas of credit policy, systems and

10 Credit Management: Principles and Practices

**TABLE 1-4   Credit Tasks Necessary for Job Advancement
As Identified by Business Credit Practitioners**

Tasks listed in order of most frequently reported as necessary for job advancement in business credit positions.

1. Attend workshops and conferences to update credit skills.
2. Establish and monitor standards of performance for credit personnel.
3. Prepare reports for corporate management.
4. Review, at least monthly, the status of collections and past-due accounts.
5. Interpret and delegate approved credit policies to subordinates.
6. Manage and control the receivables portfolio by direct involvement with accounts.
7. Formulate and apply controls to ensure that credit operations conform to standards.
8. Plan a program for the systematic follow-up of collecting accounts receivable.
9. Keep corporate management informed of the status of the accounts receivable portfolio.
10. Experiment with alternative business procedures to correct recurring problems.

Source: An Identification and Analysis of Tasks Performed by Trade Credit Personnel, Charles Gahala, Doctoral Dissertation at Northern Illinois University, DeKalb, Ill., 1983.

---

procedures, and human resources. Training for credit personnel should focus upon fulfilling these needs.[4]

ADDITIONAL RESEARCH EXAMINING THE TASKS PERFORMED BY BUSINESS CREDIT MANAGERS

Several pieces of related research were used to update the list of credit tasks that was formed in 1983. The most recent efforts to update the credit tasks are summarized below. Additional details concerning the responses can be found in four separate issues of *Business Credit*. Please see the Chapter 1 Appendix (page 20) to examine the most current list of business credit tasks.

The Pilot Study. The original listing of business credit management tasks was developed in my 1984 doctoral dissertation at Northern Illinois University. In 2004 there was a request from the Association of Credit Executives (ACE) to update my research; the ACE group participated in a pilot study to update the list of credit tasks.

---

[4] For a more detailed description of the original research related to credit management tasks, see Charles L. Gahala, *Tasks of Business Credit Personnel* (Columbia, Md.: Credit Research Foundation, February 1985).

ACE is a group of 35 corporate credit managers, each employed in a different industry and each of whom has several years of experience at Fortune 500 type companies. In 2002, ACE members were asked to review and update the listing of tasks performed by credit managers. The specific tasks identified 28 years ago are still being performed today; however, there are some significant changes reported in the way in which the tasks are being performed. The key changes that were identified by ACE members appear in Table 1-5.

Note that the changes identified by ACE members are not changes in the specific tasks being performed. ACE members validated the tasks. The tasks are simply being performed in different ways. There was considerable discussion concerning the refinement of the wording for specific tasks and the addition of new tasks. The resulting list of tasks was then used to conduct further research.

TABLE 1-5   **Changes in Performing Credit Tasks Identified by ACE Corporate Credit Managers**
(Changes are not listed in any particular order of importance.)

1. The credit crunch has become a major force that has caused more emphasis to be placed upon risk management.
2. Credit personnel should develop competence in all functional areas of a business in order to work with other departments, as members of cross-functional teams. This will enable credit managers to contribute as agents of change to improve operations.
3. There have been significant improvements in both the speed of accessing credit information and in the quality of its content.
4. Credit managers have a better image than they had 25 years ago.
5. Many routine tasks have been automated; this allows for the credit function to be more streamlined.
6. Fewer clerical credit employees are needed; credit managers spend more time focusing on non-routine aspects of the credit function. According to one credit manager, this reflects a shift toward being a manager of credit and away from being a credit manager.
7. Ethics need to be emphasized in light of the Enron, WorldCom and Global Crossing type accounting shenanigans during the first years of the 21st century and then the Lehman Brothers, Bear Stearns and AIG real estate marketplace blowout that led to a major credit crunch later during the decade.
8. Pressures from employers who subscribe to the profit motive place demands to deliver the credit function in a cost-efficient manner.
9. A need to stay current in the credit profession is essential to be considered for promotion because the changes that shape the profession are coming more quickly than years ago.
10. Financial analysis tools are more sophisticated and require a higher level of technical competence.

The Cross-Industry National Study. Cross-Industry is being used to describe the fact that credit managers participating in the research represented a wide variety of industries. The business credit task list from the pilot study was further refined by 175 business credit managers at the NACM Credit Congress held in Phoenix, Arizona, during June 2004. The Chapter 1 Appendix (page 20) contains the complete list of revised credit tasks.

The results of these opinions obtained from business credit managers produced an updated listing of business credit management tasks, which was published in January 2005 in a *Business Credit* article titled "What Do Credit Managers Do?" This article detailed the results of the findings that provide credit managers with a specific focus on a revised list of 70 business credit tasks.

Two Regional Studies. The updated list of credit tasks that was used at the 2004 NACM Credit Congress was also used to gather data at two regional credit conferences where the author of this article was an invited guest speaker. The purpose of the additional research was to find out if there were any regional variations in task performance.

The Gateway Credit Conference was held in St. Louis in September 2005, and the Central Region Credit Conference was held in Chicago in October 2005. To learn more about the specific findings at the two regional credit conferences, please see the January 2006 issue of *Business Credit*. Suffice it to say that all credit managers are not the same; there is some regional variation in the performance of credit tasks.

The Industry Study. Credit managers in a specific industry may have industry-specific needs that differ from the needs of credit managers in general. In order to examine the potential for industry-specific variation, the National Paper Packaging Industry Group was surveyed. In September 2006, industry group members were asked to identify the credit tasks essential for job advancement in the paper packaging industry. The paper packaging industry can be classified as being capital intensive. Accounts receivable are generally one of the largest assets on the balance sheet for companies in the paper packaging industry.

An examination of tasks essential for job advancement can be beneficial to any industry. In particular, the task listing could be useful to public companies that are examined for internal control weaknesses that could be reported by auditors under Sarbanes-Oxley Act disclosure requirements. There is some potential to improve credit management internal controls through an examination of the tasks being performed at a particular company.

Findings. The results of the research indicate that the credit managers from the National Paper Packaging Industry Group can sometimes disagree with the opinions of the cross-industry credit managers. Of the 70 tasks, 36 are perceived to be essential for job advancement by at least half of the paper packaging industry respondents while 25 of the tasks are perceived to be essential for job advancement by at least half of the cross-industry respondents. Perhaps the National Paper Packaging Industry Group has higher expectations for job advancement than credit managers in general? The detailed results of this research can be examined in the February 2006 issue of *Business Credit.*

Tasks performed by business credit managers are dynamic by nature. While the listing of credit tasks is an ongoing work in progress and thus is incomplete, it still is a potentially useful way to begin to examine the credit profession. The range of tasks performed at one company in comparison to another company can vary widely. There is a need to examine other industries to learn more about the variation in industry task performance.

There is considerable potential to identify training and education-related goals through the use of the task analysis. Moreover, individual companies can establish standards of performance to identify competency levels for credit personnel. The skills essential for the successful completion of essential tasks should be an ongoing focus for practitioners. A complete updated listing of the 70 business credit tasks can be found in the Chapter 1 Appendix.

The changes in the credit profession are clearly pointing toward a more highly educated credit manager. These changes identified by ACE members have been addressed and integrated into this edition of the textbook. For example, each chapter includes a Credit Management Online section at the end of the chapter. More contemporary financial tools are integrated into chapters. The real challenge to credit personnel will be to keep pace with the changes that will affect the performance of credit tasks.

NATIONAL ASSOCIATION OF CREDIT MANAGEMENT

An essential ingredient necessary to categorize an occupation as a profession is a strong professional association. As one of the oldest and largest business organizations in the United States, the National Association of Credit Management (NACM) provides business credit grantors with an essential vehicle to stay in touch with changes affecting credit management. NACM's basic goal is to increase profits for member companies through more efficient and effective credit management. Key activities that contribute to achieving this basic goal are:

- Providing additional training through educational programs, annual conferences, seminars and the national convention
- Supporting sound legislation and regulation
- Investigating and preventing fraud
- Offering government receivables assistance
- Improving international credit practices
- Publishing a national magazine
- Offering a library of publications to meet reference needs

NACM has more than 15,000 members located throughout the United States. NACM Affiliated Associations offer valuable services at the local level to assist in the effective management of their member companies' accounts receivable portfolios. These credit management resources include but are not limited to:

- Business collections
- Industry credit groups
- National, regional and local business credit reporting
- Distressed business services
- A wide variety of educational seminars, workshops and classes

Professionalism through Education

In 2009 NACM launched the web-based Credit Learning Center (CLC), which facilitates training for the essential skills needed in the credit profession. The CLC provides the opportunity to access education-related benefits 24/7. Other resources geared toward education include a resource library that can be accessed through the NACM website.

The education-related needs of credit personnel are met through a variety of NACM resources. Formal programs, such as the Graduate School of Credit and Financial Management (GSCFM), are coordinated by the NACM Education Department. There are also self-study courses, workshops and seminars at the NACM Credit Congress and on-site certificate sessions held at the NACM-National office to meet the needs of credit managers. Additionally, NACM hosts online courses, teleconferences and webinars that focus on current issues and topics in credit management. Through the Credit Administration Program (CAP) and the Advanced Credit Administration Program (ACAP), many NACM Affiliates offer courses that count toward professional designations.

The Credit and Financial Development Division (CFDD) is a division of NACM with chapters across the United States that gives NACM members additional opportunities to focus upon education and networking. The commitment to excellence at both the national and local levels can be attested to by the many awards and scholarships given to credit practitioners to further enhance excellence in the credit profession..

Professional Certification

NACM makes available a professional certification program for those who wish to demonstrate competence in the credit profession. The case for certification centers upon a long-term commitment to a career coupled with a significant potential for an increase in salary. Moreover, an ongoing certification process can help practitioners keep current within a profession. Professionals are recognized by maintaining standards of excellence. To paraphrase Lewis Carroll, sometimes credit managers need to do all of the running that they can just to stay in the same place.

NACM makes four specific designations available to business credit personnel: the Certified Credit and Risk Analyst^{SM} (CCRA); the Credit Business Associate^{SM} (CBA); the Credit Business Fellow^{SM} (CBF); and, for most credit managers, the highest level credential, the Certified Credit Executive® (CCE). For credit practitioners, these designations represent professional competence and personal achievement.

FCIB, the premier association for executives in Finance, Credit and International Business, launched two additional designations geared toward the international credit professional: the Certified International Credit Professional^{SM} (CICP) and the International Certified Credit Executive^{SM} (ICCE). Senior credit executives can demonstrate a specialized competence in international credit by obtaining the CICP and ICCE credentials. International skills have become particularly important due to the growth in international trade. These designations reflect the demand for certain credit managers to develop a specialized international competence that is distinct from NACM's four designations.

For more information about designation requirements, contact the NACM Education Department at www.nacm.org/ or 410-740-5560 or FCIB at www.fcibglobal.com/ or 410-423-1840.

CHAPTER 1: FOLLOW-UP

Recap of Important Concepts

1. There are six criteria that can be used to gauge the professional status of an occupation. Credit managers have earned the status of being categorized as professionals.

2. Credit managers should be aware of the details contained in the NACM-developed Canons of Business Credit Ethics and strive to conduct all activities at the highest level of ethical conduct possible.

3. According to Dr. Edward K. Strong, credit managers tend to have general business interests as opposed to a narrow interest in a particular area of business. Strong has identified specific occupations that are similar to, and other occupations that are divergent from, the interests of credit managers. Having an aptitude for credit management is essential to enjoying a career in the profession.

4. Credit managers have identified certain tasks that are essential to gain initial employment in business credit positions. In addition, they have identified other tasks that are essential to job advancement in the profession. These tasks can be useful for recruiting and training purposes. The wide range of tasks performed by credit managers mandates keeping in touch with change. Data gathered from the NACM Credit Congress, two regional credit conferences, the Association of Credit Executives (ACE) and one industry study were useful in terms of updating and validating the tasks performed by credit managers.

5. NACM and its affiliates provide numerous services to credit professionals. Credit managers should become aware of the various services available to them. Becoming actively involved in a professional association can be one of the most professionally enriching experiences available to a credit manager.

6. The title "credit manager" is used loosely, much like the title "accountant." In order to evidence competency necessary to complete credit-related tasks, NACM designations—the CCRA, CBA, CBF and CCE—have been developed. Through FCIB, the CICP and ICCE designations are now available. Credit practitioners can achieve recognition as professionals by completing the requirements necessary for professional designations.

Review/Discussion Questions

1. What criteria can be used to gauge whether an occupation qualifies for professional status? Do you believe that all credit practitioners should be categorized as professionals? If yes, explain why; if not, why not?
2. Which occupations tend to have interests that are similar to those of credit managers? Which occupations tend to have dissimilar interests? How can an aptitude for occupational interest be useful to a credit manager?
3. Why are the Canons of Business Credit Ethics important? Are there any specific canons that are not appropriate? If yes, why? Should there be an additional canon added to the list?
4. Choose one of the 10 changes identified by the Association of Credit Executives (ACE) in Table 1-5. How is this change shaping the way in which you perform on the job? Discuss how you can learn more about how other companies are dealing with this change. (Note: instructors may want to make this assignment focus on one particular change for discussion purposes in a classroom.)
5. What are the requirements to become a CBA? What are the requirements to become a CBF? (Please make use of the NACM website to garner specific details necessary to develop your response.)

Test Your Knowledge

1. Why are ethical standards important to credit management? Give three examples of principles that can be used to govern business ethics in credit management.
2. How can a credit manager contribute to the general welfare of society? Be specific.
3. Write a job specification for the position of credit manager. What specific education requirements, experience requirements and other special personal characteristics are appropriate for a credit manager? Please develop separate specifications for an *entry-level* credit analyst and for a credit analyst with *five years* of experience.
4. What types of educational opportunities are available that can contribute to the skills required in credit management? Try to identify specific credit-related opportunities rather than those available through high school or college courses.
5. You are a corporate credit manager who is trying to fill an entry-level position for a credit analyst. Which tasks are typically

performed by someone who is seeking initial employment in a credit management position? How can this knowledge be useful to a corporate credit manager?

6. You are a corporate credit manager who is trying to develop a training program for regional credit managers. What types of tasks should become a focal point for credit managers seeking job advancement in credit management positions? How can this information be useful to a corporate credit manager?

7. Identify three changes that are now occurring in the credit profession. Rank each of the changes in their order of importance. Justify your rank order. Be specific.

8. What are the continuing education requirements necessary to retain a CCE designation? What are the requirements to maintain the CICP designation? (Please make use of the NACM and FCIB websites to develop your response.)

Credit Management Online

Numerous websites can be of use to credit personnel. A few of the sites that are related to the content in each chapter will be recommended.

www.bls.gov/data/—The Bureau of Labor Statistics is the federal government site that contains information on inflation, employment and regional resources.

www.choosetosave.org/calculators/—Choose to Save has an array of nifty financial calculators and other links to useful personal finance topics.

www.crfonline.org/—The Credit Research Foundation (CRF) fulfills the role of enhancing research and education for business credit grantors. CRF has a number of publications of interest to credit managers.

www.fcibglobal.com/—FCIB is the trade association for executives employed in finance, credit and international business. The website is loaded with education-related opportunities for credit managers.

www.federalreserve.gov/—This is the link to the Federal Reserve System's home page. The beige book provides regional economic data.

www.financiallit.org/—The Institute for Financial Literacy offers education-related content and resources aimed at the consumer.

www.nacm.org/—The National Association of Credit Management site provides an overview of NACM membership, publications, activities, resources (such as the NACM blog, *eNews* and the Credit Managers'

Index) and services (including Secured Transaction Services). There are several links to topics of interest useful for credit managers at all levels.

online.wsj.com/home-page/—I like to joke with students and tell them that *"The Wall Street Journal* will be your textbook for the rest of your business career."

References Useful for Further Reading

Beckman, Theodore N. *Credits and Collections in Theory and Practice.* New York: McGraw-Hill Book Company Inc., 1924.

Bumgarner, Jerry. "NACM Business Credit Compensation Survey Results." *Business Credit* (November/December 2008): 6-7.

"CICP Designation Spreading Throughout the Globe." *Business Credit* (May 2010): 44-45.

Gahala, Charles L. "An Identification and Analysis of Tasks Performed by Trade Credit Personnel." Ed.D. dissertation, Northern Illinois University, 1983.

Gahala, Charles L. "An Identification of the Tasks Essential for Job Advancement in Business Credit." *Business Credit* (January 2006): 23-27.

Gahala, Charles L. "The CICP Professional Designation Available Through the FCIB: A Focus upon the Process and Content Used to Test Proficiency in International Finance." *The Journal of Contemporary Business Issues* (Spring 2008).

Gahala, Charles L. "What Do Credit Managers Do?" *Business Credit* (January 2005): 36-39.

McMann, John G. "How I Learned Trade Credit Risk Management." *Business Credit* (March 2007): 32-33.

Mota, Diana. "Designations Propel Credit Professionals, Their Companies Forward." *Business Credit* (January 2017): 22-23.

Mota, Diana. "MVPs: Most Valuable Professionals." *Business Credit* (June 2015): 18-20.

Popham, Estelle L., Adele Frisbee Schrag, and Wanda Blackhus. *A Teaching-Learning System for Business Education.* New York: McGraw-Hill, 1975.

Strong, Edward K. *Credit Management and the Strong Vocational Interest Test.* New York: Credit Research Foundation and National Association of Credit Management, n.d.

Trunzo, Giuseppe, CICP. "The Credit Management Revolution." *Business Credit* (June 2017): 14-15.

APPENDIX: A List of 70 Business Credit Tasks
Five Categories with 14 Tasks in Each

A. Credit Investigation Tasks
1. Obtain a completed and signed credit application from potential new customers in order to launch a request for credit.
2. Verify the exact name of the specific obligor.
3. Conduct the investigation professionally while limiting the extent of the credit investigation to the parameters of optimizing corporate profitability.
4. Utilize the Internet to support credit investigations.
5. Draw down and analyze reports from credit reporting agencies.
6. Contact banks and trade creditors to investigate credit references.
7. Obtain and analyze financial statement information to support credit decision-making.
8. Make field contacts by personally visiting customers or communicating with sales personnel to obtain a better perspective of the customer ability to support the credit investigation pertaining to both new and existing customers.
9. Extend credit to customers in accordance with an approval hierarchy established internally through corporate policy.
10. Participate actively in industry credit group activities.
11. Implement a credit-scoring model that includes relevant scorecards in order to evaluate the creditworthiness used to support credit decision-making.
12. Factor into the decision to extend credit-relevant factors such as the customer market, the overall economy and the specific industry to alter the stringency for extending or denying credit.
13. Utilize and communicate credit limits/lines in accordance with internal corporate policy.
14. Update the credit information essential to maintain existing accounts on an ongoing basis.

B. Accounts Receivable Portfolio Tasks
1. Manage and control the receivables portfolio by direct involvement with accounts.
2. Update and archive credit files on a regular basis.
3. Explain to customers the various types of credit arrangements such as open account credit, secured credit, installment credit or special arrangements.
4. Clarify for customers and sales personnel specific concerns such as credit policy, the use of lines of credit, unearned cash discounts or late payment service charges.

5. Monitor and analyze customer deductions and open account credits to determine if problem patterns are evident.
6. Monitor internal invoicing and the application of cash received to strive to optimize cash flow from customers.
7. Email or write personal letters to prospective or existing customers to clarify credit policy.
8. Write customer appreciation letters or encourage inactive account holders to resume making purchases.
9. Respond professionally to requests for credit references.
10. Prepare reports for corporate management to include topics such as customer deductions, days sales outstanding and cash flow forecasts.
11. Prepare an aging of accounts receivable and then regularly review the problem accounts with a particular focus upon both size and aging.
12. Interpret computer generated reports to detect trends or problems and then take corrective action.
13. Utilize Electronic Data Interchange (EDI) and Electronic Fund Transfers (EFT) to the fullest extent possible in a cost-efficient manner.
14. Prepare reports on the costs of collecting, carrying or screening accounts receivable to examine both customer profitability and the effect upon credit department economic value added.

C. Distressed-Debtor and Secured Creditor Related Tasks
1. Discuss delinquent accounts with sales personnel.
2. Provide reports and then furnish essential details to upper-level management on the status of severe problem accounts.
3. Place a hold on an existing account and then communicate the hold in an appropriate manner.
4. Perform lien searches of public filings that pertain to either new or existing customers.
5. Obtain specific collateral for accounts by perfecting liens on personal or real property; this may entail filing financing statements under the Uniform Commercial Code (UCC) or recording a lien with the appropriate county.
6. Obtain letters of credit to reduce the risk related to specific accounts.
7. Obtain personal or corporate guarantees to support the extension of credit to specific accounts.
8. Obtain credit insurance to protect against the potential for customer non-payment.

9. Obtain a pledge of stocks or bonds or use warehouse receipts to secure marginal accounts.
10. Convert an open account receivable to a note receivable that could be set up to be collateralized and interest bearing.
11. Represent the company at creditors' meetings that relate to a bankruptcy proceeding, a bulk sale or an assignment for the benefit of creditors.
12. Arrange for the placement of accounts with collection agencies or the filing of lawsuits with attorneys.
13. File proof of claim forms and then follow up with bankruptcy proceedings.
14. Establish a reserve for bad debts in accordance with established corporate policy.

D. Credit Department Operational Tasks
1. Establish and communicate credit policy for subordinates and then monitor the enforcement of policy for its effect upon both internal and external interfaces.
2. Write job descriptions and job specifications for credit department personnel.
3. Maintain and update a credit department manual.
4. Coordinate the needs of the credit department with other departments such as IT, sales personnel, manufacturing and merchandising personnel, and accounting personnel.
5. Choose credit department personnel for participation with cross-functional work teams.
6. Obtain the approval from the treasurer, vice president of finance or other appropriate superior for accepting notes, compromise settlements (these can include less than payment in full or an extension of repayment) or the write-off of specific accounts to bad debt.
7. Establish and monitor the standards of performance for credit personnel.
8. Recommend changes that pertain to credit department employee salaries, job reclassifications and terminations.
9. Establish and update credit department training and education programs.
10. Recruit, select and promote individuals for credit positions based upon the qualifications of the applicants, maintaining diversity and the needs of the department.

11. Coordinate a mentoring program and provide feedback to credit department personnel.
12. Attend workshops to update both knowledge and skills on a regular basis.
13. Keep all credit department personnel apprised of changes in key legislation such as the Sarbanes-Oxley Act.
14. Benchmark the credit department performance in comparison to Credit Research Foundation studies or other comparable data.

E. General Credit Management Tasks
1. Monitor credit department personnel to ensure that all tasks are performed in an ethical manner.
2. Contribute to the cash management function through various activities, such as using wire transfers and lockboxes, to accelerate the inflows from customers.
3. Keep corporate management informed concerning the status of the receivables portfolio.
4. Supervise collection correspondence and records retention.
5. Supervise personnel so that the appropriate computer utilization is adhered to by all credit personnel.
6. Supervise the management of accounts receivables including unused customer credits and refunds.
7. Plan and implement a dynamic program for the systematic follow-up of collecting past due accounts.
8. Experiment with alternative business procedures to correct recurring problems.
9. Study customer and internal relationships in an attempt to improve the goodwill of the credit department.
10. Keep informed of new ideas through membership in national credit organizations such as NACM.
11. Evaluate software packages that relate to credit management.
12. Participate actively in Enterprise Resource Planning (ERP) activities.
13. Ensure compliance and full cooperation with both external and internal auditors.
14. Provide an evaluation of suppliers for the purchasing department.

Chapter 2

ORGANIZING THE CREDIT FUNCTION

"The most common standard by which credit and A/R organizations are measured is days sales outstanding. However, it is also the most misunderstood and thus misused metric in our field. Used with other performance metrics such as best possible DSO and average days delinquent, the information becomes much more meaningful for the person evaluating the conditions of the accounts receivable."[1]

Terry Callahan, CCE
President, Credit Research Foundation

Organizing the credit function requires establishing goals. Specific goals are broken down into focal points, which are then examined in order to be standardized. Finally, the side effects of anticipated action are interwoven into other departments within the organization.

For example, a company may develop the goal of reducing bad debts. One focal point that could lead to a reduction in bad debts would be to require a completed credit application from all new customers. This focal point could be examined by developing an optimal credit application. The sales force would need to cooperate by implementing the requirement of obtaining a completed application from all new customers. The side effects might create conflict with sales personnel or customers, yet the ultimate results could lead to a reduction in bad debts.

Organizing the credit function requires a vision. While credit managers are often immersed in daily duties, the overall profitability of a business should remain as the core of specific credit management objectives. The purpose of Chapter 2 is to identify critical management focal points essential to organizing the credit function.

The **Key Learning Objectives** contained in Chapter 2 are:

1. Understand the role of benchmarking the credit function.
2. Examine alternative organization structures that can be used to administer the credit function.

---

[1] Terry Callahan, "Benchmarking to Measure Your Performance," *Business Credit* (November/December 2007): 52.

3. Recognize the importance of keeping individual credit department personnel motivated.
4. Consider tasks that can be performed through the use of Business Process Outsourcing.
5. Identify specific credit-related tasks that can derive benefits through automation.

The reader may be asking this question: What do benchmarking, organization structure, motivating credit department personnel, business process outsourcing and automation have in common? By addressing these focal points separately and in combination, a credit department can be designed to perform at an optimal level. Due to shifts in needs coupled with changes in technology, there is a need for an ongoing focus.

BENCHMARKING

Quantitative measures that can be used to gauge the effectiveness of credit department performance can be obtained by benchmarking certain departmental focal points. As a management tool, benchmarking can be conducted by using either an external or an internal approach. The *external approach* to benchmarking entails emulating the best business practices of other credit departments. A company may compare itself to an industry average or to a strong corporate role model in an attempt to pinpoint areas that can be improved upon. External benchmarking is limited by the availability of comparable cost data and by difficulties that surface when a firm operates in more than one industry.

An *internal approach* to benchmarking focuses upon comparing current results to historical norms. The internal approach is limited to a focus on performance measurement for one company. Trends can be established by using the internal approach. Moreover, when a change is made in credit department operations, such as a department downsizing, the results of the change can be quantitatively examined.

Benchmarking performance measures should be quantifiable. Examples of specific credit-related measures that can be used for benchmarking purposes include: (1) aging schedules, (2) credit department expenses per employee, (3) percentage bad debt expenses, (4) days sales outstanding and (5) best possible days sales outstanding.

TABLE 2-1   Accounts Receivable Aging Schedule

| | Clark Products | | Riedel Limited | |
Status	Amount	Percentage	Amount	Percentage
Current	$17,000,000	85 %	$16,000,000	67 %
1-30 Days	2,000,000	10	2,000,000	8
31-60	800,000	4	2,000,000	8
Over 60 Days	200,000	1	4,000,000	17
Total AR	**$20,000,000**	**100 %**	**$24,000,000**	**100 %**

Aging Schedules

The purpose of an *aging schedule* is to break down accounts receivable by the age of the accounts. An aging schedule can be prepared to include all receivables by a corporation, or it can be prepared by using specific criteria. For example, an aging can be prepared for a division, product line, geographic area or sales territory. A monthly aging schedule should be compared to the results obtained 12 months earlier when there is any seasonality in sales.

Table 2-1 shows an aging schedule for Clark Products and for a competitor, Riedel Limited. The aging shows that 10% of the Clark Products receivables are 1-30 days past due while only 8% of Riedel Limited receivables are 1-30 days past due. However, a closer look at the aging shows that Clark Products could serve as an excellent benchmark company for Riedel Limited to emulate.

The aging schedule pinpoints problems in the Riedel Limited receivables; management clearly needs to investigate the problems and perhaps tighten up credit policy at Riedel Limited. The situation could be addressed by using a team from accounting, sales and credit in order to identify and correct problems.

Certain local NACM Affiliates coordinate industry credit groups; they act as a clearinghouse to develop an aging schedule for an industry. An individual member of the credit group can then compare an aging to the industry as a benchmark for performance. New goals that bring Riedel Limited more in line with Clark Products can be established.

Credit Department Expenses Per Employee

Credit department operations should focus on cost containment. The allocation of expenses to the credit department can vary from company to company, so intercompany comparisons can be misleading. However, the internal approach to benchmarking using credit department expenses per employee can be revealing. Total expenses include direct and indirect expenses, including payroll, credit reports, technology-related costs, training, travel and overhead.

Credit department expenses per employee can be calculated by dividing total annual operating expenses by the total number of employees in the department. Trends are important to pinpoint. Moreover, individual operating units and even individual credit offices can be examined separately. The results of benchmarking credit department expenses per employee should be interpreted carefully. The allocation of specific expenses will have a pronounced impact on the results.

For example, if one company allocates cash application expenses to the accounting department while another company allocates similar cash application expenses to the credit department, then the validity of making sound decisions concerning cost containment will become complicated and potentially misleading.

Percentage Bad Debt Expenses

The actual bad debts written off during a year divided by the annual sales volume provides the percentage bad debt expense. This information is available for public companies so external benchmarking can be used. In addition, internal benchmarking can be used to identify trends for the company as a whole or for individual operating units within a company.

The calculation used to benchmark bad debts is relatively simple, yet the interpretation of the results can be tricky. For example, bad debts are closely linked to overall corporate goals. A company experiencing a high growth rate in sales may also experience an increase in the bad debt expense. The important focal point becomes whether the increase in sales raises profits enough to offset the increase in bad debts. By benchmarking a change in the trend for bad debt, the management should be drawn into an evaluation of the effectiveness of the credit policy. Credit policy should be examined in light of overall corporate profitability.

Days Sales Outstanding

Equation 2-1 shows a formula used to calculate *days sales outstanding (DSO)*. This formula will be used to calculate DSO in Equation 2-2.

Equation 2-1: Use of Total Receivables

$$DSO = \frac{\text{Total Accounts Receivable}}{\text{Credit Sales During Period}} \times \text{Number of Days in Period}$$

For a company that has total receivables of $8 million and annual credit sales of $50 million, the DSO would be calculated as follows:

Equation 2-2: DSO Example

$$DSO = \frac{\$8,000,000}{\$50,000,000} \times 365 = 58 \text{ Days}$$

The results derived in Equation 2-2 show accounts receivable divided by sales per day are used to generate a DSO of 58 days. Most companies try to control their investment in receivables; DSO is useful to gauge this investment of funds into accounts receivable. Using the DSO as a benchmark of performance, however, can be misleading. Credit managers do not control sales terms; an increase in sales when terms are changed could give decision makers misleading information. Consequently, the best possible DSO is often more useful for benchmarking purposes.

Best Possible Days Sales Outstanding

The *best possible days sales outstanding (BPDSO)* is particularly useful for benchmarking purposes using the internal approach. This measure can be used for monthly, quarterly or annual periods. The essential difference between BPDSO and DSO is that the BPDSO uses *current* (those receivables not yet due) rather than *total* receivables in the calculation. Equation 2-3 shows the formula used to calculate BPDSO.

Equation 2-3: Use of Current Receivables

$$BPDSO = \frac{\text{Current Accounts Receivables}}{\text{Credit Sales During Period}} \times \text{Number of Days in Period}$$

For example, if current accounts receivables are $6 million and credit sales during the year are $50 million, the BPDSO would be 44 days. Equation 2-4 shows the example of the BPDSO calculation.

Equation 2-4: BPDSO Example

$$BPDSO = \frac{\$6,000,000}{\$50,000,000} \times 365 = 44 \text{ Days}$$

TABLE 2-2   Benchmarking Performance Measures

Measure	Firm Being Analyzed	Industry Average	Best in Industry
1. Aging Schedule			
Current	67%	70%	85%
10-30 Days Past Due	8	12	10
31-60 Days Past Due	8	10	4
Over 60 Days Past Due	17	8	1
2. Credit Department Expenses Per Employee	$60,000	$65,000	$70,000
3. Percentage Bad Debts	4%	3%	1%
4. Days Sales Outstanding (DSO)	58 Days	50 Days	34 Days
5. Best Possible DSO	30 Days	30 Days	30 Days

The results of Equation 2-4 show a BPDSO of 44 days. When comparing the results of Equation 2-4 to the results of Equation 2-2 for the DSO, the *average days delinquent (ADD)* can be obtained. The DSO of 58 days minus the BPDSO of 44 days provides an ADD of 14 days. By using the BPDSO to obtain the ADD, the impact of any change in terms of sales is taken into consideration.

Table 2-2 summarizes the aforementioned measures used for benchmarking purposes. Management should consider emulating the company that can produce the best results in an industry, or consider using the industry norm, when analyzing the results. This type of comparison helps to pinpoint areas that need attention when organizing the credit function.

By making use of an *external approach* to benchmarking, an outside resource is used to provide the data to which comparisons can be made. The Credit Research Foundation (CRF) conducts an annual benchmarking survey of credit managers. CRF members furnish data for which CRF acts as a confidential clearinghouse to develop industry results. Credit managers can learn more about the CRF benchmarking process by contacting CRF at www.crfonline.org/. Customized benchmarking papers are available from CRF and can be used to implement the benchmarking management technique.

Organizing the credit function starts with a careful self-examination, and benchmarking can accomplish that objective. Benchmarking the performance measures for the credit function is potentially revealing and useful when reviewing the organization of the credit function.

DEVELOPING JOB SPECIFICATIONS FOR THE CREDIT FUNCTION

Developing job specifications for the credit function requires assigning authority and responsibility. The extent to which authority is concentrated or dispersed depends upon individual circumstances. The goal of organizing the credit function is to engineer the most effective results possible.

A small business normally has a relatively simple organizational structure. Credit operations might be concentrated in one location, enabling the credit department to work closely with other departments. However, as the size of the business increases, the organization of the credit department can become more complex.

An *organization chart* shows the nature over which authority exists and where decision making should be made. Table 2-3 presents an organization chart that employs a functional assignment of authority and responsibility. The credit manager reports to a treasurer who empowers the credit manager with the authority and responsibility to control credit operations. There could be a number of additional layers in an organization chart for a large business.

The credit manager in Table 2-3 could have management layers that report to him or her. For example, regional credit managers could report directly to the credit manager. The regional credit managers may have area credit managers who report directly to them. Zone managers could

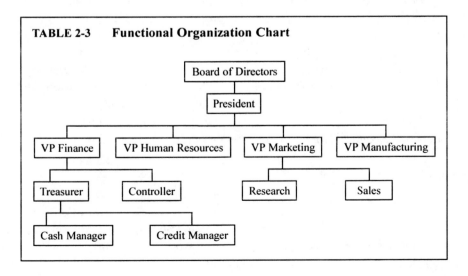

TABLE 2-3 Functional Organization Chart

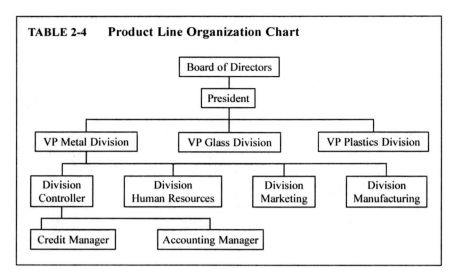

TABLE 2-4   Product Line Organization Chart

report directly to area managers. For many companies, there has been a trend to decrease the number of layers in the organization structure.

An organization chart also can be structured by product so that several divisions or subsidiary units of an individual company can operate more autonomously. Table 2-4 presents an organization chart that is structured by product line. When product expertise is essential, an organization chart structured by product can be effective.

In the organization chart in Table 2-4, each division could have a division credit manager. The division credit manager could develop a specialization in industry-specific product knowledge. The credit manager could then be located at division headquarters to develop a close working relationship with other managers in that division.

Should a company use an organization chart that is structured by function or an organization chart established by product line? Often the crux of the decision is centered upon using a centralized or decentralized approach to management. There are several factors that influence the decision to centralize or decentralize operations.

Advantages of Centralized Credit Operations

1. *Maximum Control.* Credit decisions are usually more consistent when a credit department is centralized. There is less likelihood that a marketing or manufacturing manager will exert pressure on the credit manager to extend credit when the credit manager is located in the corporate headquarters.

2. ***Reduced Training.*** The ability to develop the skills essential to manage credit can be fostered with consistency. Specific tools used for training credit analysts can be utilized more easily in a centralized credit department. Credit personnel are better able to clearly understand specific credit-related tasks because there is an opportunity to work closely with other credit managers who can guide credit personnel through complex applications.

3. ***Economies of Scale.*** A centralized credit operation may require fewer credit personnel. Moreover, when divisions have common accounts, the likelihood of duplicating credit analysis is reduced.

4. ***More Uniform Policy Implementation.*** Credit policy is more likely to be interpreted consistently when a credit department is centralized. The proximity of a corporate credit manager to clarify policy and support decisions provides an improved opportunity for uniform credit decisions. However, there are advantages to dispersing credit operations to various locations.

Advantages of Decentralized Credit Operations

1. ***Improved Customer Rapport.*** Customers may perceive credit decision making more favorably. Credit personnel may be more aware of the local business conditions.

2. ***Closer Interdepartmental Relationships.*** When a credit manager is at the same location as sales managers and operating managers, communication often improves. Managers may become more responsive in certain situations. Interdepartmental conflict can be reduced.

3. ***Reduced Response Time.*** In general, the larger an organization, the greater the number of decisions that need to be made. In a decentralized credit environment, credit managers may be in a more self-sufficient position, which allows credit decisions to be made in a more timely manner.

A company may use a combination of centralized and decentralized operations. In most cases, the company-specific situation dictates the degree to which credit can be decentralized. For example, if a product requires substantial product knowledge and profit margins are high, a company may lean toward decentralization. Corporate politics also play a key role in the decision to decentralize. When division managers are rewarded based on profitability, the division vice president may insist on a decentralized credit operation to maintain more control over credit decisions.

MOTIVATING CREDIT PERSONNEL

During an era of a national credit crunch, fear can become a dysfunctional yet powerful motivator. Cash flow problems often result in increased demands placed upon credit managers. Maintaining a highly motivated credit department is critically important to the credit function.

Credit managers who perceive their situations as unfavorable are in a position to compromise on ethical standards. Serious morale problems can result in behavior that jeopardizes the integrity of the credit function. Table 2-5 contains examples of dysfunctional behavior that clearly compromises the ethics of the credit profession.

Credit managers are involved in a number of diverse situations in which ethics can be compromised. There is plenty of gray area in each of the situations identified in Table 2-5.

Ethical behavior can easily be traced to motivation, which is often complex. For example, although faced with a heavy workload, some credit managers would prefer to play golf than put in more time. Other more complicated situations may require more personal time off due to family responsibilities. Employees who have more flexibility in their work schedules may experience higher levels of motivation and an increase in job satisfaction.

TABLE 2-5   Compromising on Credit Ethics: Dysfunctional Behavior

1. Cut deals with customers for extended terms arrangements.
2. Program a computer so that certain customers are not billed late payment service charges.
3. Pad an expense account.
4. Accept a gift from a collection agency in return for forwarding accounts for collection.
5. Absorb an unearned cash discount, showing favoritism to certain customers.
6. Mislead management with a past due report that omits certain past due accounts.
7. Forge personal credentials on a job application.
8. Order a credit report for a friend who does not have a subscription with the credit reporting agency.
9. Wing it when someone calls to request credit information on an existing customer.
10. Treat subordinates unfairly in a job review, showing favoritism to cronies.

Credit managers can be motivated in a number of ways. Abraham Maslow created a motivation-related hierarchy of needs in 1954.[2] The basic human needs identified by Maslow, in an ascending order of importance, have stood the test of time. These needs can be used as a starting point when considering motivation.

1. *Physiological Needs.* Basic needs used to sustain human life—such as food, water, clothing, shelter, sleep and sexual satisfaction—comprise physiological needs. Other incentives will not motivate a person until physiological needs have been satisfied. For example, if a member of the credit department is in dire need of sleep, the individual's work will suffer. A salary increase may not serve to motivate the employee.

2. *Security or Safety Needs.* The threat of physical danger or loss of job is the second level in the hierarchy of needs. Rumors of a corporate downsizing can create serious motivational problems.

3. *Affiliation or Acceptance Needs.* The need to feel accepted is the next level in Maslow's hierarchy of needs. A credit manager who is ostracized by other credit department members will have trouble contributing to the overall objectives of the department.

4. *Esteem Needs.* After the first three levels of the hierarchy are satisfied, the need to develop self-confidence, status and prestige should be fulfilled. Sometimes a corner office, a laptop computer or a job title can contribute to fulfilling this need.

5. *Self-Actualization Needs.* This particular need is a focus on becoming all of what one is capable of becoming. Obtaining the CCE designation could be a temporary goal for certain credit managers; after the CCE is obtained, an individual would then identify a new goal to stay motivated.

There is clearly a need to keep credit personnel motivated. Yet practical suggestions are often as effective as theoretically based motivational techniques. Situations often dictate appropriate motivational strategies. The payoffs from a highly motivated credit department can be surprisingly beneficial; yet the problems from a dysfunctional credit department can become devastating.

---

[2] Abraham Maslow, *Motivation and Personality* (New York: Harper and Brothers, 1954).

TABLE 2-6   **Credit Department Motivation**

1. Promote an atmosphere of contribution by giving managers more power.
2. Encourage education-related activities by providing time away from the job and financial support.
3. Develop a salary system that is based on performance, not just seniority.
4. Ask a credit person to perform a new task and provide essential support to complete the task.
5. Provide an opportunity to make lateral moves.
6. Allow for some flextime in the work week.
7. Encourage innovation in the completion of credit tasks.
8. Promote balance among job-related interests and outside interests.

When credit department turnover is high or employee absenteeism is on the rise, employee morale is often at low ebb. There is a need to investigate the cause of the morale problem and to confront the situation using numerous strategies.

Table 2-6 provides a few options that may be used to motivate credit department employees. The motivators identified in this table are general in nature. Readers are encouraged to creatively identify examples for each motivator.

Salaries in credit management have been increasing steadily. There are industry and regional variations that have an impact. The geographic region, size of receivables portfolio, employer revenue, education and professional certifications can also influence salaries of credit employees.

The credit function should be engineered to provide credit department employees with a competitive compensation package. There is evidence to suggest that salary does not always motivate employees. Yet, the absence of providing a competitive salary structure can lead to motivational problems.

BUSINESS PROCESS OUTSOURCING

Historically, certain types of credit tasks have been temporarily or permanently performed by outside vendors. This practice is known as outsourcing. For example, a collection agency could be assigned certain problem accounts, a lawyer could be retained to file a lawsuit or a bank could be used to expedite the receipt of payments via a lockbox system. These types of tasks have been widely used by credit personnel in order to gain expertise for the completion of tasks or to try to contain costs.

Business process outsourcing (BPO) entails the use of long-term contracts usually for the performance of non-core business processes that are to be performed by outside companies. In November 1999, BP-Amoco entered into contract in excess of $1 billion to outsource its finance function to PricewaterhouseCoopers. BPO decisions such as this one are often driven by four major goals: (1) the potential to gain access to new technology, simultaneously freeing up funds needed for the technology, (2) the emphasis on cutting costs to enhance profits, (3) the potential to gain management expertise in areas where the expertise is in short supply and (4) the potential to provide managers with an increase in time to use for other more complex core business tasks.

Certain credit-related processes lend themselves nicely to BPO. Processes such as routine collection activity, lien searches, cash application, deduction follow-up, credit investigation and documentation for letters of credit can benefit from the use of BPO. Each process should be examined individually.

Ultimately, the entire credit function could be outsourced. Too often the decision to outsource comes from the top-down approach initiated by top-level management. Credit managers should contribute to the decision-making process. In order for credit managers to contribute to the decision-making process, the costs of servicing credit-related processes and the value added by the credit department or outsourcing firm should be scrutinized.

The quantitative analysis of BPO decisions is similar to a make-or-buy decision that is often included as part of the second course in principles of accounting. This type of analysis identifies incremental cost differences based upon the alternatives of outsourcing or not outsourcing. For example, if a company performs the credit task of performing lien searches, it will need to incur costs such as a portion of credit department salaries, the allocation of fixed costs and overhead for office space and resources, and variable costs associated with each lien search. These costs could be compared to the costs of outsourcing the task of performing lien searches. The alternative with the lower costs pinpoints the potential cost reduction.

The qualitative aspects of a BPO decision are much more difficult to analyze. Several questions that entail the use of sound judgment need to be posed. Will the outsourced process be handled in a more reliable manner? Will there be any cultural or language barriers? Will there be any differences in the quality and results of the processes being outsourced?

For example, if there is an opportunity to outsource credit investigations, a business with many similar small-balance customers could provide BPO with an edge due to economies of scale. However, for a business with large-balance accounts there is often considerable product and industry expertise that may require close personal contact essential to properly complete the credit investigation; this situation might favor handling credit investigations internally.

BPO can conjure up negative feelings from existing employees. The threat of a downsizing if the BPO decision is implemented poses a dilemma. In certain situations, BPO can actually contribute to an increase in costs. Moreover, if credit managers have more time to focus on non-mundane tasks, then the BPO decision could be welcomed by existing personnel.

There has been a shift toward focusing upon value added rather than cost reduction when considering a BPO decision. Since management of the credit function varies widely from company to company, the decision to use BPO is one more tool that credit managers should become adept at analyzing. In the final analysis, BPO is being driven by the automation of business activities.

AUTOMATING CREDIT ACTIVITIES

Organizing the credit function includes harnessing technological change to facilitate credit processes. Many credit departments have taken a process focus to integrate technology into the credit function. When an existing process is enhanced, a *total quality management (TQM)* approach is being used. When new processes become the focal point, a *reengineering* approach is being used.

Harnessing technology with cost-efficient results will be an ongoing challenge. Automated systems have the potential to cause information overload. While automated systems certainly have the potential to process more information, they do not have the ability to synthesize knowledge. Therefore, credit managers will have to roll up their sleeves and get their hands dirty digging for new ways to harness technology.

The expertise essential to tap into the wealth of information available through new technology is in short supply. Many credit managers will have to gain access to new ideas by going outside of their own firms. Potential sources of ideas include industry credit groups, local NACM Affiliates, local colleges, trade journals, consultants and companies that provide various products.

The array of new products and processes is simply too long to list. Some of the more important credit-related applications that can assist the credit manager are worth noting, however. Individual providers for specific products often use catchy labels on products that can cause some confusion. Table 2-7 provides process-related technological focal points for credit managers.

The process-related focal points contained in Table 2-7 provide topics where technology can be used to produce process reengineering. By relating the topic to actual performance through a benchmarking measure, credit managers can identify certain areas that need improvement. The real challenge is to harness technology in a cost-efficient way. For example, migration toward a shared services environment can be particularly useful. Making use of remotely hosted software rather than company-owned servers can simply be more cost-efficient. The side effects can necessitate a change in the organization structure, which often has an impact on employee morale.

An integrated resource planning system, such as *SAP* or *PeopleSoft*, can be particularly useful to those companies that operate in a global environment. Business units can gain access to a centralized repository of data that can be more readily integrated into the management of credit. For example, the total corporate exposure by country or by customer can be readily garnered.

The key focal points in organizing the credit function include benchmarking, organization structure, motivation of credit department personnel, business process outsourcing and automation. The focal points need to be designed both individually and in combination. Change is inevitable. The ability to function at an optimal level of efficiency is the ongoing goal of the credit function. Sometimes the process of striving to reach the goal can become as important as actually achieving the goal.

Several credit departments have moved toward developing a team approach to the organization of work. For example, a team approach could combine sales, credit, accounting and customer service responsibilities. A team member who takes an order can be responsible to make sure that the order is filled properly. When the customer sends in a payment, another team member also ensures that the cash is applied properly and any discrepancies are quickly recovered. Credit personnel keep sales personnel informed of problems if they arise.

Another organizational focal point for credit managers is total quality management (TQM). The goal of striving for zero defects by doing a job properly is an attitude that TQM fosters. Internal resources are directed

40

Credit Management: Principles and Practices

**TABLE 2-7   Process-Related Technological Focal Points
for Credit Managers**

Process	Intended Focus
1. Automated Electronic Invoicing	Prompt, accurate invoices with complete access available to credit managers at their workstations.
2. Automated Collection Systems	Collection parameters automatically identify timing and mode of collection while tracking results.
3. Credit Reporting	Online access to credit reports for customers.
4. Credit Scoring/Order Approval	Risk analysis to provide an evaluation of customer creditworthiness.
5. Electronic Credit File	Online maintenance of customer credit information.
6. Electronic Documentation Search	Retrieval of lien information and corporate registration.
7. Financial Analysis	A wide range of analysis tasks such as ratio analysis, common-size analysis and pro forma construction; industry comparisons are readily available.
8. Management Reports	Specific reports generated based upon parameters furnished.
9. Portfolio Analysis	Sort receivables for risk analysis purposes by product, operating unit or geographical area.
10. Short Payment Analysis/ Channel Deductions	Sort customer deductions by size, product, territory or cause, and then channel an immediate follow up.

---

toward producing zero defects through preventive maintenance. TQM can be useful by benchmarking a credit department's core expenses: screening costs, collection costs and bad debts.

Cost-effective innovative performance is at the heart of organizing the credit function. Credit personnel could consider using the checklist that begins on page 85 to map activities to initiate a study to determine if there is need to reengineer the organization of credit function.

CHAPTER 2: FOLLOW-UP

Recap of Important Concepts

1. The credit function can be organized by focusing on developing processes that allow the credit function to operate at an optimal level.
2. Benchmarking is an effective management tool for examining the credit function. The approach used can be external or internal. External benchmarking compares the results of a company to those of a superior competitor or to an industry. Internal benchmarking examines the performance of a company over time to identify trends.
3. Specific criteria used to benchmark the credit function include aging schedules, credit department expenses per employee, percentage bad debt expenses, days sales outstanding (DSO) and best possible days sales outstanding (BPDSO).
4. The credit function can be organized by focusing on assigning authority and responsibility. An organization chart is often developed by using business functions or product line.
5. The credit function is often centralized. Advantages of a centralized organization structure include maximum control, reduced training, economics of scale and uniform credit policy implementation. For certain reasons, many companies often use a mix of centralized and decentralized credit operations.
6. When credit department morale is at low ebb, there is a danger that credit personnel behavior will become dysfunctional. Credit personnel may find themselves in positions where professional ethics can be compromised.
7. Business Process Outsourcing (BPO) entails the use of outside companies to perform certain processes. Certain credit activities can be outsourced in an attempt to benefit from technological expertise or in cost-reduction efforts. BPO can also be useful when the credit department workload becomes overwhelming.
8. Abraham Maslow's hierarchy of needs is one of many motivational theories. Maslow's theory is based upon fulfilling low-level needs prior to considering higher level needs. Motivational theory can be a useful starting point when considering morale problems. There are also a number of practical approaches that can be used to motivate employees.

9. Salaries in credit management positions have been on the rise. Credit department employee salaries are influenced by several factors including size of receivables portfolio, number of active accounts, number of credit people supervised, region, industry, education, number of years with the company and number of years in credit.
10. The ability of credit departments to harness technological change will remain a major concern throughout the decade. Certain activities in the credit department lend themselves to changes in the way in which they are performed.

Review/Discussion Questions

1. What does it mean to benchmark the credit function? Discuss the usefulness of specific measures that can be used to benchmark the credit function.
2. Where can one obtain benchmarking data to use for the management of the credit function?
3. Identify a danger signal where the credit department appears to be lacking in morale.
4. What has been the trend in salaries for personnel in credit management positions? Why do you think the trend is moving in this direction?
5. The following questions pertain to the MGC Company:
   (a) Calculate the Days Sales Outstanding during the year if total receivables at the end of the year are $20 million and annual sales are $100 million.
   (b) Calculate the Best Possible Days Sales Outstanding if current receivables are $15 million and sales during the year are $100 million.
   (c) What is the Average Days Delinquent when comparing your results in (a) to (b) above?
6. Draw an organization chart for the credit function at your place of employment or for any selected business.
7. Is your credit function set up on a centralized or decentralized basis?
8. What forces are contributing to the surge in Business Process Outsourcing?
9. What credit processes lend themselves to the use of BPO?
10. What caveats should credit managers be aware of when considering BPO?

Test Your Knowledge

1. Provide three examples of unethical behavior by a credit manager.
2. How is the percentage bad debts expense calculated for a company?
3. What is the difference between a centralized and a decentralized credit function? Which approach is better?
4. What is the purpose of an organization chart?
5. Explain Maslow's hierarchy of needs theory. How can this theory be useful to a corporate credit manager?
6. What processes in the credit function tend to be excellent focal points for using technological innovation? Try to identify an example where a credit department should be able to reengineer a specific process.
7. Compare and contrast internal benchmarking and external benchmarking. Support your response with examples.
8. What are some of the advantages of using a centralized credit function as opposed to a decentralized credit function?
9. You are hired as a corporate credit manager by a medium-sized company. You notice that morale in the credit department is low. What specific tactics could be useful to provide the credit department with a motivational lift?
10. Business Process Outsourcing (BPO) needs to be examined both quantitatively and qualitatively. Deduction management is a credit-related process that could benefit from BPO. What quantitative and qualitative factors will shape the decision to use BPO for deduction management?

Credit Management Online

www.crfonline.org/surveys/surveys.asp/—The Credit Research Foundation benchmarking study of the credit and accounts receivable functions is available for purchase at this website. There are free sample statistics that demonstrate the potential use of benchmarking at this site.

www.fcibglobal.com/—The CICP credential available through FCIB-NACM is detailed on this site. The criteria concerning eligibility and the nature of the exam are outlined. An application form can be downloaded.

http://nacm.org/certification.html/—This website provides the details for the four credentials available from NACM to credit personnel: CCRA, CBA, CBF and CCE. Qualifications, study guides and exam dates are available here.

http://nacm.org/services/credit-career-center.html/—This website provides information for job seekers, employers and recruiters.

www.nacmchicago.org/—As the website for a local NACM Affiliate and NACM Connect which spans eight states, this online material describes the potential activities for credit personnel to get involved with at the local level. Membership, services, educational activities, local board membership and local committees are highlights of this site.

www.roberthalffinance.com/—Robert Half International makes available a list of open jobs in finance and credit that can be used to identify positions in credit management by location. An annual salary survey can be obtained that shows the salaries for those employed in accounting and finance positions.

References Useful for Further Reading

Barron, Jacob. "NACM Survey Illuminates Credit Department Organization Styles." *NACM eNews* (January 5, 2010).

Callahan, Terry. "Benchmarking to Measure Your Performance." *Business Credit* (November/December 2007): 50-52.

Diana, Tom. "What's Ahead in Business Credit Technology?" *Business Credit* (October 2006): 32-33.

EBSCO Publishing. *Business Source Elite.* (May 29, 2010): https://library.usao.edu/home/blogs/kbrown/business-source-elite-database-upgraded-business-source-complete/.

"FTC Data Security Tips." *Business Credit* (October 2007): 36-38.

Gahala, Charles. "Financial Tools of Analysis: Business Process Outsourcing." *The National Credit Review* (March 2001).

Gahala, Charles. "Practical 'Best Practices' to Integrate Benchmarking into the Credit Department." *Business Credit* (November/December 2007): 28, 30.

Horner, Chris, Ed. *Credit and Collections Benchmarks & Analysis 2010.* Newark, NJ: IOMA Business Intelligence at Work, 2010.

Institute of Credit Management. "DSO Benchmarking." *Credit Management* (May 2009): 18.

Lehman, Jennifer. "Ever-Evolving Technology: Where Do New Platforms and Software Fit into the Credit Profession?" *Business Credit* (March 2016): 18-20.

Leopold, Markus, Paolo Vanini, and Silvan Ebnoether. "Optimal Credit Limit Management Under Different Information Regimes." *Journal of Banking & Finance*, Vol. 30, No. 2 (February 2006): 463-487.

Mota, Diana. "Getting the Most Out of an Industry Trade Group as Benchmarking Tool." *Business Credit* (September/October 2016): 16-18.

Mota, Diana. "MVPs: Most Valuable Professionals." *Business Credit* (June 2015): 18-20.

"NACM 2008 Business Credit Compensation Survey." NACM and Cascade Employers Association (May 2008).

Nelson, Craig. "Are Savings Enough? A Benchmarking Framework for Maximizing Your Deal." *Business Credit* (November/December 2009): 45-46.

Trkman, Peter. "The Critical Success Factors of Business Process Management." *International Journal of Information Management*, Vol. 30, No. 2 (April 2010): 125-134.

Trunzo, Giuseppe, CICP. "The Credit Management Revolution." *Business Credit* (June 2017): 14-15.

Wimley, C.J. "Emerging Trends in Technology." *Business Credit* (October 2007): 30-33.

Chapter 3

CREDIT MANAGEMENT IN A GLOBAL MARKETPLACE

"What's striking is that we've had recessions before, we've had serious recessions, but this one took more out of GDP numbers than we've ever seen. This is truly a global recession."[1]

Chris Kuehl, Ph.D.
Managing Director, Armada Corporate Intelligence
and NACM Economic Advisor

The expansion of U.S. international trade went from 9% of U.S. gross domestic product (GDP) in 1960 to 28% of GDP in 2015 according to the World Bank. The significant increase in international trade makes it essential to take a global approach to credit management. World markets simply have become more interdependent.

The ability to compete in a global marketplace has become a necessity. International trade is expected to continue to grow due to the adoption of the euro as the common currency in 19 European countries. Furthermore, huge markets in countries such as China and India are opening up to foreign trade. Agreements such as the North American Free Trade Agreement (NAFTA) and the Uruguay Round of the General Agreement on Tariffs and Trade (GATT) have also contributed significantly to the growth in trade.

At a time when many U.S. companies have witnessed a decline in domestic markets, certain international markets have been able to grow. Academics refer to this as the negative correlation benefits between marketplaces that can contribute to a stability of earnings. The higher the negative correlation between markets, the greater the reduction in risk. In this context, global trade can actually create a degree of risk reduction through diversification benefits.

---

[1] Jacob Barron, "Rating the Regions: A Look at What 2010 Has in Store for Global Trade," *Business Credit* (March 2010): 44-49.

48

The purpose of Chapter 3 is to provide a foundation for credit management in a global marketplace. The **Key Learning Objectives** in Chapter 3 are:

1. Recognize risks that are unique to operating in a global marketplace.
2. Identify credit analysis focal points that are useful when analyzing sovereign governments and foreign companies.
3. Examine the opportunity to control credit risk through the use of export credit insurance.
4. Utilize strategies that can be helpful to manage foreign exchange risk.

Those firms with comparative advantages in identifiable markets will have the best opportunities to excel in a global marketplace. Credit managers also play a vital role by contributing to the management of risk. Risk management is emerging as the most important ingredient essential to success in a global marketplace.

The subject of credit management in a global marketplace is deliberately introduced early in this textbook. In addition, specific international topics are integrated into later chapters in the book. The intention is to develop a global way of thinking concerning credit-related subject matter. The topic is so important that the Finance, Credit and International Business Association (FCIB) and NACM have developed the Certified International Credit Professional (CICP) and International Certified Credit Executive (ICCE) designations in response to the demand for the unique skills essential to manage credit in a global marketplace.

A CHANGE IN WORLD GROWTH

Significant risks are reflected by changes in the growth rates. For example, in 2009 the World Trade Organization (WTO) reported the sharpest decline in world trade in more than 70 years. Due to an international credit crunch, risk control will continue to be the major focus for global credit management for years to come.

The data in Table 3-1 show that the U.S. Gross Domestic Product (GDP) grew at a 2.2% rate during 2015, and only a 1.6% rate during 2016. The GDP growth rate in Asia was 4.2% in 2015 and 4.1% during 2016, showing almost no change. In South and Central America, the GDP in 2015 was -0.9% and -2.0% in 2016. The change in growth pinpoints changes in risk.

3: Credit Management in a Global Marketplace   49

TABLE 3-1	**World Trade Organization**								
	International Trade Statistics								
	GDP			**Exports**			**Imports**		
	2014	2015	2016	2014	2015	2016	2014	2015	2016
Vol. world mdse trade [a]	2.7	2.6	1.3						
Real GDP [b]	2.6	2.6	2.3						
Developed economies	1.7	2.2	1.6	2.4	2.7	1.4	3.6	4.7	2.0
Developing economies [c]	4.2	3.5	3.5	3.0	2.0	1.3	1.7	0.5	0.2
North America	2.4	2.5	1.6	4.2	0.7	0.5	4.8	6.7	0.4
South and Central Ameria	0.6	-0.9	-2.0	-2.2	2.5	2.0	-2.4	-5.8	-8.7
Europe	1.6	2.2	1.9	2.0	3.6	1.4	3.2	4.3	3.1
Asia	4.0	4.2	4.1	4.3	1.1	1.8	3.0	2.9	2.0
Other regions [d]	2.5	1.1	1.7	0.9	4.3	0.3	-0.9	-5.1	-2.4

a Average of exports and imports.
b Real GDP at market exchange rates.
c Includes the Commonwealth of Independent States (CIS) including associate and former member states.
d Other regions comprise Africa, CIS and Middle East.

Sources: World Trade Organization Secretariat for trade; consensus estamates for GDP, with data source from the International Monetary Fund, Organisation for Economic Co-operation and Development, United Nations, Economist Intelligence Unit and a variety of national sources. Press Release dated April 12, 2017.

The data in Table 3-1 pinpoint differences in growth rates for GDP, exports and imports during 2014, 2015 and 2016. For example, the data in Table 3-1 show that North American exports increased by only 0.5% during 2016 while world exports increased by 1.3% during the same year. On the other hand, North American imports increased by 0.4% in 2016 while imports into South and Central America declined by -8.7% rate. The important point to note is that international trade brings with it an increase both in opportunity and in risk.

RISK IN A GLOBAL MARKETPLACE

For most of the topics in this book, the material is applicable to both domestic and global operations. However, there are several types of risk that are unique to managing credit in a global marketplace. These risks need to be examined carefully by credit managers who are involved with evaluating diverse business practices in foreign countries.

The framework in which international credit operates is based upon conventions, laws, culture, mores and regulations. This framework provides the mechanism to consider risk while establishing credit arrangements. Credit managers face the challenge of understanding how specific factors contribute to risk within an international framework.

For example, the practice of countertrade is somewhat similar to bartering; this can be a cashless process that provides a mechanism to avoid foreign exchange currency risk. Countertrade arrangements vary widely. However, countertrade can create new types of risk depending upon the buyback or compensation agreement. The increase in risk comes from the willingness of the foreign government to release products or to impose licensing agreements.

The practice of forfaiting is another example of a credit tool that can be used to reduce risk while at the same time imposing new risks that need to be examined carefully. *Forfait* has a French derivation; it implies the purchase of a negotiable instrument (such as a promissory note or a letter of credit) from an exporter on a non-recourse arrangement. The practice of forfaiting is somewhat popular in Europe. If a letter of credit is used as the payment mechanism to fund an export, then the exporting company could discount the letter of credit from a financial institution that then has the responsibility to collect the funds. The new risks for the credit manager using forfaiting involve significant documentation complexities.

Determining the level of risk is essential to conducting business in any country. There are six categories of risk that are unique when operating in a global marketplace: (1) political risk, (2) cultural and language risk, (3) legal risk, (4) bank liquidity coupled with bank capital adequacy risk, (5) foreign exchange risk and (6) country risk. Each type of risk contributes to the complexity of decisions made by credit managers.

Political Risk

Political and social forces often contribute to the ability and willingness of a debtor to honor obligations. An individual nation can exercise considerable control over business operations. Political risk includes the risk of expropriation of assets without compensation. Other examples of political risk include radical ideological shifts, rioting, terrorism against personnel or property and military coups.

Political risk can be assessed by examining the history of a particular country. Factors such as government stability and social conditions influence political risk. In addition, external factors such as ideological orientation and participation in international organizations may be examined to assess political risk.

Cultural and Language Risk

Unique cultural heritages and values can influence the ability to operate successfully in a global environment. At times, cultural norms can conflict with managerial values. For example, the attitude toward alcohol in certain Arab countries may restrict consumption. In some cultures, women may not be accepted as business executives in the same way in which they are accepted in the United States; this can influence negotiation strategy. Even the dress code can create a barrier to open negotiation.

U.S. credit practitioners can be at a disadvantage if they are not fluent in foreign languages. In Canada, there are divisions between the French- and English-speaking populations. Language risk can be potentially catastrophic. Although more and more foreign business practitioners use the English language, the credit manager who can master local languages holds a distinct advantage.

The risk of making a translation error should not be underestimated. Experienced credit managers often will require two translations to reduce translation errors. Some U.S. credit managers use both a bilingual English-speaking native and a bilingual foreign translator from the host country to compare translations. Translators often have trouble with technical terms.

Language can also be muddled by misunderstood gestures or even confused through unspoken words. The conversational distance may be smaller in the Middle East. A Japanese businessperson may be nodding yes but really thinking no; he or she may be trying to appear polite and agreeable.

In certain countries, the Muslim religion often necessitates a need to include financing that incorporates compliance to Sharia'a or Islamic Law. Taking the time to learn the principles of compliance to Sharia'a can go a long way toward fostering sound business relationships with devout Muslims.

For some credit managers, the issue of receiving or providing gifts and payments to obtain cooperation is a major concern. Although it is common practice in international business to exchange gifts, this issue can become murky. When is a credit manager bribing a public official? When is a private party really asking for an extortion payment? Americans are governed by the Foreign Corrupt Practices Act, which pertains to questionable business practices that relate to bribes and illegal payments. Global credit managers should become familiar with this Act. The U.S. Department of Commerce includes a lesson on the Foreign Corrupt Practices Act in *A Basic Guide to Exporting*, at www.export.gov/article?id=U-S-Foreign-Corrupt-Practices-Act/.

Legal Risk

When credit practitioners enter into business agreements, the laws of the host country govern business transactions. This means that litigation for nonpayment and potential judgments are governed by business practices in the foreign country.

Both the European Community and the United Nations have conventions established for contract disputes when parties from two or more countries are involved. It is also possible to have disputes arbitrated in centers such as Geneva, London, Paris, Hong Kong or New York. The use of conventions or arbitration clauses should be stipulated in agreements before problems arise. Otherwise, the laws of the host country will govern disputes.

There are also numerous types of governmental laws that can become barriers to international trade:

- *Embargoes* are used to prohibit products that originate from certain specified countries.
- *Quotas* are used to limit the dollar value or quantity for specified products.
- *Tariffs* are fees charged to import goods into a country.
- *Customs* can be a way to limit entry by imposing documentation requirements or assessing fees on imports.
- *Anti-dumping regulations* are used to prohibit the sale of products at below-cost pricing.
- *Health and safety regulations* pertain to product, packaging and labeling requirements.
- *Antitrust laws* are commonly referred to as restrictive trade practices in other countries.
- *Tax laws* may vary widely from country to country. Consumption taxes, value added taxes, income taxes and capital gains taxes each mandate compliance with host country codes.

Legal risk in international trade is being reduced through agreements such as the North American Free Trade Agreement (NAFTA) and the General Agreement on Tariffs and Trade (GATT). Together, the NAFTA and GATT agreements are a movement toward deregulation that has resulted in an increase in world trade.

NAFTA is the agreement that promotes free trade among Canada, Mexico and the United States. All three countries can potentially benefit from reduced costs, more competitive prices and an increase in global trading power. The long-range view is that NAFTA is an economic reform that is facilitating trade among the three countries. However, there are operating details that need to be carefully scrutinized.

The World Trade Organization (WTO) is an international organization consisting of 164 member countries. The WTO is headquartered in Geneva, Switzerland. The WTO's role is to establish trade agreements, monitor trade policies and handle trade disputes among member nations. The WTO was created by GATT in the Uruguay Round of negotiations.

GATT is an international trade agreement that acts as a mechanism for regulating international trade and trade negotiations. The first GATT agreement, entered into by 23 nations, went into effect in 1948. The Uruguay Round of the GATT agreement was signed by more than 120 countries in 1994. The Uruguay Round of GATT was negotiated over a seven-year period; the results have contributed to the growth in world merchandise trade. The Uruguay Round contributed to the formation of the General Agreement on Trade in Services (GATS), which is being negotiated. GATS' focus is to create an agreement for trade pertaining to accounting, advertising, computer, engineering, education, financial and other services.

One factor that has slowed down the expected growth in international trade relates to the agency issue. The agency issue suggests that there may be a conflict of interests among employees, stockholders, managers (agents) and creditors. In the United States, there is a general belief that the actions that maximize the price of stock also benefit society in general. However, in countries where there are severe social problems, the interests of stockholders are not always a primary concern. The results of the conflict—often caused by social problems—can have a fallout in a debtor's willingness to service obligations. The interests of agents other than stockholders can dominate trade issues.

Bank Liquidity and Bank Capital Adequacy Risk

Another factor that has limited the growth in international trade pertains to the health of the international banking system. In particular, bank liquidity and bank capital adequacy experienced serious shortcomings during the credit crunch from 2008 and continuing into

2010. Basel, Switzerland is a town where a series of negotiations concerning bank capital adequacy have taken place. Central banks and regulators from 27 countries agreed to rules concerning the maintenance of bank capital.

The Basel Accord agreements (Basel I and Basel II) set the rules for banks to maintain a certain level of equity capital. Basel I, which was established in 1988 set the standards for minimum capital requirements for banks. Then Basel II, implemented in 2009, relaxed the rules for bank capital standards by allowing banks considerable flexibility to develop their own formulas to determine capital adequacy. Many experts agree that Basel II was a failure.

At the height of the credit crunch in January 2008, banks around the world were caught up in a spiral of risk-taking that led to a liquidity crunch and serious problems with bank capital adequacy The concern had been that customer loan defaults were increasing, which placed numerous banks in a precarious position as they tried to adhere to the Basel agreement. On September 13, 2010, the Basel III international agreement was reached. The newest Basel Accord is aimed at stabilizing the global financial system. The agreement is focused on cutting bank risk taking and developing firmer capital adequacy guidelines to protect the international banking system. Financial institutions have been in need of more rigorous rules so that the institutions are better able to survive an economic downturn.

Much focus has been placed upon stress tests to determine bank viability. A stress test is similar to using scenario analysis in corporate finance. Risk can be examined by modeling the effect of changing economic conditions. For example, plausible changes in variables such as household debt levels, unemployment, the loss of a key customer and real estate valuations can each be examined. By linking the changes in key variables to the impact upon bank capital adequacy, the risk of a bank surviving an economic downturn can be examined. Stress tests have sounded an alarm to the international financial community for banks to focus upon a need to increase bank capital.

Foreign Exchange Risk

Credit transactions in a global marketplace are denominated in various currencies. Foreign exchange risk is the risk that the exchange rate used to change one currency into another currency will fluctuate. The potential loss due to a fluctuating currency value is of particular importance to credit managers. This subject will be more fully developed in the last section of this chapter.

Political risk, cultural and language risk, legal risk and foreign exchange risk each pose unique problems to a global credit manager. In addition, there is business risk inherent in international trade. The next section of this chapter will identify focal points that are useful when extending credit to a sovereign government or foreign business.

Country Risk

Perhaps the single most limiting factor that retards the growth in international trade is the availability of credit. When credit availability is associated with the obligation of a sovereign government, country risk should be examined. Country risk can be defined as the probability that a loss could be incurred due to events that are under the control of the government. Country risk is a function of political, social and economic circumstances.

Country risk can become complicated for credit analysis purposes because the analysis includes a number of variables that are not normally analyzed by most credit managers. Some credit managers set a country credit limit in order to restrict exposure. Table 3-2 contains a list of focal points for credit managers to consider when analyzing country risk.

The focal points contained in Table 3-2 are a good starting point for country risk analysis. Country risk analysis reports are also available from the Export-Import Bank of the United States. Individual country restrictions can be reviewed at www.exim.gov/. There are also commercial providers who can provide credit insurance by country. FCIB, Dun & Bradstreet, Standard & Poor's and certain major money center banks prepare reports that can be useful for credit analysis purposes.

Default on governmental debt is normally restructured. One of the best gauges to use concerning future governmental obligations is to examine performance on past credit obligations. Sometimes credit managers can reduce their exposure by obtaining guarantees from governmental agencies in the host country. In other cases, export insurance can be used to control credit risk in many foreign countries.

Just as banks have seen a focus upon stress tests during the global credit crunch of 2008 to 2010, countries are also seeing a heightened focus being placed upon stress tests to examine risk. In particular, Greece, Spain and Italy have seen major gradual increases in country sovereign debt obligations. At issue is the ability of a government to

TABLE 3-2	**Country Risk Analysis Focal Points**

I. Political Risk Assessment
  A. Political System: Structure and Evolution
  B. Stability of Leadership
  C. Cooperation with International Bodies
  D. Geopolitical Importance to Western Bloc Countries

II. Social Risk Assessment
  A. Disparity of Income; Per Capita Income
  B. Unemployment Levels
  C. Environmental/Governmental Regulation
  D. Social Order
  E. Population Growth Rate
  F. Infrastructure/Transportation Problems

III. Economic Risk Assessment
  A. Balance of Payments Flexibility
  B. Inflation Rate/Interest Rates
  C. Natural Resources/Degree of Product Diversification
  D. Growth Rate in Output of Goods and Services
  E. Ability to Service Debt Burden
  F. Ability to Attract Investment
  G. Current Taxation Levels; Flexibility in Future Taxation Levels

service its debt. The stress tests focus upon varying scenarios to determine the viability of meeting financial obligations. The social and political side effects will certainly shape the availability of credit within countries.

FOREIGN COMPANY ANALYSIS

Credit analysis for a foreign business is similar to analyzing a domestic business, but there are a few important differences. First, the country in which the business is located influences the ability to extend credit to the business. Second, there is a potential for currency fluctuation, which creates an added risk. Finally, the details available by using various sources of credit information are similar to, but somewhat different than, using domestic sources.

When analyzing credit information on a foreign business, there are a number of potential sources to utilize. These sources include resources from FCIB as well as financial statement information, bank references and commercial agency reports. Chapter 7 will include coverage of commercial agency reports. A few comments concerning the use of international sources of information are included in this chapter.

FCIB. This international arm of NACM is a leading producer of payment records for foreign businesses in more than 176 countries. FCIB members are able to obtain actual credit experience by industry and geographic region. Country and political risk reports are also available through FCIB. There are more than 1,000 corporate members of FCIB. FCIB resources can be examined at www.fcibglobal.com/.

FCIB publishes a Monthly International Credit and Collection Survey that includes extensive payment records. The FCIB website allows non-members access to the highlights of survey results. Credit information is reported twice a year by continent. The country information that is readily available to non-members includes: method of transacting business, average number of days for which credit is granted, the number of accounts and the average payment delay. FCIB members also have access to much more detailed information.

Non-U.S. Financial Statements. Credit managers should be aware that both the format for non-U.S. financial statements and the principles of accounting used to prepare financial statements in other countries are different than those used in the United States. (A financial statement drawn from a company in Great Britain may look like you are driving on the wrong side of the road because the assets can appear toward the right column and the liabilities toward the left column in a horizontal balance sheet.)

Since diverse accounting conventions are applied to varying business practices, the results can be easily misinterpreted. For example, Japanese firms tend to use more financial leverage than U.S. firms. Moreover, Japanese firms tend to enter long-term supply contracts and invest in the stock of their suppliers. These differences can result in some unusual gains and losses in an income statement due to fluctuating interest rates and stock market volatility.

There is a movement toward globalizing financial accounting rules through the use of International Financial Reporting Standards (IFRS), which will be discussed in Chapter 9 later in this book.

Bank References. The availability of information through foreign bank references tends to be more limited in foreign countries than in the United States. In many instances, foreign banks will not share information with suppliers. As a result, credit managers often contact their U.S. bank, which can then contact a correspondent foreign bank to obtain a reference for the credit manager. The U.S. bank often charges a fee for obtaining the reference by increasing the compensating balance requirement on the credit manager's business account.

Not only do sources of information on foreign businesses differ from domestic accounts, the terms of sale may also vary. Due to increased competitiveness in transacting global business, open account terms are becoming more popular in international business. However, trust between the buyer and creditor is sometimes not sufficient to establish open account terms. Certain less creditworthy customers may be reluctant to pay cash in advance. For those customers who do not justify open account terms, export sales can be supported through the use of a letter of credit as a payment mechanism.

EXPORT LETTERS OF CREDIT

Letters of credit allow customers to substitute their creditworthiness for the creditworthiness of an issuing bank. Letters of credit are somewhat similar to other types of secured transactions. Chapter 11 in this book contains a thorough discussion of both standby and documentary letters of credit. Documentary letters of credit pertain to both import and export letters of credit.

Credit managers should realize that the foreign customer initiates the letter of credit. The customer's bank issues the letter of credit to an advising bank in the United States. If the credit manager is not comfortable with the creditworthiness of the foreign bank, he or she should request a confirmation of the letter of credit by a U.S. bank. The confirmation allows the credit manager to rely on the creditworthiness of the confirming bank.

The exporter should carefully examine each letter of credit, checking to see if the stated terms and conditions are acceptable. If there are any unacceptable terms or conditions, the creditor should request an amendment to the letter of credit. Any documentation discrepancy is grounds for a bank to refuse the responsibility to comply. Letters of credit should stipulate that they are subject to the Uniform Customs and Practices for Documentary Credits (UCP 600), which is the sixth revision of the original UCP that was enacted in 1933.

The most common problems concerning letters of credit that are encountered by exporters include: (1) an insufficient dollar amount to cover the credit, (2) an expiration date on the letter of credit that has passed and (3) an inability to meet the shipping date specified in the

3: Credit Management in a Global Marketplace

TABLE 3-3 Common Documentation Discrepancies in Export Letters of Credit

- Documents inconsistent with each other.
- Documents presented more than 21 days after date of shipment (or other presentation period specified in the letter of credit).
- Full set of bills of lading not presented or other required documents missing.
- Draft drawn incorrectly or for the wrong amount.
- Draft not signed or not endorsed.
- Invoice does not describe merchandise in exact accordance with the letter of credit.
- Invoice does not show the same shipping terms as specified in the letter of credit.
- Invoice includes charges inconsistent with the shipping terms in the letter of credit.
- Invoice not made out in the name of the applicant shown in the letter of credit.
- Insufficient insurance amount or coverage does not include the risks specified by the letter of credit.
- Insurance certificate or policy not endorsed.
- Insurance certificate dated later than the shipment date. (Acceptable if coverage is warehouse-to-warehouse.)
- Bill of lading not clean (defective condition of goods or packaging indicated).
- Bill of lading does not clearly indicate the name and capacity of the signer and who the carrier is. (Must be signed "ABC Co. as carrier" or "XYZ Co., as agent for ABC Co., the carrier.")
- Bill of lading not correctly endorsed (if endorsement is required).
- Multimodal bill of lading presented when letter of credit calls for port-to-port (or simply "ocean") bill of lading; "on board" notation does not include the name of the vessel and the port of lading.
- Multimodal bill of lading presented when shipping terms are FOB (i.e., port-to-port).
- Bill of lading not marked "freight prepaid" or "freight collect" as required under the credit or in agreement with the invoice and shipping terms.
- Not all documents show license numbers, letter of credit numbers or other identification required in the credit.
- Documents not signed in accordance with letter of credit terms (any documents called a "certificate" must be signed).

Source: Walter Baker, Vice President, Bank of America, N.T. & S.A., Exchanging Documents for Money, Chicago, Ill., 1994, pp. 28-29. (Used with specific permission of author.)

letter of credit. Table 3-3 contains a list of the most common discrepancies that surface when banks examine a letter of credit.

These discrepancies can be used as a partial checklist for particular concerns on letter of credit transactions. When a letter of credit arrangement does not appear to be a viable alternative, credit managers can seek to arrange other terms. When a letter of credit is not available, a credit manager can consider obtaining export trade and political risk insurance in order to manage risk.

EXPORT CREDIT INSURANCE

A credit manager can use export credit insurance to control risk on export sales. The insurance company covers the credit so that in the event of a default by a foreign customer, the insurance company will fund the loss. Export credit insurance often includes an agreed-upon deductible amount for claims.

Many countries have established governmental agencies or private consortiums of insurance companies that insure debt obligations. In the Unites States, the Foreign Credit Insurance Association (FCIA) is a private association that includes many commercial insurance companies. The FCIA works closely with Export-Import Bank (Ex-Im Bank), which is an agency of the U.S. government.

Exporters may purchase insurance to cover various types of business transactions through the FCIA. Commercial risk due to a customer default can be covered; political risk coverage also is available through the FCIA. The FCIA website can be reviewed at www.fcia.com/ to learn more about the services available.

The Export-Import Bank publishes a country limitation schedule that includes exceptions and limitations for coverage. Policies can be structured to meet the needs of credit managers. Protection against political or commercial nonpayment is available through Ex-Im Bank. The actual insurance can be purchased to cover a large, one-shot deal or may be structured to provide blanket coverage in a particular country. The insurance coverage can be short term in nature, or it can be arranged over a long period of time. Insurance can be purchased to cover leased goods, goods shipped on consignment, services or recurring shipments of goods to a single customer. Since the insurance policies can be structured in many ways, the website at www.exim.gov/ is a useful starting point.

Commercial and political risk insurance is also available through private insurance companies. For example the big three of the credit insurance industry are Atradius, Coface and Euler Hermes. Each provides trade and political risk insurance. Their websites can serve as useful tools: www.atradius.us/ (Atradius U.S.), www.coface-usa.com/ (Coface North America) and www.eulerhermes.com/ (Euler Hermes ACI).

A typical experienced manufacturer with significant interests in undeveloped countries may benefit from the use of credit insurance. The insurance provides protection against large, unexpected losses. The websites noted above provide helpful information to learn more about the use and availability of credit insurance to support exports.

Due to the increasing competitiveness caused by operating in a global marketplace, the selling terms available may create opportunities to increase sales. If a customer is unwilling to pay cash or provide a letter of credit, credit insurance may afford an option essential to control risk.

FOREIGN EXCHANGE RISK

One of the most important differences between domestic and international credit management is that international transactions are often conducted in currencies other than U.S. dollars. Through the years, U.S. credit managers have often conducted international business in dollars. Historically, the dollar has been considered a safe haven with almost universal acceptance. However, the ability to conduct international transactions in U.S. dollars is not always in the best interest of the U.S. exporter. Other currencies are gaining in international stature, particularly the euro.

The euro is the currency now used by 19 of the 28 European Union member states as their national currency. Adoption of the euro facilitates trade. The European countries that have adopted the euro as their currency include: Austria, Belgium, Cyprus, Estonia, Finland, France, Germany, Greece, Ireland, Italy, Latvia, Lithuania, Luxembourg, Malta, the Netherlands, Portugal, Slovakia, Slovenia and Spain. Foreign exchange risk has decreased for the trade between members of these 19 countries.

Foreign exchange risk is caused by a fluctuation in the price of a unit of one country's currency in relationship to the price of the currency in another country. At issue is the transfer of purchasing power using different currencies. For a U.S. exporter, when a sale is made, either the U.S. exporter or the business in a foreign country will bear the foreign exchange risk.

For example, consider the case in which a U.S. exporter sells a product to a firm in Japan. If the transaction is arranged in yen, the U.S. exporter must accept payment from the Japanese business in yen and then convert the yen to dollars. If the transaction is arranged in dollars, the Japanese business must convert the yen to dollars in order to pay the U.S. exporter. In either case, foreign exchange risk exists for one of the participants in the transaction.

If the U.S. business insisted upon conducting an export in dollars, the Japanese customer would bear the exchange rate risk. A concern is that the Japanese customer could demand a price concession to bear the exchange rate risk; even worse yet, the Japanese business may change suppliers and purchase from an Australian business that is willing to bear the exchange rate risk.

An international credit manager should be adept at managing exchange rate risk. The basic principles that apply to collecting domestic receivables also apply to collecting international receivables. The key difference is that cash flow is maximized in a cost-efficient way by managing foreign exchange risk in a global marketplace.

In order to manage foreign exchange risk, it is essential for credit managers to focus on key points. These points include: (1) understand the differences between using spot and forward market rates, (2) recognize that vehicle currencies are more readily convertible than soft currencies, (3) consider market forces that cause currencies to fluctuate, (4) recognize an opportunity to hedge a transaction and (5) understand some of the services available from banks to assist in the management of foreign exchange risk.

Spot vs. Forward Rates

The spot rate of exchange is the actual exchange rate between two currencies for their immediate trade. Table 3-4 contains exchange rates at the close of business on May 17, 2017. Exchange rates can be found in *The Wall Street Journal* or in the financial section of most metropolitan newspapers. An online source at www.xe.com/ucc/ can be useful as a currency converter. The rates contained in Table 3-4 are subject to change on an ongoing updated daily basis.

TABLE 3-4   Sample Spot Exchange Rates*

Country	Currency	U.S. Dollars Needed to Buy One Unit	Units of Foreign Currency Per U.S. Dollar
Germany	Euro	1.11554	.89648
Great Britain	Pound	1.29640	.77139
Japan	Yen	.00901	110.959
Canada	Dollar	.73456	1.36135
Mexico	Peso	.05338	18.7342

*Data accessed on May 17, 2017.

The data in Table 3-4 show that on May 17, 2017, one U.S. dollar was equivalent to 1.11554 euros. At the time that this book was being written, the euro had been falling in comparison to the U.S. dollar due to an economic crisis in certain countries that use the euro as their currency. The drop in the euro could make a vacation to Europe less expensive for an American visiting Europe but more expensive for a European visiting the United States.

The forward rates of exchange represent the cost to obtain a commitment to deliver or to accept an agreed amount of a specific currency on a specific date. Standard forward contracts are typically established for 30, 60, 90 or 180 days. Forward contracts trade in the over-the-counter marketplace. However, money center banks can help to arrange the details concerning time intervals for forward contracts. Exchange rates are established at the time that a forward contract is entered into.

The Chicago Mercantile Exchange (CME) provides the largest marketplace in the world for futures contracts in various currencies. The typical contract is for six months. Futures contracts are issued on a quarterly basis. Futures contracts are standardized contracts, whereas forward contracts can be tailored to individual transactions between parties. Both types of contracts are quite useful as a mode to reduce currency risk. However, futures contracts have an excellent secondary market whereas forward contracts have a very limited secondary market. The CME website, www.cmegroup.com/, is useful for quotes and for educational purposes concerning futures contracts.

Currency Convertibility

Currencies such as the U.S. dollar, the euro, the British pound and the Japanese yen are considered to be bellwether currencies, or vehicle currencies, because other countries frequently use them to conduct business.

There are certain currencies—known as soft currencies—that are not easily converted into dollars. The Ecuadorian sucre or the Pakistan rupee might be considered soft currencies. When dealing with soft currencies, each one could be converted into dollars. The dollar is then used as a vehicle currency so that an Ecuadorian business can export to Pakistan through the use of dollars. It is important to become familiar with legal and tax situations when dealing in a country with a soft currency. Certain currencies may have a limited convertibility; other countries may place controls on the flow of capital.

Market Forces

Currencies fluctuate based upon several market-related forces. The central bank in a country may defend a currency when market forces are driving down a currency's purchasing power. Fiscal policy also will influence exchange rates. Forces such as the rate of inflation, the balance of trade, tariffs, taxation policies or a war can influence currency exchange rates.

Most credit managers realize that they are unable to control the forces that shape currency exchange rates. Therefore, credit managers should identify ways to control the risk associated with exchange rate fluctuation. A hedge can be used to control risk.

Hedging a Transaction

The safest way to conduct an export credit arrangement is to conduct the transaction in U.S. dollars. When a transaction is conducted in a foreign currency, credit managers should consider a hedge transaction by using a currency futures contract. This entails entering into a futures contract to hedge a position in a foreign currency.

Financial currency futures are traded on the Chicago Mercantile Exchange in their Globex around-the-clock electronic marketplace (www.cmegroup.com/globex/trade-on-cme-globex.html/). The International Monetary Market (IMM) has experienced exceptional growth since trading first began in 1972. Futures contracts typically have four delivery months each year.

A U.S. exporter could enter into a business transaction that is denominated in Japanese yen. If the contract is entered into in June but payment is not expected until September, the U.S. exporter would bear the risk of currency fluctuation. In order to control the currency fluctuation risk, the credit manager could purchase a September currency futures contract available through the IMM. This would allow the U.S. exporter to lock in the exchange rate today for the funds to be received in September. In this case, the credit manager is said to be in a hedged position.

Table 3-5 provides a sample currency hedge for a U.S. exporter. This example pinpoints the risk for an export denominated in a foreign currency. The Chicago Mercantile Exchange has seminars and courses available online that can be a useful way to hone the skills essential to trading futures contracts.

3: Credit Management in a Global Marketplace

TABLE 3-5   Sample Currency Futures Hedge

1. A U.S. exporter sells 1,000,000 aluminum beverage cans to a Japanese customer for 9,252,500 yen. Today's exchange rate is 92.5250 yen per U.S. dollar. However, payment will be made in 90 days.

2. If the sale was made for cash today, the U.S. exporter would obtain 9,252,500 yen ÷ 92.5250 yen = $100,000 for the aluminum beverage cans. (This is the spot rate of exchange on June 3, 2010.)

3. If the cans are actually paid for in 90 days, the U.S. exporter would be paid using an updated exchange rate. If the yen fell against the dollar to a point where on September 3, 2010, it takes 140 yen to purchase one U.S. dollar, the U.S. exporter would obtain 9,252,500 yen ÷ 140 = $66,089.28

4. The exporter could have entered into a currency futures contract to avoid the more than $30,000 currency exchange loss. This loss represents the difference between the original spot price ($100,000) and the actual payment ($66,089.28).

5. Over 99% of all futures contracts are closed out through the use of a reversing trade. The exporter would pay a fee to purchase the futures contract (perhaps $50) and also pay brokerage commissions when buying and reversing the futures contract. In addition, there are margin requirements to be maintained during the period in which the contract is held.

Banking Services

Banks often are an excellent source of information concerning the management of international payments. Concentration banking involves the use of lockbox services in countries where there is a large volume of transactions. These situations allow banks to collect in-country using local accounts to speed up the availability of funds. Concentration banking is useful when economies of scale can be used to take advantage of detailed cash management services. The details of specific transactions can be made available quickly through electronic means. Due to bank transaction costs, the use of concentration banking may not be appropriate for small companies.

Banks also are an excellent source for exchange rate quotations. Banks often act as an intermediary to arrange forward contracts for company-specific needs. Moreover, large banks conduct training sessions and provide materials that can be particularly useful for credit managers. Several large U.S. money center banks are at the leading edge of using technology to assist credit managers in a global marketplace.

CONCLUSIONS

Due to the tremendous increase in global trade, credit managers will need to develop a global way of thinking. Since U.S. exports often create an increase in credit risk, the use of letters of credit often requires specialized educational needs for credit personnel. While only about 1% of U.S. exports are insured, the FCIA, through Export-Import Bank, can provide a vehicle to reduce risk in certain situations. Credit insurance is growing in use due to the credit crunch. Commercial banks can provide considerable assistance to credit personnel in the areas of currency hedging and the use of letters of credit.

CHAPTER 3: FOLLOW-UP

Recap of Important Concepts

1. U.S. exports have grown from 9% of GDP in 1960 to 28% of GDP in 2015. The adoption of the euro by 19 European countries, the opening of new markets such as China and India, and international free trade agreements such as NAFTA and the Uruguay Round of GATT suggest that the growth in international trade will continue.

2. Credit managers play a vital role in managing the risk associated with the growth in international trade. Many of the basic responsibilities of credit managers in a global marketplace are similar to those in a domestic marketplace. However, there are several specific responsibilities that can be directly traced to operating in a global marketplace.

3. There are a number of risks that credit managers need to control. Specific risks that are inherent to international trade include: political risk, cultural and language risk, legal risk, bank liquidity risk coupled with bank capital adequacy risk and foreign exchange risk. The use of stress tests to assess risk has become more common to assess the risk for banks and for countries.

4. Political risk includes the risk of expropriation of assets. Credit managers should monitor ideological shifts, social unrest, acts of terrorism, government stability and general social conditions in order to assess the level of political risk.

5. Cultural and language risk should not be underestimated. Priorities should be placed on the ability to speak the language used in the host country, the accuracy of translation and unique cultural influences. Corporate policy concerning gifts should be clear. The Foreign Corrupt Practices Act governs questionable business practices such as the payment of bribes.

6. The laws of the host country generally govern business dealings. However, it is possible to use conventions or arbitration clauses in agreements to cover specific potential future disputes.

7. Host countries can create barriers to international trade. Specific concerns include: embargoes, quotas, tariffs, customs, anti-dumping laws, health and safety requirements, restrictive trade practices and tax laws. Both NAFTA and the Uruguay Round of GATT represent a movement toward deregulation in global markets. However, the Basel III Accord may lead to more regulation in the banking industry.

8. Country risk is the probability that a loss could be incurred by events that are under the control of the government. Social, political and economic focal points should be analyzed to assess country risk. Stress tests are a more contemporary approach now being used to assess country risk.

9. The analysis of the creditworthiness of a foreign business is similar to analyzing a domestic business. However, financial statements are constructed by using different accounting conventions. FCIB and money-center banks are excellent sources of information. Moreover, credit reporting agencies have improved the availability and quality of reports pertaining to foreign businesses.

10. Letters of credit are a commonly used vehicle to arrange for payments in a global market. There are a number of potential documentation discrepancies that relate to using export letters of credit.

11. Export credit insurance can protect the interests of credit managers through political risk insurance and commercial insurance. The Export-Import Bank of the United States (Ex-Im Bank), FCIA and other private companies offer ways to reduce risk through the use of export credit insurance.

12. Foreign exchange risk is the risk that is caused by a fluctuation in the price of a unit of one country's currency in comparison to the price of a currency in another country. Global credit managers should be concerned with controlling foreign exchange risk.

13. Credit managers can hedge their position in a business transaction denominated in a foreign currency by entering into a futures contract. This allows the credit manager to control the exposure in exchange rate risk.

14. Banks provide a wide range of services to help credit managers operate effectively in a global marketplace. The use of technology, the improvement in cash flow and the actual training of credit managers represent important services available from large banks.

Review/Discussion Questions

1. What is political risk? Identify examples of political risk. Which countries do you believe have a high level of political risk today?

2. What is cultural and language risk? Are there any foreign countries in which the cultural norms may cause problems for credit managers? Give examples to support your answer.

3: Credit Management in a Global Marketplace

69

3. Provide an example of governmental laws that are barriers to international trade. What is the global trend in terms of barriers to international trade? Try to identify major agreements to support your response.
4. What is country risk? Identify several focal points used to evaluate county risk.
5. Identify the nature of problems that credit managers encounter when they analyze credit information concerning a foreign customer.
6. Why is the health of the banking system important to credit managers?
7. If Mexican pesos sell for $.08260 per peso, how many pesos would it take to buy one U.S. dollar?

Test Your Knowledge

1. Why is it important for credit managers to develop a global perspective to managing credit?
2. What is an export letter of credit?
3. What is a tariff? How would an increase in a tariff influence international trade?
4. What is foreign exchange risk?
5. What does the term "expropriation" mean? How can a credit manager try to assess the potential for expropriation?
6. The use of gifts is common in international business. Why should a credit manager be concerned about accepting or giving gifts?
7. What do the Basel Accord agreements focus upon? Why are these agreements important to the international business community?
8. Identify at least six common document discrepancies that occur when using documentary letters of credit.
9. How can export credit insurance protect the interests of credit managers on export sales? Be specific.
10. How can a credit manager control foreign exchange risk? Identify a vehicle that can be used to reduce foreign exchange risk.

Credit Management Online

www.atradius.us/—The Atradius website is an excellent source for information concerning credit insurance.

www.cmegroup.com/—The Chicago Mercantile Exchange is the largest futures exchange in the world. This site can be useful for currency quotes and education concerning hedging futures contracts.

70   Credit Management: Principles and Practices

www.coface-usa.com/—The Coface website is another excellent resource for information concerning credit insurance.

www.eulerhermes.com/—Likewise, the Euler Hermes website provides useful materials about credit insurance.

www.globaloffset.org/—This is the website for the Global Offset and Countertrade Association. The terminology, legal concerns and mechanics of countertrade are explained in detail.

www.exim.gov/—The website for the Export-Import Bank of the United States provides guidelines for exporting to particular countries as well as information about insurance availability and related costs. The country limitation schedule is particularly noteworthy.

www.fcibglobal.com/—This is the home page for the Association of Executives in Finance, Credit and International Business (FCIB). The 1,200 FCIB member corporations, located in 55 countries, are listed. Products and services geared to meet the needs of exporters can be examined; details concerning the CICP designation can also be reviewed.

www.ft.com/—*The Financial Times* is the European equivalent to *The Wall Street Journal*. The site contains market information, world news and contemporary topics of interest.

www.unzco.com/—The U.S. Department of Commerce guidelines for international trade are located at this site, which also offers a basic guide to exporting. There are trade publications and white papers available as well. There is considerable information that could be quite useful for training purposes.

www.wto.org/—The World Trade Organization website offers considerable economic research and statistics that can be useful to credit managers. The WTO is based in Geneva, Switzerland; trade agreements and a forum for disputes that arise in the 164 member countries can also be examined on this site.

www.xe.com/—This is a handy website for currency conversions, which provides drop-down menus to convert one currency into another.

References Useful for Further Reading

Barron, Jacob. "Rating the Regions: A Look at What 2010 Has in Store for Global Trade." *Business Credit* (March 2010): 44-47.

Barron, Jacob. "A Wrench in the Gears? Basel II, the Credit Crunch and an Economic Slump: What Export Credit Professionals Should Know." *Business Credit* (May 2008): 48-51.

Board of Governors of the Federal Reserve System. *The Supervisory Capital Assessment Program: Design and Implementation.* (April 24 2009): 1-18. (*Explanatory note*: See this report to learn more about the mechanics of the stress tests used by the Federal Reserve to evaluate the capital adequacy for the largest U.S. banks.)

Caouette, John B., et al. *Managing Credit Risk: The Great Challenge for Global Financial Markets*, 2nd Ed. Wiley: Hoboken, NJ, 2008.

Carr, Matthew. "Thinking Globally, Working Locally." *Business Credit* (June 2009): 20-24.

Diana, Tom. "Export Sales Can Be Fraught with Legal Peril." *Business Credit* (May 2007): 54-57.

Diana, Tom. "Selling with Sharia'a Compliant Financing." *Business Credit* (February 2007): 52-53.

"FCIB and the U.S. Department of Commerce Release Updated Trade Finance Guide." *Business Credit* (June 2008): 29.

Gahala, Charles. "Establishing Payment Arrangements to Support Export Sales." *Blueprints: The Produce Professionals Quarterly Journal* (July/August/September 2006): 60-63.

Gahala, Charles. "The FCIB Online Course in International Credit and Risk Management." *Business Credit* (March 2007): 52-53.

Goudy, Gene. "2007 Credit Insurance Update." *Business Credit* (March 2007): 60-63.

Goudy, Gene. "Credit Insurance Update–2009." *Business Credit* (March 2009): 20-25.

Grogan, Larry, CCE, CICP. "Making Good Credit Decisions Even without Advanced International Expertise." *Business Credit* (April 2016): 26-27.

Koch, John. "Integration of U.S. Small Businesses into the Export Trade Sector Using Available Trade Finance Tools and Resources: Part 1." *Business Credit* (October 2007): 66-69.

Koch, John. "Integration of U.S. Small Businesses into the Export Trade Sector Using Available Trade Finance Tools and Resources: Part 2." *Business Credit* (November/December 2007): 64-68.

Lehman, Jennifer. "International, Interconnected: The Role Automation Should Play in Global Business." *Business Credit* (November/December 2015): 30-33.

Lustig, Carole. "Forfaiting: A European Customer Finance Technique Comes to the U.S." *Business Credit* (November/December 1998): 26-29.

Mota, Diana. "Trends and Developments in Trade Credit Insurance Coming Quicker than Ever." *Business Credit* (January 2017): 14-15.

Onaran, Yalman. "The Global Battle Over New Rules for Banks." *Bloomberg Businessweek* (May 31, 2010): 41-42.

Shappell, Brian, CBA, CICP. "Credit Insurance Not an Export-Specific Risk Mitigator." *Business Credit* (June 2016): 4-5.

Shappell, Brian. "Unveiling Opportunity: Economic Potential Comes with Vagueness, Potential Risk in Islamic Finance." *Business Credit* (June 2010): 4-7.

Shoulton, Byron. "What's Happening Globally?" *Business Credit* (June 2010): 20-21.

Stern, Nicholas. "Letter of Credit Basics: Some Expert Tips to Avoid Common Mistakes." *Business Credit* (April 2017): 36-37.

West, Dan. "Countertrade: Part 1 of 2." *Business Credit* (April 2001): 64-67.

West, Dan. "Countertrade: Part 2 of 2." *Business Credit* (September 2001): 42-46.

Wilkerson, Jim, Kenneth Spong, and Jon Christenson. "Financial Stability Reports: How Useful During a Financial Crisis?" *Federal Reserve Bank of Kansas City* (First Quarter 2010): 41-70.

Part II

Credit Policy and the Extension of Credit

Chapter 4

MANAGING CREDIT POLICY

"Why have a policy? Recent events have made a valid, consistently enforced policy a necessity for every business, including alleged corporate malfeasance and the willingness of courts to impose sanctions for failure to produce documents in litigation."[1]

Kavita Knowles, Esq.
Fullerton & Knowles P.C.

Accounts receivable represent about 25% of a typical company's total assets. The ability to manage this key asset depends upon the formation and implementation of effective credit policy. Due to the complex nature of credit policy, credit managers should look beyond individual customers in a way that reflects an understanding of just how credit fits into overall corporate goals.

Policies that guide the credit function are developed and monitored within the context of a corporate strategic-planning framework. Specific credit policies are formulated to achieve corporate goals, and credit procedures often help to clarify operating decisions. The mix of specific policies and procedures used to coordinate the credit function are as complex as those of any functional area of business.

The purpose of this chapter is to give you an overview of credit policy and procedures. A hands-on guide for developing credit policy can be accomplished by performing a thorough credit department policy and procedure audit. The audit can be completed by using the checklist provided at the end of this chapter.

The **Key Learning Objectives** in Chapter 4 are:

1. Recognize the role of the credit function in the strategic planning process.
2. Focus upon four key credit department objectives.
3. Define credit policy recognizing that credit policy can have both benefits and limitations.

---

[1] Kavita Knowles, "What You Should Know About Electronic Document Retention," *Business Credit* (October 2008): 32.

4. Gain an understanding of receivables portfolio analysis.
5. Appreciate the potential use of Economic Value Added (EVA) as a gauge to evaluate policy management effectiveness.
6. Identify specific focal points for which credit department policy and procedures could be developed.
7. Use bad debts as a focal point to examine credit policy and procedures.

STRATEGIC PLANNING AND THE ROLE OF THE CREDIT FUNCTION

In a discussion between two credit managers, one credit manager stated that a particular credit policy had worked very well. The other credit manager, however, stated that the same policy was one that would be impossible to consider. Why? The reason is simple: not all corporate markets, products or goals are the same.

Moreover, not all credit managers perform exactly the same tasks. Some credit managers perfect liens under the Uniform Commercial Code (UCC); others do not. Some credit managers use letters of credit; others do not. Consequently, for very good reasons, the credit function varies in terms of policy and procedures from company to company and industry to industry.

Strategic planning is the key ingredient that underlies credit policy and procedures. Strategic planning entails the coordination of long-range plans with a particular focus upon strategies, controls and desired results. There are, of course, a number of external and internal factors that contribute to the overall strategic plan.

External factors such as social, political, economic, legal, technological and competitive pressures impact upon a strategic plan. These external forces are assessed in light of internal factors such as production capacity, technology availability, financial strength, human resources and marketing. The ultimate goal of strategic management is to evaluate these interrelated factors and assess their impact upon risk and reward, which translates into profit or loss.

Judgment always plays a key role in formulating a strategic plan. The tie-in for credit managers is the need to develop credit policies and procedures that remain flexible enough to adapt to the constant change in the interrelated variables, which is part of the strategic planning process.

For example, one company could decide to liberalize credit terms by lending money to customers to boost sales and profits. At the same time, another company could decide to tighten credit policy by eliminating credit cards. The two companies would be moving in the opposite directions with credit policy, yet both companies could improve profits.

The role of strategic planning underlies the framework from which credit policy is formulated. Clearly defined goals impact upon accounts receivable to shape the resulting credit policy. Consequently, the objective of the credit manager is to achieve a desirable balance between changing and conflicting goals.

FOUR KEY CREDIT DEPARTMENT OBJECTIVES

Why have a credit department? Ask any credit person or college student to respond to this question, and then be prepared for some very unexpected surprises. Actually, there are four key credit department objectives to consider when responding to this question. A balanced scorecard can be used to recognize the optimal trade-off to use to balance the four credit department objectives. The balanced scorecard approach can also integrate other functional areas into the planning process. Cross-functional work teams can be used to carry operating strategies through the organization.

1. Develop an Optimal Level of Sales

There is an old axiom that states, "Develop sales-minded credit managers and credit-minded sales managers." This axiom highlights a focus upon balancing corporate goals.

This objective can be considered in light of credit policies and procedures used to sell to marginal accounts. The increased sales will usually broaden the market base and affect corporate profits. Internal controls and a high level of skill in exercising judgment are important in selling marginal accounts. Properly managed, these accounts can frequently contribute substantially to profits.

2. Minimize the Carrying Costs for Accounts Receivables

Average days receivables, better known as days sales outstanding (DSO), is a key focal point measuring credit department effectiveness. A corporate treasurer monitors DSO closely. Table 4-1 will be used to illustrate the importance of allowing the DSO to increase. DSO can be

TABLE 4-1	DSO Calculation	
DSO Step 1: Calculate Sales Per Day		
Annual Sales		$730,000,000
Divide by Days in Year	÷	365
To Obtain Sales Per Day		$2,000,000
DSO Step 2: Calculate DSO		
Average Receivables		$80,000,000
Divide by Sales Per Day	÷	2,000,000
To Obtain DSO		40 Days

calculated in two steps to illustrate the importance of monitoring a change in DSO.

Using the data in Table 4-1, the DSO is 40 days. If the DSO went up to 50 days, the treasurer would need a $20,000,000 source of funds (10 day increase in DSO times $2,000,000 Sales Per Day). The treasurer would use the firm's weighted average cost of capital to calculate the cost of the DSO increase. If the cost of capital for a firm is 12%, it would cost the firm $2,400,000 per year to carry the receivables an extra 10 days throughout the year ($20,000,000 × .12 = $2,400,000).

Credit controls can be used to tighten or loosen credit policy that will cause the DSO to change. Is it better to have a shorter DSO? Is it better to have a longer DSO? It depends!

A shorter DSO is preferred when all other things stay the same. However, if tighter credit controls result in a reduction in sales revenue, those controls need to be thoroughly evaluated in light of their overall contribution to profits.

The challenge to evaluate a DSO as being the optimal DSO is ongoing. As strategic planning goals interact with changes in both external and internal forces, credit managers may need to modify credit policy. These skills usually require considerable experience in credit management.

3. Minimize Bad Debt Losses

Every time a sale is made and goods are shipped to a customer, the risk of incurring a bad debt occurs. The key factor is the assessment of the level of risk in relation to the potential return. If bad debts are abnormally low, credit policy may be too restrictive. On the other hand, there is another old axiom that states, "A sale is not completed until the cash is in the drawer."

4: Managing Credit Policy

TABLE 4-2	Increase in Sales Needed to Offset Bad Debt	
Bad Debt Write Off Amount	Profit Margin Percent	New Sales Needed to Offset Bad Debt
$ 1,000	2%	$ 50,000
10,000	2%	500,000
100,000	2%	5,000,000
1,000	5%	20,000
10,000	5%	200,000
100,000	5%	2,000,000

The data in Table 4-2 indicate the incremental new sales that must be originated in order to offset a bad debt. The incremental new sales needed is obtained by dividing the bad debt amount by the profit margin percentage. For example, if a company with a 2% profit margin writes off $10,000 to bad debts, that company must find $500,000 in incremental new sales in order to offset the bad debt.

Credit managers are left with several questions. What is the profit margin of a product being sold? Are new sales readily available? How aggressive should the extension of credit be to marginal accounts? Is an economic or industry change going to cause a change in potential bad debts? The answers to these questions can certainly have an impact upon credit policy and procedures.

4. Monitor the Costs Incurred by the Credit Department

Some of the specific costs borne by the credit department include technology, staffing, equipment, space, debt recovery, credit reporting and training. Lax credit controls may result in costs that erode the credit department's contribution to profits. Consequently, controls need to be established to ensure that the credit department is functioning at a high level of efficiency.

Across-the-board cost cutting often fails to appreciate where the efficiency levers are located. Learning just where the credit department efficiency levers are located is a major challenge. There is a mandate to tie credit policy and procedures to cost control. Updating procedures mandates experimenting with new techniques that employ the investment into technology. The completion of credit tasks more efficiently is an ultimate goal. A corporate chieftain who evaluates credit department cost efficiency does not always know what to look for. As a matter of fact, most employees outside of the credit department may not even recognize essential credit-related costs. Therefore, credit managers need to link credit policy and procedures closely to cost controls.

ESTABLISHING CREDIT POLICY

The four key credit department objectives can provide a useful basis for identifying specific policy topics. To reiterate, they are: (1) develop an optimal level of sales, (2) minimize the carrying costs for accounts receivables, (3) minimize bad debt losses and (4) monitor the costs incurred by the credit department. Because every company has a different strategic plan, judgment becomes the dominant factor when considering policy needs. These objectives can serve as a starting point for developing a credit department mission statement.

Credit managers can determine operational constraints at individual companies in order to establish the procedures used to implement specific policies. For example, there could be a corporate policy that requires credit limits to be assigned for all customers. An individual company sets policy to determine how the credit limits should be used: rigidly or flexibly. An individual company also decides to whom the credit limits are communicated. Should the sales department know credit limits? Is the customer made aware of credit limits? The answers to these questions can vary from company to company.

Credit policy can be defined as a general course of action used to guide frequently encountered situations designed to achieve strategic objectives. Effective policy can help to ensure uniformity within an organization. More importantly, effective credit policy enhances corporate profitability. To illustrate, suppose that a person pulls into a mini market and buys $25 worth of gas. Employees at the mini market need to understand its credit policy. Is a personal check acceptable? Can a bank credit card be used? Can a customer pay with a $100 bill? In the absence of policy, these questions could be tough to answer; employees would make inconsistent decisions and customers could become upset.

There are potential criticisms concerning the use of credit policy. Occasionally, credit policy is viewed as a straightjacket that impedes flexibility. Another complaint leveled at credit policy is that it is too time-consuming to develop. One final criticism of credit policy is that the policy can lead to disputes with other department managers or customers.

While each of the criticisms of credit policy may have some merit, the benefits of credit policy far outweigh the drawbacks. For example, consider the policy of charging late payment interest. Customers paying

4: Managing Credit Policy 81

late without interest charges use supplier money. This policy may generate complaints. Yet, the policy charging late payment interest can also contribute to corporate profitability.

SIGNS THAT INDICATE
A NEED TO REVIEW CREDIT POLICY

Both external and internal forces can signal the need to modify credit policy. For example, on January 19, 2017, Janet Yellen, chairman of the Federal Reserve, made a presentation during which she stated, "I would mention the potential for changes in policy to affect the economic outlook. At this time, the size, timing and composition of such changes remain uncertain."[2] The Fed was inferring that monetary policy would remain loose as long as inflation was kept under wraps. (The Fed had been loosening monetary policy while working through the credit crunch that included numerous financial difficulties.)

For business credit grantors, a number of warning signals may point out a need to review what is going on in the credit department in regard to policy. A few of the warning signals that may necessitate a policy shift include:

- A recession (could signal more potential bad debts)
- Employer profit margins tightening
- Change in competitive forces
- Change in social or political forces
- Excessive inventory levels
- An increase in bad debts as a percent of sales
- An increase in the DSO period
- An increase in credit department employee turnover
- Credit department budget problems
- An employer recapitalization

This list could continue on and on. However, the key factor to keep in mind is that good judgment underlies any need to alter credit policy and procedure. The need for a shift in policy should be monitored on an ongoing basis. Existing policies can be reaffirmed or altered as conditions require.

---

[2] Chairman Janet Yellen. "The Economic Outlook and the Conduct of Monetary Policy." Presentation made at the Stanford Institute for Economic Policy Research, Stanford California (January 19, 2017).

In May 2009, the Credit Research Foundation released the results of a survey that examined the impact of the credit crisis on credit department operations. The survey results, reported by 1,032 respondents, indicated that 93% of the respondents believed that customers were relying upon suppliers more than in the past years for working capital needs. Further, the results indicated that 59% of the respondents were tightening credit policy and that 66% were tightening collection policy.[3]

The review of credit policy needs to extend beyond the "if it ain't broke, don't fix it" mentality. The pace of changes in business conditions mandates regular review of credit policy. Professionalism in credit management necessitates keeping credit policy current.

RECEIVABLES PORTFOLIO ANALYSIS

Credit management has considerable potential to tap into information technology, and some credit departments have made great strides in this area. In particular, there is an opportunity to manage the entire receivables portfolio as an investment that can contribute to the overall profitability of a firm. Portfolio management can be used to evaluate risk and returns by breaking down the impact of a policy change upon the value added by the credit function.

Internal and external forces shape changes within the receivables portfolio. The portfolio should be monitored for shifts in risk and profitability. For example, credit scoring models can be used to screen customers. As the aging of receivables is lengthening, the scores being used to qualify for credit approvals may have to be increased. Overall corporate goals need to be recognized and then balanced.

Another situation might involve a company deciding to expand sales. The accompanying anticipated changes in portfolio carrying costs and bad debts should be monitored. Will the increase in sales offset the increase in carrying costs and bad debts? Policy may have to be altered to optimize the risk-reward trade-off.

Policy changes need to focus upon balancing the risk-reward trade-off at individual firms. Analyzing the overall receivables portfolio is an effort to look beyond the individual accounts receivable; an effort is being made to see the forest beyond the trees. Benchmarking goals can be used as guidelines for portfolio analysis. Credit managers should view

---

[3] *Study on the Economic Impact of the Credit Crisis on Business Credit and Accounts Receivables.* Credit Research Foundation (May 2009): 6.

receivables portfolio analysis as a tool that can enhance the value added by the credit function.

ECONOMIC VALUE ADDED

One approach that can be used to demonstrate the value added by the credit function is through the use of Economic Value Added (EVA). A number of large companies use EVA to evaluate managers. Conceptually, EVA is similar to the Net Present Value capital budgeting technique; the real strength of EVA is that even non-financial managers find EVA to be relatively easy to understand.

EVA has become a buzzword in finance. EVA can be defined as net operating profit after taxes less the after-tax cost of capital. When considering an income statement, the operating profit is what is left when cost of goods sold and operating expenses are deducted from sales. The operating profit is used on an after-tax basis.

The after-tax cost of capital includes charges for both interest expense related to debt capital and a cost for equity capital. The charge for equity capital is calculated by using one of several possible methods. Most college finance books demonstrate the cost of equity through the capital asset pricing model approach, the dividend yield plus growth rate approach, and the bond yield plus risk premium approach.

Table 4-3 illustrates the calculation of EVA for the Cardinal Company. The bond yield plus risk premium approach is used to calculate the cost for equity capital. Since equity capital is riskier than debt capital, a risk premium of about 4% is added to a firm's bond interest rate. The bond interest rate is often related to a credit rating from Moody's or Standard & Poor's. The example in the table shows that the Cardinal Company has a bond rating that allows it to borrow at 10%. The cost of debt is 10% and the cost of equity is 10% plus 4% to arrive at 14%.

The example in Table 4-3 assumes that Cardinal Company is capitalized by using $5,000,000 in debt capital and $5,000,000 in equity capital. The interest expense is 10% of $5,000,000 or $500,000; the charge for equity is calculated by using the bond yield plus risk premium approach. The 4% risk premium is added to the cost of debt to obtain 14% for the cost of equity. The 14% cost of equity is assessed upon $5,000,000 of equity employed to obtain $700,000. The table flows just like an income statement except that there is a cost for equity funds that were used by the Cardinal Company during the period.

TABLE 4-3	Economic Value Added Calculation Illustration	

The Cardinal Company

Sales	$10,000,000
Cost of Sales	3,000,000
Gross Profit	7,000,000
Operating Expenses	4,000,000
Operating Profit	3,000000
Interest Expenses	500,000

(Debt Capital: 10% of $5,000,000 in debt capital employed during the period)

Profit before Tax	2,500,000
Income Tax (30% Rate)	750,000
Income after Tax	1,750,000
Charge for Equity	700,000

(Equity Capital: 14% of $5,000,000 in equity capital employed during the period)

Economic Value Added	$1,050,000

The EVA calculation in Table 4-3 illustrates that there is a charge of $700,000 for equity capital that accountants overlook in an income statement. The cost of equity is taken into consideration through the EVA calculation.

Corporations can use EVA to evaluate divisions, profit centers or even individual managers. EVA would not be useful in certain situations such as e-commerce companies. It works best for "old economy" type companies. Individual credit managers may be able to recognize that by cutting the investment in receivables, EVA is sometimes enhanced. However, if the investment in receivables is due to a sales increase, EVA might be enhanced by an increase in the receivables portfolio.

The purpose of EVA is to measure the value created for the owners of the firm. Credit policy should also focus upon creating value for the owners of the firm. When credit managers can demonstrate that they create value for a firm by increasing the EVA, they are often rewarded with performance bonuses. The challenge to credit managers is to develop credit policy in a way that strikes an optimal balance between the four key credit department objectives; this will allow the EVA to be maximized.

THE CREDIT DEPARTMENT POLICY AUDIT

Each credit department is different. The purpose of a credit department policy audit is twofold. First, the audit should examine the specific tasks now being performed within the credit function. Second, the audit can be used to consider the effectiveness of current credit department activity in conjunction with what the credit department could potentially contribute to overall corporate profitability.

The audit list can be used as a starting point for topics that are essential to consider when formulating credit policy. This list demonstrates the wide range of tasks performed by credit managers. The skills used to complete credit tasks are as varied and sophisticated as those skills needed in any other business-related occupation.

The complexity of each topic precludes writing one policy statement that could fit all companies. These focal points need to be digested in relationship to strategic planning objectives.

Credit department policies and procedures are allocated to each of the four key credit department objectives presented earlier in this chapter. For college students, this list may help to answer the question "What do credit managers focus upon in their day-to-day activities?" For credit practitioners, this list may be helpful when considering the question "What could credit managers be focusing upon?"

Credit Department Policy Subject Matter Checklist

I. Credit policies and procedures that focus upon development of an optimal level of sales.
    A. New customer policy and procedures.
        1. Credit application with each request. (A sample should be provided in the company's credit manual.)
        2. Procedures that outline expected turnaround time for making a credit decision on new accounts.
        3. Procedures that outline the specific mode for communicating the request for credit and credit decision.
        4. Responsibility for establishing and keeping current credit department files. (The nature of the contents should be included in each file.)
        5. Policy for the creation, retention and destruction of customer records.
        6. Policy for authorizing and communicating credit limits.

B. Policies and procedures that relate to terms of sales.
1. Terms established by industry; clear communication internally and to customer.
2. A discount chargeback policy; procedures for follow-up consistently applied and monitored.
3. A late payment service charge policy; procedures for follow-up consistently applied and monitored.
4. A policy for requests for extended term arrangements, with necessary approvals clearly specified.
5. A blanket approval policy. (Small orders below a specified amount are either cash or automatically approved.)
6. A policy and procedure for consignment sales.
7. A policy for export sales and letters of credit.
8. A policy for terms for sales to a debtor-in-possession in Chapter 11 bankruptcies.
C. Policy and procedures that govern credit investigations.
1. A sign-off policy for responsibility of the control of account developed by the size of account.
2. Use of credit-reporting agencies clarified by the specific requirements for types of reports to be utilized.
3. Policy and procedures that outline obtaining bank references detailing the type of information needed.
4. Policy and procedures that outline obtaining trade references with details of information needed.
5. Financial statement requests from customers and procedures for the analysis of statements with key focal points.
6. Policies and procedures that govern the use of collateral. (Include sample documentation, specify authorized signatures and clarify the safeguarding of documents held in storage.)
   a. Perfecting liens under Article 9 of the UCC
   b. Guarantees (personal and corporate)
   c. Warehouse receipts
   d. Letters of credit (details by types of LC)
   e. Subordination agreements
   f. Lien searches
   g. Pledge of stocks, bonds or certificates of deposit
   h. Mechanic's liens

II. Credit policies and procedures that focus upon minimizing the carrying costs of receivables.
   A. Follow-up system for past-due accounts.
      1. Responsibility and time interval for initial follow-up.
      2. A systematic program for additional follow-up.
      3. Use of the computer for monthly statements or automated dunning letters.
      4. Policy and procedures for holding orders and NSF checks.
      5. Policy for deductions and open credits.
      6. Policy for personal visits. (Written summary report required.)
      7. Policy for the exchange of credit information related to customer payment experience.
      8. Policy for unauthorized shipments.
      9. Policy and procedures for cash application.
      10. Policy and procedures for electronic fund transfers.
   B. Internal credit department reports. (Assign responsibility, clarify timing and include a distribution list for each report.)
      1. Aging of receivables. (Do all items age out?)
      2. Over credit limits report.
      3. Reports on open items by category and age (deductions, credits, unearned discounts, service charges).
      4. Highly leveraged transaction report.
      5. Report for accounts with collection agencies or in litigation.
      6. Bad debt write-off report and reserve for bad debt report.
      7. Travel and expense reports.

III. Credit policies and procedures that focus upon minimizing bad debt losses.
   A. Policy for conversion of an open account to a note. (Interest bearing? Collateralized?)
   B. Policy and procedures governing customer counseling.
   C. Policy for use of collection agencies.
   D. Policy related to the use of outside attorneys and lawsuits.
   E. Policy and procedures related to customer bankruptcy, bulk sales and assignments for the benefit of creditors.
   F. Policy for credit manager participation on creditors' committees.
   G. Authorization for accounts written off to bad debts.

IV. Credit policies and procedures that focus upon credit department organization and cost containment.

A. A formal organization chart that clarifies the positions of each member of the credit department. (Authority and responsibility should be clear.)
B. Policies and procedures that govern human resources within the credit department.
1. Recruiting and hiring guidelines.
   a. Educational requirements by position
   b. Experience requirements by position
2. Training and development guidelines.
   a. Performance review criteria with procedures for a regular periodic performance review
   b. Membership in professional organizations
   c. Workshop and tuition reimbursement guidelines
   d. Promotion and termination guidelines
   e. Benchmarking (consider use of CRF research)
C. Credit department budget guidelines.
1. Responsibility for preparation and content.
2. Specific items for which policies and procedures need to be developed.
   a. Salaries/incentives
   b. Space and equipment
   c. Supplies
   d. Training and education
   e. Travel and entertainment
   f. Collection/investigation expenses
   g. Computer hardware and software
   h. Internet usage (appropriate websites to visit)

POLICY AND PROCEDURES USED TO ESTABLISH BAD DEBT RESERVES AND WRITE-OFFS

The credit policy audit provides a broad framework to use to identify focal points for which policy and procedures are needed. In order to appreciate the need to adopt procedures to guide the implementation of credit policy, bad debt reserves will be used as a focal point.

Individual companies accrue for the likelihood of customers not repaying debt. For example, those accounts operating in bankruptcy or those accounts that have been placed with a collection agency need to be placed under consideration as potential bad debts. The criteria used to establish a bad debt reserve has received considerable scrutiny because bad debt reserves are often a key credit management focal point of the Sarbanes-Oxley (SOX) legislation, which will be discussed more fully in Chapter 5.

Some credit managers like to use a gut feel for the accounts that need to be added to the bad debt reserve. Auditors should be challenging the specific accounts for which accruals in the bad debt reserve have been set up, or sometimes auditors should be challenging why certain accounts have not been set up in the bad debt reserve.

Credit managers try to pinpoint accounts likely to default, yet the process to estimate bad debts is not exact. Three methods are often used to set up the bad debt reserve:

1. An aging of the accounts receivable is often used as a method for establishing the reserve,
2. A process of using a percentage of credit sales is commonly used or
3. A process that focuses upon the percentage of the ending balance in accounts receivable is also often used.

Sometimes an industry average or a combination of the three methods is used. A process for writing off accounts receivable as bad debts needs to be used. Usually a process of using specific account identification (the direct write-off method) or a percentage of sales (the allowance method) is chosen. The allowance method can be established in two ways: the Income Statement Method, which estimates bad debts as a percentage of net credit sales, or the Balance Sheet Method, which relies upon an estimate of the uncollectible accounts determined by an analysis of the accounts receivable. Some companies may use a combination of specific account identification and a percentage of sales.

The reserve for bad debts shows up in an account often called the "allowance for doubtful accounts," which appears in the balance sheet as a contra asset. If actual bad debts exceed the balance that has been set up in the allowance for doubtful accounts, then the reserve in the account is overdrawn and an additional bad debt expense must be recognized.

Bad debts have been used here as an example of a key credit policy focal point. The procedures used to implement the policy can vary. The fundamental point is for credit managers to use a consistent approach and then to review the effectiveness of the policy and procedures on a regular basis.

CHAPTER 4: FOLLOW-UP

Recap of Important Concepts

1. Credit policy is a general course of action used to guide frequently encountered situations designed to achieve strategic objectives.
2. Effective credit policy should balance overall corporate goals. A credit department focus should consider countervailing forces such as sales levels, receivables carrying costs, bad debt write-offs and credit department costs.
3. Credit policy is dynamic. Both internal and external forces shape the need to monitor credit policy on an ongoing basis. Policy needs to be tightened or loosened through strategic and tactical planning.
4. Any discussion of credit policy should consider the potential drawbacks. Credit policy is sometimes considered a straightjacket, too time-consuming to develop and difficult to implement. These drawbacks need to be examined carefully when establishing credit policy.
5. Credit managers perform a wide range of tasks that should be governed by policies. Disparate corporate objectives preclude writing one set of policy statements that could be used by all companies.
6. There is an evolving focus being placed upon receivables portfolio management. By looking at the overall portfolio, credit managers are more likely to enhance departmental contributions to profits.
7. Economic Value Added (EVA) can be a useful tool to measure credit department contributions to ownership wealth.
8. A credit department audit should provide a useful starting point for the development of credit policies. Chapter 4 includes a lengthy checklist of potential credit department policy subject matter. Credit policies should be considered with overall corporate profitability as the underlying objective.
9. The process of setting up a bad debt reserve and then actually writing accounts off to bad debts can be a useful focus to learn more about establishing credit policy and procedures.

Review/Discussion Questions

1. Describe how the credit function should fit into the strategic planning process.

2. For a company with a 1% profit margin and $5,000 written off to bad debts, how much in incremented new sales must be generated in order to offset the bad debt?
3. What risk does a credit manager take when tightening up on credit policy? What risk is taken when credit policy is loosened?
4. What is receivables portfolio management? How can portfolio management be used as an approach to reach credit department goals?
5. How does EVA differ from traditional profit in an income statement?
6. How can a credit department audit be useful for establishing credit policies?
7. How can bad debt reserves be established?
8. What needs to be done when the allowance for doubtful accounts is not sufficient to cover the actual accounts that are written off to bad debt?

Test Your Knowledge

1. What is meant by a credit manager's reference to "optimal credit policy"?
2. Try to identify specific changes in credit policy that can be viewed as tightening credit policy. What signs can a credit manager look for that might necessitate a need to tighten credit policy?
3. What criticism is commonly leveled at the development of credit policy? Try to cite specific examples of criticism that could be leveled at credit policy changes. How can a credit manager prepare to handle the anticipated criticism?
4. Define credit policy.
5. How would the policy toward conducting a credit investigation differ for a company with numerous small balance accounts compared to a company with only a few large balance accounts?
6. What are the pros and cons of using a liberal credit policy?
7. Calculate the EVA for The Wire Brush Company based upon the following parameters:
   - Annual sales are $50,000,000.
   - Cost of sales are $15,000,000.
   - Operating expenses are also $15,000,000.
   - The company has a 40% tax rate.
   - Assets are $20,000,000.
   - Liabilities are $15,000,000.

- The company can borrow at a 9% interest rate.
- A 4% risk premium exists for equity capital .

8. When should an account be written off to bad debt?
9. What are the approaches that are often used to write an account off to bad debt?

Case Study

You have just been hired as a corporate credit manager for Puget Sound Packaging Corporation. Your employer has annual sales of $200 million. The corporate treasurer hired you to fix a situation where credit policy is non-existent or out of control.

Your new employer is nicely positioned in a growth industry. Profit margins for Puget Sound Packaging are not as high as those for competitors in the industry. The economy is in a slow growth stage.

Your task as the new corporate credit manager is to establish credit policy. In developing your response, identify specific credit policies that you believe are essential to the credit function. Your response should identify focal points. Try not to get hung up in procedures, but rather focus your response upon "optimal" policies so that the credit function can operate effectively.

Credit Management Online

www.crfonline.org/—The Credit Research Foundation publishes numerous occasional papers. Among the studies offered, the National Summary of Trade Accounts Receivables has been published quarterly since 1958.

www.federalreserve.gov/monetarypolicy/beige-book-default. htm/—The Federal Reserve Board website offers the Beige Book Report on the current status of the U.S. economy. The report is published eight times per year and provides economic details that are available by district. The Beige Book contains detailed information on current economic conditions as a means to identify signs of improvement or declines in economic activity.

corporate.morningstar.com/—Morningstar, Inc., hosts a website that contains cost of capital analysis for more than 5,000 companies, 300 industries and 145 countries. This site is geared toward advanced financial analysis, which can be quite useful for EVA analysis. Morningstar also publishes credit ratings and credit reports.

www.sternstewart.com/—This site is hosted by Stern Stewart & Co., which is credited with developing EVA as a tool for the analysis of companies. There is an EVA tutor and a wealth of information available concerning EVA.

References Useful for Further Reading

Barron, Jacob. "On the Same Team: Tales from the Sales-Credit Schism." *Business Credit* (September 2008): 40-42.

Bernanke, Ben. "Monetary Policy and the Housing Bubble." Presentation Made at the Annual Meeting of the American Economic Association, Atlanta, Georgia. January 3, 2010.

Bohn, Jeffrey R. and Roger M. Stein. *Active Credit Portfolio Management in Practice.* Hoboken, NJ: Wiley, 2009.

Credit Research Foundation. *Determining Bad Debt Reserves and Accounting for Bad Debts.* (April 2006): 1-7.

Credit Research Foundation. *Study on the Economic Impact of the Credit Crisis on Business Credit and Accounts Receivables.* (May 2009): 1-11.

Gahala, Charles. "Financial Tools of Analysis: The Economic Value Added." *National Credit News* (November 2000): 12-13.

Golub, Bennett W., and Conan C. Crum. "Risk Management Lessons Worth Remembering from the Credit Crisis of 2007-2009." *Journal of Portfolio Management* (Spring 2010): 21-44.

Grundke, Peter. "Top-down Approaches for Integrated Risk Management: How Accurate Are They?" *European Journal of Operational Research*, Vol. 203 (June 2010): 662-672.

"How to Create a Smart Credit Policy." *Inc. Guidebook*, Vol. 1, No. 11: 1-4.

Johnson, Tom. "Keeping Credit Policy Relevant in Today's Business World." *Business Credit* (March 2000): 23-26.

Kiviat, Barbara. "The Paperless Chase: Companies Are Pushing to Send Only Online Statements." *Time* (November 13, 2009): 104.

Knowles, Kavita. "What You Should Know About Electronic Document Retention." *Business Credit* (October 2008): 32-34.

Mills, William. "Risk Management." *Mortgage Banking* (March 2010): 77.

Parisi, Jeff. "How to Be More Strategic in Your Organization." *Business Credit* (June 2010): 12, 14.

Shappell, Brian, CBA, CICP. "Your Best Policy: The Importance of, Adherence to Internal Credit Policies Slipping? It Shouldn't Be!" *Business Credit* (May 2015): 34-37.

Stephens, Harry. "Paper Statements—Asset or Liability?" *Business Credit* (October 2008): 58-59.

Subran, Ludovic. "DSO: One in Four Companies Pay after 90 Days." *Business Credit* (September/October 2016): 19.

Thorpe, Paula, ACI. "Why Have a Credit Policy?" *Business Credit* (June 2011): 32-37.

Chapter 5

LEGISLATION AND REGULATIONS PERTINENT TO BUSINESS CREDIT DECISION-MAKING

"I have frequently remarked at lectures and in articles about the extent to which credit professionals are exposed to legal issues as part of their daily duties. It would certainly not be an overstatement that a company's credit department has more exposure to legal matters than most other departments, possibly with the exception of the legal department."[1]

Bruce Nathan, Esq.
Partner at Lowenstein Sandler LLP

A major challenge to business credit grantors is posed through the need to cope with external forces. Government legislation and regulation shape credit decisions. Legislation and regulation not only create and protect the rights of creditors but also impose limitations on business activities.

This chapter will examine government legislation that is pertinent to credit decision-making. Social responsibility and professionalism are common threads that weave credit managers toward compliance. Failure to comply with federal and state laws can result in severe reprisal.

There is a clear-cut need to become aware of specific government legislation and regulations that are pertinent to business credit. Moreover, policies and procedures should be in place to ensure that all credit department personnel are acting within the boundaries of the law. Credit managers should consider governmental legislation from the dual perspective of taking advantage of legal rights and for compliance within legal boundaries.

The **Key Learning Objectives** in Chapter 5 are:

1. Recognize some of the key ingredients contained in the Dodd-Frank Wall Street Reform and Consumer Protection Act, which was signed into law on July 21, 2010.

---

[1] Bruce Nathan, "The ABCs of Legal Issues Encountered by Credit Professionals," *Business Credit* (February 2007): 18.

2. Identify antitrust legislation with a particular focus upon antitrust laws such as the Robinson-Patman Act.
3. Clarify the pertinent aspects of the Securities and Exchange Commission's Sarbanes-Oxley Act.
4. Introduce the Federal Trade Commission's "Red Flags Rules," which furnish guidelines for a new set of regulations that have important implications for business credit grantors.
5. Examine consumer credit protection legislation with the application geared toward business credit decision-making.
6. Understand the Law of Usury together with an examination of an annual percentage rate (APR) yardstick applied to simple, discount and add-on interest rates.
7. Provide an overview of the Prompt Pay Act with a focus upon government payments to creditors.

THE DODD-FRANK WALL STREET REFORM AND CONSUMER PROTECTION ACT OF 2010

How quickly the winds of change can shift the economic landscape. The Great Recession was triggered by a financial collapse in the commercial and investment banking sector during 2007. The fallout has been catastrophic.

- During 2009 and again during 2010, more than 100 commercial banks failed in the United States.
- Credit conditions tightened and led to a lack of funding availability for both consumers and businesses, to an extent that had not been seen since the Great Depression of the 1930s.
- Foreclosures became a common practice in real estate; residential real estate values dropped to the extent that an estimated one quarter of all mortgage holders were "under water," suggesting that more was owed on the mortgage than the market value of the home.
- More than eight million Americans lost their jobs.
- Key business titans such as Bear Stearns, Lehman Brothers, Merrill Lynch, Countrywide Financial, Washington Mutual, IndyMac, American International Group (AIG), General Motors and Chrysler either went bankrupt or were taken over.
- Several large financial intermediaries were rescued through a federal government bailout that included the $700 billion Troubled Asset Relief Program (commonly referred to as TARP).

In response to the financial collapse, on July 21, 2010, President Barack Obama signed into law the Dodd-Frank Wall Street Reform and Consumer Protection Act of 2010, more commonly known as the Dodd-Frank Reform Bill. There was a considerable amount of horse trading prior to the passage of the legislation. The complexity of the new law is reflected in its length; it fills more than 2,300 pages.

It will take several years for the law's impact to play out in the economy. However, it has four key focal points. The following material covers these points, whose titles are drawn from the White House website (www.whitehouse.gov/blog/2010/07/21/president-obama-signs-wall-street-reform-no-easy-task).

Holding Wall Street Accountable

Complex loans made through derivatives such as credit default swaps (CDSs) became a hot product. CDSs are a derivative where an obligation is backed by a type of credit insurance that guarantees repayment of the debt. Perhaps due to the insurance, credit rating agencies gave an AAA credit rating to several real estate-related swaps pertaining to the issues. The extent of the size of the marketplace lacked transparency because many trades were not made on organized exchanges.

Profits for financial intermediaries were enticing. The growth in hedge funds occurred, evidenced by $39 billion outstanding in 1990 to more than $2 trillion outstanding in 2007. The hedge fund bubble had an impact upon many participants: Fannie Mae, Freddie Mac, commercial banks and investments banks, which were led by a new breed of analysts known as the "Quants."

The new law suggests that banks and other market participants should not be "too big too fail." Moreover, the Volcker Rule, named after former Federal Reserve Chairman Paul Volcker, suggests that since banks benefit from FDIC insurance, they need limits on the amount of capital that can be invested into risky trades.

Protecting American Families
from Unfair, Abusive Financial Practices

During the buildup to the Great Recession, complex real estate loans were devised for consumers. Predatory lending included loans with adjustable rates and resets on the interest rate that resulted in exorbitant payments. Real estate appraisals were sometimes fictitious. Borrowers were sometimes not qualified based upon income levels and home affordability.

A new Bureau of Consumer Financial Protection was established by the Dodd-Frank Reform Bill. As a result, clear rules set by lenders in plain language should be established. Fees should not be hidden. Appraisals should be regulated more clearly. A stricter credit investigation should be conducted pertaining to the borrower's creditworthiness.

Closing the Gaps in Our Financial System

Gaps in the regulatory system that failed to restrict AIG should no longer exist. Large banks should not be in a position to be bailed out by the federal government. The "too big to fail" situation should no longer exist. A bankruptcy court in a Chapter 11 proceeding should not allow for a claimant to move ahead of another claim as some have argued was done through the bankruptcy plan approved in the General Motors Chapter 11 proceeding. There should be restrictions on banks making risky bets with their capital.

Hundreds of new rules affecting financial regulation were implemented. For example, the Dodd-Frank Reform Bill requires stronger capital requirements for banks. Banks are now limited to the extent of their investing in private equity funds and hedge funds. The focus upon the "too big to fail issue" remains to be seen over a period of time.

Reform is Critical to Market Certainty and Stable Growth

There are several key summary focal points in the Dodd-Frank Reform Bill. Concerns such as making the accountability for regulation and supervision more clear, developing stronger capital buffers for market participants to weather through financial storms, reducing the concentration of risk and providing more transparency in derivatives trading are each key ingredients.

The Dodd-Frank Reform Bill is complex. It will take years for the changes to unfold. A capitalistic economy relies upon confidence from market participants. It is a vital first step toward instilling the confidence needed to affect economic recovery. Credit managers will need to recognize the new legislation as a form of government intrusion that is necessary for the improved operation of the economy.

The rest of this chapter will be much more specific in terms of addressing the needs of business credit managers.

AN OVERVIEW OF ANTITRUST REGULATION

In the late 1800s, the U.S. economy moved away from an agricultural base and toward a manufacturing base. Although common law had forbidden monopolistic restraint of trade, business practices that had been destructive toward small firms were widespread. Price-cutting collusion among companies was a common mechanism used to drive competitors out of business.

The commerce clause in the Constitution gave Congress the power to enact antitrust laws. Antitrust legislation is aimed at prohibiting price fixing, price discrimination and group boycotting. Congress enacted each of the following antitrust acts: (1) the Sherman Antitrust Act of 1890, (2) the Clayton Act of 1914, (3) the Federal Trade Commission Act of 1914 and (4) the Robinson-Patman Act of 1936.

The Sherman Act

In 1890, the Sherman Act became the first of the antitrust laws. The Sherman Act was aimed at two focal points: (1) the prevention of attempts to monopolize and (2) the prevention of conspiracies in restraint of trade. The basic philosophy arising from the Sherman Act is that an industrial concentration of power is not desirable.

The language "restraint of trade" has always caused confusion. Most importantly, for credit managers it had not been clear under which specific circumstances they could be guilty of conspiracy. In the case of *Catalano Inc. v. Target Sales Inc.*, the U.S. Supreme Court made it clear that credit terms are a component of price, so far as the antitrust statutes are concerned. Therefore, credit managers who agreed with competitors to fix credit terms are in violation of the Act.

The Clayton Act

In 1914, the Clayton Act was passed by Congress. The purpose of the Clayton Act was to strengthen the Sherman Act by making illegal practices more specific. For example, the Clayton Act prohibits interlocking directorates that result when a member of the board of directors also sits on a competitor's board.

The Clayton Act includes a provision that prohibits price discrimination for commodities. A seller may discriminate in price in order to meet competition or when differences in quality, quantity or costs of transportation exist. This provision was later amended by the Robinson-Patman Act.

The Federal Trade Commission Act

Congress also enacted the Federal Trade Commission Act in 1914. This Act created the Federal Trade Commission (FTC). In 1938, the Wheeler-Lea. Amendment empowered the FTC to oversee unfair and deceptive business practices.

The FTC is particularly focused upon consumer protection. Changes in technology and the growth in the importance of intellectual property have contributed to a plethora of problems. For example, there have been numerous consumer complaints concerning cyber-fraud, identity theft, pyramid schemes, deceptive business opportunities and credit repair schemes. The FTC has a mission to protect American consumers against such deceptive practices.

The Robinson-Patman Act

The Robinson-Patman Act of 1936 is every bit as important as the Sherman Act for credit managers. The Robinson-Patman Act forbids price discrimination where the effect of such price discrimination may be to substantially reduce competition or to create a monopoly.

As *Catalano* has held, credit terms fixed by credit managers are construed as equal to price. Upon complying with rigid requirements, credit managers may meet equal terms offered by a competitor. This could include offering a discount or granting extended payment terms. Documentation that verifies competitive terms must be obtained. More importantly, a credit manager may not obtain the information regarding the competitive terms from its competitor. The documentation should come from the customer or some third-party source. Arranging terms with competitors would be a clear violation of the antitrust statutes. As an aside, a credit manager should recognize that there is an increase in credit risk when extended terms are used.

Discounts and late payment service charges should also be considered a part of terms. The Robinson-Patman Act does allow for a seller to reflect certain cost savings in price. For example, certain quantity discounts could be a reason for a difference in price if the cost difference is supported by proof. This type of discount should be made available to all customers.

Attorney Wanda Borges specified four elements that must exist for an action to be deemed a conspiracy that results in a restraint of trade. The four elements include: (1) there must be knowledge of the parties, (2) a common purpose, (3) an actual restraint of trade and (4) intent to restrain

5: Legislation and Regulation

101

TABLE 5-1   Antitrust Guidelines for Credit Managers

1. Do contact your corporate attorney when qualms or questions concerning antitrust arise.
2. Do develop internal policy in consultation with legal counsel that clearly adheres to antitrust legislation.
3. Do extend or deny credit to customers based upon uniform standards of creditworthiness. Stay uniform when charging back unearned discounts and when assessing late payment service charges.
4. Do not attempt to influence the credit decisions made by other credit managers outside of your organization.
5. Do not discuss future terms, future actions or hearsay comments when exchanging credit information with other credit managers. Only exchange factual credit information.
6. Do not collude with any competitor when establishing credit terms, and do not discuss any pricing policy with a competitor.

---

trade.[2] According to Borges, credit managers should keep in mind what price fixing is all about.

Table 5-1 provides some general antitrust guidelines for credit managers. These practical suggestions can help guide credit decisions. Specific guidelines are available on the FTC website (https://www.ftc.gov/tips-advice/competition-guidance/guide-antitrust-laws).

Despite all of the admonishments, the U.S. Supreme Court determined in 1926 that the exchange of completed and factual information concerning terms and other credit information is legal. Any agreement to fix terms will be judged harshly under federal antitrust standards. The penalties for violations are severe and can include a fine, imprisonment and monetary damages awarded to injured parties.

THE SARBANES-OXLEY ACT

The Sarbanes-Oxley Act was passed in 2002 and is commonly referred to as SOX. The Act was a result of several accounting scandals that gained their notoriety from problems at companies such as Enron, WorldCom, Global Crossing and Sunbeam. The intention of SOX is to protect investors in public companies from the problems that can result from inaccurate or unreliable corporate disclosures.

The Securities and Exchange Commission (SEC) has been charged with the responsibility to oversee SOX reporting requirements. SOX

---

[2] Wanda Borges, "Antitrust Issues Explained," *Business Credit* (November/December 2006): 12.

resulted in a mandate for senior employees to take personal responsibility for the accuracy and completeness of financial information that is reported to the public. While SOX has received praise for increasing investor confidence in financial statements, SOX-related tasks have also resulted in internal control requirements that have filtered down to credit managers.

Section 404 of SOX mandates that rules for establishing responsibility be developed. The mandate pertains to setting up and then maintaining internal controls for financial reporting purposes. Certain credit managers have been asked to sign off on SOX documentation.

Auditors require that there should not be any misstatement of material facts. Credit managers should not let slip by anything that does not seem to be right about the way in which credit and receivables are being reported. SOX affords protections to someone willing to report wrongdoing.

Record keeping is an important safeguard to support SOX enforcement. Important documentation to retain include credit applications, loan documents, analyses, financial data and copies of communications such as memoranda, letters and emails. The SEC recommends that documents be retained for seven years. Its website (www.sec.gov/spotlight/sarbanes-oxley.htm) furnishes pertinent details concerning SOX.

THE RED FLAGS RULES

In 2009, there were more than 11 million identity fraud victims in the United States. In a manner similar to an official tossing a flag at a football game to indicate a penalty, the Federal Trade Commission (FTC) developed a set of guidelines for businesses to use as "Red Flags" to identify potential signs of fraud and prevent identity theft. The FTC was directed to develop the Red Flags Rules under the Fair and Accurate Credit Transaction Act (FACT Act/FACTA) passed by Congress. As of July 21, 2011, the SEC and the CFTC took over from the FTC enforcement of the Red Flag Rules involving business-to-business transactions.

The Red Flags Rules require creditors and financial institutions to address the risk of identity theft. For those companies that are covered, the FTC specified a four-step process to comply with the "Red Flags." The process should be a written corporate policy.

First, a company should identify the Red Flags that are likely to surface at their own business. For example, the way in which accounts are opened, the manner in which someone can gain access to account information, suspicious documents or the use of personal codes that can be used to gain access to an account.

Second, the policy should focus upon setting up a set of procedures to use to detect any Red Flags. This can be done in several ways. For example, a company should verify the authenticity of the party opening a new account, verify a change of address or confirm that the person being dealt with is in fact the appropriate person.

Third, if there are Red Flags that surface, something needs to be done to reduce the potential harm being caused and to remedy the situation. Appropriate policy might include contacting the customer, changing the password or closing the account.

Finally, the FTC Red Flags Rules recognize a need to update the policy regularly. Changes in technology occur so swiftly that identity thieves can easily change tactics to attempt to circumvent internal corporate safeguards.

One of the issues raised concerning the Red Flags Rules is who within a company should be responsible for setting up and implementing the internal oversight for the policy. At Benedictine University in March 2010, a group of corporate credit managers met to examine the Red Flags Rules. Not only did several attendees express concerns about having the ultimate responsibility within a firm, but an in-house corporate attorney, a vice president of finance and an in-house corporate technology manager also discussed their concerns for oversight. Perhaps the responsibility for adherence to the Rules needs to be shared?

A set of sample guidelines for developing an internal Red Flags Rules policy is included in the March 2009 issue of *Business Credit*. FTC guidelines are also available online to help credit managers with Red Flags' Rules implementation (https://www.ftc.gov/tips-advice/business-center/guidance/fighting-identity-theft-red-flags-rule-how-guide-business).

CONSUMER CREDIT LEGISLATION PERTINENT TO BUSINESS CREDIT

During the past 30 years, Congress has enacted comprehensive consumer credit protection legislation. Laws such as the (1) Equal Credit Opportunity Act, (2) Fair Credit Reporting Act, (3) Fair Debt Collection Practices Act, (4) Truth in Lending Law and (5) Fair Credit Billing Act each govern consumer credit. However, business credit grantors are affected by certain aspects of consumer credit legislation.

In addition, credit managers should be familiar with three other laws that have broader relevance to consumer and business credit: (1) the Law of Usury, (2) the Gramm-Leach-Bliley Act and the (3) Prompt Payment Act.

The Equal Credit Opportunity Act and Regulation B

The Equal Credit Opportunity Act (ECOA) went into effect in 1975. The purpose of the ECOA is to prohibit discrimination by creditors. Issued in 1977 by the Federal Reserve Board, Regulation B is the mechanism used to implement the ECOA.

All credit grantors should be aware of Regulation B. The requirements for adherence to Regulation B are stricter where consumers are concerned. Nevertheless, business credit grantors are also required to adhere to the provisions of Regulation B.

The ECOA makes it unlawful for any creditor to discriminate with respect to the extension of credit against an applicant on the basis of sex, race, color, creed, national origin, age or marital status. Strict adherence to this prohibition means that:

1. A creditor is prohibited from inquiring about an applicant's childbearing capacity or birth control practices, race, color, national origin, age or religion.
2. A creditor may inquire about marital status only if an applicant lives in a community property state or if an applicant requests unsecured credit and relies in part upon property that the applicant owns jointly with another person. The purpose of the inquiry would be to satisfy the creditor's standards of creditworthiness, or to assure the creditor of having the ability to move against the property in question if a debt becomes unpaid.

Regulation B was amended with its changes effective April 15, 2003. The official staff commentary also was amended. Some language in the official staff commentary is most helpful, in particular, to trade credit grantors. Mandatory compliance with amendments began April 15, 2004.

The following material summarizes the provisions to be followed by business trade creditors. Adherence to the ECOA and Regulation B is closely scrutinized when an "adverse credit decision" is made. The definition of an "adverse credit decision" is:

- A refusal to grant credit in substantially the amount or on substantially the terms requested in an application unless the creditor makes a counteroffer (to grant credit in a different amount or on other terms) and the applicant uses or expressly accepts the credit offered.

- A termination of an unfavorable change in the terms of an account that does not affect all or substantially all of a class of the creditor's accounts.
- A refusal to increase the amount of credit available to an applicant who has made an application for an increase.

Business credit grantors must give an applicant a statement as to the adverse action taken, orally or in writing, within a reasonable period of time. Business credit grantors must also provide the ECOA anti-discrimination statement to the applicants that says, "The federal Equal Credit Opportunity Act prohibits creditors from discriminating against credit applicants on the basis of race, color, religion, national origin, sex, marital status, age (provided the applicant has the capacity to enter into a binding contract); because all or part of the applicant's income derives from any public assistance program; or because the applicant has in good faith exercised any right under the Consumer Credit Protection Act. The federal agency that administers compliance with this law concerning this creditor is the Federal Trade Commission, Equal Credit Opportunity, Washington, DC 20580." (www.consumer.ftc.gov/articles/0347-your-equal-credit-opportunity-rights)

While trade credit is referenced in Regulation B, only the Official Staff Commentary gives definition to "trade credit" and it is defined generally as "limited to a financing arrangement that involves a buyer and a seller—such as a supplier who finances the sale of equipment, supplies, or inventory; it does not apply to an extension of credit by a bank or other financial institution for the financing of such terms."

With regard to the extension of (i) trade credit or (ii) business credit to a business that had gross revenues in excess of $1 million in its preceding fiscal year (or for credit incident to a factoring agreement), a creditor shall:

1. Notify the applicant, within a reasonable time, orally or in writing; and
2. If an applicant makes a written request for the reasons behind the credit decision within 60 days of being notified of the adverse action, then the creditor must provide to the applicant a written statement of the reasons for the adverse action together with the requisite ECOA notice.

The issue of obtaining a signature or a personal guarantee from a spouse remains a great concern. The amended Regulation B states: "A creditor shall not require the signature of an applicant's spouse or other person, other than a joint applicant, on any credit instrument if the applicant qualifies under the creditor's standards of creditworthiness for the amount and terms of the credit requested. A creditor shall not deem the submission of a joint financial statement or other evidence of jointly held assets as an application for joint credit."

Regulation B is very specific as to when a spouse's signature may be required. It states: "If a married applicant requests unsecured credit and resides in a community property state, or if the property upon which the applicant is relying is located in such a state, a creditor may require the signature of the spouse on any instrument necessary, or reasonably believed by creditor to be necessary, under applicable state law to make the community property available to satisfy the debt in the event of default if:

(i) Applicable state law denies the applicant power to manage or control sufficient community property to qualify for the amount of credit requested under the creditor's standards of creditworthiness; and

(ii) The applicant does not have sufficient separate property to qualify for the amount of credit requested without regard to community property."

The Fair Credit Reporting Act

The Fair Credit Reporting Act (FCRA) has been in effect since 1971. The FCRA applies to the extension of consumer credit and is also potentially important to business credit grantors. The Federal Trade Commission (FTC) enforces the FCRA.

There are consumer credit reports on nearly 90% of American adults. Under the FCRA, a consumer who is denied credit due to information in a credit report has the right to inspect the credit report.

Two issues have given consumer credit reports a dubious reputation. First, the incidence of errors in the reports could be excessive. Second, a consumer's right to privacy may not be protected when credit reporting agencies sell their database to interested marketers and other subscribers.

The FCRA was amended in 1997. Business credit grantors should be concerned with the authorization of a consumer report. A business transaction in which an individual has accepted personal liability for business debt, such as in the case of a sole proprietor, partner or guarantor, does provide a permissible purpose under Section 604 of the FCRA to obtain and use a consumer credit report. Under the FCRA, a creditor must certify to the consumer credit reporting agency that there is a permissible purpose for obtaning the consumer credit report. In the case where a business creditor obtains a personal guarantee, the creditor may order a consumer report without prior written authorization from the guarantor.

In a situation where an employer would like to order a consumer credit report on a current or prospective employee, the written consent of the current or prospective employee should be obtained. Usually the human resources department will handle the necessary authorization documentation.

Business credit grantors who deal with consumers on an occasional basis must be mindful of the FCRA requirements. One may obtain a consumer report only under the following circumstances:

- In response to the order of a court having jurisdiction to issue such an order, or a subpoena issued in connection with proceedings before a federal grand jury.
- In accordance with the written instructions or permission of the consumer to whom it relates.
- In connection with a legitimate business need for the information.

The Fair Debt Collection Practices Act

In 1978, Congress passed the Fair Debt Collection Practices Act (FDCPA). This law pertains to personal debt collected by collection agencies and attorneys from consumers, and works toward preventing abusive collection practices. Under the FDCPA, debt collectors are prohibited from harassing, furnishing false statements and making abusive or threatening statements.

This law is aimed at consumer credit. The Federal Trade Commission website for the Act (www.ftc.gov/enforcement/rules/rulemaking-regulatory-reform-proceedings/fair-debt-collection-practices-act-text) can be useful to gain a more complete understanding of the details of this law.

The Truth in Lending Act and Regulation Z

The Truth in Lending Act mandates disclosure of credit terms to consumers. The purpose of the Truth in Lending Act is to allow consumers to make educated credit decisions through the use of comparable credit terms. The Truth in Lending Law does not govern maximum interest rates; federal and state usury laws establish maximum interest rates.

Standard disclosure forms include the total dollar amount of finance charges and also the annual percentage rate (APR). This information is required by the Act. The finance charge must disclose interest as well as any ancillary fees, credit insurance and points. Moreover, prepayment penalties, default provisions and specific collateral are included in disclosure requirements. The APR is basically a simple interest rate that is calculated through an actuarial method. The calculation of an APR will be explained later in this chapter.

A backlash against deceitful practices in the credit card industry resulted in changes to Regulation Z, which went into effect on February 22, 2010. The changes focus upon harmful practices used in consumer finance; the intent of the changes is to protect consumers. Those credit managers who are involved in consumer finance can review details about the changes on the Federal Reserve Board website (www. federalreserve.gov/creditcard/).

The Fair Credit Billing Act

In 1975, the Truth in Lending Act was amended to create the Fair Credit Billing Act. The intention of this law is to take the hassle out of billing errors for consumers. Creditors are required to correct errors promptly while at the same time preventing the errors from showing up on consumer credit reports.

Since this law was designed for consumer credit, discussion is limited. For more information about the Fair Credit Billing Act, please refer to the Federal Reserve Board website and its *Consumer Handbook to Credit Protection Laws* (http://www.federalreserve.gov/pubs/consumerhdbk/default.htm).

The Law of Usury

The Law of usury is one of the most complex laws that can affect all types of credit grantors. Under the legal doctrine established in England in 1774, the sale of goods and services was not governed by usury law. This doctrine held true in the United States until individual states began to establish usury laws during the 1950s and 1960s. At this time, usury law became applicable to the sale of goods and services.

Today, credit managers should be concerned with both federal and state usury laws. Severe penalties exist for charging an interest rate that is higher than the governing usury ceiling. Penalties often vary. For example, in some states a creditor will forfeit interest; in other states a creditor will forfeit all principal; while in other states, a creditor will forfeit twice the amount of all interest.

Usury is the interest rate charged that is in excess of the governing legal rate of interest. Various situations create different usury ceilings. For example, the usury ceiling for credit sales that are secured by liens on residential property may not be the same as the usury ceiling that governs service charges linked to interest on a note.

Business creditors sometimes use terms such as *finance charge* or *service charge* instead of interest. When these terms are used in conjunction with the extension of credit and slow-paying debtors, the terms then have the same meaning. Usury laws may be applicable; state laws determine potential usury applications for slow-paying debtors.

Another concern for business creditors is compound interest. Compound interest is the charging of interest on interest. Specific state laws vary concerning whether or not compound interest may be assessed.

Credit managers are urged to refer to the most recent edition of the *Manual of Credit and Commercial Laws* to ascertain the application of federal and state usury ceilings. This reference is updated on an as-needed basis. Specific court cases and individual state laws are available for detailed application of the law of usury.

Interest Rate Calculations

Most credit managers encounter situations where a complete understanding of the basic mathematics of interest rate calculations is essential. Usury laws mandate an understanding of interest rate calculations. The Truth in Lending Law requires lenders to disclose an APR to consumer borrowers.

An APR is derived through an actuarial method. An actuarial method is one in which the present value of the payments is equal to the loan's cash value. The laws that govern APR do not in all cases define APR as the effective rate of interest.

Three types of interest rates are commonly used by business credit grantors: (1) simple interest, (2) discount interest and (3) add-on interest. Seemingly minor misunderstandings concerning the type of interest can lead to major differences in the effective rate of interest. The following examples look at three types of commonly used interest rates through the use of an APR yardstick.

Simple Interest in Dollars. The interest that is assessed to a loan based upon the amount borrowed is the simple interest in dollars. By using the formula of Principal × Rate × Time, the simple interest dollar amount is obtained. For example, a $1,000 loan at 10% simple interest for 60 days would accumulate interest of $16.44, as shown in Equation 5-1 below:

Equation 5-1. Simple Interest Example

$$\$1,000 \times .10 \times \frac{60}{365} = \$16.44$$

Note that a 365-day year was used. Sometimes a 360-day year, which is known as a banker's year, is used. The impact of using a banker's year would result in slightly higher interest amount.

Simple Interest Expressed in APR. When a credit manager is looking for the APR on a loan for one year, the calculation is relatively easy. Simply divide the interest in dollars by the principal. Equation 5-2 below shows the calculation of a one-year loan for $1,000 at a 10% rate of interest (APR).

Equation 5-2. Simple Interest Expressed in APR

$$\frac{\$100}{\$1,000} = 10\% = APR$$

When the loan period is for a number of days less than one year, the magic of compounding must be taken into consideration. For a 60-day loan, the loan could be repeated six times during a year. Because of the impact of compounding, the APR would increase. For example, the formula and corresponding results for a 60-day loan for $1,000 at a stated rate of 10% are shown in Equation 5-3.

Equation 5-3. Simple Interest APR for Less Than One Year

$$(1 + \frac{\text{Stated Rate}}{T})^{T} - 1.0 = (1 + \frac{.10}{6})^{6} - 1.0 = 10.46\% = APR$$

The "T" in Equation 5-3 represents the number of times that the loan can be replicated in one year. The equation shows that the stated rate is 10% but that the APR is 10.46%. Since the lender receives the principal in 60 days and the loan can be replicated six times during the year, the APR is higher.

Discount Interest. When a credit manager converts an open account to a note and the face of the note includes both principal and interest, the note is set up on a discount basis. Discount refers to the inclusion of interest and principal in the maturity value. Therefore, the maturity value must be "discounted" in order to determine the principal. The difference between the maturity value and the principal is the interest.

Discount interest will have the effect of increasing the APR. Examples will be shown to illustrate the APR for a full year discount loan in Equation 5-4 and then for a discount loan term for less than one full year in Equation 5-5. Equation 5-4 shows an APR of 11.1% for a one-year loan with a stated rate of 10% set up on a discount basis.

Equation 5-4. Example of Discount Interest

$$\frac{\text{Stated Rate \%}}{1 - \text{Stated Rate \%}} \text{ or } \frac{.10}{1 - .10} + 11.1\% = \text{APR}$$

Equation 5-5 shows the APR for a discount-type loan arrangement with a stated rate of 10% for a two-month period. Note that the interest dollar amount is used in this equation rather than the stated rate of interest that was used in Equation 5-4.

Equation 5-5. Example of Discount Interest Less Than One Year

$$(1.0 + \frac{\text{Interest}}{\text{Face} - \text{Interest}})^T - 1.0 = (1.0 + \frac{\$16.67}{\$1,000 - 16.67})^6 - 1.0 = 10.61\% \text{ APR}$$

Equation 5-5 shows that $16.67 in interest ($1,000 \times .10 \times \frac{60}{360}$) is charged on a two-month loan with a stated rate of 10%. The impact of setting up the loan on a discount basis is to increase the APR to 10.61%. The "T" in this equation represents the number of compounding periods per year.

Add-On Interest. Installment loans used in certain industries often charge interest by using an add-on interest rate. The construction equipment industry, the automobile industry and the appliance industry often use add-on rates. Add-on interest is paid on the original principal of the loan throughout the life of the loan. Other interest rates recognize the amortization of principal during a loan. The effect of using an add-on rate is to nearly double the stated rate of interest.

An illustration of a three-year $10,000 loan at 10% add-on will be used to demonstrate add-on interest. A three-step calculation will be used.

Step One: $\$10,000 \times 10\% \times 3 = \$3,000 = $ Total Interest
Step Two: $\$10,000 + \$3,000 = \$13,000 = $ Principal + Interest
Step Three: $\$13,000 \div 36 = \$361.11$ Monthly Payment

The three-step calculation shows that a $10,000 installment loan for three years at 10% add-on requires 36 monthly payments of $361.11. In order to get an approximate APR for this loan, use Equation 5-6 below.

Equation 5-6. Approximate APR

$$\frac{\text{Average Annual Interest}}{\text{Principal} \div 2} - \frac{\$3,000 \div 3}{\$10,000 \div 2} - \frac{\$1,000}{\$5,000} = 20\%$$

Equation 5-6 gives an approximate APR for the 10% add-on loan as a 20% APR. The approach used in this equation slightly overstates the actual APR.

Interest Rate Related Concerns

Errors in interest calculations can vary from minor to significant. Usury is a potential hazard with severe penalties for violations. Customers sometimes demand to know how interest has been assessed. Therefore, both legal and practical motives exist for the formulation and communication of policies related to interest rate calculations.

Simple interest is often used to assess service charges for an open account that is paid late. When is the account made aware of this policy? When does the interest start accruing? Does the account that chronically pays late have interest assessed on unpaid service charge invoices? Are all customers being treated equally? These are policy questions that have potential usury implications.

Sometimes a large customer that is experiencing cash flow problems asks to have an open account converted to a note. The note should clearly include the type of interest being used. Notes that require monthly interest payments are often set up on a simple interest basis. Notes that are set up with principal and interest payable at maturity are often set up on a discount basis. A policy governing this area should exist. Sample notes and interest rate calculations should be included in a credit policy manual.

A letter of credit that requires a time draft becomes a banker's acceptance when the bank accepts the vendor's documentation. Many corporate treasurers prefer to discount the banker's acceptance to make the funds available immediately upon acceptance. Discount interest is usually assessed when a banker's acceptance is discounted. A policy to double-check the numbers should be in place.

Finally, interest rates should not remain static. As the rate of inflation and the cost of money fluctuates, interest rate levels need to be altered. Some credit managers prefer to peg interest rates to an index, such as the prime rate, in order to reduce interest rate risk. In theory, the prime rate is the lowest rate available from a large money-center bank to a very creditworthy short-term business borrower. When interest rates are tied to prime, usury ceilings should be carefully used as a rate cap on any applicable loan.

Credit professionals often use computers to assess interest rates. The type of interest rate used and specific legal concerns should underlie the computer applications. Interest rate concerns need to be updated on an ongoing basis.

The Gramm-Leach-Bliley Act

On November 12, 1999, the Gramm-Leach-Bliley Act (GLB) was signed into law by President Bill Clinton. GLB replaced the antiquated Depression-era Glass-Steagall Act. GLB is a comprehensive overhaul of the regulations that guide financial institutions. The long-standing barriers between commercial banking, investment banking and insurance were virtually eliminated.

GLB contains guidelines that protect consumers from the disclosure of information released to third parties. Two provisions of GLB provide the operative guidelines concerning the protection of personal information: Section 502 and Section 503.

Section 502 governs the release of nonpublic personal information. Financial institutions must provide consumers with a notice that informs consumers that information may be disclosed to a third party; consumers are then given the opportunity to keep the information from being disclosed by completing a non-disclosure option.

Section 503 requires financial institutions to divulge their policies concerning the disclosure of personal financial information. This disclosure is made when an account is opened and then at least once annually.

GLB has been under some harsh criticism during 2010. The credit crunch of 2008-2010 can be linked to marketplace issues that many trace to GLB as sharing at least a portion of the responsibility. Several financial intermediaries experienced a severe crisis in capital when real estate markets imploded in 2008. Did deregulation (the elimination of Glass-Steagall) contribute to the turmoil in financial markets?

Both the U.S. Senate and the U.S. House had approved bills to address concerns with GLB. The legislation intended to reform financial markets, the Dodd-Frank Act, was finalized during the summer of 2010. There was heightened anticipation for the implementation of the biggest legislative overhaul of financial markets since the Great Depression.

Prompt Payment Act

President Ronald Reagan signed federal legislation for the Prompt Payment Act into law in 1982. A major amendment to the 1982 Act went into effect in 1989. In addition, most states have enacted laws that are similar to the federal Prompt Payment Act.

The purpose of prompt payment legislation is simple. For most businesses, cash flow is essential for survival. The government is a very unusual customer; credit risk is minimal, but a bureaucracy laden with paperwork requirements and personnel inefficiency can delay payments. The cost of carrying government agencies should not be allowed to shift to the private sector.

Prompt payment laws are aimed at requiring both federal and state government agencies to pay for goods or services in a timely manner. The amended federal act clarifies the responsibilities for both the government and suppliers. The nuts-and-bolts utilization of prompt payment legislation is well worth the effort of mastering the details.

Stipulations included in the federal prompt payment legislation are as follows:

1. A seven-day constructive acceptance period exists for the government to inspect shipments or work performed. The government also has seven days from the receipt of invoices to review invoices.
2. The deadline for earning cash discounts is determined from the date of an invoice.
3. Remittance information should be included with government checks so that creditors can properly identify what is being paid.
4. Interest for late payments is payable for goods or services if payments are made more than 15 days after a 30-day payment period, except for meat or meat-food products, which call for interest if payments are three days beyond a seven-day payment period, or for perishable agricultural products, which call for

interest if payments are made five days beyond a 10-day payment period.

5. The interest obligation begins one day after the appropriate due date. Interest rates are set by the Treasury Department and can change every six months, on January 1 or July 1. Late payment interest should be paid automatically by the federal government without a supplier request.

6. In the event that late payment interest is not paid, creditors need to write a letter that includes specific details for both late interest and an additional penalty on top of the late interest. This request should be made by creditors within 40 days of receiving a late payment.

Prompt payment legislation was revised on September 29, 1999. Although still not perfect, this legislation provides credit managers with a highly desirable mechanism that can be used to induce prompt payment. At a minimum, prompt payment legislation provides a potential tool to use to induce payment from the government in a timely manner or to require the payment of interest.

Federal interest rates are adjusted semi-annually. For the period beginning January 17, 2017 through June 17, 2017, the rate of interest was 2.5%. There is a spreadsheet at the Prompt Pay website that will calculate the interest cost to the government. The site address is www.fiscal.treasury.gov/fsservices/gov/pmt/promptPayment/rates.htm.

CHAPTER 5: FOLLOW-UP

Recap of Important Concepts

1. Sound business practice requires adherence to government legislation and regulation. Credit managers are motivated to comply with laws through both social responsibility and the threat of government reprisal.
2. Antitrust laws have been enacted to prevent conspiracies in restraint of trade. Credit managers should become familiar with the potential application of antitrust legislation to credit management-related situations. In particular, an understanding of the Robinson-Patman Act and how it applies to setting and enforcing terms should be clear.
3. The Sarbanes-Oxley Act (SOX) is focused upon providing accurate and complete information to the users of financial statements for public companies. There are certain responsibilities under SOX that can trickle down to the credit manager level.
4. Due to the rapid increase in identity theft, the FTC developed the Red Flags Rules. Credit managers should be prepared for a new set of responsibilities related to following these new requirements.
5. Consumer credit legislation can be pertinent to business credit grantors. The Equal Credit Opportunity Act prohibits discriminatory practices when extending any type of credit. The ECOA also imposes certain requirements upon business credit grantors that pertain to the modification of adverse credit decisions and the retention of credit records.
6. Any business credit grantor who occasionally deals with a consumer needs to become familiar with the Fair Credit Reporting Act. Consumers who are denied credit based upon a consumer credit report are to be notified of the source and nature of the information upon which the denial was based.
7. The Truth in Lending Act mandates disclosure of credit terms to consumers. Part of the disclosure requirement includes the interest rate expressed as an APR.
8. Usury is the rate of interest charged that is in excess of the governing legal rate of interest. The utilization of usury laws is governed by state laws that include a wide number of applications and penalties.
9. Most credit managers encounter numerous situations where an understanding of the mathematics of interest rate calculations is

5: Legislation and Regulation   117

essential. Simple interest, discount interest and add-on interest can each be converted into an APR.

10. The Gramm-Leach-Bliley Act imposes broad disclosure requirements concerning consumer financial privacy for financial institutions.

11. Prompt payment legislation is aimed at requirements that pertain to federal and state governmental agencies. Credit managers should become familiar with their rights and responsibilities under the prompt payment laws.

Review/Discussion Questions

1. Describe how credit policy and procedures can be useful tools to foster decisions consistent with the compliance of government legislation.

2. How is antitrust legislation important to credit decision-making? Try to identify specific situations where credit managers could be susceptible to an antitrust violation.

3. What types of information can a credit manager legally share with a competitor when exchanging credit information?

4. Can a credit manager ever be in violation of requirements under the Sarbanes-Oxley Act? If so, furnish an example of a potential violation. If not, why not?

5. Why are the Red Flags Rules a potential concern for credit managers?

6. What types of discrimination are prohibited by the Equal Credit Opportunity Act? Does this part of the ECOA apply to business credit grantors?

7. What requirements apply to records retention concerning the ECOA? How do non-trade business creditors differ from trade business creditors concerning adverse credit decisions?

8. What is the purpose of the Fair Credit Reporting Act?

9. What is the purpose of the Truth in Lending Act?

10. What is usury? Who governs usury laws?

11. What problems can a business credit manager encounter that are governed by the law of usury?

12. Perform each of the following interest rate calculations:
    a. Calculate the simple interest on a three-month loan in the amount of $10,000 with a simple interest rate of 7%.
    b. How much is the APR in (a) above?

118   Credit Management: Principles and Practices

   c. How much is the APR for a loan made on discount basis that has a 12% stated rate of interest?

   d. Calculate the monthly payment for a five-year loan that has a principal of $20,000 and a 7% add-on interest rate.

   e. What is the approximate APR for the loan made in (d) above?

13. What is the purpose of the Prompt Payment Act?

14. Are the stipulations that govern prompt payment legislation more in favor of the government or the creditor? Support your response with sound reasoning.

15. How could the Gramm-Leach-Bliley Act constrain sharing of consumer credit information available from financial institutions?

Test Your Knowledge

1. Briefly describe each of the following:
   - a. Sherman Act
   - b. Clayton Act
   - c. Robinson-Patman Act
   - d. Fair Credit Reporting Act
2. What is the purpose of the Sarbanes-Oxley Act?
3. What safeguards can a credit manager take to comply with the requirements of the Sarbanes-Oxley Act?
4. Provide an overview of the four steps suggested by the FTC concerning the development of a Red Flags Rules internal corporate policy. Provide specific suggestions for adherence to each step.
5. What is usury?
6. Describe the basic intention and guidelines that pertain to the Prompt Payment Act.
7. How does the Equal Credit Opportunity Act apply to business creditors? Be thorough.
8. How can a credit manager stay within the guidelines of the Robinson-Patman Act when considering a request for an extended term arrangement?
9. Why is antitrust legislation important to credit decision-making? Try to identify specific situations where credit managers could be susceptible to an antitrust violation.
10. What is the purpose of the Fair Credit Reporting Act?

Credit Management Online

www.clla.org/—The Commercial Law League of America website contains a considerable amount of information concerning legislation that is important to credit management.

www.creditworthy.com/—This website offers links to the application of several federal laws that are important to credit management.

www.federalreserve.gov/creditcard/—Credit card laws can be examined at this site, which is maintained by the Board of Governors of the Federal Reserve Board.

www.federalreserve.gov/supervisionreg/reglisting.htm—This website provides information about Federal Reserve Board regulation as well as application and compliance issues. Both the Truth in Lending Act and Equal Credit Opportunity Act can be examined.

www.fiscal.treasury.gov/fsservices/gov/pmt/promptPayment/rates.htm—The Prompt Payment Act website provides a financial calculator to determine the interest that can be charged to the U.S. government; this site also includes links to other information concerning the Prompt Payment Act.

www.ftc.gov/—Using the Federal Trade Commission (FTC) website, visitors can examine antitrust concerns and guidance for business applications.

www.ftc.gov/tips-advice/competition-guidance/guide-antitrust-laws—The FTC's *Guide to Anti-trust Laws* can be downloaded from this site. In particular, the links to content "Dealings in the Supply Chain," "Dealings with Competitors" and "Price Discrimination: Robinson-Patman Violations" should be of interest to credit managers.

www.ftc.gov/tips-advice/business-center/privacy-and-security/gramm-leach-bliley-act—A fact sheet for businesses pertaining to the FTC's financial privacy requirements from the Gramm-Leach-Bliley Act is available at this link.

www.nacm.org/—The site map for the NACM website can be used to examine bills and recaps for legislative affairs and governmental advocacy issues which are pertinent to credit management.

www.sec.gov/spotlight/sarbanes-oxley.htm—This link to the U.S. Securities and Exchange Commission website provides details about the implementation of internal control reporting provisions of the Sarbanes-Oxley Act.

www.sifma.org/—The Securities Industry and Financial Markets Association provides considerable information about federal government regulation. In particular, the Gramm-Leach-Bliley Act can be examined on this website.

www.whitehouse.gov/wallstreetreform/—This web address will take you directly to the White House site that includes a thorough discussion of the Dodd-Frank Reform Bill of 2010.

References Useful for Further Reading

Barron, Jacob. "Legislative Lookout: Measures Proposed and Enacted That Could Affect B2B Credit." *Business Credit* (May 2010): 22-25.

Barron, Jacob. "More Beneath the Surface: What the Recently-enacted CARD Act Left Out." *Business Credit* (April 2010): 6, 8.

Barron, Jacob. "Tables Begin to Turn on SOX." *Business Credit* (March 2007): 29.

Blakeley, Scott, Esq. and Virginia Soderman, CCE. "Credit Scoring: Assessing the Risk, Making the Sale and Complying with the Law." *Business Credit* (June 2014): 30-32.

Blakeley, Scott, Esq. and Norman Taylor, CCE. "The Credit Team's Best Practices with the U.S. Federal Antitrust Laws." *Business Credit* (November/December 2014): 36-41.

Borges, Wanda, Esq. "Antitrust Issues Explained in NACM Teleconference." *Business Credit* (November/December 2006): 12.

Borges, Wanda, Esq. "Commercial vs. Consumer Transactions: Clarifying the Use of Personal Guaranties and Cosignors." *Business Credit* (December 2014): 8-10.

Borges, Wanda. "NACM Teleconference Explains Basic SOX Facts." *Business Credit* (October 2006): 46.

Bradley, Brian. "Red Flags, Grey Areas." *Business Credit* (October 2008): 48-49.

Federal Trade Commission. "Price Discrimination: Robinson-Patman Violations." *FTC Guide to Antitrust Laws* (June 2010): www.ftc.gov/tips-advice/competition-guidance/guide-antitrust-laws.

"Get Ready for the FTC's Red Flags Regulations and Guidelines." *Business Credit* (March 2009): 62-68.

Hadley, Tony. "Regulations in the Commercial Environment: What's Out There?" *Business Credit* (May 2015): 52-54.

"In Rush to Protect Computer Files, Old-Fashioned File Cabinets Are An Open Invitation to Data Thieves." *Business Credit* (October 2006): 47.

Jacob, Katy. "Two Cheers for the Monetary Control Act." *The Federal Reserve Bank of Chicago* (June 2010): www.chicagofed.org/publications/chicago-fed-letter/2010/june-275.

Lewis, Michael. *The Big Short*. New York: W.W. Norton and Company, 2010.

National Association of Credit Management. *Manual of Credit and Commercial Laws*, Current edition. Columbia, Md.

Nathan, Bruce. "The ABCs of Legal Issues Encountered by Credit Professionals." *Business Credit* (February 2007): 18-19, 22-23.

No More Delays for Small Businesses on SOX Compliance." *Business Credit* (November/December 2009): 49.

Patterson, Scott. *The Quants*. New York: Crown Business, 2010.

Paulson, Henry. *On the Brink*. New York: Hachette Book Group, 2010.

Prater, Connie. "What the New Credit Card Law Means for You." creditcards.com (June 14, 2012): www.creditcards.com/credit-card-news/new-credit-card-law-1282.php.

"Protiviti Warns: No Avoiding SEC's SOX Compliance for Smaller Public Companies." *Business Credit* (September/October 2009): 45.

Tang, Carolyn. "Red Flag Warning: How Will the FTC's Red Flags Rules Impact You?" *Insight* (May/June 2010): 20-21.

Tatelbaum, Charles M. "Flash! The Equal Credit Opportunity Act Applies to Commercial Credit Grantors." *P.D. News* (January 1998): 1-3.

Tatelbaum, Charles M. "Gramm-Leach-Bliley Act Impacts Business Credit." *Business Credit* (June 2001): 6.

Tatelbaum, Charles M. "Impact of Amended Fair Credit Reporting." *The Credit Report* (December 1997): 1-3.

Thorne, Deborah. "The Equal Credit Opportunity Act: Avoid the Pitfalls." *Business Credit* (March 2008): 10-13.

Chapter 6

CONDUCTING THE CREDIT INVESTIGATION

"NACM's July 2008 monthly survey posed an important question: 'Do you use a proprietary credit scoring system in your day-to-day evaluation of accounts?' The survey showed that a majority of respondents do not use a proprietary system with 67.8% of participants responding 'No' and a still significant 32.2% of respondents answering 'yes.'"[1]

Jacob Barron, CICP, NACM staff writer
Reporting on the July 2008 NACM Survey

The term "credit" has a Latin derivation, *credere*, that when literally translated means to believe in or to trust. For most credit managers, the decision to believe in a customer comes down to both the ability and the willingness of a customer to pay. Pressures to reduce costs, accompanied by an explosion in the availability of improved information resources, have shaped major changes in performing a credit investigation.

Conducting a credit investigation is one of the most common tasks performed by credit managers. Yet the factors that shape the extension of credit can vary widely from company to company. The ultimate goal of a credit investigation is to assess customer business risk so that shareholder wealth can be maximized for the credit manager's employer.

Credit decision-making is dynamic. As internal concerns and external forces change, a credit manager will ultimately be in a position to tighten or loosen controls that affect the extension of credit. The ability to assess customer risk is the skill that enables credit managers to confront the dynamics of credit decision-making.

Successful credit investigations are earmarked by linking internal controls to the evaluation of external information sources. The goal is to establish effective policy and procedures.

The **Key Learning Objectives** contained in Chapter 6 are:

---

[1] Jacob Barron, "Credit Scoring: Why Some Do and Some Don't," *Business Credit* (October 2008): 54.

1. Examine internal concerns pertinent to conducting a credit investigation.
2. Identify numerous potential sources of credit information.
3. Focus on the essential aspects of a bank reference, trade reference and industry credit group.
4. Analyze the potential use of empirical credit scoring in a business credit environment.
5. Recognize the importance of monitoring existing credit lines.

Later in this book, we will build on the credit investigation. Chapter 7 will focus on the use of external business credit reporting companies. In Chapter 8, our focus will shift toward maintaining customer relationships. In Chapters 9 and 10, we will examine the importance of financial statements for the credit manager.

THE FIVE Cs OF CREDIT

The ultimate decision to grant or to deny credit rests in the hands of the credit manager. The irony of gathering and interpreting objective credit information is that the final decision is always somewhat subjective. Sound judgment becomes the most important skill for credit managers to develop.

Historically, the *Five Cs of Credit* have provided a foundation to broaden the credit manager's focus. The ability to analyze each of the Five Cs can provide a well-rounded focus. The Five Cs include:

1. *Character.* Many credit managers believe that this is the most important of the Five Cs. Does a customer honor commitments? Have there been any prior problems with management? Character reflects one's willingness to pay. The customer, sales person, bank loan officer and other suppliers are useful to the credit manager when evaluating character.
2. *Capital.* Financial statement analysis provides the basis to evaluate capital. Focal points include liquidity, cash flow, financial leverage and asset management. An analysis of capital can provide an objective appraisal for a customer's ability to pay creditors.
3. *Capacity.* Does the debtor have the legal capacity to bind a corporation? Is each functional area of the business properly managed: financial, marketing, production and accounting? Capacity is a subjective indicator for a debtor's ability to pay. Credit managers can consider the length of time a customer has

been in business and the legal composition of the business as a reflection of capacity.

4. *Conditions.* The term "conditions" refers to a broad-based focus that extends beyond customer analysis. Changes in tax policy, industry analysis, economic conditions and geographic area can each become focal points for credit decision-making.

5. *Collateral.* Debtor support in terms of specific assets used as collateral can enhance a customer's creditworthiness. Resources such as liens on specific assets, letters of credit, pledges of stock or bonds, and personal or corporate guarantees can each afford an opportunity to ultimately extend credit.

The Five Cs of Credit can be used as a starting point to assist credit decisions. Internal corporate goals need to be balanced with the Five Cs. Credit practitioners should have knowledge of the various resources and the ability to extract the most from their investigation.

PROCESSING APPLICATIONS FOR CREDIT

Most business transactions occur on a credit basis. Both screening new accounts and monitoring existing accounts require credit analysis skills that command a great deal of judgment. In order to effectively process numerous applications for credit, the following focal points are essential: (1) establishing internal controls, (2) recognizing the legal form of the debtor entity, (3) limiting the extent of the credit investigation and (4) identifying essential sources of credit information.

The Credit Application

The credit-sales relationship is the foundation for credit controls that govern new accounts. There is a need to establish internal controls for order processing, especially for new accounts. When an initial order comes into the credit department, the order should be logged in. The responsibility for the credit decision should be clear. Any non-routine circumstances should be communicated.

In most orders from new customers, a credit application should be required. The credit department uses the application for an efficient processing of the order. A carefully developed credit application not only provides the foundation for processing orders from new customers but also has the potential to furnish the foundation of knowledge essential for effective ongoing administration of accounts.

126   Credit Management: Principles and Practices

When a new customer is seeking credit, the credit manager has some leverage to request information that may be more difficult to obtain later. Credit managers are urged to include any necessary information essential to processing the application on their credit application form. The credit application should be completed in its entirety and then signed by the applicant. (See the Chapter 6 Appendix for a sample credit application.)

When credit departments have a need for a quick turnaround time in making their credit decision, the information furnished on an application is vital. Sometimes information culled from a credit application provides much of the data that is essential to use in a credit-scoring model.

The needs of a particular credit department can vary widely. Some credit applications include a built-in personal guarantee form. Other applications include a requirement to furnish a financial statement. Perhaps tax exemption information or an opportunity for comments from a customer or a sales person can prove to be helpful. The point is that credit managers need to develop an application form that works.

Recognizing the Legal Form of the Debtor Entity

The name on the credit application needs to be verified. The legal name of the obligor is critical. When uncertainty concerning the legal name exists, the Corporation Division at the Secretary of State's Office should be contacted to verify the name. Once the name on the credit application is verified, the focus should be placed squarely upon the creditworthiness of the specific obligor. Most entities take on one of three legal forms: proprietorship, partnership or corporation. However, there are distinguishing modes of operation that can become important such as subsidiary, division, limited liability corporation, an "S" corporation or a joint venture.

The *proprietorship* form has the most number of entities in existence, but the corporate form generates significantly more revenue. A proprietor has unlimited personal liability. All *partnerships* are required to have at least one general partner who also has personal liability. However, limited partners do not have personal liability. For a *corporation*, there is no personal liability from stockholders unless creditors obtain a personal guarantee or there have been certain acts of fraud.

When dealing with a corporation, creditors should be aware of the legal difference between a *division* and a *subsidiary*. A division is an arm of the corporation in which the legal entity is the entire corporation. On the other hand, a subsidiary exists separate and apart from the parent

6: Conducting the Credit Investigation

company; creditors can consider requesting a corporate guarantee and a board of directors' resolution that authorizes the corporate guarantee in cases when the subsidiary cannot stand on its own creditworthiness.

A *limited liability corporation* (LLC) allows stockholders to be protected from personal liability while at the same time provides certain tax advantages that are associated with partnerships. There has been a resent surge in the number of businesses operating as an LLC legal entity. The reduction in investor risk has made the LLC a popular type of entity. Particular industries are characterized by having many LLC entities: accounting practices, medical practices and legal firms. The LLC entity creates the risk that is similar to that of other corporations; personal guarantees should be considered when dealing with an LLC.

Regular corporations are referred to as *"C"* corporations. An *"S"* corporation (formerly known as a subchapter "S" corporation) has the status of a partnership for tax purposes. For corporations that qualify by meeting IRS requirements such as 35 or fewer shareholders, the shareholders are taxed on profits at their own marginal rates; there is no double taxation on corporate profits and dividends as there is for the "C" corporation. Creditors should view "S" corporations in a manner similar to "C" corporations for obligations.

With the explosion in international trade, numerous companies have decided to partner with a business to form a *joint venture*. Joint ventures create an obligation for the joint venture entity. Therefore, credit managers need to be careful about legal responsibility; only the joint venture itself, not the businesses that have invested in the joint venture, has liability for joint venture obligations. This might create a need to consider a corporate guarantee from the joint venture investor companies.

Both the name and type of entity of the obligor should be clarified. Once this is done, the credit manager should consider the extent to which the credit obligation will be conducted.

Limiting the Extent of the Investigation

Cost containment is a key focus for credit management. A credit manager can expend considerable time and costs while conducting a credit investigation. The credit manager's time can be viewed as an opportunity cost. In addition, the direct costs associated with the credit investigation can add up; credit reports, phone calls, postage expense and customer visits will each contribute to credit investigation costs.

Credit policies and procedures should be developed that balance the costs and benefits of thorough credit analysis. The extent of the credit investigation is governed by each of the following factors:

1. The profit potential on the product, if high, can justify a more thorough credit investigation.
2. When there is potential for a long-term supplier relationship, a more thorough investigation is cost justifiable. On the other hand, a one-shot deal may not provide the opportunity to recoup credit investigation costs.
3. A large dollar order can justify an in-depth credit investigation. On the other hand, some companies have a blanket policy for small orders so that credit investigation costs are better controlled.
4. The business risk of the customer can often pinpoint the need to go further or stop with a credit investigation. For example, an application from Microsoft or WalMart might be quickly approved. An application from an obscure company may require substantial time and the use of numerous sources of credit information.
5. The nature of the sale can influence a credit investigation. An export sale may require the need to set up a letter of credit. A long-term secured credit sale could require extensive analysis of the collateral and the need to perfect a lien.
6. The time frame in which a credit decision must be made can vary from one hour to several weeks. Time imposes constraints on the extent of a credit investigation.

Controls that govern credit investigations need to be flexible. Situations dictate a cost/benefit focus that considers each factor mentioned in this section. Credit managers need to hone the skill of taking a credit investigation as far as it has to go.

Identifying Essential Sources of Credit Information

Credit managers do not use all sources of information for each of their customers. However, most credit managers encounter certain situations where they want to play a trump card. This is when the knowledge of any existing potential source of credit information can prove to be vital to the ultimate decision.

Table 6-1 provides an extensive list of resources that can prove useful during a credit investigation. The bread-and-butter resources will be thoroughly discussed. Those sources of credit information that are not

6: Conducting the Credit Investigation

129

> **TABLE 6-1   Potential Sources of Credit Information**
>
> - The Customer
> - Your Own Sales Representative
> - Business Credit Reporting Agencies:
>   - CreditNet.com   - Experian
>   - Dun & Bradstreet   - NACM Affiliates
> - Customer Financial Statements
> - Trade References
> - Bank Reference from Customer
> - Industry Credit Groups
> - Use of Creditor's Own Bank to Conduct Investigation
> - Securities and Exchange Commission (10-Ks, etc.)
> - U.S. Department of Commerce: Commercial Services
> - Public Records (liens, lawsuits) (State and County)
> - Utility Companies
> - Consumer Credit Reporting Agencies:
>   - Equifax   - TransUnion
>   - Experian
> - Bond Rating Agencies:
>   - Moody's   - Fitch's Investors Service
>   - Standard & Poor's   - Duff & Phelps
> - The Value Line Directory (Company and industry reports)
> - Morningstar (Investment-related tools and reports)
> - U.S. Bankruptcy Courts
> - Better Business Bureau
> - FCIB (International resources and reports)
> - Export-Import Bank of the United States
> - Customer's Accountant
> - Customer's Insurance Company
> - Various Trade Journals

often used have been identified in order to plant a seed. There are numerous potential resources, any one of which can make or break a decision to extend credit.

ANALYZING BUSINESS CREDIT INFORMATION

In the previous section of this chapter, our focus was placed upon establishing internal controls, limiting the extent of credit investigations and identifying sources of credit information. In this section of Chapter 6, our focus will turn toward utilizing key sources of business credit information. The specific key sources to be analyzed include: (1) bank references, (2) trade references and (3) industry credit groups.

Bank References

The 2009 calendar year ended with the steepest decline in bank lending since 1942. The severe recession of 2008-2009 resulted in an explosion in the FDIC watch list for potential bank failures to 702 banks. The struggling banking industry curtailed loans in all major categories.

The side effects of a weak bank-lending environment have been felt by business credit managers. More customers have been asking for extended terms. Suppliers have been dealing with more slow payers. Bankruptcies have increased. These side effects pinpoint the importance of more closely monitoring customer bank relationships.

The commercial loan officer who handles a prospective customer's account is usually the appropriate contact for a bank reference. Invariably, the loan officer will have a close relationship with the customer. The banker may be in a position of wanting to strengthen a borrower's loan relationship, so the banker will usually want suppliers to ship to the bank's customers.

In order to obtain the most information from a bank reference, the trade creditor needs to understand the code of ethics used to exchange credit information. Moreover, the trade creditor should also know which questions to pose to the banker in order to obtain the most meaningful information. Banks have experimented with the practice of charging trade creditors for a reference. This practice has not become widespread due to the number of bank customer complaints.

Risk Management Association (RMA), formerly called Robert Morris Associates, is a trade association for commercial bankers. RMA has established a code of ethics for exchanging credit references. Table 6-2 contains the seven principles that are used for the exchange of credit information. Credit managers are urged to abide by these principles both when obtaining and furnishing information. Both RMA and NACM have approved the principles outlined in Table 6-2.

Bankers often provide financial information in general ranges. This is due to the normal fluctuation in deposit and loan balances. Table 6-3 contains the *RMA General Figure Ranges*, which are used by bankers when exchanging financial data.

The diligence of the credit manager in posing pertinent questions to a bank loan officer should not be underestimated. Most accounts will be categorized as satisfactory. Credit managers need to know more than the fact that a satisfactory relationship exists to evaluate a potential customer.

Some of the information that can be obtained from a banker includes:

6: Conducting the Credit Investigation   131

TABLE 6-2   **Statement of Principles**
for the Exchange of Credit Information

1. Confidentiality is the cardinal principle in the exchange of credit information. The identity of inquirers and sources should not be disclosed without their permission.
2. All parties involved in the exchange of credit information must base inquiries and replies on fact.
3. The purpose of the inquiry and the amount involved should be clearly stated.
4. If the purpose of an inquiry involves actual or contemplated litigation, the inquirer should clearly disclose this fact.
5. The inquirer should make every effort to determine the subject's bank(s) of account before placing an inquiry.
6. Proper identification should be provided in all credit communications.
7. Replies should be prompt and contain sufficient facts commensurate with the purpose and amount of the inquiry. If specific questions cannot be answered, the reasons should be clearly stated.

TABLE 6-3   RMA General Figure Ranges

To ensure accuracy and consistency when exchanging credit information, the RMA General Figure Ranges should be used. It may be necessary, at times, to clarify these terms so that the inquirer and respondent are "speaking the same language."

Low 4 figures	=	$1,000 to $1,999
Moderate 4 figures	=	$2,000 to $3,999
Medium 4 figures	=	$4,000 to $6,999
High 4 figures	=	$7,000 to $9,999

The ranges are adjustable to accommodate all amounts in the following manner:

"Normal"	=	Under $100
"3 figures"	=	From $100 to $999
"4 figures"	=	From $1,000 to $9,999
"5 figures"	=	From $10,000 to $99,999
"6 figures"	=	From $100,000 to $999,999
"7 figures"	=	From $1,000,000 to $9,999,999

---

1. When was the account opened?
2. What is the average checking account balance?
3. Have there been any NSF checks?
4. Can the banker furnish details about the type of loans?
5. What are the current balance and payment record on the loans?
6. What is the specific collateral on the loans? (Try to obtain the nature of the financing arrangement.)

132   Credit Management: Principles and Practices

7. Have there been any personal guarantees? (Was a personal financial statement made available?)
8. Are there any inter-company customer-related transactions? (If so, please specify.)
9. Has the bank ever issued a standby letter of credit on this customer's behalf?
10. Does the bank have a current financial statement? (Will the banker share any of the numbers?)
11. What is the trend of the customer's operations?
12. Can the banker express an opinion for the overall account and/or management?

The 12 pieces of information listed are a good starting point. Each of the points can be developed more fully by posing follow-up questions. Bankers may not be in a position to volunteer derogatory information unless a credit manager frames the appropriate question.

Sometimes bankers will be reluctant to furnish information over the phone. A written inquiry can prove to be sufficient. It has become much more common for the creditor to have to go back to a credit applicant and ask the applicant to authorize his or her banker to release the requested credit information.

A bank reference has the potential to be the most fruitful information obtained by a creditor. Bankers may reside in the same town as a customer. The bank loan officer is usually thoroughly aware of a borrower's situation. The key to a successful bank reference is the ability to pose the essential questions to the right person at the bank.

Trade References

Trade references provide a vital piece of information to creditors: the willingness of a customer to pay. Actual payment experience is an excellent indication of future payment patterns. The exchange of factual information should be the focus of a credit reference. *Reciprocity* is a key ingredient when considering the exchange of information.

Many pieces of information obtained from a bank reference apply to trade references. In addition to the topics introduced for bank references, a supplier can be questioned concerning various aspects of customer relations. For example, have orders ever been held? Are discount charge-backs a problem? Have there been any disputes? When was the last sale made to this customer? What is the current status of the account?

In most situations, credit managers can pick up the phone and obtain a trade reference. However, some creditors have a policy of not releasing information over the telephone; they respond only to written inquires. Other companies may want to ensure that the caller is not fictitious, so they will call back to the creditor with the reference. An electronic exchange of information can be efficient. Keep records of the nature and details of inquiries furnished and received.

Sometimes the practice of reciprocity is not honored. Professionalism is diluted when a creditor refuses to give out information over the phone, and then at a later date, turns around and requests a reference over the telephone. Credit practitioners should strive to maintain reciprocity in order to maintain a high level of professional status.

Industry Credit Groups

Industry credit groups provide a forum whereby many years of experience can be shared, thereby enabling one to stay current with change. The factors that affect one company tend to have a similar effect upon other companies in the same industry. Direct involvement and interchange with other credit managers in the same industry can often be the most valuable source of information available.

The primary purpose of an industry credit group is to exchange factual historical information among members who share a common customer base. In addition to sharing factual information, industry groups have an educational side wherein they address professional concerns that range from organizational issues to computer systems to participation on creditors' committees. The opportunity to interchange data and keep current with changes underlies most educational activity.

Each industry group generally establishes bylaws as a means to clarify its activities. Groups are careful to set forth principles that ensure that no discrimination exists in any activities. Factors for the group to clarify include: member dues, number of meetings per year, type of reports to exchange, election of group officers and an agenda for any credit education-related topics. Written credit reports, oral account discussion and education-related activities are ongoing benefits of group membership.

Written Industry Credit Reports

Most industry credit groups will clear or report on accounts on a regular basis. Credit managers typically request information for a slow payment record, a first order, a change of ownership or any extraordinary concern.

Most written credit reports are custom designed. The reports will show payment patterns that are typical within an industry. The written credit reports are generally discussed at the next industry group meeting. Some industry groups clear all past-due accounts, while other groups will limit the number of accounts thereby allowing for more in-depth discussion.

Oral Account Discussion by an Industry

The primary advantage of an oral interchange of payment history is the freshness of the information. Discussion of accounts represents a key focus of the formal industry group meetings. Superior-quality historical factual information is exchanged in confidence. Personal contact among credit managers promotes a cooperative attitude. Perhaps the oral exchange of current factual information fosters more group trust than any other single activity.

In addition to obtaining typical payment history, credit managers can address practical procedural questions. For example, when can a customer be reached? Who is really making the decision to pay when a customer is called for payment? What numbers will the government require before sending a payment? Are any other credit managers experiencing quality claim concerns? Are deductions typical? Experienced credit managers can furnish answers to these questions. One can readily understand why credit managers recognize that the benefits of an industry group are vital.

Education-Related Activities at Industry Group Meetings

The opportunity for credit managers to gather with a group of peers is important to recognize. Credit managers need to keep abreast of changes and discuss how their jobs will be affected by socioeconomic developments. In the education portion of meetings, industry groups may ask a member to lead a discussion on a particular topic of interest to the group. At times, outside speakers are used to address common concerns. Varying topics of industry specific concerns are reviewed during these discussions such as:

- *Technological Breakthroughs.* Examples include the use of electronic funds transfers (EFT), the Internet, credit scoring models, electronic data interchange, enterprise resource planning (ERP) and computer software utilization.
- *Demographic Shifts.* Changing demographics have an effect on customer performance within specific industries.

6: Conducting the Credit Investigation

- *Corporate Restructuring.* Credit managers are faced with dual concerns because both customers and employers are going through a restructuring process. Either concern could be an important agenda item at an industry meeting.
- *International Trade Concerns.* Banks, freight forwarders or government agencies can recommend and provide potential guest speakers on timely topics. A focus by continent and/or country would be relevant to certain industries. The use of letters of credit or other export terms represent viable topics in the area of international trade.
- *Macroeconomic Forces.* For example, a change in the gross national product affects the auto industry much more than the food industry. The economic impact of proposed government legislation may prove to be a cause for credit managers to oppose or support specific legislation as a collective body.

The written reports, oral discussion of accounts and education-related activities tend to be indispensable and tangible benefits of industry credit groups. Active participation is a key ingredient of an industry credit group. An individual relatively new to credit management has the opportunity to gain a practical edge in applying credit skills. One can learn from seasoned credit managers who have taken on leadership roles. For both the individual new to credit and the seasoned credit manager, an industry group can provide a mechanism for personal growth.

AN ANALYSIS OF CREDIT SCORING SYSTEMS

The use of *credit scoring* has exploded into the business credit environment. The reasons are simple. Scaling down the credit department is a common reality that has been experienced by many credit managers. The cost-cutting trend suggests that credit managers simply have less time to manage more accounts. Simultaneously, there have been significant improvements and developmental cost reductions related to business credit scoring systems. Many business credit managers are now employing some type of a credit scoring systems.

The focus upon credit scoring in a business credit management reduces the need for human judgment. Judgmental credit analysis relies upon a credit analyst's ability to gather and interpret customer-related information. Credit scoring systems rely upon scorecards to replace the judgment exercised by a credit analyst. While the need for human

136 Credit Management: Principles and Practices

judgment to override the scoring system will always be there, the benefits of computer scoring can be significant.

Credit scoring systems attempt to assign points to a number of variables that characterize customers. The points are then totaled in order to generate decisions relating to the extension of credit. In order to provide credit managers with guidelines to consider the use of a credit scoring system, the following areas will be discussed.

1. An overview of the development of credit scoring and the mechanics of three types of credit scoring models.
2. A demonstration of a simplistic credit scoring model.
3. An identification of the benefits achieved through a properly developed credit scoring system.
4. Critical discussion of the major drawbacks related to credit scoring systems as they pertain to business credit grantors.

The Development and Mechanics of Credit Scoring Systems

Credit scoring systems have progressed significantly since they were first used during the 1930s, when mail-order businesses used numerical systems to make an accept/reject decision. The early credit scoring systems were based upon a trial-and-error experimental process. The underlying basis of the credit decision was made by accumulating points rather than a credit manager exercising judgment.

Significant technological improvements have been the key to many business creditors implementing credit scoring systems. The improvements in computer technology have allowed creditors to identify predictor variables from a large sample of customers. The predictor variables are assigned point values. Credit extension decisions are then based upon a customer's accumulation of points. Using this tool can help the credit manager arrive at more consistent credit decisions.

Credit scoring can be based upon any of three different approaches to developing the scoring model: (1) behavioral models, (2) rules-based models or (3) neural models. The models are each concerned with developing a prediction of nonpayment or for the prediction of a bankruptcy. The models are used to generate scorecards; some credit managers use several scorecards for various industries.

Behavioral Models. Behavioral-based scoring systems require a substantial pool of customers. Customer records are scrutinized for anywhere from 20 to 200 specific factors on each customer. Certain factors are identified as predictive variables, which are then analyzed by using multiple discriminate analysis or multivariate regression analysis. The analysis is concerned strictly with statistical predictability applicable to a designated number of accounts.[2]

Rules-Based Models. At the heart of a rules-based model is the application of a set of rules. The rules tend to be relatively simplistic in nature. For example, several readily available variables—such as D&B rating, number of years in business, standard industrial classification (SIC) code and public record information—could be assigned weights. The weights are then used on a scorecard that determines creditworthiness. New accounts might be in need of garnering more points until they can establish themselves as creditworthy.

Neural Models. The basis of a neural-based credit scoring model is the use of a computer to combine mathematics with logic. The model employs the parallel processing of math-based historical experiences and logic-based patterns. The model is engineered through the use of a substantial number of processing elements similar to the neurons that influence the human brain. The processing elements are layered based upon experience. Eventually the neurons signal the credit decision. (*See* the *Credit and Financial Management Review*, Fourth Quarter 2001, to review an academic study of neural-based credit scoring.)

A Demonstration of a Credit Scoring Model

In order to furnish a simplistic example of a rules-based scoring model, a creditor could analyze each customer by examining 100 various factors. Perhaps only 10 of the 100 factors are statistically significant. The 10 statistically significant factors are then combined with judgmental factors that predict willingness to pay, such as payment history and trade references.

Implementation of a credit scoring system does not necessarily eliminate the need for judgment. In many cases, business credit grantors use a two-tiered system that streamlines the use of judgment. For example, in a 10-factor system with each factor weighted equally (usually factors have different weights) at 10 points, a credit manager could automatically approve all accounts scoring above 80 points, reject all accounts below 50 points, or exercise judgment on all accounts scoring between 50 and 80 points. The weights enable the credit manager

---

[2] Edward Altman, *Corporate Financial Distress* (New York: Wiley Publishing Co., 1983). Readers are urged to review Altman's Z-score models for a thorough discussion of statistical procedures. Although designed for bankruptcy prediction, the process is conceptually similar in credit scoring models.

138   Credit Management: Principles and Practices

to determine the odds that the new account will turn out to be a favorable or unfavorable risk.

A credit manager could easily tighten or loosen credit approval policy by moving the points for the cutoffs. A more restrictive credit policy would simply move the minimum level of points to 60 from 50. Under certain conditions, the credit manager may want to exercise judgment on more accounts. The judgment area could widen to include scores between 45 and 85 points to be used as the revised cutoff levels for review.

Cutoffs are set based upon the probability of payment. The cutoff levels should be monitored and reviewed on a regular basis in order to maintain optimal control. In doing so, the credit manager identifies and accumulates everything known about the population under consideration.

Credit Scoring Examples

Table 6-4 contains a sample of the type of system that is used for credit scoring on an individual. The sample is based upon the use of a rules-based analysis for historical bad debt losses. Certain predictor variables are identified and then weighted on a scorecard. The total score is then used to accept or reject new credit applicants.

There are eight variables that have been introduced through the use of eight questions in Table 6-4. Based upon the points scored for each question, applicants can be evaluated for creditworthiness. Variables such as annual income are weighted based upon actual loss experience with previous bad debts.

The scores can be used to predict the probability of a bad debt. For example, Table 6-4 shows that an applicant who scored a 75 would be in the top 30% of all credit applicants and have a 2% probability of becoming a bad debt.

A company could set up its credit policy using a system similar to the example in Table 6-4. Perhaps 4% is an acceptable bad debt threshold. Then scores above 50 would be acceptable as a cutoff. Another approach could call for accepting all scores above 70; any score between 20 and 69 could be reviewed by a credit manager, who might order a credit report on which to base a decision; and all scores below 20 could be rejected. Parameters could be adjusted based upon experience. If credit policy is tightened, simply raise cutoffs.

Table 6-5 shows a hypothetical credit scorecard that can be used if there are many applications from small balance companies. The variables are identified and weighted by using numerous data from historical bad

6: Conducting the Credit Investigation 139

TABLE 6-4   Credit Scoring Scorecard for an Individual

Points Earned

_____ 1. How much is your annual income?
   0 to $20,000 (-10) $20,001 to $35,000 (5)
   $35,001 to $70,000 (10)   Over $70,000 (15)

_____ 2. How many years have you been employed at your current job?
   less than 1 (-15)   1-2 (2)   3-5 (10)   Over 5 (16)

_____ 3. What is your highest education level?
   No H.S. diploma (-10)   H.S. diploma (5)   College grad (10)

_____ 4. What is your current living arrangement?
   Own home (15)   Rent (2)   Other (0)

_____ 5. What is your age?
   Under 24 (5)   24-33 (10)   34-42 (4)   43-51 (15)   Over 51 (20)

_____ 6. Do you have a bank credit card?
   Yes (10)   No (0)

_____ 7. How many other credit cards do you own?
   0 (5)   1-4 (10)   5-10 (12)   Over 10 (4)

_____ 8. Do you have a telephone?
   Yes (10)   No (0)

Using the Scores for Each Applicant

Score	Layer	Probability of Bad Debt %
100-108	Top 5%	.5%
85-99	15%	1%
70-84	30%	2%
50-69	50%	4%
20-49	75%	6%
Less than 20	100%	10%

---

debts. The system is not meant to be a panacea; credit analysts should have the ability to override the system when judgment is used.

For the company with many applications in small dollar amounts, the system used in Table 6-5 can be practical. If bad debt results are not successful, the system should be combined with other sources of credit information. The time and costs associated with credit investigations can be drastically reduced. Moreover, if the system is properly designed, bad debts can be reduced.

140   Credit Management: Principles and Practices

TABLE 6-5   Credit Scoring Scorecard for Corporate Applicants

Points Earned

_____ 1. How many years has the business been in operation?
         0-1 (0)   1-4 (-5)   5-8 (6)   Over 8 (20)

_____ 2. What is the payment history of the customer to your company?
         Discount/prompt (20)   Slow 30 days (5)
         Slow over 30 days (-8)   No payment experience (0)

_____ 3. What is the payment history of the customer to other suppliers?
         Discount/prompt (20)   Slow 30 days (5)
         Slow over 30 days (-8)   No payment experience (0)

_____ 4. Is there a bank loan outstanding?
         Yes (10)   No (0)

_____ 5. During the past year, in what direction have profits changed?
         Increased (9)   No change (0)   Decreased (-5)

_____ 6. During the past year, in what direction have sales changed?
         Increased (6)   No change (0)   Decreased (-4)

_____ 7. What is the rating available from a credit reporting agency?
         (Use composite)
         1 (15)   2 (5)   3 (0)   4 (-6)   Not rated (0)

_____ 8. Has any of the existing management team ever been affiliated with
         a previous bankruptcy?
         Yes (-20)   No (0)

Using the Scores for Each Applicant

Score	Layer	Probability of Bad Debt %
75-100	Top 10%	.1%
65-74	Top 25%	1%
40-64	Top 50%	2%
20-39	Top 75%	5%
Less than 20	Top 100%	18%

Potential Benefits Achieved
Through Effective Credit Scoring Systems

Credit scoring systems can provide a number of favorable outcomes:

1. *Reduced Credit Investigation Costs.* The cost of credit reports for each current and potential customer can be prohibitive. A properly designed credit scoring system may substantially reduce the need for credit reports. In particular, credit grantors who handle a high

volume of new accounts benefit from the reduced investigation costs.

2. ***Reduced Response Time for New Accounts.*** For large credit departments, judgmental systems may create situations for credit managers to exercise judgment that is applied inconsistently. A scoring system facilitates consistency with the improved clarity of pertinent factors and the empirical assignment of weights useful when assessing the factors. The response time can be reduced with improved results.

3. ***Improved Management Control.*** When the economy slips toward a recession, corporate policy may become more conservative. The point system cutoffs can easily be moved to reflect a tighter credit policy. Conversely, controls can be loosened by lowering the number of points necessary to qualify for credit.

4. ***A Potential for Reduced Discrimination.*** The Equal Credit Opportunity Act prohibits discrimination on the basis of race, color, sex, religion, national origin and immigration status when using a credit scoring system. However, the Act states that age may be used in a credit scoring system when "the system is demonstrably and statistically sound." Furthermore, experts believe that a judgmental system is more difficult to defend against discrimination claims. A scoring system by nature is purely objective.

The potential benefits of credit scoring systems underlie their widespread use. Literally millions of credit decisions made by thousands of credit grantors are based upon credit scoring models each year. While an NACM survey of almost 3,000 credit managers indicated that about a third of the respondents are using credit scoring models, expect the percentage rate for users to escalate as improvements in technology continue.

Problems Related to Credit Scoring Systems

Business credit grantors should recognize the serious practical drawbacks that relate to credit scoring systems. Major drawbacks suggest that credit scoring should not be attempted in certain circumstances. Potential drawbacks include:

1. ***An Insufficient Pool of Customers.*** When a business has relatively few customers or very large balance customers, a credit scoring system may not be appropriate.

2. ***A Heterogeneous Pool of Customers.*** Business credit grantors may sell into markets that vary so substantially that judgment is essential. Statistical analysis may not be able to identify variables that can consistently predict repayment, or variable weights may not adequately identify an accept or reject decision. For example, how much weight should be given to a previous bankruptcy? Credit managers are making use of multiple scorecards to try to confront the problem of a heterogeneous pool of customers.

3. ***The Obsolescence of Historical Information.*** The nature of credit scoring systems is to develop predictor factors based upon historical performance. What happened in the past, however, may not occur in the future. As dollar exposure per account increases, the risk of relying upon historical information becomes greater. One particular problem that occurred during the recession in 2008 and 2009 is that the credit scores lagged behind the quick deterioration in the economy.

4. ***The Prohibitive Cost of Developing a Scoring System.*** Scoring system costs have declined dramatically during the past few years. However, a less expensive generic type of a system may prove to be ineffective as a risk assessment tool. Moreover, the system may need to be modified on a regular basis. A cost benefit analysis may be difficult to interpret. Shortcuts should be avoided if benefits are to be achieved.

5. ***Statistical Difficulties.*** Statistics relating to credit scoring systems are as complex as any that the credit manager can expect to encounter. Problems relate to obsolete data, insufficient data, selection of predictor variables and the weighing of predictor variables. There has been a trend away from the use of multiple discriminate analyses toward the use of models based upon logistic regression. For more information on statistical problems, see the article by Robert Eisenbeis.[3]

Any one of the five problems identified could cause a particular credit grantor to dismiss the potential utilization of a credit scoring system. However, only when the problems are carefully weighed against the potential benefits can a proper decision be rendered.

The software used, the support available from the internal IT department and top management "buy-in" can each lead to a more

---

[3] Robert A. Eisenbeis, "Pitfalls in the Application of Discriminant Analysis in Business, Finance, and Economics," *The Journal of Finance* (June 1977): 875-900.

congruent integration of credit scoring. The important question to consider is: What are the benefits inherent in using credit scoring as a risk assessment tool? The response is that each credit manager needs to find the best way to assess risk in a cost-effective manner in order to optimize profits. Business credit grantors have made tremendous inroads in utilizing scoring systems efficiently.

MONITORING EXISTING ACCOUNTS

The information used to analyze new customers may be more extensive than for long-term customers. At issue is the difficulty of balancing the costs of updating credit information against the benefits of more closely monitoring risk. Existing customers need to be monitored.

Moody's and Standard and Poor's, among other ratings agencies, have been widely criticized for the high credit ratings they gave to certain collateralized debt obligations. The fallout in the real estate market came quickly. The downward pressure to lower ratings did not come quickly enough for many bond investors.

Credit managers should review accounts on a regular basis. Changes in the overall economy, within an industry or at a particular company can trigger a need to consider quick revisions in a supplier relationship. Specific software can be used to alert credit managers to a change in payment patterns. There are also companies that will alert credit managers to changes in publicly available information. Yet many problems go undetected until it is too late to benefit from placing a hold on orders for a deteriorating account.

Bust-Outs present a particularly difficult type of a problem. A bust-out is a scheme to deliberately defraud creditors. The bust-out handles payments by paying in a timely manner early in a relationship and then later, when large orders are placed, files for bankruptcy. Bust-outs are not easy to detect. When credit information includes a false corporate name or address, or when a customer places a very substantial order after having placed several small orders, credit managers should be skeptical. A thorough credit investigation is in order.

Conducting credit investigations for existing customers on an ongoing basis may entail more skill than is needed with new customers. It can be quite difficult to work out of a deteriorating situation. The personal judgment used during negotiation requires fresh information and significant creativity. Conducting a thorough credit investigation may never be more important.

CHAPTER 6: FOLLOW-UP

Recap of Important Concepts

1. Historically, the Five Cs of Credit have been used as a starting point to conduct a credit investigation. The Five Cs should be combined with an analysis of internal concerns that are pertinent to making decisions. Internal controls that foster a cohesive credit-sales relationship should be developed. A functional credit application and an effective system of communicating can provide the sound foundation that is necessary to conduct a credit investigation.

2. Alternative sources of credit information should be used to the extent necessary. A cost/benefit approach becomes the driving force in utilizing potential credit information sources. Chapter 6 includes a lengthy list of potential resources. In addition, several practical factors are identified that can be used to limit the extent of the credit investigation.

3. Banks can be one of the most useful sources of credit information. Credit managers should abide by the RMA's Code of Ethics when exchanging information. Creditors should be familiar with the appropriate types of questions to pose to bankers; framing the proper questions can lead to the development of pertinent information.

4. Credit references from trade suppliers reflect a potential customer's payment history. Reciprocity and the RMA's Code of Ethics should be honored when using trade references.

5. For some credit managers, industry credit groups are the single best source of credit information. Both the discussion of open accounts and the ability to clear accounts with other suppliers in written reports provide useful information for credit investigation purposes. Industry groups also provide a unique opportunity to keep abreast with change through education-related activities.

6. Empirical credit scoring systems are growing in popularity with business credit grantors. The growth is fostered by improvements in computer systems. There are benefits and problems related to credit scoring systems that need to be carefully examined when considering the use of a credit scoring system.

7. There is a need to update credit information on existing accounts on a regular basis. The costs and benefits of monitoring risk is a role that credit managers need to address.

Review/Discussion Questions

1. What information should be included on a credit application? Why?
2. Why is it important to limit the extent to which a credit investigation is conducted? What factors might limit the investigation?
3. Discuss the use of each individual source of potential credit information. (This question is intended for business practitioners.)
4. Why is there a need to establish principles for the exchange of credit information?
5. Why is a bank loan officer an appropriate resource for a credit investigation? What questions should be introduced during a telephone conversation used to obtain a bank reference?
6. Explain the banking phrase "mod 5," as used in the RMA gerenal figure ranges. Give an example of a mod 5 balance.
7. What is the cardinal principle in the exchange of credit information?
8. Why is it important to verify the exact legal name for a new customer? How can the legal name be verified?
9. What internal controls can be used to facilitate the credit investigation process?
10. What type of business credit grantor is most likely to use a computer credit scoring system?
11. a. Use Table 6-4 to score each of the following credit applications:

	(1) Mike Huffy	(2) Benji Workman	(3) Anita Luk
Annual Income:	$18,000	$47,000	$29,000
Years at Employer:	Less than one	10	4
Education Level:	H.S. Diploma	College Grad	College Grad
Living Arrangement:	Rents	Owns	Rents
Age:	Under 24	45	34
Credit Card Bank:	None	Yes	Yes
Other Credit Cards:	None	5	None
Telephone Status:	None	Yes	Yes
Score:	_____	_____	_____

    b. Based upon the following credit policy, would you grant credit to any of the applicants?

       Approve scores above 75
       Investigate score between 40 and 74
       Reject scores below 40

    c. What are some of the benefits and pitfalls of using a credit scoring approach to granting credit?

    d. If a credit manager wanted to loosen credit policy, what changes could be made when using a credit scoring system? What factors could cause the policy to be loosened?

Test Your Knowledge

1. Explain each of the Five Cs of Credit.
2. List 10 potential sources of credit information.
3. What are the RMA principles that are used to exchange credit information? Describe the RMA general figure ranges in detail.
4. Describe in detail the information available from a trade supplier when obtaining a credit reference.
5. How can industry credit groups be useful to a credit manager?
6. What are the factors that should be considered when investigating the usefulness of a computer credit scoring system? Should the factors be weighted equally? Be thorough.
7. Provide an overview of the three approaches that can be used to develop credit scoring systems.
8. What is a bust-out? Are there any precautions that a creditor can take to reduce the likelihood of being burned in a bust-out?
9. Is there a difference in the obligation created by a division of a company in comparison to a subsidiary? If so, why is this difference important?
10. Why have LLC corporations grown in importance? Can credit managers do anything to limit risk when dealing with an LLC corporation?

Credit Management Online

www.crfonline.org/publications/abstracts.asp/—The Credit Research Foundation publishes articles and books that delve into various aspects of credit analysis. Abstracts can be reviewed; copies of articles can be ordered online.

www.export.gov/ and **www.buyusa.gov/**—Both websites provide extensive information about exporting.

www.export.gov/salesandmarketing/—Using the U.S. Department of Commerce website, one can obtain credit reports on overseas companies, among other resources. (Click on the "Market Research" link.)

www.moodys.com/—Moody's has ratings for more than 170,000 corporate, government and structured finance securities.

www.myfico.com/—This link will take you to information on FICO scores which were developed by Fair Isaac Corporation. The FICO scores are credit scores often used in consumer credit.

www.nacm.org/knowledge-learning-center.html/—This link will take you to information that pertains to the credit industry, which is available on the National Association of Credit Management website.

www.rmahq.org/—The Risk Management Association (RMA) is a bank trade association formerly known as the Robert Morris Associates. There are numerous publications, including the *RMA Journal*, that can be referenced from a wide range of useful topics.

www.dnb.com/—D&B has a database of credit-related articles and other useful credit-related resources on the the website.

www.standardandpoors.com/—Standard and Poor's can provide an assessment of credit analysis methodologies used for credit ratings. This website defines credit ratings, provides default studies and describes recent actions taken that concern bond credit rating changes. The Case-Shiller monthly home price indices are available, as well.

References Useful for Further Reading

Anderson, Raymond. *The Credit Scoring Toolkit: Theory and Practice for Retail Credit Risk Management and Decision Automation.* Oxford: Oxford University Press, 2007.

"The January 2017 Senior Loan Officer Opinion Survey on Bank Lending Practices." The Federal Reserve Bank (January 2017): https://www.federalreserve.gov/boarddocs/snloansurvey/201702/default.htm.

Altman, Edward I. *Corporate Financial Distress: A Complete Guide to Predicting, Avoiding, and Dealing with Bankruptcy.* New York: Wiley Publishing Co., 1983.

Barron, Jacob. "Credit Scoring: Why Some Do and Some Don't." *Business Credit* (October 2008): 54-55.

Bernanke, Ben. "Speech by Chairman Ben S. Bernanke at the Meeting on Addressing the Financing Needs of Michigan's Small Businesses." Detroit, Michigan (June 3, 2010).

Blakeley, Scott, Esq. and Virginia Soderman, CCE. "Credit Scoring: Assessing the Risk, Making the Sale and Complying with the Law." *Business Credit* (June 2014): 30-32.

Critenden, Michael R. and Marshall Eckblad. "Lending Falls at an Epic Pace." *The Wall Street Journal* (February 24, 2010): A1.

"Developing an Internal Credit Score for Businesses." NACM GSCFM Class of 2015. *Business Credit* (September/October 2015): 52-54.

Diana, Tom. "Credit Scoring—Not Just for Rocket Scientists." *Business Credit* (March 2007): 12-14.

Eisenbeis, Robert A. "Pitfalls in the Application of Discriminant Analysis in Business, Finance, and Economics." *The Journal of Finance* Vol. XXXII No. 3 (June 1977): 875-900.

Fensterstock, Albert. "A Brief History of Credit Scoring." *CRF News* Issue 4 (2009): 5-7.

Gahala, Charles L. "Changing the Face of Credit Management: Credit Scoring Models at the R. R. Donnelley Company." *National Credit News* (April 2002): 3-4.

Gomez, Camilo. "How Much Credit?" *Business Credit* (March 2007): 18-20.

Grogan, Larry, CCE, CICP. "Making Good Credit Decisions Even without Advanced International Expertise." *Business Credit* (April 2016): 26-27.

Hardekopf, Bill. "The History of Credit Cards." *Business Credit* (May 2010): 50-51.

Jones, Stewart, and David A. Hensher, Eds. *Advances in Credit Risk Modelling and Corporate Bankruptcy Prediction.* Cambridge, UK: Cambridge University Press, 2008.

Maltby, Emily. "When Business Credit Scores Get Murky." *The Wall Street Journal* (March 4, 2010): B6.

"NACM Survey Shows Proprietary Scoring Inappropriate, Impractical for Many Respondents." *Business Credit* (September 2008): 9.

O'Hare, Eileen. "Controlling Decisions with Statistical Portfolio Scoring." *Business Credit* (November/December 2007): 10-12.

Siddiqi, Naeem. *Credit Risk Scorecards: Developing and Implementing Intelligent Credit Scoring.* Hoboken, NJ: Wiley, 2006.

Simon, Jeremy M. "FICO Reveals How Common Credit Mistakes Affect Scores." (July 13, 2010): http://www.creditcards.com/credit-card-news/fico-credit-score-points-mistakes-1270.php.

Stuart, Alix. "Giving Credit Risk Its Due." *CFO* (August 14, 2009): http://ww2.cfo.com/risk-compliance/2009/08/giving-credit-risk-its-due/.

Thorne, Deborah. "Credit Applications: Useful Tools in Knowing Your Customer and in Binding Your Customer to Contractual Terms." *Business Credit* (February 2008): 30-33.

Yegorova, Irena, Bruce H. Andrews, John B. Jensen, and Steven Walczak. "A Successful Neural Network-based Methodology for Predicting Small Business Loan Default." *The Credit and Financial Management Review,* Vol. 7, No. 4, Fourth Quarter 2001.

6: Conducting the Credit Investigation

149

APPENDIX: Sample Credit Application

© Copyright NACM MidAmerica, P.O. Box 60626, Oklahoma City, OK 73146. All rights reserved.

Date _____

A. APPLICANT

Legal Business Name _____
(List all Trade Names, DBA's and/or Divisions or Subsidiaries)

Street Address _____ City _____ State _____ Zip _____
Mailing Address _____ City _____ State _____ Zip _____
Phone _____ Fax _____ Email _____
Ship-to Address _____
Estimated Annual Sales _____ Person to contact about account _____
Amt. of Credit Req. $_____ Type of Business _____ How Long in Business _____

B. BUSINESS INFORMATION

FEIN (Federal Tax Identification No.) (if applicable) _____ or SS# _____
☐ Sole Proprietorship _____
☐ Partnership   Partner _____ Partner _____
☐ Corporation/LLC   President/Member _____ VP/Member_____
   (Circle one)   Secretary/Member _____ Treas./Member _____
☐ Other: LP / LLP / Joint Venture / Trust
   Principal/Partner/Trustee _____ Principal/Partner/Trustee _____
Sales Tax Exemption Certificate ☐ Yes   ☐ No (*if yes, enclose signed certificate or copy*)

C. BANKING INFORMATION

Bank_____Phone_____
Address _____ City _____ State _____ Zip _____
Officer Contact _____ Acct. No. _____ Type of Acct._____

I hereby authorize bank named above to release information requested for the purpose of obtaining and/or reviewing credit.

_____   _____
Signature   Date

D. TRADE REFERENCES (Please provide three references)

	Name	Contact	Address
1.			
2.			
3			

The preceding information is for the purpose of obtaining credit and is warranted to be true. I/We hereby authorize [**Your Co. Name**] to investigate all references and customary credit information sources including consumer credit reporting repositories (*see* Consent to Obtain Consumer Credit Report below) regarding my/our credit and financial responsibility for the purpose of obtaining credit and for periodic review for the purpose of maintaining the credit relationship.

CREDIT POLICY: Statements are rendered as of the [**Your Co. Terms**]. COD restrictions may be placed on any past due account.

CREDIT TERMS: All invoices are due [**Your Co. Terms**]. A service charge of 1½% per month, or 18% per annum may be assessed on delinquent invoices but not to at any time exceed the highest legal rate of interest legally allowed.

VENUE: All amounts due for purchases from [**Your Co. Name**] are payable at [**Your Co. Address**]. It is further understood that this agreement is entered into in the state of _____ county of _____ and is governed by the laws of the state of _____.

CHANGE OF OWNERSHIP: I/We understand that we must notify [**Your Co. Name**] in writing and by certified mail of any change in ownership, the name of the business or structure of the business under which credit is established.

150　Credit Management: Principles and Practices

COLLECTION AND ATTORNEY'S FEES: In the event of default, and if this account is turned over to an agency and/or an attorney for collection, the undersigned agrees to pay all reasonable attorney's fees, and/or costs of collection whether or not suit is filed.

CERTIFICATE OF USE: I/We certify that this request is for the extension of credit for business purposes only and not for the extension of credit for personal, family or household purposes.

AUTHORITY OF SIGNATURE AND TITLE: The person executing this agreement has the authority to bind the customer and is authorized by the customer to enter into the credit application terms and conditions:

Firm Name _____

By _____ Title _____

By _____ Title _____

PERSONAL GUARANTEE

For valuable consideration, the receipt of which is acknowledged, including but not limited to the extension of credit by [Your Co. Name] to _____ the undersigned, individually, jointly and severally, unconditionally guarantee(s) to [Your Co. Name] the full and prompt payment _____, of all obligations which Guarantor presently or hereafter may have to [Co. Name] and payment when due of all sums presently or hereafter owing by Guarantor to [Co. Name] Guarantor agrees to indemnify [Co. Name] against any losses [Co. Name] may sustain and expenses [Co. Name] may incur as a result of any failure of Guarantor to perform including reasonable attorney's fees and all costs and other expenses incurred in collecting or compromising any indebtedness of debtor guaranteed hereunder or in enforcing this guarantee against guarantor. This shall be a continuing guarantee. Diligence, Demand, Protest or notice of any kind is waived. It shall remain in full force until guarantor delivers to [Co. Name] written notice revoking it as to indebtedness incurred subsequent to such delivery. Such delivery shall not affect any of guarantors obligations hereunder with respect to indebtedness heretofore incurred.

CONSENT TO OBTAIN CONSUMER CREDIT REPORT

The undersigned individual who is principal proprietor or partner of the entity applying for business credit, and therefore desirous of a business relationship with [Your Co. Name], recognizing that his or her individual credit history may be a factor in the evaluation of the credit history of the applicant, hereby consents to the use of the consumer credit report of the undersigned by [Your Co. Name] as may be necessary in the credit evaluation process and for periodic review for the purpose of maintaining the credit relationship.

Sign Name	Print Name	Date
Sign Name	Print Name	Date

The undersigned personal guarantor, recognizing that his or her individual credit history may be a necessary factor in the evaluation of this personal guarantee, hereby consents to and authorizes the use of a consumer credit report on the undersigned, by the above named business credit grantor, from time to time as may be needed, in the credit evaluation process.

Sign Name	Print Name	Date
Sign Name	Print Name	Date

Witness

The federal Equal Credit Opportunity Act (ECOA) prohibits creditors from discriminating against credit applicants on the basis of race, color, religion, national origin, sex, marital status, age (provided the applicant has the capacity to enter into a binding contract); because all or part of the applicant's income derives from any public assistance program; or because the applicant has, in good faith, exercised any right under the Consumer Credit Protection Act. The federal agency that administers compliance with law concerning this creditor is the Federal Trade Commission, Division of Credit Practices, 600 Pennsylvania Avenue, NW, Washington, DC 20580.

Chapter 7

BUSINESS CREDIT REPORTING

"The first delivery system for credit information was verbal.... Subscribers sent out their confidential clerks or came themselves, to the Mercantile Agency, to have credit letters read aloud."[1]

Travis B. Blackman
(describing credit reports circa 1850)

More than 160 years have passed since the type of early credit reports described by Travis Blackman has been used. Football players have changed from the early years of professional football. Today, players are bigger, faster and stronger than ever before. In a much more pronounced way, business credit reporting services have changed as well. Due to the Internet, business credit reports have become easier to access, and the reports contain much more pertinent information.

Business credit reporting companies provide detailed credit information for a fee. Because the business that orders the report does not conduct the investigation contained in the report, the report is referred to as an ***indirect source*** of credit information.

The use of credit information services should entail an evaluation of the benefits provided by the information weighed against the costs of the information. The costs of business credit reports are based upon the fees charged by the credit reporting agency, the type of report ordered and the quantity of reports ordered. The fees for ordering reports are often posted on the reporting agency's website when downloading reports from the Internet.

Credit reporting services can provide substantial benefits. The turnaround time for a credit investigation is often instantaneous. Monitoring key accounts can be more closely controlled. Costs for completing a credit investigation can be reduced. Moreover, the quality of information now available in business credit reports can often exceed

---

[1] Travis B. Blackman, *The Story of Dun & Bradstreet* (Murray Hill, N.J.: D&B Information Services, 1991), 3.

the information available if conducting a routine in-house credit investigation.

The **Key Learning Objectives** in Chapter 7 are to:

1. Provide an overview of business credit reporting services.
2. Examine the nature of a D&B rating, and the sections of a D&B Business Information Report.
3. Analyze the information available in an Experian Credit Advantage Report.
4. Identify business credit reports that are available from other credit reporting companies.
5. Become familiar with the use of consumer credit reports for business credit reporting purposes.
6. Provide an overview of the FICO score and the VantageScore often used in personal credit.

BUSINESS CREDIT REPORTING SERVICES

An indirect credit investigation can save time while often furnishing superior information, in comparison to a credit investigation performed directly by a credit analyst. A cost benefit analysis should be performed to determine the needs of an individual user. One focal point should include a close look at the information needed to support screening new accounts and monitoring existing accounts.

For example, when considering relatively small balance accounts, a full report may not be necessary. The costs of the full report might be hard to justify. Perhaps just a snapshot of a business could be sufficient. On the other hand, for marginal accounts or key accounts, a full report might be essential.

Another focal point might be placed upon avoiding the duplication of information. Particularly in decentralized credit environments or multi-divisional companies, there is a potential to order more than one report on the same customer. This can drive costs to excessive levels.

There was once a time when D&B seemed to have a virtual monopoly on the business credit reporting industry. Both domestic and international competitors, however, have made significant inroads in the business credit reporting industry. The result is a marketplace that is more responsive to the needs of credit professionals.

Various types of concerns—such as a lack of clarity in the fee structure, a one-report-fits-all-user-needs mentality and a lack of compatibility in technology needs—seem to have been addressed. For credit managers, the results can be characterized as being quite beneficial. Yet there is a new problem of product differentiation that now takes on more importance than ever. This new problem will be addressed by examining individual credit reporting companies in this chapter.

D&B Corp.

D&B Corp. was formerly known as the Dun & Bradstreet Corporation. The company was split into three separate companies when Moody's Investment Services and R.H. Donnelley were spun off. Now D&B more fully focuses on its role of providing business credit information services. D&B is generally considered to be the world leader in providing high-quality business credit information, yet some credit managers believe that the leadership edge is shrinking.

The origin of D&B can be traced to Lewis Tappan, who founded the Mercantile Agency in New York in 1841. One of Tappan's employees, R.G. Dun, purchased the Mercantile Agency in 1851 and then changed the business name to R.G. Dun and Co. John M. Bradstreet founded a rival credit agency in Cincinnati in 1849. The two firms merged in 1933 to form what is now called D&B Corp.

There have been four former U.S. Presidents employed at D&B early in their careers: Abraham Lincoln, Ulysses S. Grant, Grover Cleveland and William McKinley. D&B's information base contains more than 265 million business records in 200 countries worldwide.

For most credit managers, there is a need to:

- Understand the nature of a D&B rating and PAYDEX score.
- Utilize the components of a D&B Business Information Report.
- Recognize the potential utility for other D&B products.

The D&B Rating

The **D&B Rating** is a system that measures a firm's size and composite credit appraisal, based upon information from a company's interim or fiscal balance sheet and an overall evaluation of the firm's creditworthiness. *See* www.dnb.com.lv/en/rating.html/.

The **5A** to **HH** rating classifications reflect a company's size based upon *net worth* or equity as computed by D&B. *See* Table 7-1. Company size can be an effective indicator of credit capacity. These Ratings are assigned to businesses that have supplied D&B with a current financial statement.

TABLE 7-1 D&B Ratings

Based on Balance Sheet Net Worth		Composite Credit Appraisal			
		High	Good	Fair	Limited
5A	$50,000,000 and over	1	2	3	4
4A	$10,000,000 to 49,999,999	1	2	3	4
3A	$1,000,000 to 9,999,999	1	2	3	4
2A	$750,000 to 999,999	1	2	3	4
1A	$500,000 to 749,999	1	2	3	4
BA	$300,000 to 499,999	1	2	3	4
BB	$200,000 to 299,999	1	2	3	4
CB	$125,000 to 199,999	1	2	3	4
CC	$75,000 to 124,999	1	2	3	4
DC	$50,000 to 74,999	1	2	3	4
DD	$35,000 to 49,999	1	2	3	4
EE	$20,000 to 34,999	1	2	3	4
FF	$10,000 to 19,999	1	2	3	4
GG	$5,000 to 9,999	1	2	3	4
HH	up to $4,999	1	2	3	4

Based on Number of Employees		Composite Credit Appraisal		
		Good	Fair	Limited
1R	10 and over	2	3	4
2R	1 to 9	2	3	4

Source: D&B Corp. website: Glossary of Terms. Recorded June 6, 2017.

The **Composite Credit Appraisal** is a rating system from 1 through 4 that makes up the second half of a company's rating and reflects D&B's overall assessment of a firm's creditworthiness. The Composite Credit Appraisal is based on D&B's analysis of company payments, financial information, public records, business age and other important factors (when available).

Note: A **2** is the highest Composite Credit Appraisal possible for a company that does not supply D&B with current financial information.

The **1R** and **2R** rating categories reflect company size based on the total number of employees for the business. They are assigned to company files that do not contain a current financial statement.

ER (Employee Range) Ratings apply to certain lines of business that do not lend themselves to classification under the D&B Rating system. Instead, these types of businesses are assigned an Employee Range symbol based on the number of people employed. No other significance should be attached to this symbol. *See* Table 7-2.

7: Business Credit Reporting Services

TABLE 7-2 D&B Employee Range Designation

Rating	Number of Employees
ER1	1,000 or more
ER2	500 to 999
ER3	100 to 499
ER4	50 to 99
ER5	20 to 49
ER6	10 to 19
ER7	5 to 9
ER8	1 to 4
ERN	Not Available

Source: D&B Corp. website: Glossary of Terms. Recorded June 6, 2017.

For example, a rating of **ER7** means there are between five and nine employees in the company. **ERN** should not be interpreted negatively. It simply means we do not have information indicating how many people are employed at this firm.

The **D&B Rating** field in a report may also display the following designations when certain conditions are present:

The '- -' **Symbol:** This represents the absence of a D&B Rating and should not be interpreted as indicating that credit should be denied. It means that the information available to D&B does not permit D&B to classify the company within a Rating Key and that further inquiry should be made before reaching a credit decision. Some reasons for using the "- -" symbol include: deficit net worth, bankruptcy proceedings, lack of sufficient payment information or incomplete history indicator.

DS (DUNS Support): This indicates that the information available to D&B does not permit D&B to classify the company using the D&B Rating Key.

INV (Investigation Being Conducted): When an INV appears, it means an investigation is being conducted on this business to get the most current details.

NQ (Not Quoted): This is generally assigned when a business has been confirmed as no longer active at the location, or when D&B is unable to confirm active operations. It may also appear on some branch reports, when the branch is located in the same city as the headquarters.

TABLE 7-3	Key to D&B PAYDEX
Paydex	Payment History
100	Payment comes 30 days sooner than terms
90	Payment comes 20 days sooner than terms
80	Payment comes on terms
70	Payment comes 15 days beyond terms
60	Payment comes 22 days beyond terms
50	Payment comes 30 days beyond terms
40	Payment comes 60 days beyond terms
30	Payment comes 90 days beyond terms
20	Payment comes 120 days beyond terms
UN	Unavailable

Source: D&B Corp. website. Recorded June 6, 2017

The D&B PAYDEX Score

PAYDEX is a business credit score. D&B analyzes a business' payment performance (i.e., if it pays its bills on time) and gives it a numerical score from 1 to 100, with 100 signifying a perfect payment history. *See* Table 7-3.

A business' D&B PAYDEX score helps lenders, vendors and suppliers determine whether to approve you for financing and on what terms. Typically, the better the score, the more generous the terms extended. This can save your business money and give you more time to pay for supplies or services, leveling out cash flow. *See* www.dandb.com/glossary/paydex/.

D&B Business Reports

There are five major categories of D&B business reports: the Business Information Report, the Credit Advisor, the Credit Concierge, the Credit eValuator Plus Report and the Credit Reporter Plus.

D&B's reports are distinguished by both the cost and details concerning the content available. *See* www.dnb.com/products/finance-credit-risk/business-credit-reports.html/.

A Focused Look at the D&B Business Information Report

Credit managers can access D&B reports online. *See* www.dnbla.com/en/business-information-reports/.

There are several types of reports available from D&B. For many credit managers, the **Business Information Report** is one of the most complete sources of credit information available. D&B assigns each entity its own DUNS number. Credit information that pertains to any report ordered is privately shared with a customer, and fees are assessed for each report.

The following headings are used by D&B in a Business Information Report:

1. *Executive Summary and Business Information.* This overview provides credit managers with a quick readout on the customer. Information includes the DUNS number, business name, address, phone number, standard industrial classification (SIC and NAICS) code, D&B rating, PAYDEX score, year started, number of employees and summary financial statement data such as annual sales and net worth plus other information.

2. *Business History and Business Registration.* These sections provide an overview of the company's ownership. Affiliated companies, a review of the operations and industry information are included. For example, a change in ownership or a bankruptcy would be reported here.

3. *Government Activity Summary.* This section details whether the company is a borrower or has administrative debt. Also, if it is a public company, exporter/importer or contractor.

4. *Operations Data, Industry Data and Family Tree.* These sections provide information about the type of business and company structure.

5. *Financial Statements.* Comparative statements and key ratios are given in addition to liabilities and assets.

6. *Indicators.* These include public filings such as judgments, liens, suits and UCC filings.

7. *PAYDEX.* D&B furnishes a PAYDEX score plus summary and detailed payment information.

A Business Information Report from D&B can provide the basis for a credit decision. Yet the ultimate accept/reject decision is always made by the credit manager. When there are errors in reports or incomplete reports, D&B should be contacted directly so that the reports can be improved upon.

Other D&B Products

There are numerous products available from D&B. A menu can be accessed at www.dnb.com/ that includes samples of the products available. The days of using only one type of report for all credit situations are over. There are products available for purchasing managers and for marketing managers. One of the best ways to appreciate the wide range of products and services available is to test the products and services on the D&B website.

Experian

Experian Information Services, Inc. began in 1976. It was formerly called TRW until it was divested by TRW and the name was changed to Experian. Most individuals recognize Experian as one of the big three companies that prepares consumer credit reports. The Experian Business Credit product line has been instrumental in driving the entire industry toward higher quality levels.

Experian now provides reports for more than 25 million (as of 2017) businesses. The Experian website is located at www.experian.com/small-business/small-business-credit.jsp/.

Experian Business Credit has several products available for credit managers. Most credit managers should become familiar with the Business Credit Advantage Report, which is Experian's most comprehensive report. Experian also has available: the ProfilePlus Report, the CreditScore Report, the BizVerify Report, Intelliscore Plus predictive business scores and International Profiles. The crux of the difference when determined which type of report to draw down from Experian should focus upon the costs of the report and the amount of information needed.

The types of Experian business reports can be compared online (www.experian.com/small-business/comparison-chart.jsp/); there are samples for each product.

The Business Credit Advantage Report

The Experian Business Credit Advantage Report can be examined online to review a fictitious company by the name of LaSalle Medical Products. Visitors can review each part of the report. Simply click on the highlighted section that is to be examined.

The Business Credit Advantage is a comprehensive business credit report that assists credit managers in making informed accept/reject decisions quickly. The unique aspect of the Business Credit Advantage is its format. Experian has developed a seven-part report based upon extensive analysis of historical payment performance. The Experian Business Credit Advantage has the following components:

1. *Executive Summary.* The executive summary includes a brief description of the business. In addition, an actual and a predicted Days Beyond Terms (DBT) are furnished. The actual DBT is a dollar-weighted average for the actual number of days that a business is using to pay its suppliers. The predicted DBT includes historical payment trends and other pertinent factors such as industry, public records and years in business. The executive summary also includes a general credit evaluation, historical payment information and any significant derogatory data.

2. *Credit Summary.* The credit summary provides a credit ranking score. Scores range from 1 through 100 with a higher number used to reflect less credit risk. The scores are developed statistically by using algorithms that are derived from three broad focal areas: (A) **Credit**, which includes information concerning trade experiences, balances in use, payment habits and trends; (B) **Public Records**, which draws information from the frequency, recency and dollar amounts that are associated with bankruptcies, liens and judgments; and (C) **Demographics**, which include factors such as the number of years the business has been on file, its standard industrial classification (SIC) code and its size.

3. *Payment Summary.* Experian uses thousands of actual accounts receivable records contributed by businesses to compile extensive trade payment information. Actual payment records are summarized by industry to obtain a monthly payment trend summarized over a six-month period and a quarterly payment trend summarized over a 15-month period.

4. *Payment Trends.* Payment patterns reflect changes during the past six months. Publicly available information such as bankruptcy, tax liens and judgments are detailed.

5. *Trade Payment Information.* Details concerning the records from individual suppliers are made available by the supplier type drawn from an industry. A summary of payment trends and a summary of inquiries are also available.

6. ***Inquiries.*** Number of inquiries by other companies about subject company in the last nine months.
7. ***Collection Filings.*** Number of open or closed collection tradelines by collection agencies. Collections activities are in detail and also summarized.
8. ***Commercial Banking, Insurance, Leasing.*** Information about commercial financial relationships with a bank, insurance company or a lessor.
9. ***Tax Lien Filings, Judgment Filings and UCC Filings.*** Any tax liens, judgments or filings under the Uniform Commercial Code (UCC) are shown in this section.

The Experian Business Credit Advantage Report can be useful when a detailed report is needed. On the other hand, if an account is healthy and stable perhaps only a report that is minimal in nature, such as a BizVerify Report, will suffice.

Other Business Credit Reporting Companies

In addition to D&B Corp. and Experian Business Credit Services, there are other credit reporting companies. Several industry-specific credit reporting services exist. There are also certain countries where credit reports are available through a host country credit reporting source. A brief overview of alternative credit reporting sources follows.

CreditNet. Brief credit reports are available from CreditNet (www. creditnet.com/), which has 14 million businesses in its database. The reports could be useful to verify existence or to find an address or telephone number.

Equifax Small Business. Although Equifax is better known for consumer credit reports, it also has a database of 91 million businesses available on its website (www.equifax.com/business/business-credit-reports-small-business/). An Equifax report will typically include a company profile, key factors, a payment index and a credit risk score.

FCIB International Credit and Country Reports. FCIB provides customized credit reports for foreign companies as well as country reports, which are available for more than 196 countries. The reports on foreign companies are developed through local credit providers in the host country. The country reports provide considerable information; a sample country report can be viewed on the FCIB website (www. fcibglobal.com/). All reports can be ordered online.

7: Business Credit Reporting Services

Graydon International. Graydon specializes in credit reporting in Europe. Graydon's database includes reports on more than 130 million companies in 190 countries. It can develop credit reports for companies in every country in the world. Graydon's reports include bank and trade references, public filings, litigation and industry comparisons. The Graydon website is located at www.graydoninternational.com/.

NACM National Trade Credit Report. Provided by the National Association of Credit Management, this report covers tradelines for over 10,000 industry group members and 40 different NACM locations. Included is company information, the predictive score, comparison charts, monthly and quarterly trending, tradelines, collection claims, alerts, financial institution data, public records, bankruptcies, UCC filings, corporate information and inquiries from other companies about the subject company. *See* http://nacm.org/ or www.tradecreditreport.com/.

CONSUMER CREDIT REPORTS

The use of consumer credit is heavily reliant upon personal credit reports. There are consumer credit reports available on more than 90% of American adults. It is important for business creditors to realize that there are circumstances when it is permissible for business credit grantors to draw a consumer report.

The Fair Credit Reporting Act (FCRA) governs consumer credit reporting. Under the FCRA, a consumer credit report may be drawn when the information is used in connection with a business credit transaction. The transaction should entail an extension of credit when an individual's personal creditworthiness supports the business transaction. A permissible purpose is required in order for a business credit grantor to draw a consumer credit report.

Three main companies are engaged in the development of consumer credit databanks: (1) Equifax, (2) Experian and (3) TransUnion. There are certain types of information that are common to each credit reporting company's personal credit report. Consumer credit reports include information such as payment history, judgments, liens and bankruptcies. Extensive use of coding systems can be useful to gain specific details for the records contained in consumer reports.

Atlanta-based Equifax, Inc., was founded in 1899. The company stock trades publicly on the New York Stock Exchange under the ticker symbol EFX. Equifax has access to more than 400 million records in the United States. Its corporate website is www.equifax.com/.

Dublin-based Experian PLC provides global information services. Its operating headquarters are based in Nottingham, England (United Kingdom); U.S. headquarters are located in Costa Mesa, California. The company provides information in 80 countries, and there are more than 890 million Americans in the Experian database. The U.S. operation was formerly a part of TRW until it was spun off. It has a strong regional presence on the West Coast.

Not only is Experian a strong competitor to D&B in business credit reporting, it is also positioned as one of the three largest consumer credit reporting companies in the world. Experian trades on the London Stock Exchange under the ticker system EXPN. Experian consumer credit reporting services can be accessed at www.experian.com/.

Chicago-based TransUnion was formerly a subsidiary of The Marmon Group, but it is now a privately held and independently owned company. TransUnion is the smallest of the three consumer credit reporting agencies. Although it has a strong regional presence in the Midwest, there are TransUnion operations in all 50 states and in 33 countries. As of June 25, 2015, the company stock trades publicly on the NYSE under the ticker symbol TRU. The corporate website is www.transunion.com/.

The three consumer credit reporting companies are each known for making use of credit scoring. All three companies are growing rapidly. A three-in-one credit report that contains information from each of the consumer credit reporting agencies is available. In addition, a free personal credit report that contains your own personal credit data can be requested once a year from each of the three credit reporting companies at the following link: www.annualcreditreport.com/.

CONSUMER CREDIT SCORING

Credit reports and credit scores are purchased by banks, credit reporting companies, credit card issuers and other types of creditors. When authorized, they can also be purchased by insurance companies and potential employers. Business credit managers can benefit from a close look at the methodology used to develop consumer credit scores.

The FICO Score. Fair Isaac Corporation has been the dominant provider of consumer credit scores, which are commonly referred to as FICO scores. They can range anywhere from 300 to 850. A higher FICO score reflects less risk to a creditor.

FICO scores are calculated by using statistical algorithms. The five general components that have been developed and weighted are as follows:

- 35% of the score derived from payment history;
- 30% from the account balances now owed;
- 15% from the length of credit history;
- 10% from the type of credit now used; and
- 10% from new credit.

Details concerning the FICO scoring components and methodology are available online at www.myfico.com/credit-education/whats-in-your-credit-score/.

The VantageScore. The three consumer credit reporting companies, Experian, Equifax and TransUnion, collaborated jointly to help to create the VantageScore for VantageScore Solutions, LLC. The model uses different algorithms from the FICO score to develop a credit score. A VantageScore can range from 501 to 990; the lower the score, the higher the credit risk. The process of characteristic normalization is used to create 12 scorecards used to assign a VantageScore. A new 13th scorecard was added to rank consumers with sparse credit histories.

Statistical algorithms that are used to obtain a VantageScore focus upon six characteristic categories of information, which are as follows:

- 40% of the score derived from payment history;
- 20% from credit amount utilization;
- 11% from recently reported balances;
- 31% from depth of credit reflected by length and types of credit;
- 5% from recent credit reflecting the number of recently opened accounts and the credit inquiries; and
- 3% from available credit.

Additional details concerning the VantageScore can be examined online at www.vantagescore.com/.

Both the FICO score and the VantageScore reflect a focus on the development of better ways to efficiently evaluate credit risk. The models can be quite effective in predicting serious future delinquencies. The methodology used to develop consumer scores has considerable potential to benefit those business creditors who are considering the development of their own models.

CHAPTER 7: FOLLOW-UP

Recap of Important Concepts

1. Credit reporting services have been in existence in the United States for more than 160 years. Both the quantity and quality of information now available in credit reports is indispensable to credit decision-making.
2. Products now available from credit reporting companies should be examined from a cost/benefit analysis approach.
3. D&B Corp. is generally considered to be the world leader in providing credit information services. Credit managers should become adept in scrutinizing D&B ratings, Business Information Reports and other D&B products. There are Business Information Reports available through D&B for more than 265 million businesses located throughout the world.
4. Since 1976, Experian has grown to become a formidable contender to D&B as the world leader in business credit reporting services. Experian furnishes several Business Credit Reports. The Business Credit Advantage Report contains extensive information that can be used to support key decisions.
5. There are other industry-specific and international credit reporting services. Credit managers should consider experimenting with various business credit reporting services to gain access to the best services to meet the needs of their particular employer.
6. There are three primary providers of consumer credit reports: Equifax, Experian and TransUnion. Under certain circumstances, business credit grantors may draw a consumer credit report to access information relevant to the extension of credit.
7. The FICO score and the VantageScore are two of the most widely used risk assessment scores in consumer credit. Business credit managers can benefit from a careful examination of the methodology used to develop consumer credit scores.

Review/Discussion Questions

1. Describe a D&B rating of BB2. Be specific.
2. What information is contained in the heading of a D&B Business Information Report?
3. How can a credit manager use D&B to assist a purchasing manager?
4. What other products are available to credit managers from D&B?

5. Describe the components of an Experian Business Credit Advantage Report.
6. How can an Experian credit ranking score be useful to a business credit grantor?
7. From whom can a credit manager obtain reports for a business outside of the United States?
8. What companies provide consumer credit reports? What type of information is disclosed in a consumer credit report?
9. Who are the major providers of consumer credit scores? What names are used for each company's score?

Test Your Knowledge

1. What does a D&B rating represent?
2. The Experian credit score is based upon the utilization of several pieces of information. What information is used to develop the score?
3. What specific type of information is contained in a D&B Business Information Report or an Experian Business Credit Advantage Report? Thoroughly summarize the types of information contained in either report.
4. Under the Fair Credit Reporting Act, when can a business credit grantor draw a report on a consumer?
5. What type of internal controls can be used to monitor the effectiveness of business credit reporting services?
6. Describe the way in which a credit manager could utilize business credit reports to assist a purchasing manager.
7. How can the FICO score or the VantageScore be useful to a business credit manager who is attempting to develop an in-house business credit scoring system?

Case Study

D&B furnishes a sample report for the Gorman Company at its corporate website. The report is 13 pages in length. Go online and type in dnb sample report. Examine the report to identify the various types of information found in the report. Is any derogatory information contained in the report?

Next, go to the website sbcr.experian.com/pdp.aspx?pg=Sample-ProfilePlusI&hdr=reportSample to view the sample report for LaSalle Medical Supply. What types of information are contained in the report? Is there any derogatory information?

Compare the types of information found in the sample reports from D&B and Experian. Do the reports differ in nature? Do you have a preference for either report? Support your response with details.

Credit Management Online

www.businesscreditusa.com/—This link will take you to Credit.net, which is a commercial site that offers reports on more than 15.5 million businesses. A free sample report can be examined at the site.

www.CreditReport.com/—This site contains a wealth of information concerning consumer credit.

www.dnb.com/—The home page for D&B Corp. is hosted at this site. D&B's many products can be reviewed, and product pricing is also included. There are samples for products with discussion of the niche that each product is intended to fill.

www.dnb.com/products/finance-credit-risk/business-credit-reports.html/—Through this D&B site, you can compare sample reports for each of the following types of D&B reports: the Business Information Report, the Credit Advisor, the Credit Concierge, the Credit eValuator Plus Report (most popular) and the Credit Reporter Plus (entry level).

www.equifax.com/—The home page for Equifax can be accessed at this link. A sample Equifax Business Credit Report is available. Three-in-one reports, which include information from Equifax, Experian and TransUnion, are demonstrated at this site.

www.experian.com/—Experian provides both consumer and business credit reports. The components of each type of report are explained and then demonstrated through the use of sample reports.

www.myfico.com/—Fair Isaac Corporation demonstrates FICO scores at this site. There is also a link to a nifty financial calculator that may be of use for numerous consumer-related financial calculations.

www.nacmmidwest.org/chicago/creditgroups.htm/—This link will take you directly to the Industry Credit Group Overview web page for NACM Midwest, where services available to industry groups have been summarized.

www.transunion.com/—Consumer credit reporting company Trans-Union Corporation hosts this website. The basic contents of a consumer credit report are described at this site.

www.vantagescore.com/—This is the home page for VantageScore, a consumer credit scoring model developed through the collaboration of Equifax, Experian and TransUnion.

References Useful for Further Reading

Blackman, Travis. *The Story of Dun & Bradstreet.* Murray Hill, NJ: Dun & Bradstreet Information Services, 1991.

Blakeley, Scott, Esq. and Virginia Soderman, CCE. "Credit Scoring: Assessing the Risk, Making the Sale and Complying with the Law." *Business Credit* (June 2014): 30-32.

The Business Information Report. Dun & Bradstreet Information Services Website: June 15, 2010.

"Characteristic Leveling Process White Paper." VantageScore (May 2006). Key in title of paper online to locate pdf of article.

Cole, Robert H., and Lon Mishler. *Consumer and Commercial Credit Management,* 11th Ed. Burr Ridge, IL: Irwin/McGraw-Hill Inc., 1997.

"D&B Announces Services for Customers to Better Predict Small Business Credit Risk." *The Wall Street Journal* (May 17, 2010). Key in title of paper online to locate pdf of article.

Goldwasser, Joan. "Shootout at the Credit Score Corral." *Kiplinger's Personal Finance* (July 2010): 58.

Hadley, Tony. "Regulations in the Commercial Environment: What's Out There?" *Business Credit* (May 2015): 52-54.

Hanessian, Brian. "Leading a Turnaround: An Interview with the Chairman of D&B." *McKinsey Quarterly* Issue 2 (2005): 82-93.

Hansen, Fay. "The Revolution in Online Credit Resources." *Business Credit* (October 2000): 26-30.

Kim, Jane J. "Credit Scores: Can You Get Them Free?" *The Wall Street Journal* (October 8, 2009).

Maltby, Emily. "When Business Credit Scores Don't Count." *The Wall Street Journal* (March 18, 2010): B6.

Schmidt, David. "Get Better Mileage for Your Information Dollars." *Business Credit* (March 2001): 66-69.

Simon, Jeremy. "FICO Reveals How Common Credit Mistakes Affect Scores." (November 29, 2009). Key in title of paper online to locate pdf of article.

Part III
Credit, Collection and Analysis

Chapter 8

A Systematic Approach to Effective Collection Activity

"Commercial collectors are facing one of the most challenging collection environments in a generation. Lurking inside those increasingly delinquent portfolios are tomorrow's deadbeats and bankrupt companies. Many of those accounts are just temporarily slowing their payments in an effort to manage cash to deal with their own downstream disruptions. How is a collector to tell the difference?"[1]

Alex Coté, Vice President of Marketing, Cortera, Inc.

One of the most difficult challenges in credit management is the management of collection activity during a credit crunch. The forces that restrict bank lending tend to contribute toward the tightening of credit in all other areas of credit. A domino effect often takes place. Customers cannot pay because their own customers cannot pay. The management of collection activities becomes more challenging than ever.

Most credit managers would agree that collection activity is central to credit management. Garnering the ultimate receipt of cash for sales that are made on a credit basis has created jobs for credit managers for many years. Technology has revolutionized collection activity. The pivotal focus should now be placed upon efficiently harnessing that technology to integrate collection activity with the overall goals of a firm.

Collection activity can be optimized by using a systematic approach that integrates multiple focal points. In a systematic approach, a credit manager recognizes the interrelationships of the many component factors that impact collections. For example, in a systematic approach, order entry, prompt and accurate billing, internal controls for screening new accounts, reports to monitor existing accounts, alternative collection strategies, deduction management and legal concerns each create a focal point both individually and collectively.

---

[1] Alex Coté, "Spring Cleaning: Improving Collections Results in a Tough Economy," *Business Credit* (May 2009): 24.

172   Credit Management: Principles and Practices

Customer knowledge acquired from conducting a credit investigation (in Chapter 6) and obtaining agency reports (in Chapter 7) are put to use in developing a comprehensive collection system in this chapter. Moreover, financial statement analysis (Chapters 9 and 10) and legal concerns (Chapters 11 and 12) each play important roles in collection activity. Therefore, credit managers are challenged with assessing multiple focal points in order to apply the concepts that are integral to an effective collection system.

A sound analysis of a collection system includes several areas of concentration. While the focus includes components of the collection system in a piecemeal approach, the actual system is interactive.

The **Key Learning Objectives** contained in Chapter 8 are:

1. Examine the technological changes that have altered the approach to collection activity.
2. Recognize the way in which various terms of sale affect the collection system.
3. Identify internal controls that can be useful in maintaining credit availability.
4. Analyze alternative modes of collection available to the credit manager.
5. Make use of reports such as the NACM Credit Managers' Index (CMI).
6. Focus on customer deductions as a component of collection activity.

INTEGRATING TECHNOLOGY INTO THE COLLECTION SYSTEM

Enterprise resource planning (ERP) embraces the use of an integrated approach to technology. Technology can be designed to perform a wide array of business applications that are compatible for the needs of various departments and users within an organization. Systems such as *PeopleSoft, SAP* and *Oracle* have been among the leaders in ERP installations.

Coupling the needs of credit managers to available ERP packages has been, and will continue to be, a major challenge. Credit and collection needs are not often among the key applications integrated into ERP systems. A complicating fact is that credit department needs can vary widely from company to company. While one ERP system will not fit the needs of all users, ERP providers have made significant improvements in their credit and collections modules.

There are also software systems that focus upon credit management that are available from companies such as SunGard (https://www. sungardas.com/en/services/managed-application-cloud/application-management-services/).

SunGard makes available the AvantGard solutions package. This package includes a number of features that focus on credit management concerns. For example, cash application, deductions management, collection management, credit screening and internal reporting can be enhanced with a good software applications package.

Credit management software application packages may be integrative with ERP systems and can be useful for specific credit-related applications. The cost-benefits of a new credit management system must be justified internally. In addition, the internal support available from the IT department is also an important consideration.

The real challenge is to obtain meaningful credit information in a timely, cost-efficient manner. Successful use of technology will free up time for credit managers to focus upon less mundane tasks. Applications can generate hit rates for cash application, credit scoring using various scorecards by industry, deduction management by types of disputes that include clear delineation of responsibility, collection management that can include payment trends and triggers detailed payment records, automated prioritized follow-ups, automated customized correspondence and management reports.

The ability to harness technology underlies the development of the rest of this chapter. Technology is useful when considering setting terms and then developing a collection management system. Managing receivables efficiently requires access to meaningful information that can be used to control risk.

TRADE CREDIT TERMS

One of the most important factors to focus upon in a collection system is establishing and then enforcing the terms of sale. Used in this context, terms of sale represent the period for which the credit is granted. Although most business transactions occur on a credit basis, the terms used in the credit period need to be carefully considered.

Many firms still use a lockbox system in order to speed up the inflow of funds available for the treasurer to use. A lockbox is a system where incoming checks are directed to a post office box which is generally a bank address. The funds are deposited in the bank and matched with the creditors outstanding balances. Credit managers are made aware of receipts via an electronic transmission of data so that their records coincide with actual payments received.

Selling terms can be readily separated into four categories: (1) cash, (2) open account, (3) special and (4) electronic payment arrangements. Since there are many variations of terms, each of the four categories will be scrutinized. Whatever terms are put to use with a customer, the terms should be clearly communicated in writing. A paper trail can be useful if an account ever needs to be litigated.

Cash Terms

Credit should be earned. When a customer is not creditworthy, cash terms become an alternative means to make a sale. There are a number of ways for a credit manager to establish cash terms. The following cash terms vary in risk:

Wire Transfer and ACH (Automated Clearing House). Rather than obtaining a check, a credit manager can negotiate for a wire transfer. A customer in a hurry for merchandise may arrange to have a bank wire funds to a creditor's bank. The fees are nominal.

Cashier's Check. This type of check is drawn by a bank on the bank's own funds.

Certified Check. A certified check is a check in which a bank guarantees that funds are on deposit when the check is certified. The bank earmarks the funds for the creditor.

Cash with Order. In a situation where goods are manufactured for a particular customer, a credit manager may want to receive payment prior to manufacturing. In this case, the check accompanies a customer's order.

Cash on Delivery (COD). The risk to a credit grantor on COD terms is that a trucker may forget to pick up the check on delivery. In addition, a customer could refuse to accept a COD shipment. These risks make other types of cash terms more acceptable to a credit grantor.

8: A Systematic Approach to Effective Collection Activity   175

Cash in Advance. A credit manager may have a customer order but feel reluctant to ship COD. In this case, cash in advance of shipment may be most appropriate.

Open Account Terms

Most businesses tend to grant customers an industry-wide set of terms. Sophisticated customers will consider their own cost of capital in order to evaluate repayment. Likewise, a credit manager should recognize that customer payment patterns govern the profitability of a sale. Terms are related to the time value of money.

Open account terms are also called ordinary terms or standard terms. Table 8-1 displays examples of commonly used open account terms. The specific terms of 1% 10N30 entitle a customer to a 1% cash discount if the customer pays in 10 days. If the customer forgoes the discount, the full amount is due on day 30.

Many credit managers send new customers a "welcome aboard" letter that includes an explanation of terms. Concise invoices should also reinforce terms. For example, if an invoice is paid by a certain date, the customer can deduct a specified cash discount. If the amount is paid after the specified discount date, the specified net amount should be paid by the net date.

A credit manager may be in a position to convince a customer that taking cash discounts can create profits. The following may prove useful.

TABLE 8-1   Examples of Open Account Terms

Terms	Explanation
Net 30	Full amount is due in 30 days.
1% 10N30	A 1% cash discount is earned if paid in 10 days; the net amount is due on day 30.
10th Prox	The full amount is due on the 10th day of the following month.
1% 10th Prox	A 1% cash discount is earned, and the discounted amount is due on the 10th of the following month.
1% 10 MOM	A 1% cash discount is earned if paid in 10 days; the net amount is due the middle of the month.
2% 15 EOM	A 2% cash discount is earned if paid in 15 days; the net amount is due at the end of the month.

The formula will provide the approximate percentage cost, on an annual basis, to forego taking discounts.

Equation 8-1. Approximate Cost Formula

$$\text{Approximate \% Cost} = \frac{\text{Discount Percent}}{100 - \text{Discount Percent}} \times \frac{365}{\text{Number of Days Until Paid} - \text{Discount Period}}$$

The formula in Equation 8-1 can be used by a creditor whose terms are 1% 10N30. The results reflect the cost expressed in an annualized percentage.

Equation 8-2. Approximate Cost Example

$$\text{Approximate \% Cost} = \frac{1}{100 - 1} \times \frac{365}{30 - 10} = .01 \times 18.25 = 18\%$$

Recognize that this is a cost to forego a discount. Funds used from day 11 to day 30 cost approximately 18%. If a customer has a source of funds such as a bank, and borrows from the bank at a rate lower than 18%, the customer can create higher profits by discounting. The cash discount becomes an incentive to pay in 10 days.

The results of Equation 8-2 are approximate. The effective annual rate is actually a bit higher. Equation 8-3 shows the calculation for the effective annual rate, which is 20%. This approach is a bit more accurate.

Equation 8-3. Actuarial Example

$$\text{The Effective Rate} = (1.01)^{18.25} - 1.0 = 20\%$$

The results calculated in Equation 8-3 use the terms of 1% 10N30, which were also used in Equation 8-2. However, the annualized rate increased from 18% to 20% due to the magic of compounding. There are 18.25 interest periods in one year ($365 \div 20$); the interest rate per period is $.01 \div .99 = .01$. Therefore, the approximate cost calculated in Equation 8-2 understates the effective rate calculated in Equation 8-3.

There are two assumptions used in these interest rate calculations. First, discounts are taken on the discount date. Second, if discounts are foregone, the full amount is paid on the net date. These parameters can be changed to coincide with actual customer payment habits.

For example, if a customer with terms of 1% 10N30 actually pays on day 60 instead of day 30, the cost is reduced. Equation 8-4 shows the cost to a customer who pays on day 60.

Equation 8-4. Approximate Cost Application

$$\text{Approximate \% Cost} = \frac{1}{100 - 1} \times \frac{365}{50} = .01 \times 7.3 = 7\%$$

Equation 8-4 shows that a customer can benefit by paying late. The approximate annualized percentage cost to forego a 1% discount and pay on day 60 is 7%. Unless a creditor charges late payment interest, or a customer experiences a supplier holding shipments due to slow payments, the customer may want to lean on a supplier and pay late.

Table 8-2 shows both approximate costs and effective costs for various credit terms. Credit managers should recognize the incentive of offering and carefully enforcing cash discounts. For terms of 3% 15N45, Table 8-2 shows that the real cost of not taking a 3% cash discount and paying the net amount on day 45 is 44%. Any customer foregoing the 3% discount may be in a position where any source of capital simply may not be available to take the discount.

The preceding examples might be useful to a corporation when considering a change in terms. A change in the discount period, the net period or the discount percentage should change customer payment habits. However, overall corporate profitability also needs to be examined.

Special Terms

The potential to create profit through the use of special terms mandates an understanding of the alternatives available. For the credit manager, there are unique risks associated with special terms. A clear understanding of any arranged special terms should be communicated among the customer, sales manager and credit manager in advance.

TABLE 8-2	Annual Percentage Costs to Customer to Forego Discounts	
Terms	Approximate % Cost	Actuarial Effective Rate
2% 10N30	36%	44%
2% 10N60	15%	16%
3% 15N45	35%	44%

Special terms arrangements can be broken down to consider a special emphasis on electronic payment arrangements.

Consignment Terms. A credit manager may find a marginal credit risk customer who has an ability to sell a product. Goods can be shipped to a consignee without passing title. When the goods are sold by the consignee, a remittance is made to the creditor. If the goods are not sold by the consignee, the consignee may return the goods to the creditor.

High-margin goods such as baseball cards or jewelry are sometimes sold on a consignment basis. In an insolvency, banks with blanket liens on inventory often claim consigned goods as collateral. Creditors who ship consigned goods should receive regular inventory reports, require insurance coverage designating the creditor as loss payee and consider perfecting a lien under the UCC (Uniform Commercial Code).

Contra Account Arrangements. When a customer is also a supplier of goods, a contra account arrangement can be useful. In the event that the customer is not a good credit risk, the credit manager should maintain a balance owed to the customer in excess to the balance due from the customer. Both shipping controls and record keeping need to be carefully maintained in a contra account arrangement.

Letters of Credit. A letter of credit allows a credit manager to substitute the credit risk of a bank for the credit risk of a customer. Standby letters of credit can be an effective tool to use when selling to a marginal account. Export letters of credit facilitate international trade. The risks associated with using letters of credit will be discussed thoroughly in Chapter 11. Payments are made under the terms that are specified in the letter of credit.

Barter Arrangements. Bartering is an exchange of goods in return for goods. Usually bartering involves the use of a clearinghouse system or a reciprocal trade agreement system. A clearinghouse accepts a creditor's merchandise in exchange for trade credits while assessing a transaction fee. The trade credits are then used to acquire goods. Creditors should be concerned about the availability of goods and the limited life of the credits when using a clearinghouse.

Reciprocal trade companies (RTCs) operate as a broker. When RTCs are used, clients exchange goods for credits. However, the company then places a bid for goods at a specified price with the RTC, who in turn acquires the goods for the specified price.

Seasonal Datings. Certain industries generate cash flows only once a year. For example, the agriculture industry generates cash flow when crops are harvested. Terms are often established that call for payments to coincide with the timing of the cash flow generated when crops are harvested and then sold. Anticipation discounts are sometimes used as an incentive to customers with seasonal datings.

Seasonal datings pose a problem because accounts receivable balances build up. The credit exposure is increased because of ongoing shipments only being paid for once per year. Anticipation incentives encourage early payment that can be viewed as a vehicle to reduce the dollar exposure in the account.

Electronic Payment Arrangements

Systems such as Electronic Invoice Presentment and Payment (EIPP) and Electronic Bill Presentment and Payment (EBPP) were developed to support automated cash inflows. EIPP refers to business-to-business transactions while EBPP refers to consumer-to-business transactions. Both EIPP and EBPP allow sellers to electronically transmit billings to customers.

Other types of electronic payment arrangements are predominant in certain industries. Prearranged systems for electronic payments can improve the predictability of cash flow. Electronic funds transfers refer to the transfer of dollars; electronic data interchange includes the transfer of the remittance advice.

There are several types of electronic payment arrangements: credit cards, debit cards, stored value cards, online payment systems, wire transfers and automated clearing house (ACH) arrangements. Standardized forms and procedures are also available. Each electronic payment arrangement will be discussed individually. In order to effectively implement electronic systems, managers across functional areas need a company-wide policy that fosters cooperation among the credit, sales, customer service, purchasing and transportation departments.

Credit Cards. Credit cards are the most common type of electronic payment. Consumer credit has been the historical bailiwick for credit card usage. Internet transactions are often paid for through credit cards. According to a study performed by CRF, credit cards are now used by more than half of the population studied in a business-to-business environment. The purchaser, seller and credit card company are linked through an electronic network. Credit cards afford convenience but at a cost to the seller.

Debit Cards. Debit cards can be used in a manner very similar to the ways in which credit cards are used. However, unlike the creation of a revolving open account when a credit card is used, the debit cardholder has funds immediately debited from an account. There is no credit created.

Stored Value Cards. A customer can purchase the right to store value in a card by prepaying. The card is used by the holder, and the monetary value is transferred to the seller. A smart card is a stored value card that allows for the electronic transfer of value from a bank to a merchant.

Online Payment Systems. The Internet has provided a unique opportunity to market products. In addition to credit cards and debit cards, online payment systems developed by companies such as PayPal, Amazon Payments and Google Wallet allow buyers to establish credit electronically. Various tools are used to support the online purchase. Authorization by the online payment service is often based upon savings accounts, checking accounts, money orders or credit cards.

Wire Transfers. The Federal Reserve allows for the quick transfer of large balances made between financial institutions through the Fedwire. Sometimes a customer with past due balances may want an order released quickly. In such situations, a credit manager can insist upon a wire transfer to clean up the past due balance prior to releasing a new shipment. Foreign exchange wire transfers are made over the Clearing House Interbank Payment System (CHIPS).

ACH Arrangements. Automated clearing house (ACH) arrangements are one of the fastest growing electronic payment mechanisms. Transactions such as utility bill payments or property taxes can be made because a payment was authorized by an individual, a business or the government, and then a bank is authorized to process the remittance electronically. Many consumers have their paychecks deposited automatically into their bank account via a type of ACH arrangement. ACH arrangements are sometimes called direct debit programs. They offer an alternative to using checks. Next-day and same-day payments are available.

CREDIT AVAILABILITY

Historically, the terms *credit limit*, *credit line* and *credit availability* have been used interchangeably. This may no longer hold true.

Creditors can potentially be held liable by customers who claim that they have been led to believe that an open-ended availability of credit exists. Creditors should consider avoiding use of "credit lines," which may imply credit will be granted up to a specified amount. Instead, creditors should use language on a credit application that clearly points out that the decision for credit availability is solely at the discretion of the vendor.

Credit managers have a number of concerns regarding credit availability. To whom is the availability of credit communicated? There are some companies that only communicate dollar limits internally. Yet at other companies, customers know that a specified amount of credit can be used.

At some companies, credit availability is used only as a threshold amount to draw attention to an account. The credit manager then can exercise judgment in terms of holding shipments or increasing the dollar exposure. Yet at other companies, the credit availability amount is an absolute threshold for exposure to a customer.

Credit authority is often established through a hierarchy. Table 8-3 presents an example of a hierarchy approach that can be used to assign levels of authority.

Table 8-3 shows that the Division Credit Manager has authority to approve credit to a customer for any amount over $50,000, up to a maximum of $200,000. In some ways, the concept of a hierarchy of credit authority is similar to a loan committee at a bank. As accounts grow larger, the potential risk should be reviewed by higher level personnel.

At many companies, credit is automatically made available to customers up to a certain amount. For example, orders below $200 may be approved by implementing a policy for blanket approval to any customer. The costs of a credit investigation and actual payment experience with small-balance accounts are important factors when considering the blanket threshold amount.

Internal controls are useful in making credit available. Systems that allow for an automatic approval of orders to large, strong companies can reduce the burden of credit personnel reviewing every purchase order. For products with a limited customer market, controls can be used to prevent all orders from entering the manufacturing process until credit is approved.

TABLE 8-3   Sample Hierarchy for Credit Authorization

Title	Dollar Authority
Assistant Credit Manager	Up to $50,000
Division Credit Manager	$50,001 to $200,000
Corporate Credit Manager	$200,001 to $500,000
Treasurer	$500,001 to $1,000,000
Vice President of Finance	More than $1,000,000

TABLE 8-4   Credit Controls for Existing Customers

Code	Classification	Explanation
A	Automatic	Accepted to process all orders.
L	Limited	Credit authorized up to a limited specific amount.
R	Refer	All orders should be referred to credit department for approval.
C	Cash	Customer payments required in advance.
H	Hold	Credit hold on orders. Do not ship.

The use of internal controls is central to the effectiveness of any credit department. Table 8-4 shows a set of codes that can be used to classify customers. The classifications are useful to expedite orders from existing customers. The codes can be distributed internally to the sales, manufacturing and transportation departments.

Table 8-4 shows that customer code "R" is called a refer account. All orders for customers with an "R" code need to be referred to the credit department for credit approval. The "R" code would be useful to control risk for a marginal account.

COLLECTION ACTIVITY

Sound collection activity entails the development of effective policy and procedures. The effectiveness is based upon knowledge of customer habits and use of alternative collection procedures. Failure to communicate clear ground rules can undermine the effectiveness of any collection activity. Records for collection activity should be maintained.

Technology is available to facilitate collection activity. Certain types of tasks that are routine in nature lend themselves to the automated applications. The specific decision rules can be developed to trigger the type of mode that is most useful for collecting; then collectors can be automatically alerted to use the appropriate follow-up. Management reports can be made available online or directly distributed to keep all interested parties aware of the current situation.

For example, accounts can be classified by size or by risk; then a particular mode of collection is deemed to be most useful. Large amounts might entail a phone call after five days past due; smaller accounts might trigger a letter after 10 days past due. The timing of an appropriate follow-up can be automated. Based upon the internally generated decision rules, an account could be placed on hold if a commitment is not honored. Sales personnel and production personnel can be alerted to any developing problems. Distinctive modes for collecting accounts include:

Concise Invoices. The accuracy and design of an invoice, and promptness in billing, are important starting points for collection activity. The name and telephone number of a vendor contact should appear on the invoice. The payment destination should be clear. If a lockbox is used, its location should allow an optimal clearing time for funds.

If a customer complains about a delay in receiving invoices, the creditor needs to investigate the problem. Sometimes a simultaneous mailing of invoices to the customer and credit manager from the billing department can pin down the problem. Technology makes it possible for a credit manager to transmit a copy of an invoice to a customer almost instantaneously.

Collection Letters. The internal policy for the initial letter should be soon after the due date. The sooner the initial contact, the higher the likelihood of collection. There are actually some companies that send out the initial collection letter on the due date.

Some companies use a series of collection letters. Other companies may use one letter and then change modes to telephone collection activity. The size of the account will shape the tactics. The intervals should be systematic. Knowledge of customer habits is crucial to follow-up practices.

Monthly Statements. Monthly statements can be a useful collection device. Some companies pay bills strictly from monthly statements; other companies discard monthly statements. A credit manager can ask customers whether or not they use monthly statements. Sometimes handwritten comments on a monthly statement personalize the statement and result in an effective collection device.

Email Messaging. An electronic message can be quite effective. Some customers are seldom in the office; most people review their email regularly so that the communication of a problem is less likely to go unnoticed. Collection systems can be used to incorporate messages automatically on the day before an invoice is due. More carefully worded messages can be triggered to be released automatically as time passes. The effectiveness of email messages is the ability to release time for credit managers to focus upon other urgent problems.

Telephone Calls. Pre-call planning is a first step. Learn what time of day and day in the week the person with authority to pay is available. Records of the conversations should be maintained in a computerized system or on a call sheet. The goal of the collection call is to get the customer to make a commitment. Any credit hold, accumulation of late charges, necessary updates to credit information and reasons for the delay should surface during the conversation. Leading questions, a strategic pause and a professional approach are key ingredients to the conversation. Hold a customer to a commitment by using an effective follow-up system.

Personal Visits. Dollar exposure can justify the costs involved with a personal visit. Visits should be carefully planned by updating credit information, communicating with sales personnel and bringing along essential documentation. Goodwill visits to large customers can be an effective way to foster improved communications. Visits to collect problem accounts should be conducted professionally. Decisions concerning any questionable topics should be deferred until after the visit. An inspection of the customer's premises can be revealing. The tone of the meeting should be firm but fair. Any commitments from the customer should be confirmed in writing and promptly followed up on.

Collection Agencies. Collection agencies can be effective because of the psychological introduction of a third party. Many collection agencies offer a 10-day period during which the agency does not charge a fee if the account pays within those 10 days of being placed for collection. Collection agency fees can be substantial. There are companies that have set up subsidiary collection agencies to act as an in-house collection tool to circumvent agency fees.

Whatever agency is used, creditors should make sure that the agency is bonded. The agency should be willing to furnish financial statements and be licensed in the states where it is collecting. The fees should be competitive. Creditors should also find out the "hit rate," which is the percentage of claims that the agency actually collects. Collection agencies should send reports regularly concerning the status of accounts placed with the agency. Finally, the agency should remit funds and provide reports in a timely manner.

Litigation. Credit managers normally negotiate a fee arrangement and check for any potential conflict of interest when seeking outside legal assistance. If a lawsuit is recommended, the attorney should indicate whether or not there are attachable assets so that the costs of litigation are justifiable. A creditor also has the option to docket a judgment to create a lien against the debtor's assets. However, a judgment does not guarantee payment. When a written agreement exists, a creditor can be reimbursed for the costs of litigation. In other cases, the costs of litigating, or the poor likelihood of recovering the debt, suggest that litigation may be fruitless.

Bad Debt Write-Offs. After all collection alternatives are exhausted, an account is written off to bad debts. Policy should require specific authorization to write an account off to bad debts. There normally should be documentation in a credit file that justifies the write-off. Auditors will often pressure credit personnel to write off an account after the account is one year old. A paper trail of collection activity can be useful as a tool to avoid future similar situations.

THE CREDIT MANAGERS' INDEX

NACM's Credit Managers' Index (CMI) is based on monthly surveys completed by approximately 1,000 credit and collection professionals from across the United States who represent a broad range of industries. CMI data have been collected since February 2002; the index was initially published in January 2003. Chris Kuehl, Ph.D., managing director of Armada Corporate Intelligence and NACM's economic adviser, compiles and analyzes survey responses for the CMI.

The CMI is a diffusion index comprised of 10 equally weighted macroeconomic items, four of which are favorable factors and six of which are unfavorable factors. The favorable factors are sales, new credit applications, dollar collections and amount of credit extended. The unfavorable factors are rejections of credit applications, accounts placed for collection, disputes, dollar amount of receivables beyond terms, dollar amount of customer deductions and filings for bankruptcy.

The CMI has gained acceptance as a benchmarking and forecasting resource; many in the business and financial community view the CMI as an economic indicator to both watch and report on.

Credit managers can use the CMI as a gauge to determine the direction of monthly changes in macroeconomic forces that help shape credit management. Credit managers should find the CMI to be quite insightful.

The value of the CMI can be clarified by comparing the details from individual company experience to the monthly changes in each CMI macroeconomic item. A careful examination of the CMI could be useful; an archive of CMI reports is available on the NACM website (nacm.org/cmi.html). *Business Credit* magazine also features a truncated version of the previous month's report.

REVIEWING THE COLLECTION SYSTEM

Both automated systems and practical judgment-based approaches can be useful in reviewing a collection system. The *automated approach* involves the use of collection scoring technology. The technology works in a manner that is similar to a credit scoring system for new accounts: it furnishes statistically based scores derived from actual experience. The results can be used to derive scores that predict the likelihood of slow payment or of incurring a bad debt. Predicted payments and bad debts can be compared to actual payments and bad debts to consider adjusting policy and procedures.

In a *judgment-based approach*, practical concerns are addressed. Collections often involve practical operating problems. The size and number of accounts can be factors in determining the optimal approach.

Any collection system needs to integrate policy and procedures that consider practical concerns. Policy should be embedded into any automated collection system. Some of the questions that need to be asked concerning collection activity include:

- How should non-sufficient funds (NSF) checks be handled? Will customers then be placed on a cash-in-advance payment arrangement for future orders?
- Will late payment service charges be used as an incentive for prompt payment? If used, are the charges billed out or are dummy billings used on an aging of receivables? At what rate is interest charged? Who monitors usury concerns?
- How is the sales department kept informed of collection problems? Will the sales department keep the credit department aware of problems?
- Are credit personnel properly trained to use the collection system? Should certain collection tasks be outsourced?
- Will a change of pattern in the collection routine improve the days sales outstanding? How tight can the pattern be made before

customers are irritated enough then lost due to being too stringent? Is the company more profitable if marginal accounts are not granted credit?

- Is there an opportunity of collecting in small claims court?
- Who selects the collection agency being used? On what basis is the collection agency selected? Who monitors the effectiveness of the agency?
- Who informs a customer that shipments are being held? When is the sales department notified?
- Who decides when an account should be written off as a bad debt?

The best training for credit managers can come from experience. There are usually circumstances that vary from account to account. Technology provides a useful starting point. Then a credit manager needs to ask questions and follow intuition while exercising judgment. A regular periodic evaluation should be made that considers the efficiency of the overall collection system.

DEDUCTIONS

Deductions are sometimes called short payments. A customer might short-pay invoices due to quality problems, transportation claims, returned goods, promotional allowances, billing errors, discount problems or other miscellaneous reasons. The responsibility for follow-up on deductions varies by company. Credit, sales, accounts receivables, customer service or a combination of departments may be responsible.

Regardless of the responsibility, deductions need a quick and systematic follow-up. There is a cost to carry deductions in receivables if the deductions are not allowed. There is also a hidden cost of using the time involved by employees who are trying to resolve deductions. The task of identifying, verifying and resolving deductions can become arduous. The follow-up system should include step-by-step procedures by the type of deduction and emphasize timing.

Reports can be a useful tool to control deductions. Deductions can be categorized by a number of factors: cause, size, age and product. Attempts should be made to pinpoint the cause of deductions and correct any internal problems. Ultimately, deductions are resolved in any one of three ways: (1) a credit can be issued for the full amount, (2) the deduction can be denied or (3) a portion of the deduction can be allowed.

There are many credit-related issues to consider concerning deductions. Some of the issues that relate to customer deductions include the following:

- Should deductions age out as past-due items on an aging of receivables? (Perhaps only certain types of deductions age out.)
- At what threshold amount should deductions be automatically absorbed? Who decides? (Consider monitoring customers who may test the system that absorbs a specific amount.)
- At what number of days beyond a discount date should unearned discounts be charged back? How is this monitored? (Some credit managers use the postmark on an envelope to monitor discounts.)
- Who monitors cash discounts for the proper amount? (Discounts should be taken on the net invoice amount, not on the gross invoice amount that includes promotional allowances.)
- Who decides whether a quality claim will be allowed? How is that decision made?

Deductions are an important customer relations concern. There are significant costs associated with carrying and resolving deductions. The timely disposition of deductions is also essential to effective collection management. The best strategies for reconciling deductions often originate from questioning the system. What caused the open items? What needs to be done to resolve open items? Can business practices be improved upon so that the process that caused the deduction to occur be avoided or resolved more expediently in the future?

Many companies use a team approach to resolve deductions. The team-based process can create an increased level of awareness that can lead to a quicker resolution to problems. Since deductions have many different causes, there is usually someone on a cross-functional team who should be closer to the root cause and better able to move forward than other team members.

In certain industries, outsourcing can offer a fast and cost-efficient approach to resolving deductions. Outsourcing is effective particularly in retailing, where promotions and pricing changes occur frequently. Outsourcing can provide a viable option to deduction resolution.

ESCHEATMENT

The law that governs abandoned or unclaimed property is referred to as *escheat law*. While escheat law follows common law practices, it is also governed by state laws. The practice of absorbing credit balances can potentially be in violation of state law. Penalties vary by state. Moreover, much attention is given to unused gift cards and uncashed checks from customers; these balances are also governed by escheat law.

Credit managers need to maintain accurate internal records for any unused credit balances. A good-faith effort should be made to return or refund any unused credit balances. The state's escheat laws then need to be followed carefully. After a period of dormancy, sometimes following the practice of transferring funds over to a state entity as escheatable property can suffice.

CHAPTER 8: FOLLOW-UP

Recap of Important Concepts

1. Technology can contribute significantly to the development of an effective collection system. Credit managers are being challenged to harness technology in a cost-efficient manner.
2. Collection activity entails the coordination of a number of factors: clear communication of terms, controls for credit authorization, an effective use of various modes of collecting and a means to reconcile account balances.
3. Selling terms can be categorized as cash, open account, special or electronic. Each set of terms should be considered from a risk-reward perspective. Credit managers should be thoroughly aware of the alternative terms and when to establish specific terms.
4. Credit authorization needs to be carefully controlled. A hierarchy can be useful for specific dollar authority levels. Internal codes should be assigned to individual accounts based upon their creditworthiness.
5. Collection activity progresses through various stages. Invoices, monthly statements, letters, email messages, telephone calls, personal visits, collection agencies, lawsuits and bad debt write-offs should each be evaluated for effectiveness. Credit managers should evaluate the efficiency of the collection system on a periodic basis.

6. NACM makes available a monthly Credit Managers' Index (CMI) that can be quite useful to gauge macroeconomic trends that are shaping changes in credit management.
7. Deductions require consistent and timely follow-up. Deductions should be identified by type. Procedures to verify and resolve open items should emphasize timing and a team approach.
7. The one essential ingredient to a collection system is effective policies and procedures. Collection guidelines should be communicated clearly and applied consistently. The controls should be reviewed regularly. Any changes in corporate goals can be integrated into the overall collection system.

Review/Discussion Questions

1. Why is a systems approach beneficial to credit managers while performing collection activity?
2. What form of cash selling terms is the most restrictive? What form of cash selling terms has the most risk?
3. a. With terms of 2% 15N45, what is the approximate annualized cost expressed as a percent to the customer who pays the net amount on day 45?
   b. If the customer with terms of 2% 15N45 is allowed to pay on day 90, how much is the approximate annualized cost expressed as a percent? (Assume no late payment charge.)
   c. What did you learn from your calculations in 3(a) and 3(b)?
4. How can credit availability become an issue with a customer? To whom is credit availability communicated within an organization?
5. What is an electronic payment system? Furnish two examples of electronic payments.
6. Explain how internal controls can be used to monitor existing customers for credit availability.
7. How can invoices be an important focal point in a collection system?
8. Explain how telephone collection activity should be influenced by the following customer responses during a collection call:
   a. An intentionally provocative response, such as "So what?" from a customer.
   b. An evasive response, such as "I'll look into it."
   c. A customer who is looking for sympathy and saying, "My customers are not paying me, so how can I pay you?"

8: A Systematic Approach to Effective Collection Activity 191

9. Are late-payment service charges a fair way to control slow-paying accounts?
10. What is the Credit Managers' Index (CMI)?
11. What is a deduction? What are some of the leading reasons that deductions are taken? What can ultimately be done to resolve a deduction?
12. What does the term *escheat* refer to? What should a credit manager do with escheatable property?

Test Your Knowledge

1. What is a consignment sale?
2. What is a contra account arrangement?
3. Provide an overview for the use of anticipation discounts.
4. How should unearned cash discounts be monitored?
5. What is the difference between a credit card and a debit card?
6. What is the purpose of using a lockbox system?
7. Discuss the role of monthly statements in collection activity.
8. What should a credit manager try to do before, during and after a customer visit?
9. What factors should a credit manager consider when selecting a collection agency?
10. A company is considering changing selling terms from 1% 10N30 to 2% 10N30. What factors should a credit manager consider if his or her employer is considering this proposed change? Be thorough.
11. What factors are used to calculate the Credit Managers' Index (CMI)? How can the CMI be useful to credit professionals?
12. What does EIPP represent in terms of a payment arrangement?
13. Why has the use of team building caught on in terms of resolving deductions?

Case Study for Discussion

Technology has changed the approach to collection activity. In what ways has technology enhanced the collection of accounts receivable? Try to pinpoint at least five specific benefits that are made available to credit managers through technological enhancements.

Have credit managers been able to use the technology properly that is available? Please consider costs, benefits and credit department goals when developing your response.

Are there any downsides to the increased reliance upon technology?

Credit Management Online

nacm.org/cmi.html—This link will take you directly to the Credit Managers' Index (CMI) located on the NACM website. Details available in the monthly CMI reflect changes in the economy that focus on specific factors that have both positive and negative influences upon credit management.

www.chicagofed.org/education/econ-classroom/fed-challenge/economic-education-resources—The Federal Reserve Bank of Chicago makes available a considerable amount of educational information concerning the use of economic resources. This link will take you directly to the Economic Education Resources page.

www.consumerfinance.gov/data-research/credit-card-data/—This site is hosted by the Consumer Financial Protection Board and provides information about credit cards, including legislative changes.

www.crfonline.org/store/—The Credit Research Foundation online store has books, monographs and occasional papers that are available at this link.

www.federalreserve.gov/—The Federal Reserve System site can be used to access any of the 12 regional banks for local research and current economic information. The Fed also provides education-related material about the U.S. payment system, check clearing, check truncation and regulation.

www.paypal.com/us/home—PayPal Inc. is a commercial site that offers online payment services, which are useful primarily for consumers and small businesses. This site is popular with Internet sellers linked through bank accounts or credit cards. Transaction costs for sellers can be reduced in comparison to using credit card companies.

www.sungard.com/resources/corporate-liquidity/brochures-datasheets/avantgard-brochure-paymentsoverview—This link will take you directly to SunGard's financial software system AvantGard.

References Useful for Further Reading

Balovich, David. "Escheat What?" *Creditworthy News* (April 27, 2010): www.creditworthy.com.

Barron, Jacob. "A Gut Feeling: The Uncertain World of Collecting on Judgments." *Business Credit* (May 2007): 50-51.

Barron, Jacob. "Come Together: Collaboration is the Key to Solving Your Company's Deduction Problems." *Business Credit* (September 2008): 16-20.

Barron, Jacob. "The Complex World of Collecting Sales and Use Tax." *Business Credit* (May 2007): 10-12.

Barron, Jacob. "How to Sell Your Claims." *Business Credit* (October 2007): 52-53.

Barron, Jacob. "Leveraging Uncle Sam: Getting the Threat of the IRS Behind Your Collection Effort." *Business Credit* (June 2008): 10-12.

Brave, Scott. "Chicago Fed National Activity Index Turns Ten: Analyzing the First Decade of Performance." *The Chicago Fed Letter*, No. 273 (April 2010).

Busch, Leon J. "Is Refund Processing Creating a Bottleneck in Your AR and AP Departments?" *Treasury & Risk* (June 2009): 16-17.

Coté, Alex. "Spring Cleaning: Improving Collections Results in a Tough Economy." *Business Credit* (May 2009): 24-28.

Diana, Tom. "International Collections: Tales from the Dark Side." *Business Credit* (September 2007): 58-62.

"EDI Products and Services." *Healthcare Financial Management* (2009): 50.

Elms, Barry. "Collecting is Selling." *Business Credit* (September 2008): 6-8.

Fusco, Adam. "Strategies for Successful Collections." *Business Credit* (May 2017): 8-9.

Gahala, Charles. "Selecting and Utilizing a Debt Collection Agency." *Business Credit* (November/December 2004): 40-41.

Hull, Terris. "FBI Convicts Several Involved in Bust-out Scheme." *Business Credit* (October 2006): 14.

Krawec, Nicholas. "Unauthorized Deductions: A Legal Perspective." *Business Credit* (September 2007): 8.

Large, Jack, and Wolff Large. "Financial Supply Chain Review 2010." *Euromoney* (March 2, 2010): 42-48.

Mason, Jon. "The Cheque's in the Post." *ICM* (April 2010): 24.

McDaniel, Pamela. "Three Critical Features of an Accounts Receivable Management Solution." *Business Credit* (March 2017): 30-31.

Mota, Diana. "Centralized Credit and Collections Still a Trend, Outsourcing Perhaps Not as Much as Feared." *Business Credit* (September/October 2015): 44-45.

Nathan, Bruce S. "Bailment or Consignment: It Makes a Difference!" *Business Credit* (November/December 2006): 26-28.

Nathan, Bruce S. "Recent Court Decisions on Consignments and Other Security Agreements: The Benefits of Aggressive Creditor Action and the Pitfalls of Failing to Document Properly!" *Business Credit* (January 2009): 46-49.

Ng, Serena, and Cari Tuna. "Big Firms Are Quick to Collect, Slow to Pay." *The Wall Street Journal* (August 31, 2009): A1.

Norwood, John M. "Cashier's Checks in the 21st Century." *Banking Law Journal* (October 2009): 848-864.

"The Payment Factory: Strengthening Compliance and Improving Internal Controls for Corporate Treasurers." White paper co-authored by SunGard and IdenTrust (June 2008): 1-10.

Sereika, Ronald, CCE. "The Importance of Building Relationships to Get Paid." *Business Credit* (February 2017): 40-42.

Stern, Nicholas. "Responding to the Psychology of the Debtor." *Business Credit* (March 2017): 28-29.

Trunzo, Giuseppe, CICP. "The Credit Management Revolution." *Business Credit* (June 2017): 14-15.

Unger, Rob. "Same Day ACH: Flexing New Muscle for Credit Professionals in Fall 2016." *Business Credit* (May 2016): 12-13.

Voorhees, R.G. "Finance in History: Bankruptcy." *CFO* (August 8, 2007): www.cfo.com/printable/article.cfm/9614341.

Wallis, Lyle. "Electronic Invoice Presentment and Payments: Automating the Billing and Receipts Process." *Business Credit* (June 2008): 38-41.

Wheeler, Chad. "Finding a Reputable Collection Agency." *Business Credit* (September 2007): 56.

Wimley, C.J. "How Companies Are Improving Cash Flow and Reducing Costs with Credit and Collections Automation." *Business Credit* (October 2008): 66-69.

Wood, Mark. "Living with Deductions: Management and Prevention." *Business Credit* (September 2007): 52-53.

Chapter 9

FINANCIAL STATEMENT ANALYSIS

"With the convergence of IFRS, I think you're going to see a much more principles-based approach to accounting as opposed to a rules-based approach, and this has a lot of significance for credit professionals."[1]

Dr. Charles Mulford
Professor of Accounting, Georgia Tech University

Financial statements can provide creditors with a wealth of information concerning a company's financial position, performance and changes that are occurring in its financial position. The challenge to credit managers is to try to keep up with the rapid pace of changes in the accounting profession to support effective decisions. Financial statement analysis is simply one of the most important topics that can be of use in credit decision-making.

Generally Accepted Accounting Principles (GAAP) can be defined as the principles of accounting that have substantial authoritative support. In the United States, GAAP has a history of applying *rules-based* standards. Its counterpart, the International Financial Reporting Standards (IFRS), has a history of applying *principles-based* standards. Credit managers will need to stay familiar with both the rules-based GAAP and the principles-based IFRS as the rules for accounting practices move toward global standards.

Whether rules or principles are being used to construct financial statements, the key focus will continue to be placed upon *questioning* the application of accounting standards to individual financial statements.

Credit managers have different ways of performing financial statement analysis. The analysis is sometimes limited to a quick eyeballing of numbers; at other times, computer analysis generates detailed, sophisticated spreadsheets. Regardless of the type of analysis, the focus should be placed upon using financial statements to support superior credit decisions.

---

[1] Jacob Barron, "In the Drop Zone," *Business Credit* (March 2008): 59.

196 Credit Management: Principles and Practices

Financial statement analysis is a subject that can be studied through the use of different focal points. The subject could certainly be a textbook in itself. In order to address the needs of credit managers, there are two chapters of this book that delve into financial statements. This chapter will lay a foundation for the more advanced topics that are contained in Chapter 10.

The **Key Learning Objectives** in Chapter 9 are:

1. Identify the role of the independent public accountant in the preparation of financial statements.
2. Examine the usefulness of common-size financial statement analysis.
3. Analyze specific financial ratios that are useful for credit decision-making.
4. Delve into contemporary measures generated through the use of financial statements; these measures can be useful for different types of credit analysis.
5. Provide an overview for the use of International Financial Reporting Standards (IFRS).
6. Focus on specific key focal points that are frequently scrutinized by credit managers when analyzing financial statements.

THE SOURCE OF FINANCIAL STATEMENTS

All public companies and many privately held businesses have their financial statements examined by independent public accountants. Independence of the audit provides reasonable assurance that financial statements are free of material departure from GAAP. Credit managers, however, should be able to recognize various types of auditors' opinions and the latitude accountants have in using alternative practices that are permitted by GAAP.

Public accountants emphasize that financial statements are prepared by management, not by public auditors. The role of the public auditor is to exercise judgment in determining the fairness of the financial statements according to GAAP. The public auditor then expresses an opinion concerning both fairness and conformity within the parameters of GAAP.

The American Institute of Certified Public Accountants (AICPA) established external auditor opinions in terms of the levels of assurance given by the independent auditor's opinion. The opinion pertains to the

9: Financial Statement Analysis   197

fairness of financial statements using the GAAP criteria established by the AICPA guidelines. There are four specific opinions.

1. *An Unqualified Opinion.* An unqualified opinion, also known as a "clean opinion," is the highest level of assurance that financial statements comply with GAAP. Auditors, who present an unqualified opinion in the third paragraph of the auditor's report, give their professional opinion that financial statements are presented fairly and are in compliance with GAAP.
2. *Qualified Opinion.* The public auditors may qualify an opinion for the following reasons: report has mistakes in accounting entries; the audit scope is limited (access is denied to certain financial data); auditor has doubts about veracity; auditor not confident report complies with GAAP or represents accounts fairly; or, a question concerning the firm's ability to operate as a going concern. In each case, grounds for giving a qualified opinion are spelled out in the auditor's report with the use of a fourth paragraph. More complete details for the qualified opinion are then inserted with a note to the financial statements.
3. *Adverse Opinion.* Financial statements that depart from GAAP to the extent that they do not present fairly the position of the firm will receive an adverse opinion.
4. *Disclaimer.* Sometimes an auditor may not be able to express an opinion concerning financial statements. If limitations are placed upon the scope of the audit, the auditor will issue a disclaimer.

Credit managers should exercise considerable judgment when reviewing financial statements and the auditor's report. When more than one accounting procedure is permitted by GAAP, remember that it is the management—not the outside auditor—who decides which practice to use. When a qualified opinion is issued, the credit manager should examine closely the related note to the audit qualification. Moreover, a an adverse opinion or a disclaimer should be recognized as posing a serious limitation on possible creditworthiness.

Failure to perform an audit at the requisite level of care has resulted in considerable litigation. When an auditor improperly gives a "clean opinion," a credit manager may be in a position to seek redress. The legal criteria have not always been clear. Under common law, there are three essentials necessary to establish auditor liability: (1) the creditor must have suffered a loss; (2) the cause of the creditor's loss must have been a reasonable reliance on a material omission or on a material misstatement in an audited financial statement; and (3) the auditor must have failed to exercise the proper level of care while performing the audit.

There have been a number of disturbing situations, such as Enron, WorldCom, Global Crossing and Sunbeam, in which accounting firms have been placed under a microscope for their questionable application of accounting standards. Several key questions came to the forefront. For example, to what extent are accountants' audit opinions influenced by consulting contracts? Should one of the largest accounting firms, Arthur Andersen, have been prosecuted for failure to comply with document retention in the audit of Enron? These and other questions are at the heart of the confidence in the role that certified public accountants (CPAs) engage in an audit.

In response to disturbing accounting practices, Congress passed the Sarbanes-Oxley Act (SOX) in 2002. SOX is discussed more fully in Chapter 5 of this book. The accounting profession has been pushed by the Securities and Exchange Commission (SEC) toward a more principles-based approach to try to prevent material misstatements of audited financial statements.

In general, public accounting firms function at a very high level of professional competence. Audited financial statements are superior to either a compilation or a review. In a compilation, the internal management team prepares the numbers in the financial statements. In a review, the auditor does not comply with normal auditing standards required by GAAP.

The source for financial statements goes beyond the focus of an audit opinion letter. Credit managers should request personal financial statements when relying upon an individual. Personal statements should be signed and dated. Asset valuation is often inflated on personal statements, so personal statements are often not as reliable as audited statements. Furthermore, some personal statements may include assets held jointly by a spouse. Credit managers should consider the appropriateness of a spousal guarantee or obtain a personal statement that eliminates assets held jointly.

All public corporations must comply with the financial disclosure mandated by the SEC. Both 10-K annual reports and 10-Q quarterly reports provide detailed financial information that is available to the public at www.sec.gov/.

9: Financial Statement Analysis

Most companies legally maintain two sets of books: one for financial accounting and a second for tax accounting. Since tax laws and financial accounting rules do not coincide, the two sets of books are usually different. Tax returns are not generally made available to the public. Credit managers may encounter customers who claim that financial statements do not exist. In these cases, a copy of a tax return may be of use.

There are occasions when the data presented in financial statements are deliberately misrepresented. Consider saving the envelopes in which financial statements are mailed. False financial statements leave a customer vulnerable to a mail fraud conviction.

COMMON-SIZE ANALYSIS

Common-size analysis is performed on the income statement and the balance sheet. To common-size an income statement, simply take each item in the income statement as a percentage of net sales. A common-size balance sheet takes each line item in the balance sheet as a percentage of total assets.

Table 9-1 presents income statement data for Blackhawk Retail Company. The income statements pertain to three annual periods; three years is a requirement for public companies in annual reports. Common-size percentages are in parentheses next to each income statement item.

The three-year common-size analysis is helpful to identify trends. Note that Blackhawk Retail Company has been decreasing cost of goods sold as a percentage of net sales. At the same time, operating expenses

TABLE 9-1	Blackhawk Retail Company Common-Size Income Statements for the Years Ended December 31: 2017, 2018 and 2019					
(000s Omitted)	2017	%	2018	%	2019	%
Net Sales	4500	(100)	4950	(100)	5450	(100)
Cost of Goods Sold	3375	(75)	3564	(72)	3870	(71)
Gross Margin	1125	(25)	1385	(28)	1580	(29)
Operating Expenses	500	(11)	594	(12)	708	(13)
Operating Income	625	(14)	791	(16)	872	(16)
Interest Expense	70	(2)	75	(2)	100	(2)
Pre-tax Profit	555	(12)	716	(14)	772	(14)
Income Tax	222	(5)	250	(5)	272	(5)
Net Income after Tax	333	(7)	466	(9)	500	(9)

TABLE 9-2	Blackhawk Retail Co. and the Industry Average Common-Size Income Statement for 12/31/19	

	Blackhawk Retail Company	Industry Average
Sales	100 %	100 %
Cost of Goods Sold	71	75
Gross Margin	29	25
Operating Expenses	13	12
Operating Income	16	13
Interest Expense	2	2
Pre-tax Profit	14	11
Income Tax	5	5
Net Income after Tax	9	6

have increased. These trends help to pinpoint the type of questions that should be posed.

For example, is gross profit up due to industry or economic conditions? Has the company changed any marketing policies such as using higher selling prices? Has the company changed suppliers or improved labor cost control? Are these changes temporary? Can selling general or administrative expenses be reduced to improve the operating results?

Common-size analysis is useful not only to spot changes or trends internally, but also to make comparisons to an industry. Table 9-2 shows the common-size income statement percentages of Blackhawk Retail Company in comparison to the industry. Industry data are available from the RMA Statement Studies or through agency credit reporting services.

The data in Table 9-2 show that Blackhawk Retail Company has been able to hold down the cost of goods sold to 71% of sales while the industry average is 75%. The difference could be due to the sales increase and an ability to distribute fixed costs to more units. However, the credit analyst may want to question numbers directly with the Blackhawk Retail Company management.

Common-size analysis is also performed on the balance sheet. Table 9-3 provides balance sheet data for Blackhawk Retail Company that include two-year end dates. The common-size percentages are in parentheses. These percentages are derived by dividing balance sheet items by total assets.

The common-size data in Table 9-3 can be useful to pinpoint changes. For example, the property plant and equipment percentage increased from 20% to 28% of total assets. A corresponding increase in secured

9: Financial Statement Analysis

TABLE 9-3 **Blackhawk Retail Company**
Common-Size Balance Sheets 12/31/18 and 12/31/19

(000s Omitted)	2018	%	2019	%
Cash	50	(3)	45	(2)
Marketable Securities	175	(12)	150	(8)
Accounts Receivables	450	(31)	650	(36)
Inventory	600	(41)	580	(32)
Total Current Assets	1,275	(87)	1,425	(78)
Property, Plant & Equipment	300	(20)	500	(28)
Less: Accumulated Depreciation	(100)	(7)	(115)	(6)
Total Assets	1,475	(100)	1,810	(100)
Accounts Payable	300	(20)	410	(23)
Accrued Wages & Taxes	100	(7)	95	(5)
Notes Payable	150	(10)	135	(7)
Total Current Liabilities	550	(37)	640	(35)
Debentures	50	(3)	45	(2)
Secured Debt	150	(10)	325	(18)
Total Liabilities	750	(51)	1,010	(56)
Retained Earnings	425	(29)	500	(28)
Common Stock	300	(20)	300	(17)
Total Equity	725	(49)	800	(45)
Total Liabilities & Equity	1,475	(100)	1,810	(100)

debt from 10% to 18% suggests that long-term secured funds were used to finance the asset acquisition. Since sales have been increasing, these changes appear to be prudent.

As a general rule, a credit analyst should always focus on large common-size items in the balance sheet. Somewhat nominal changes in the common-size percentage for large line items can be important. For example, Table 9-3 shows that accounts payable increased from 20% to 23% as a common-size line item. This increase could be indicative of a slowdown in payments to suppliers.

The company common-size data should also be compared to industry data when analyzing a balance sheet. The analysis is similar to income statement analysis. However, balance sheet analysis provides useful information concerning how funds are invested and where the funds are obtained.

The data in Table 9-4 show the common-size balance sheet for Blackhawk Retail Company and the industry averages. The balance sheet percentages for the industry average can vary by the size of the

202
Credit Management: Principles and Practices

TABLE 9-4	Blackhawk Retail Co. and the Industry Average Common-Size Balance Sheets 12/31/19	
(000s Omitted)	Blackhawk Retail Company %	Industry Average %
Cash	2	4
Marketable Securities	8	4
Accounts Receivable	36	32
Inventory	32	40
Total Current Assets	78	80
Property, Plant & Equipment	28	25
Less Accumulated Depreciation	(6)	(5)
Total Assets	100%	100%
Accounts Payable	23	25
Accrued Wages & Taxes	5	6
Notes Payable	7	10
Total Current Liabilities	35	41
Debentures	2	0
Secured Debt	18	20
Total Liabilities	56	61
Retained Earnings	28	19
Common Stock	17	20
Total Equity	45	39
Total Liabilities & Equity	100%	100%

company. For example, small companies may use more debt, carry more receivables or have fewer dollars invested in property, plant and equipment assets. Credit analysts should exercise caution using industry data. Comparably sized companies are essential when undertaking an industry common-size analysis.

Table 9-4 data show side-by-side, company-to-industry common-size balance sheets. This type of analysis can be revealing. For example, the Blackhawk Retail Company invests 36% of assets into accounts receivables while the industry invests only 32% of assets into receivables. Is this difference reflective of extended selling terms, lax enforcement of collection activity or the extension of credit to marginal accounts?

Common-size analysis is particularly effective as a means for pinpointing items that should be questioned. The superior credit analyst is capable of making inter-relationships among the numbers. Asking the right questions can often lead to meaningful financial statement interpretation. Common-size analysis can lead to superior questions essential to sound credit decisions.

RATIO ANALYSIS

Ratio analysis is used to provide insights concerning the financial position of a business. In accounting, there are rules established by GAAP to prepare financial statements. No such rules exist for the formulas used in ratio analysis or the interpretation of financial ratios.

For a given corporation, Value Line, Moody's, Standard & Poor's and RMA each may furnish a different number for earnings per share. The differences are caused by nuances used by analysts when performing the calculations. For credit managers, the key is to be consistent in applying formulas so that they are useful for comparative purposes. Several of the websites at the end of this chapter furnish ratios and industry norms that can be downloaded.

Ratio analysis is straightforward. Credit managers should look for trends over time for a particular company. In addition, the individual ratios should be compared to a benchmark for a specific industry.

Ratio analysis can be easily broken down into the following categories: (1) liquidity ratios, (2) asset management ratios, (3) debt management ratios and (4) profitability ratios. Three ratios have been carefully selected from each category based upon their broad usage by credit managers. There are more than 60 financial ratios that can be used to analyze statements. Credit analysts may employ industry-specific ratios or variations of the ratios presented for company-specific utility.

Liquidity Ratios

The liquidity ratios are particularly important to short-term creditors. Liquidity measures short-term solvency. The liquidity ratios include: (A) Current Ratio, (B) Quick Ratio and (C) Payables Deferral Period. These ratios will be calculated using the 2019 data for the Blackhawk Retail Company.

A. **Current Ratio** $= \dfrac{\text{Total Current Assets}}{\text{Total Current Liabilities}} = \dfrac{1,425}{640} = \mathbf{2.2}$

The numerator in the Current Ratio is usually cash, marketable securities, accounts receivables and inventory. Some credit managers include prepaid expenses; other credit managers feel that prepaid

204 Credit Management: Principles and Practices

expenses should not be categorized as a current asset. The denominator of the Current Ratio represents all debt due within a 12-month period.

A Current Ratio of 2.2 suggests that there is $2.20 in current assets for every dollar in current debt, which is usually a good sign. However, a high Current Ratio is not necessarily good. For example, if a business lets receivables age out and does not turn inventory, the Current Ratio will go up while operations are deteriorating. The credit analyst needs to make a few inter-relationships in order to properly interpret the Current Ratio.

B. **Quick Ratio** $= \dfrac{\text{Quick Assets}}{\text{Current Liabilities}} = \dfrac{845}{640} = \mathbf{1.3}$

Sometimes the Quick Ratio is called the Acid Test Ratio. This ratio is a more stringent measure of liquidity than the Current Ratio. The numerator includes current assets less inventory; the inventory is subtracted because it is the least liquid of the current assets.

A Quick Ratio of 1.3 suggests that Blackhawk Retail Company should have the ability to service short-term debt without selling off inventory. As is the case for all ratios, the Quick Ratio should be monitored for trends from year to year and also compared to an industry norm.

C. **Payables Deferral Period** $= \dfrac{\text{Accounts Payable}}{\text{Purchases Per Day}} = \dfrac{410}{3,870 \div 365} = \mathbf{38.7\ Days}$

The accounts payable deferral period provides a basis for judging a company's willingness to pay its short-term creditors. The numerator is the accounts payable at year end. The denominator is the annual purchases divided by 365 days to get Purchases per Day. Purchases for a manufacturing company can be found in a multi-step income statement where they are part of the cost of goods sold.

The Payables Deferral Period of 38.7 days for Blackhawk Retail Company is generally favorable. The results should be compared to general terms in an industry and general payment habits within an industry. When companies encounter liquidity problems, the Payables Deferral Period usually lengthens.

Asset Management Ratios

For most companies, the largest assets in the balance sheet include accounts receivable, inventory and fixed assets. Three ratios that can be used to measure the effectiveness of asset management are: (D) the DSO

Period, (E) the Inventory Carrying Period and (F) the Fixed Asset Turnover. Each of these three ratios will be calculated using the 2019 data for the Blackhawk Retail Company.

D. **DSO Period** $= \dfrac{\text{Accounts Receivable}}{\text{Sales Per Day}} = \dfrac{650}{5,450 \div 365} =$ **43.5 Days**

There are a number of ways to calculate the Days Sales Outstanding (DSO). In this example, the numerator is the ending accounts receivable balance and the denominator is the annual sales divided by 365 days. The results show that accounts receivable are collected in 43.5 days.

The DSO is closely related to terms of sales and credit policy. As terms lengthen, the DSO period will also be longer. If credit policy is lax, the DSO will also stretch out.

E. $\dfrac{\textbf{Inventory}}{\textbf{Carrying Period}} = \dfrac{\text{Inventory}}{\begin{array}{c}\text{Cost of Goods}\\ \text{Sold Per Day}\end{array}} = \dfrac{580}{3,870 \div 365} =$ **54.7 Days**

The Inventory Carrying Period (ICP) provides the average number of days over which goods are held in inventory. The numerator is the ending inventory. The denominator is the cost of goods sold divided by the number of days in a year. Some credit analysts prefer to use an average inventory in the numerator and sales (rather than cost of goods sold) in the denominator.

In the Blackhawk Retail Company example, the results show that goods are held for 54.7 days. Some analysts prefer to use turns per year; simply divide 365 days by 54.7 days to get 6.67 turns per year. Seasonal buildup is common in many industries. However, when the ICP lengthens, credit analysts should be aware of a potential problem moving the inventory.

F. **Fixed Asset Turnover** $= \dfrac{\text{Sales}}{\text{Fixed Assets}} = \dfrac{5,450}{385} =$ **14 Times**

The Fixed Asset Turnover is calculated by dividing net sales by net fixed assets. Net fixed assets include gross fixed assets less any accumulated depreciation. The Fixed Asset Turnover for Blackhawk Retail Company is 14 times. This ratio is often difficult to interpret.

A high Fixed Asset Turnover may suggest that a company is doing a good job generating sales with assets. On the other hand, if the Fixed Asset Turnover is higher because fixed assets are not being replaced, the company could be heading for trouble in the long run. Also, a company that leases fixed assets may have a misleading Fixed Asset Turnover. Several inter-relationships need to be made to properly interpret the Fixed Asset Turnover ratio.

Debt Management Ratios

Debt Management Ratios are of particular importance to long-term creditors. They include: (G) Debt to Equity Ratio, (H) Times Interest Earned Ratio and (I) Fixed Charge Coverage. Examples that explain the importance of debt management ratios will be used for the Blackhawk Retail Company in 2019.

G. **Debt to Equity Ratio** $= \dfrac{\text{Total Liabilities}}{\text{Shareholders Equity}} = \dfrac{1,010}{800} = \textbf{1.3}$

The Debt to Equity Ratio is a measure of financial leverage. Some credit analysts subtract intangible assets from the shareholders equity in the denominator to obtain a tangible net worth rather than using total shareholders equity.

The results of 1.3 suggest that the creditors of Blackhawk Retail Company have more invested in the business than the owners. This is not unusual. The extent that leverage is used varies by industry.

H. **Times Interest Earned** $= \dfrac{\text{Operating Profit}}{\text{Interest Expense}} = \dfrac{872}{100} = \textbf{8.7}$

The Times Interest Earned Ratio (TIE) is of particular importance to bondholders. The TIE suggests the likelihood of servicing or defaulting on debt. The numerator is the operating profit, which is sometimes referred to as earnings before interest and taxes (EBIT). The denominator is the interest expense line item from the income statement.

A TIE of 8.7 suggests that the Blackhawk Retail Company is generating enough operating profit to cover interest 8.7 times. The lower the TIE, the greater the risk of insolvency. As the TIE approaches 1.0, the debt should be restructured or a default is looming.

I. **Fixed Charge Coverage** $= \dfrac{\text{Operating Profit}}{\dfrac{\text{Interest}}{\text{Expense}} + \dfrac{\text{Lease}}{\text{Obligation}} + \dfrac{\text{SFP}}{(1-\text{TR})}} = \dfrac{872}{120.4} = \textbf{7.2}$

The Fixed Charge Coverage (FCC) is particularly important when a business does a lot of lease financing that appears off the balance sheet. The numerator is the operating profit. The denominator is the interest expense, any lease obligation payable during the year and the sinking

9: Financial Statement Analysis

207

fund provision (SFP) on an after-tax basis. A sinking fund represents the retirement of principal during the year.

The lease obligation and sinking fund provision are usually found in footnotes to the financial statements; they are being given without looking at the footnotes to the financial statements because the footnotes have not been furnished. The numbers being furnished are $5 for the lease obligation and $10 for the sinking fund. The tax rate comes from calculating taxes paid divided by pretax income; these numbers are found in Table 9-1 for the income statement. The numbers used to calculate the tax rate are $272 paid in taxes divided by the pre-tax income which are $772 to derive the 35.2% tax rate used in the formula, which is expressed in decimal form as .352.

Illustrating the Blackhawk Retail Company during 2019, the operating profit is $872 divided by (the interest expense of $100 plus the lease expenses of $5 and plus the after tax sinking fund of $15.4) to derive an FCC of 7.2. The FCC suggests that the company has enough funds to cover its fixed charges 7.2 times.

The FCC calculation is important to creditors in certain industries such as photocopying machines, airlines, rails and heavy equipment where a lot of leasing occurs. As in the case of the TIE ratio, the higher the FCC ratio, the safer the business.

Profitability Ratios

Profitability ratios are important to all creditors and investors in a business. Three of the most widely used profitability ratios include: (J) Profit Margin, (K) Return on Assets and (L) Return on Equity. Each ratio will be described using data from Blackhawk Retail Company in 2019.

$$J. \textbf{ Profit Margin } = \frac{\text{Net Income after Tax}}{\text{Net Sales}} = \frac{500}{5,450} = \textbf{9\%}$$

The Profit Margin is sometimes referred to as the bottom line margin or the net profit margin. The calculation is simply net income after tax divided by net sales. Recognition of revenue and deferring of expenses can have a significant impact on the Profit Margin.

The 9% Profit Margin calculated for Blackhawk Retail Company should be compared to an industry. Jewelry stores tend to have high margins while grocery stores have tight margins. Cyclical industries tend to have margins that vary with the stage in the business cycle.

K. **Return on Assets** $= \dfrac{\text{Net Income after Tax}}{\text{Total Assets}} = \dfrac{500}{1,810} = $ **28%**

The Return on Assets (ROA) is a reflection of management's ability to deploy assets profitably. This ratio is calculated by dividing net income after tax by total assets. Since accountants do not place a value on human resources as an asset in the balance sheet, small firms or firms that are not capital-intensive may have much higher ROAs than capital-intensive businesses.

The ROA of 28% for Blackhawk Retail Company is a favorable reflection on management's ability to deploy assets profitably.

L. **Return on Equity** $= \dfrac{\text{Net Income after Tax}}{\text{Shareholders Equity}} = \dfrac{500}{800} = $ **63%**

The Return on Equity (ROE) reflects the percentage return being generated by a business for the owners of the business. (The actual return to the owners would come in the form of dividends plus profits derived from the sale of stock that has appreciated in value.) ROE is important because it reflects an ability to raise additional capital.

The Blackhawk Retail Company has an unusually high ROE. Sometimes small businesses do not have a lot of equity capital so the ROE can then be quite misleading. For a typical business, the ROE is closer to 15%.

Summary of Ratios

The 12 ratios used to analyze the Blackhawk Retail Company are summarized in Table 9-5. In particular, ratios are a useful tool in terms of appreciating the ability of a company to service creditors. The ratios can signal problems. Credit analysts have the responsibility to question the results. In general, the results of the ratio analysis for the Blackhawk Retail Company are favorable when compared to the industry.

FINANCIAL TOOLS OF ANALYSIS

There are a number of tools that can be used to analyze financial statements other than common-size analysis and ratio analysis. In order to better grasp the potential using financial statements, four tools will be introduced: (1) concept of Zero Working Capital, (2) DuPont Analysis, (3) Basic Defensive Interval and (4) Sustainable Growth. These tools illustrate the potential for credit managers to become creative. Knowing

9: Financial Statement Analysis — 209

TABLE 9-5   Summary of Financial Ratios

		Blackhawk Retail Co.	Industry Average
1.	**Liquidity Ratios**		
	A. Current Ratio $= \dfrac{\text{Current Assets}}{\text{Current Liabilities}}$	2.2X	2.0X
	B. Quick Ratio $= \dfrac{\text{Cash + Marketable Securities + AR}}{\text{Current Liabilities}}$	1.3X	1.0X
	C. Payables Deferral Period $= \dfrac{\text{Accounts Payable}}{\text{Purchases Per Day}}$	38.7 Days	40 Days
2.	**Asset Management Ratios**		
	D. DSO Period $= \dfrac{\text{Accounts Receivable}}{\text{Sales Per Day}}$	43.5 Days	42 Days
	E. Inventory Carrying $= \dfrac{\text{Inventory}}{\text{Cost of Goods Sold Per Day}}$	54.7 Days	60 Days
	F. Fixed Asset Turnover $= \dfrac{\text{Sales}}{\text{Fixed Assets}}$	14X	12X
3.	**Debt Management Ratios**		
	G. Debt to Equity $= \dfrac{\text{Total Liabilities}}{\text{Shareholders Equity}}$	1.3X	1.6X
	H. Times Interest Earned $= \dfrac{\text{Operating Profit}}{\text{Interest Expense}}$	8.7X	6.5X
	I. Fixed Charge Coverage $= \dfrac{\text{Operating Profit}}{\text{Exp. \quad Oblig. } (1 - TR)}$	7.2X	6.5X
4.	**Profitability Ratios**		
	J. Profit Margin $= \dfrac{\text{Net Income after Tax}}{\text{Net Sales}}$	9%	6%
	K. Return on Assets $= \dfrac{\text{Net Income after Tax}}{\text{Total Assets}}$	28%	18%
	L. Return on Equity $= \dfrac{\text{Net Income after Tax}}{\text{Shareholders Equity}}$	63%	30%

both how and when to use a particular tool requires the use of a considerable amount of judgment.

Zero Working Capital

Net working capital is the difference between current assets and current liabilities. An average company invests about 20 cents into net working capital for each dollar in sales. If a treasurer can cut down on the investment into net working capital, the costs to carry the net working capital can be reduced.

The concept of zero working capital is attained when current assets less current liabilities are equal; then the net working capital is zero. A treasurer could strive to cut down on the level of current assets or increase the level of current liabilities to move toward the goal of zero working capital. Attaining zero net working capital may not be feasible; yet it becomes an important focal point because of the cost of capital associated with carrying working capital. It also creates problems for operating managers.

For example, cutting the DSO and moving toward just-in-time inventory then delaying the payments on accounts payable could each contribute to moving a treasurer toward a goal of zero working capital. The side effect is that it is a challenge to cut DSO and inventory carrying periods. Moreover, suppliers could be upset if accounts payable are not being paid in a timely manner.

The primary purpose for introducing zero working capital is to suggest a need to look beyond a number and appreciate the cause for the number being what it is. Zero working capital needs to be analyzed to get at the cause for the situation. If it is deliberate, it can make a business more profitable. On the other hand, zero working capital can also reflect severe liquidity problems and a looming bankruptcy. The challenge is for credit managers to recognize the root cause of the situation.

DuPont Analysis

The internal management at the E.I. DuPont de Nemours and Company is credited with creating an approach to financial statement analysis. DuPont Analysis has a primary purpose of getting the users of financial statements to recognize that one financial ratio can actually be influenced by several possible focal points. There are actually two equations that have been handed down as components of DuPont Analysis.

The *first DuPont Equation* focuses upon Return on Equity (ROE). The equation is shown below:

$$\textbf{ROE} = \frac{\text{Net Income after Tax}}{\text{Total Assets}} \times \frac{\text{Total Assets}}{\text{Common Equity}}$$

The owners of a business are usually interested in improving their ROE. The equation suggests that the ROE can be improved upon if the individual components are examined. The next step would be to consider focal points that lead to increasing the ROE such as changing pricing, cutting expenses, cutting asset levels or using more debt.

The Blackhawk Retail Company will be used to illustrate the DuPont calculation. The 2019 Income Statement from Table 9-1 and the 2019 Balance Sheet found in Table 9-3 will be used. The ROE is calculated by dividing the net income after tax of $500 by the total equity of $800 to arrive at an ROE of 63%. The same result is obtained by using the DuPont Equation below:

$$\text{DuPont Equation: } \mathbf{ROE} = \frac{500}{1,810} \times \frac{1,810}{800} = \mathbf{63\%}$$

The *second DuPont Equation* is often referred to as the *Extended DuPont Equation*. This equation also focuses upon ROE; however, the equation includes more potential focal points. The Extended DuPont Equation is shown below:

$$\mathbf{ROE} = \frac{\text{Net Income}}{\text{Sales}} \times \frac{\text{Sales}}{\text{Total Assets}} \times \frac{\text{Total Assets}}{\text{Common Equity}}$$

To illustrate the Extended DuPont Equation, the 2019 Income Statement in Table 9-1 and the 2019 Balance Sheet in Table 9-3 for Blackhawk Retail are used below:

$$\text{Extended DuPont: } \mathbf{ROE} = \frac{500}{5,450} \times \frac{5,450}{1,810} \times \frac{1,810}{800} = \mathbf{63\%}$$
$$\text{Equation}$$

By examining the components that are used in the Extended DuPont Equation, a broad-based focus can be examined in order to improve the ROE. For example, the profit margin could be improved, asset turnover could be improved or the company could use more financial leverage. This approach allows management to consider various goals to improve the return on equity.

DuPont Analysis is an approach that involves critical thinking. Too often, financial analysis can become mechanical in nature. By providing multiple focal points, critical thinking skills are demonstrated to be fundamental to financial analysis. This broad-based focus involving critical thinking is the main purpose for illustrating the DuPont Equations.

Basic Defensive Interval

Various tools can be used to analyze companies. The *Basic Defensive Interval (BDI)* can be useful as a tool to measure the severity of a liquidity problem in a given situation. For example, the liquidity of e-commerce companies is sometimes marginal; they tend to burn through cash quickly without generating profits. BDI can be useful to gauge the severity of their liquidity problems.

BDI involves a straightforward, two-step calculation. The first step is to calculate the daily operating expenses, which include cost of sales and operating expenses divided by the number of days in an accounting period. The second step is to divide the defensive assets—which include cash, marketable securities and accounts receivable—by the daily operating expenses derived in step one. Cash, marketable securities and accounts receivable are also called "quick assets"; they represent access to cash in a short period of time.

To illustrate the BDI, the 2019 Income Statement in Table 9-1 and the 2019 Balance Sheet in Table 9-3 for Blackhawk Retail will be used.

Step 1.	Cost of Goods Sold	3,870
	Operating Expenses	708
	Daily Operating Expenses	4,578 ÷ 365 = 12.54

Step 2.	Cash	45
	Marketable Securities	150
	Accounts Receivable	650
	Defensive Assets	845 ÷ 12.54 = 67.38 days

The Basic Defensive Interval for Blackhawk Retail is 67.38 days. The BDI suggests that if sales fall off, there is enough liquidity to cover expenses for a little over two months. Markets for products can dry up in a hurry. Creditors would want to know whether or not Blackhawk Retail management has alternative sources of liquidity.

The main reason for studying BDI is to point out that certain financial tools can take prominence in particular instances. For example, the BDI could be crucial to a credit manager when a business loses a key customer or in a situation where a marketplace dries up overnight. Credit managers need to become proficient in using tools such as the BDI. Proficiency often comes through experience.

Sustainable Growth

Sustainable growth is often used by economists to examine the changes in a country's economy. The ability of a business to continually expand is often a key focal point when analyzing its customers. Businesses that grow rapidly often experience serious growing pains. By focusing upon sustainable growth credit, managers have another useful tool.

Sustainable growth provides the maximum rate at which sales can expand through the support from internally generated funds. Too often, businesses fail to adequately plan for expansion because they did not line up the necessary external funds. Trade creditors often suffer as a consequence because the funds are not available to service obligations.

The calculation is relatively straightforward. Sustainable growth is calculated by multiplying the Return on Equity by the Earnings Retention Rate. The Return on Equity is calculated by dividing net income after tax by common shareholders equity from the prior year. Using the prior year is a departure from the ROE calculation that is typically used; the prior year ROE is used because the calculation is future oriented. The earnings retention is calculated by subtracting dividends from the net income after tax for the current year and then dividing by the net income after tax from the current year.

Blackhawk Retail will be used to demonstrate sustainable growth. The data from the 2019 Income Statement in Table 9-1 and the 2018 and 2019 Balance Sheets found in Table 9-3 will be used. The dividends are not in the financial statements; assume that dividends are 75% of the earnings for Blackhawk Retail.

$$\text{Return on Equity} = \frac{2019 \text{ Net Income}}{2018 \text{ Common Equity}} = \frac{500}{725} = 69\%$$

$$\text{Retention Rate} = \frac{2019 \text{ Net Income less 2019 Dividends}}{2019 \text{ Net Income}}$$

$$\text{Retention Rate} = \frac{500 - 375}{500} = 25\%$$

Sustainable Growth = ROE × Retention Rate = 69% × 25% = **17%**

The sustainable growth rate for Blackhawk Retail is 17%. This suggests that if the expected growth rate is higher than 17%, the company will need external funds or it will have to make changes in certain operating policies.

The main purpose for introducing sustainable growth is to point out the fact that a calculation can be used to pinpoint questions that credit mangers should be asking. For example, are external funds available to support growth? If debt is to be used, how much risk will be created with a higher debt load to service? Does management have flexibility in altering operations if the growth does not materialize? If the managers for your customers have not considered such questions, the management may not be competent.

Financial analysis skills unfold gradually. The four tools used in this section—Zero Working Capital, DuPont Analysis, Basic Defensive Interval and Sustainable Growth—serve as examples of the types of critical thinking that are potentially applied to credit analysis. Other tools will be explored in the next chapter of this book. Not only do these skills require critical thinking, but they also require the need to keep current with changes in the accounting profession. There are numerous potential accounting-related stumbling blocks that credit managers should be prepared to encounter.

INTERNATIONAL FINANCIAL REPORTING STANDARDS

The use of one set of accounting rules would enhance the comparability of financial statements from companies throughout the world. In 1973, the International Accounting Standards Board (IASB) was formed by 10 nations to work toward establishing a set of international accounting standards. The process of developing international accounting rules is slowly approaching fruition. International Financial Reporting Standards (IFRS) are now required in over 125 jurisdictions (as of 2017) with many others permitting their use. In January 2017, the chair of the SEC said it continues to support efforts by the Financial Accounting Standards Board (FASB) and IASB to converge accounting standards.

The U.S. uses a set of accounting guidelines commonly referred to as Generally Accepted Accounting Principles (GAAP), which are represented by 25,000 pages of rules. IFRS include 2,500 pages of rules; IFRS requires the use of more judgment in the application of accounting standards.

GAAP is looked upon as the "Gold Standard" for definitive accounting rules. In general, GAAP is considered to be more rules-based, while IFRS is perceived to be more principles-based. GAAP has been around longer and is more comprehensive in nature. IFRS may furnish the benefit of lowering accounting costs because reporting will be standardized. Moreover, IFRS will enhance the comparability of financial statements for creditors and investors.

Differences exist between GAAP and IFRS, including: the application of accrual accounting; recognition of revenue; accounting for inventory; revaluation of property plant and equipment; impairment of tangible and intangible assets; consolidation of financial statements; and, in the statement of income, how earnings per share and development costs (expenses) are represented. For credit managers, workshops, articles or online courses may be the easiest way to stay abreast with the transition to IFRS.

PROBLEMS USING FINANCIAL STATEMENTS

The bankruptcy filings for Enron, Global Crossing and WorldCom have one common denominator: accounting issues. In order to use financial statements to make credit decisions, several types of accounting issues and problems must be addressed. Problems range from access to timely information and the way in which accountants report information, to the actual interpretation of the information available. Credit managers need to become adept at identifying potential red flags and posing questions.

Scrutinizing Footnotes. Footnotes should disclose pertinent accounting information such as inventory valuation, depreciation policies, contingent liabilities, off-balance sheet financing and the disclosure of certain pertinent events. For many smaller businesses, the credit analyst simply does not have footnotes available. When footnotes are available, they should be carefully scrutinized. Yet, the obligations for special purpose entities that were used by Enron Corporation could not be easily detected. Enron's financial statements were so misleading that the company had to restate prior years' financial statements, which wiped out reported profits and led to one of the largest bankruptcy filings in U.S. history.

Marking to Market. Asset values for marketable securities and loan valuations should be carried in the balance sheet at the lower of cost or market value. This is an application of the accounting principle of conservatism. The goal is greater transparency in financial statements. Fair value measurements have been required by the Statement of Financial Accounting Standards (SFAS) 157 since the fiscal year ending after November 15, 2007.

Revenue Recognition. Recognizing revenue that is not earned can mislead the users of financial statements. For example, Global Crossing used a vehicle called a "swap" to recognize an increase in revenue. In essence, the swap entailed trading rights to the use of cable resources with other firms. Accounting rules allowed the swaps to be categorized as revenue, misleading investors and contributing to a bankruptcy filing. Xerox Corporation is another business that erred in revenue recognition. Xerox booked more than $3 billion in revenue prematurely; the company was forced to restate financial statements from the previous four-year period.

Improperly Capitalizing Expenses. Expenses should be matched to the accounting period in which revenue is recognized. WorldCom is an example of the improper capitalization of expenses. WorldCom may have hidden $3.8 billion in expenses, which were capitalized as assets that then showed up improperly in their balance sheet. Recognition of the expenses would have wiped out profits. WorldCom filed a Chapter 11 bankruptcy in July 2002. The WorldCom bankruptcy remains the largest non-financial bankruptcy for a public company in U.S. history, surpassing both the General Motors Corporation (June 2009) and Enron (December 2001). Sometimes profits are an illusion; credit managers would be hard-pressed to detect a WorldCom type of accounting irregularity.

Changes in Accounting Rules. The Financial Accounting Standards Board (FASB) issues rules that public accountants must adhere to. For example, FASB 141 and FASB 142 established new standards to account for the valuation of business combinations and the amortization of goodwill.

The new rules require that acquisition goodwill have an annual test for the impairment of goodwill. This means that goodwill being amortized can vary significantly from year to year. This accounting rule could have a significant impact on the income statement. This type of rule change makes trend analysis difficult.

Book Value vs. Market Value. Land purchased 50 years ago that is carried at book value may be undervalued. Credit analysts should cultivate a habit of questioning the valuations used by accountants. Liquidation value is usually substantially lower than book value. Moreover, market value could be higher than either book value or liquidation value. Market value is often based upon appraisals, which can vary widely depending upon the aggressiveness of the appraisal.

Extraordinary Items. Significant write-offs of losses or recognition of gains can make comparisons difficult. One issue that relates to this topic is the decision of the American Institute of Certified Public Accountants (AICPA) to exclude losses and costs from the September 11, 2001 disasters from extraordinary items. The logic of categorizing costs as extraordinary is not always clear.

Timing Issues. The accounting period in which revenue is recognized and expenses are reported should be questioned. Moreover, the balance sheet does not always indicate the true timing of all future cash flow. For example, deferred taxes may be recognized if an asset is sold or they may be perpetuated if the asset is retained.

Industry Comparisons. A number of problems can surface when comparing a company to an industry. New economy businesses differ from old economy businesses. For a seasonal industry, if the fiscal year-ends do not coincide, then the comparisons can be very misleading. When accounting practices vary, comparisons can also be misleading. Finally, if a company operates in several industries, the business may need to be broken down into segments to make a valid industry comparison. When a credit manager is extending credit to a subsidiary of a company, the financial statement should be a consolidating statement. A consolidating statement shows the individual subsidiary's position. A consolidated statement combines the subsidiary with the parent.

Technology Issues. Maintenance of records and the use of electronic audit trails are both issues in accounting that carry over to credit managers. Arthur Andersen was found guilty of document shredding in the Enron case, which led to the accounting firm's demise. Credit managers need to cooperate with both external and internal auditors when their firm is being audited. A disaster-recovery mechanism should be in place. Technology-related education and training should receive a high priority. Information security should be in place to maintain the privacy of credit department records.

Accounting problems and issues require the ongoing attention of credit personnel. Perhaps the best way to keep in touch with the various types of accounting concerns is to attend professional meetings. Both NACM and many of its local Affiliates have seminars that deal with accounting issues on a regular basis.

CHAPTER 9: FOLLOW-UP

Recap of Important Concepts

1. For credit managers, GAAP is sometimes an obstacle to overcome. Since auditors have considerable latitude in reporting financial statements, credit analysts need to become adept at recognizing accounting procedures. Moreover, since accounting rules change, credit analysts need to keep in touch with the new standards used by auditors.

2. The reliability of financial statements varies widely. Audited statements should be scrutinized for the type of auditor's opinion. Personal statements should be signed and dated. The reliability of unaudited statements leaves the credit analyst with much less confidence in depending on financial statements.

3. Common-size analysis is an effective approach to financial statement analysis. Common-sizing an income statement and a balance sheet over three years can establish operating trends. Industry data are readily available to make comparisons using common-size data.

4. Financial ratios can be used to provide detailed insights into the creditworthiness of a business. Ratios can be compared to an industry to reveal the strengths and weaknesses of a business.

5. Liquidity ratios are particularly important to short-term creditors. The Current Ratio, Quick Ratio and Payables Deferral Period provide insights into the liquidity of a business.

6. Asset Management Ratios are used to measure the effectiveness of management. The Days Sales Outstanding, Inventory Carrying Period and Fixed Asset Turnover provide a barometer of the management for the largest assets on the balance sheet.

7. Debt Management Ratios are important to long-term creditors. The Debt to Equity Ratio, Times Interest Earned and Fixed Charge Coverage ratios indicate a firm's ability to manage debt.

8. Profitability Ratios tend to show the effectiveness of the overall management of the business. The Profit Margin, Return on Assets and Return on Equity provide an indication of the capability of the managers running the firm.

9. Several financial tools of analysis are couched in the use of financial statements. Zero Working Capital is a way of thinking. A controller may be deliberately slowing down payments to increase profitability at the expense of suppliers.

9: Financial Statement Analysis

10. DuPont Analysis broadens the approach to using ratio analysis. DuPont Analysis can be used to shape decisions internally. A credit analyst could use DuPont Analysis to identify the root cause of certain problems.
11. The Basic Defensive Interval can be used to take a close look at liquidity. Creditors are often most concerned with short-term solvency. This calculation is particularly relevant for an e-commerce company that experiences a rapid cash-burn rate.
12. The sustainable growth calculation can be used to analyze companies that are growing rapidly. These are often the types of companies that will experience growing pains in the near future.
13. IFRS is required in more than 125 countries; it seems to be only a matter of time in which IFRS will become the standard accounting rules used in the U.S. The implication to credit managers is that learning more about IFRS can only be helpful in terms of keeping up with the coming changes.
14. Financial statement analysis can become quite sophisticated. Interpreting footnotes, recognizing accounting rules and changes in accounting practices each pose unique reporting problems that need to be recognized and then carefully interpreted.

Review/Discussion Questions

1. In terms of being the most reliable, which auditor's opinion is the best one available?
2. What problems tend to surface when credit managers rely upon personal financial statements?
3. Why should a credit manager consider saving the envelopes in which financial statements are mailed?
4. Data for Ming Research Company and its industry appear below:

	Ming Research in $	Industry Average in %
Cash	10,000	4%
Accounts Receivable	260,000	33%
Inventory	200,000	33%
Net Fixed Assets	150,000	30%
Accounts Payable	250,000	25%
Long-term Debt	250,000	25%
Common Equity	120,000	50%
Sales	1,200,000	100%

Cost of Goods Sold	850,000	65%
Operating Expenses	200,000	15%
Interest Expense	100,000	10%
Income Tax	20,000	4%
Net Income After Tax	30,000	6%

   a. Calculate the common-size balance sheet and income statement for Ming Research.

   b. How does the Ming Research common-size analysis compare to the industry? Be specific.

   c. Calculate the four ratios in Table 9-5 for Ming Research.

   d. Discuss the financial position of Ming Research by identifying any strengths and weaknesses that you perceive.

5. Select an annual report of your choice.

   a. Common-size the balance sheet and the income statement for two years. What changes have occurred in the percentages?

   b. Perform a ratio analysis for the two most recent years. Comment on any changes or trends that you can recognize.

   c. Compare the results from your selected company to an appropriate industry. Comment on any differences that you deem to be important.

   d. Discuss the overall strengths and weaknesses of the company that you have selected.

6. Which of the tools of analysis discussed in the chapter do you believe is most useful to a credit analyst? The tools discussed were Zero Working Capital, DuPont Analysis, the Basic Defensive Interval and the Sustainable Growth Model. Please support your choice with sound reasoning.

Test Your Knowledge

1. Explain why a balance sheet is an important source of financial information for a credit manager.

2. How can an income statement be a useful tool for credit analysis purposes?

3. Give examples of ratios that can be used to analyze a company for each of the following:

   a. Liquidity

   b. Asset Management

   c. Debt Management

   d. Profitability

9: Financial Statement Analysis

4. Provide the formula and discuss the usefulness of each of the following:
   a. Quick Ratio
   b. Debt to Equity Ratio
   c. Fixed Asset Turnover
   d. Times Interest Earned
   e. Return on Assets

5. What are some of the problems encountered by a credit analyst when trying to make an industry comparison? Be specific in your response.

6. Carefully summarize each of the four audit opinions used by public accounting firms. Focus your response on the reliability of the opinions.

7. Days Sales Outstanding can generate some misleading interpretation. Discuss the potential limitation of DSO when sales volume is changing.

8. While analyzing the footnotes to a customer's financial statement, you detect a large lease obligation. What impact does the lease have upon your credit analysis? Is there any ratio useful to creditors that takes the lease obligation into consideration? If so, explain.

9. A new customer has submitted an unaudited financial statement to you. As a credit analyst, are there any means available to you to verify any of the assets or liabilities that appear in the balance sheet?

10. An existing customer of yours submits a current financial statement. The statement shows a substantial increase in inventory as a common-size percentage. What questions would you like to pose to your customer concerning the change in inventory?

11. You receive an audited financial statement from a new customer. After comparing the common-size income statement to companies of similar size in the same industry, you notice that the "Cost of Goods Sold" is much lower than the industry norm. What questions would you pose to your new customer concerning this difference?

12. Select an annual report of your choice and perform the following calculations (instructors should consider the use of one particular company if this question is to be reviewed via an in-class discussion):
    a. Determine the Net Working Capital.
    b. Perform a DuPont Analysis.
    c. Calculate the Basic Defensive Interval.
    d. Calculate the Sustainable Growth Rate.

Based upon your calculations, pose three questions for each calculation (12 total questions) that you would like to ask the treasurer of the company.

13. What are some of the differences between GAAP and IFRS? Which approach is better?

Credit Management Online

www.aicpa.org/—This link will take you to the website for the American Institute of Certified Public Accountants. Accounting issues that may be of concern to the credit profession can be examined through the many resources available on the site.

biz.yahoo.com/p/s_conameu.html—This link will take you to the Yahoo! Finance Industry Browser. By using the sector browser, you can access an individual industry to examine comparative data for public companies.

www.businessweek.com/—This is a commercial site hosted by *Bloomberg Businessweek* that provides certain information free of charge. *Bloomberg Businessweek* offers quick access to current business news and stock market information.

ww2.cfo.com/—Hosted by *CFO* magazine, this site offers articles that pertain to issues such as accounting, auditing, GAAP, cash management, risk management, regulation and education.

www.dnb.com/—D&B has several financial statement-related products available that are geared toward meeting the needs of credit managers. Financial ratio information, together with information on industry norms, can also be purchased under D&B subscription arrangements.

www.edgar-online.com/—This site offers a subscription service to public company financial information and is not affiliated with the U.S. Securities and Exchange Commission.

www.fasb.org/—The Financial Accounting Standards Board (FASB) is a private-sector organization that establishes the standards used in public accounting and reporting. FASB rules are important to creditors who review audited financial statements.

finance.yahoo.com/—Yahoo makes comparative data available by company, industry, sector and S&P 500. The information is free of charge. Numerous ratios are calculated and made available by typing in the ticker symbol for publicly traded companies.

www.hoovers.com/—Hoovers makes available current market, industry and company information. There are reports on 1,000 industries and 85 million companies available on the site. Brokerage firm reports can also be purchased at this site. Hoovers is owned by D&B.

www.rmahq.org/RMA/—The Risk Management Association (RMA), representing the banking industry, provides annual statement studies to subscribers. Common-size data together with numerous financial ratios are available. The ratios are broken into quartiles by SIC code.

www.sec.gov/—The U.S. Securities and Exchange Commission hosts this site. Public companies are required to furnish financial information, which can be accessed for free on this site. There is a quick tutorial for the Electronic Data Gathering, Analysis and Retrival system (EDGAR) www.sec.gov/page/everythingedgar to help users become familiar with the information available. Accounting rules and enforcement actions can be reviewed as well.

www.standardandpoors.com/home/en/us—This is the site for corporate and industry information available from Standard and Poor's. There is extensive information available for companies that publicly issue corporate or municipal debt.

www.valueline.com/—This is the site for Value Line, where company and industry reports are made available. The site caters to the investment community and offers numerous research reports that can be helpful.

www.zacks.com/—Zacks is a commercial site that provides free information on the stock market as well as financial ratio information on public companies. A ticker symbol is used to look at the company profile.

References Useful for Further Reading

"Advanced Issues in Financial Statement Analysis." *Business Credit* (September 2008): 35.

Bhimani, Alnoor, Mohamed Azzim Gulamhussen, and Samuel Lopes. "The Effectiveness of the Auditor's Going-Concern Evaluation as an External Governance Mechanism: Evidence from Loan Defaults." *The International Journal of Accounting*, Vol. 44, No. 3 (September 2009): 239-255.

Barron, Jacob. "Credit Basics: Financial Analysis." *Business Credit* (March 2007): 48-49.

Barron, Jacob. "Getting a Head Start: Preparing for the Switch to an International Accounting Standard." *Business Credit* (January 2009): 16-17.

Barron, Jacob. "In the Drop Zone." *Business Credit* (March 2008): 58-61.Bouillon, Marvin L. "Rev. of *Crash Course in Accounting & Financial Statement Analysis*," by Matan Feldman and Arkady Libman. *Issues in Accounting Education* 22.3 (August 2007): 539.

Carr, Matthew. "Seeking to Understand New Accounting Standards Impact in the Credit Market Chaos." *Business Credit* (January 2008): 68.

Carr, Matthew. "Taking the Fear Out of Financial Statements." *Business Credit* (June 2009): 6-8.

Colomer, Nora. "FASB Proposes New Mark-to-Market Regulation." *High Yield Report* (May 31, 2010): 14.

Dennis, Michael. "Key Financial Ratios for the Credit Department." *Business Credit* (November/December 2006): 62.

"Developing an Internal Credit Score for Businesses." NACM GSCFM Class of 2015. *Business Credit* (September/October 2015): 52-54.

Emery, Gary W. "Sustainable Growth for Credit Analysis." *Business Credit* (February 2000): 35-39.

Gallinger, George. "The Defensive Interval: A Better Liquidity Measure." *Business Credit* (September 1997): 26-28.

Gordon, Elizabeth A., et al. "Auditing Related Party Transactions: A Literature Overview and Research Synthesis." *Accounting Horizons*, Vol. 21, No. 1 (March 2007): 81-102.

Grogan, Larry, CCE, CICP. "Making Good Credit Decisions Even without Advanced International Expertise." *Business Credit* (April 2016): 26-27.

Gujarathi, Mahendra R. "Sachiko Corporation: A Case in International Financial Statement Analysis." *Issues in Accounting Education*, Vol. 23, No. 1 (February 2008): 77-101.

Hammersley, Jacqueline S., E. Michael Bamber, and Tina D. Carpenter. "The Influence of Documentation Specificity and Priming on Auditors' Fraud Risk Assessments and Evidence Evaluation Decisions." *The Accounting Review*, Vol. 85, No. 2 (March 2010): 547-571.

"Intermediate Financial Statement Analysis: Interpretation & Credit Risk Assessment." *Business Credit* (November/December 2009): 39.

Landy, Heather. "FASB Plan Could Have a Seismic Impact." *American Banker* (May 27, 2010): 1-2.

Laux, Christian, and Christian Leuz. "Did Fair-Value Accounting Contribute to the Financial Crisis?" *Journal of Economic Perspectives* Vol. 24 No. 1 (Winter 2010): 93-118.

Linthicum, Cheryl, Austin L. Reitenga, and Juan Manuel Sanchez. "Social Responsibility and Corporate Reputation: The Case of the Arthur Andersen Enron Audit Failure." *Journal of Accounting & Public Policy* (March 2010): 160-176.

McCarthy, Mary Pat. "Ten Must-Do's for the Audit Committee This Year." *Directorship* (February 2009): 71.

McCarthy, Mary Pat. "Ten To-Do's for Audit Committees in 2010." *Directorship* (February 2010): 73.

MacNamara, Joseph, CCE, CICP. "Fraud, Accounting Scandals and the Effect on Trade Credit." *Business Credit* (April 2015): 48-49.

"New Accounting Standard Effective January 2108." *Business Credit* (June 2017): 17.

Patrisso, Janice. "SEC Statement Provides Plan for 2011 Decision on IFRS Implementation in the U.S." *Financial Executive* (May 2010): 14-15.

Pounder, Bruce. "IFRS Risk: Not What You Think." *CFO* (May 14, 2010): www.cfo.com/printable/article.cfm/14497802.

Rodriguez, Kristine Blenkhorn. "One World, One Standard: International Financial Reporting Standards Are Crossing the Globe." *ICPA Insight* (January/February 2009): 29-31.

Schneider, Arnold. "Internal Audit Issues Facing Corporate Audit Committees." *Journal of Applied Business Research* (March/April 2009): 105-118.

Soliman, Mark T. "The Use of DuPont Analysis by Market Participants." *The Accounting Review*, Vol. 83, No. 3 (November 3, 2008): 823-853.

Stern, Nicholas. "Using Forensic Accounting to Spot Inconsistencies, Potential Fraud." *Business Credit* (September/October 2016): 4-5.

Subran, Ludovic. "DSO: One in Four Companies Pay after 90 Days." *Business Credit* (September/October 2016): 19.

Swamy, M.R.K. "Financial Management Call for New Approach to Ethical-based Financial Statement Analysis." *Journal of Financial Management & Analysis*, Vol. 22, No. 2 (July-December 2009): 70-84.

Wilson, Arlette C., and Dan Heitger. "Running the Annual Tests for Impairment of Acquisition Goodwill." *Mergers and Acquisitions* Vol. 1, Issue 11 (November 2001): 38-40.

Chapter 10

CASH FLOW ANALYSIS AND VALUATION ESSENTIALS

"Current business and trade credit extended daily is $40 billion. It is the lubricant of the economy."[1]

Jim Wise, Attorney and Managing Partner
PACE-Capstone

The massive use of business and trade credit contributes significantly to the viability of the U.S. economy. Over 60% of small businesses and the majority of business-to-business (B2B) sellers in the U.S. use trade credit. In order to manage this credit, cash flow analysis is an indispensible tool.

In a climate where accounting rules are routinely questioned, an understanding of the application of cash flow to credit decision-making is more important than ever. Cash flow analysis builds upon the concepts introduced in the preceding chapter. Through the use of cash flow analysis, a credit analyst can become more fully aware about the operations of any business. Moreover, one of the most useful applications for cash flow analysis is the application to corporate valuation, which can drive the viability of many financial decisions.

The study of cash flow is couched in sound financial analysis skills. Corporate valuation tools have become important focal points. Valuations are often based upon corporate profits that have the potential to drive management into using aggressive accounting techniques.

The **Key Learning Objectives** in Chapter 10 are to:

1. Understand the various definitions and terms commonly referred to as cash flow.
2. Analyze a balance sheet using specific cash flow analysis tools.
3. Examine focal points for the analysis of the statement of cash flows.

---

[1] Jim Wise, quoted in an article authored by Jacob Barron and Tom Diana, "NACM Tackles Issues Before Congress," *Business Credit* (May 2007): 88.

228 Credit Management: Principles and Practices

4. Focus on the income statement by using a discounted cash flow model as a tool to analyze a leveraged buyout.
5. Introduce the basics of corporate stock valuation techniques, which can be useful to credit managers.
6. Examine cash flow-based tools, which are useful to credit managers in measuring liquidity and bankruptcy prediction.

CASH FLOW

The specific definition for *cash flow* can vary. An economist might define cash flow as the actual cash entering or leaving the firm. An accountant could refer to cash flow as the net income after tax plus the non-cash operating expenses. For most companies, the non-cash operating expenses are depreciation, but sometimes depletion, amortization and deferred taxes are included as non-cash operating expenses. The study of cash flow analysis draws heavily from the areas of accounting and finance.

For the credit analyst, cash flow represents internally generated funds that can be used to service debt. There are a number of transactions that can make an income statement misleading. For example, expenses could have been reported but not yet paid. Revenue could have been earned but not yet received. Therefore, the income statement often varies significantly from the actual cash inflows and outflows of a firm. The actual cash flows are what are important to the creditor.

Earnings before interest, taxes, depreciation and amortization is often referred to as ***EBITDA***. The use of EBITDA has become a popular measure to gauge funds available to service debt. However, EBITDA has been discredited to some degree because it does not consider non-cash expenses due to an increase in accounts receivable or inventory. EBITDA also fails to consider debt service, such as the retirement of principal and interest.

One trend in financial marketplaces has been to focus upon *free cash flow*. Historically, the definition of free cash flow has been the cash flow less dividends. A more contemporary definition of free cash flow is the cash flow that remains after subtracting all dividends and all capital budgeting expenditures that are essential to allow the firm to operate as a going concern; this definition is much more widely embraced by the financial community. The contemporary definition of free cash flow recognizes the fact that fixed assets must be replenished over time in order for operations to continue in the long run.

10: Cash Flow Analysis and Valuation Essentials

Cash flow analysis tools are a particularly important focal point for credit analysts. Cash flow analysis of individual financial statements is often quite revealing. The next three sections of this chapter will provide useful tools of analysis for the balance sheet, statement of cash flows and income statement.

CASH FLOW ANALYSIS AND THE BALANCE SHEET

Cash flow analysis is often complex. In order to facilitate mastering the essentials of cash flow analysis, specific focal points for analysis will be identified. The most important tools of analysis that pertain to the balance sheet are: (1) the sources-and-uses-of-funds concept and (2) the Cash Conversion Cycle. A detailed discussion of both tools follows.

Sources-and-Uses-of-Funds Concept

The *sources-and-uses-of-funds concept* focuses upon change in balance sheet accounts. All changes in account balances represent either a source or a use of funds. The total "sources" must equal the total "uses" during any given accounting period when analyzing the balance sheet.

Sources and uses can be readily categorized by using the following concepts:

Source
- A decrease in any asset account
- An increase in any liability or equity account

Use
- An increase in any asset account
- A decrease in any liability or equity account

Table 10-1 provides a balance sheet for Wright Production Company. The columns represent the January 1 balances, the December 31 balances, and the sources or uses of funds during the period. Note that the total sources must equal the total uses.

Using a balance sheet analysis, a credit analyst can identify specific account changes and then use analysis skills to determine whether the changes are favorable or unfavorable. For example, long-term bonds were retired using mainly short-term debt. Is the change due to favorable interest rates? Will the short-term debt have to be refunded? If so, what is the likelihood of a bank pulling the plug on a short-term line?

230 Credit Management: Principles and Practices

TABLE 10-1	Wright Production Company Balance Sheet Analysis of Sources/Uses			
	Jan. 1	Dec. 31	Source	Use
Cash	10	15		5
Short-term Investment	15	10	5	
Accounts Receivables	205	190	15	
Inventory	230	240		10
Fixed Assets (Gross)	200	220		20
Accumulated Depreciation	60	70	10	
Land	40	40		
Accounts Payable	200	210	10	
Accruals	70	65		5
Short-term Debt	130	170	40	
Bonds	100	50		50
Common Stock	100	100		
Retained Earnings	40	50	10	—
Total Sources and Uses			90	90

Note that in Table 10-1, the totals for the current assets and the total assets are left off the analysis of sources and uses. This prevents double counting any changes.

An analysis of the balance sheet using a sources-and-uses-of-funds approach is usually helpful to identify where a business is heading. All of the sources and uses that are pinpointed in this type of analysis carry through to a firm's statement of cash flows. This statement will be discussed later in the chapter.

One caveat concerning sources and uses may need an explanation. Although "Accumulated Depreciation" is an asset account, when this account increases, a source is generated; when accumulated depreciation decreases, funds are used. This is because accumulated depreciation is a contra-asset. The rules for a source and use are revised for any contra-account. In a very similar way, the rules for debits and credits change when working with contra-accounts in accounting.

Cash Conversion Cycle

For most companies, the two largest current assets in a balance sheet are accounts receivable and inventory. The largest current liability is usually accounts payable. The *Cash Conversion Cycle* considers the time over which receivables, inventory and payables flow through a business. The survival of many businesses can hinge upon a change in the Cash Conversion Cycle.

The Cash Conversion Cycle is a straightforward calculation. Three of the ratios presented in Chapter 9 are used to calculate a firm's Cash Conversion Cycle. The following equation can be used to calculate the Cash Conversion Cycle:

$$\textbf{Cash Conversion Cycle} = \text{Days Sales Outstanding} + \text{Inventory Carrying Period} - \text{Payables Deferral Period}$$

For example, if a business has a DSO of 35 days, an average inventory of 45 days and an average accounts payable deferral period of 30 days, the Cash Conversion Cycle would be 50 days. The business would work toward shortening the Cash Conversion Cycle without losing sales. Credit analysts should note that by increasing the payables deferral period to 40 days, the Cash Conversion Cycle would be cut to 40 days.

The accounting purist may note that the elements of the Cash Conversion Cycle are not pure offsets. In other words, the size of receivables, inventory and payables are not equal, so the results are in need of practical interpretation. Yet the Cash Conversion Cycle can often serve as an alarm to creditors by pinpointing a severe problem in working capital management.

Each year, *CFO* magazine publishes an annual research study that furnishes the Cash Conversion Cycle for industries and for public companies within each industry. The results of the *CFO* research can be useful to benchmark performance by focusing upon the Cash Conversion Cycle within an industry. Data for 2015 can be accessed on the *CFO* website: ww2.cfo.com/cash-management/2015/06/barely-working-capital/.

CREDIT ANALYSIS
OF THE STATEMENT OF CASH FLOWS

In November 1987, the Financial Accounting Standards Board (FASB) issued statement number 95, which required a specific financial document known as the statement of cash flows (SCF). FASB has been issuing the statement rules that govern financial accounting since 1972. The statement of cash flows replaced the statement of changes in financial position.

The purpose of the *statement of cash flows* is to provide information about a company's cash receipts and payments during an accounting period. The statement is broken down into three types of activities: operating, investing and financing.

1. **Operating Activities.** These activities affect net income. They include cash inflows such as cash receipts from customers. Cash outflows such as wages, expenses and taxes are also included. In effect, operating activities have the impact of changing the income statement from an accrual basis to a cash basis.

2. **Investing Activities.** The acquisition or divestiture of long-term assets and marketable securities are reported in this section. Loans are also reported in this section.

3. **Financing Activities.** The issuance of stock or bonds is an inflow in this section. Any stock repurchases, debt retirement or dividend payments are outflows in this section. An analysis of financing activities can help to detect a change in the use of financial leverage.

The statement of cash flows can be prepared using either of two formats: the direct method or the indirect method. The direct method adjusts each item in the income statement from an accrual basis to a cash basis. Table 10-2 shows the operating section of a SCF using the direct method.

Table 10-2 shows that net cash flow from operations is $3,000 when using the direct method. Credit analysts should note that an income statement format is used when the direct method is used.

TABLE 10-2	Direct Method Operating Activities Section SCF		
Cash Flow from Operating Activities:			
Cash Receipts:			
Sales Revenue	$10,000		
Interest/Dividend Received	100		
		10,100	
Cash Payments:			
Purchases	3,000		
Operating Expenses	3,000		
Interest Payments	100		
Income Tax	1,000		
		7,100	
Net Cash Flow from Operations		**$3,000**	

10: Cash Flow Analysis and Valuation Essentials

TABLE 10-3	**Indirect Method**	
	Operating Activities Section SCF	
Cash Flow from Operating Activities:		
Net Income		$2,000
Adjustments to reconcile		
net income to net cash provided		
from operation activities:		
Depreciation	1,000	
Decrease in Account Receivable	4,000	
Increase in Inventory	(1,000)	
Decrease in Accounts Payable	(2,000)	
Decrease in Taxes	(1,000)	
Net Adjustments		1,000
Net Cash Flow from Operations		**$3,000**

Most large companies use the indirect method to prepare the statement of cash flows. The two methods produce the same results. The difference is in the individual line items that are listed in the operating activities section of the statement. The indirect method does not adjust all of the income statement items necessary to convert from accrual to cash accounting. Instead, only activities that impact the adjustment of net income to net cash flow from operations are reported separately.

The indirect method is demonstrated in Table 10-3. The net cash flow from operating activities is $3,000. This amount will always be the same when the results of the direct or indirect methods are compared.

The investing and financing activities sections are the same under either the direct or indirect method. A complete statement of cash flows is presented in Table 10-4.

The statement of cash flows in Table 10-4 shows a complete statement through the use of the indirect method. Most credit analysts tend to scrutinize the statement to see if funds are being generated internally or externally. In addition, credit analysts may be able to detect a mismatch of funds. For example, if long-term assets are being funded with short-term liabilities, there is an increase in interest rate risk.

Certain ratios can become useful to the analysis of the statement of cash flows. One such ratio is cash flow from operating activities divided by interest expense. The higher the ratio, the better the debtor's ability to service debt. Another important ratio for trade creditors to consider is the ratio of cash flow from operating activities divided by the total current

234   Credit Management: Principles and Practices

TABLE 10-4   **The Bowman Company**
Statement of Cash Flows
for the Year Ended December 31, 2019

Cash Flows from Operating Activities:		
Net Income		$2,000
Adjustments to reconcile net income to		
net cash provided by operating activities:		
Depreciation	1,000	
Decrease in Accounts Receivable	4,000	
Increase in Inventory	(1,000)	
Decrease in Accounts Payable	(2,000)	
Decrease in Taxes	(1,000)	
Net Adjustments		1,000
Net Cash Flow from Operating Activities		3,000
Cash Flows from Investing Activities:		
Purchase of Equipment	(5,000)	
Proceeds from Sale of Land	2,000	
Net Cash Provided by Investing Activities		(3,000)
Cash Flows from Financing Activities:		
Proceeds from Issuing Stock	3,000	
Dividends Paid	(1,000)	
Net Cash Provided from Financing Activities		2,000
Net Increase in Cash		2,000
Cash at Beginning of Year		3,000
Cash at End of Year		$5,000

---

liabilities in the balance sheet. The results provide a measure of a debtor's ability to service short-term credit obligations.

The formatting differences can make the statement of cash flows appear to be complex. However, if credit analysts can keep in mind that the purpose of the statement is simply to identify sources and uses of cash, the analysis is simplified. By breaking the statement into three sections, credit analysts can concentrate on the pertinent changes that have taken place in a business.

PRO FORMA CASH FLOW ANALYSIS
OF THE INCOME STATEMENT

In order to provide a clear explanation of valuation techniques, a cash flow model will be introduced. The cash flow model is commonly used

10: Cash Flow Analysis and Valuation Essentials

235

to value corporations in a merger, initial public offering (IPO), division spin-off or leveraged buyout (LBO). This model is widely used in valuing corporate assets. It will be demonstrated through the use of an LBO analysis.

A cash flow model is based upon the development of pro forma income statements. The basis of the model is that the value of any asset is the future cash flows discounted to obtain their net present value. An iterative process can be used by changing key variables. By changing these key variables, the riskiness of the transaction can be more fully understood. This is done by using a computer model that is run over and over to obtain a range of values for a firm.

An understanding of the basic principles of corporate finance is essential to working with concepts related to discounted cash flow models. Students who have not taken a finance course can gain a more thorough appreciation of these concepts by referring to a college-level finance textbook. In particular, the present value concept, cost of capital and capital budgeting chapters introduce essential skills useful to perform this type of analysis.

A financial analyst might use a model that extends out over a 10-year period so that long-term risk can be scrutinized. For simplicity, a four-year model will be demonstrated. The model will be used to value an LBO candidate by projecting out future income statements. The projected net cash flows will then be discounted back to time zero to obtain their net present value.

Application of a Cash Flow Model to an LBO

Cash flow models have numerous applications. One of the most common applications of a cash flow model is LBO analysis. By focusing upon an LBO, the merit of considering numerous pieces of information will be demonstrated. Once the quantitative model is developed, the next focus will be placed upon the equally important qualitative concerns. An assessment of the overall approach will then be discussed.

The pro forma income statements in Table 10-5 show projected net cash flows in each year under analysis. Note that in 2022 there is an extra line item, called the *terminal value*, of $517. This amount is the expected value of the LBO Candidate Co. at the end of 2022. The terminal value is calculated on the following page.

LBO Candidate Co.
Calculation of the Terminal Value in 2022

$$\text{Value of LBO Candidate in 2022} = \frac{\$94(1.10)}{.30 - .10} = \$517$$

The numerator in the above equation is obtained by multiplying the free cash flow in the terminal year of analysis, which is $94 in 2022, by the whole number one plus the assumed growth rate after 2022, which is estimated at 10%. The denominator is the cost of equity for the LBO candidate, estimated to be 30%, less the growth rate after the terminal year of 10%. The value of the LBO candidate at the end of the analysis time horizon in 2022 is *$517*.

Calculation of the Present Value of the LBO Candidate

The final step in the valuation of the LBO Candidate Co. is to discount the net cash flows. Since the cash flows represent flows to equity investors, the appropriate discount rate is the cost of equity. In this example, the cost of equity capital is 30%, which shows up in the denominator. This rate of *30%* indicates that **equity investors require a 30% return**. As market conditions change, this discount rate changes. The risk is reflected in the discount rate; more risk increases the discount rate. When risk perceptions went through the roof in 2008, the required rate of return escalated to levels where it was almost impossible to do an LBO.

The numerators in the equation for the final step use the net cash flow, which is the bottom line of the pro forma statements in Table 10-5. The denominators provide the present value of the projected cash flows; this is done to consider the time value of money. The following equation shows the cash flows discounted at the cost of equity in order to obtain the value of the LBO Candidate Co.

LBO Candidate Co.
Discounting the Net Cash Flows (in Thousands)

$$\frac{70}{(1.30)^1} + \frac{77}{(1.30)^2} + \frac{85}{(1.30)^3} + \frac{611}{(1.30)^4} = \$386$$

The discounted cash flow analysis suggests that the LBO Candidate is worth *$386*. The $386 represents the value of the target business to the equity investor, assuming all inputs are accurate. A major error in an estimate used in the analysis or a change in specific projections for a key variable could result in serious errors in the valuation.

10: Cash Flow Analysis and Valuation Essentials

TABLE 10-5   **LBO Candidate Company**
Projected Post LBO Income Statements

(000s Omitted)	2019	2020	2021	2022
Sales[1]	1,000	1,100	1,210	1,330
Cost of Goods Sold[2]	500	550	605	665
Gross Profit	500	550	605	665
Operating Expense[3]	200	220	242	266
Operating Profit	300	330	363	399
Interest Expense[4]	100	110	120	130
Net Income before Tax	200	330	243	269
Income Tax[5]	60	66	73	81
Net Income after Tax	140	154	170	188
Retentions[6]	70	77	85	94
Free Cash Flow	70	77	85	94
Terminal Value[7]				517
Net Cash Flow	**70**	**77**	**85**	**611**

[1] Sales growth is estimated at 10% per year.
[2] The Cost of Goods Sold is estimated at 50% of sales.
[3] Operating Expenses are estimated at 20% of sales.
[4] Interest Expenses should include both interest before and after the LBO.
[5] Income Tax is estimated at 30% of pre-tax income.
[6] Retentions are used to fund growth and are roughly equal to annual depreciation expense.
[7] The Terminal Value is the estimated value of the LBO candidate at the end of the final year being analyzed.

There are practical concerns when working with pro forma analysis. The best LBO candidates have stable and predictable cash flows in each year of analysis. However, this is often not the case. For example, one LBO candidate that ran into problems included a 30% growth rate in net cash flows; however, the actual cash flows that occurred went down 7% after the LBO.

There are two popular risk assessment techniques that credit analysts may consider when using cash flow models. These techniques are sensitivity analysis and scenario analysis. Both techniques entail reconstructing the pro formas.

Sensitivity analysis involves changing one key variable, such as sales growth, to determine the result on the net cash flow for an LBO candidate, a merger target or a business valuation. Other variables that may be changed include expenses such as interest rates, operating expenses and tax rates. The discount rate is also subject to change.

When several variables are changed simultaneously, the process is called *scenario analysis*. For example, if sales go down, expenses go up

238 Credit Management: Principles and Practices

and the economy falters, a worst-case scenario would result. For credit analysts, the likelihood of a change in key variables demands use of considerable judgment.

A money center banker suggested that her staff run the scenario analysis on an average transaction 200 times just to see how risk might play out. Once a computer model is set up, it is relatively easy to rerun scenarios; simply change variables such as the growth rate in sales, changes in key costs, changes in interest rates, changes in the economy or changes in profit margins.

The cash flow model used to evaluate an LBO is the same type of a model that can be used to value common stock, a merger target, an initial public offering (IPO) or a division spin-off. However, there are several other approaches used to perform this type of valuation. The important point to focus upon is that if revenue or expense estimates are off, the valuation will not be accurate. The transaction could then unravel.

Qualitative Concerns in an LBO

There is no one standard definition for an LBO. An LBO could be defined as any situation where a corporation changes its capital structure by substituting debt for equity. The important implication to credit managers is recognition of a high-risk situation. Some credit managers maintain a watch list of all LBO accounts in the accounts receivables and then keep their own top management informed of the performance of the accounts.

When a company borrows money, retires stock and pays a substantial dividend to prevent a takeover, the transaction is called a leveraged cash out (LCO). The risk inherent in an LCO can be just as great as the risk inherent in an LBO. A division spin-off could also result in an under-capitalized business. An understanding of the details of high-risk accounts mandates internal policies and controls to monitor total exposure. Knowledge of the qualitative details of LBO funding is essential to dealing effectively with highly leveraged transactions.

The funds provided in the majority of LBO transactions essentially come from three sources and follow a three-tier layering that involves varying degrees of risk for the participants.

1. *Senior Bank Debt.* Commercial banks are the provider of 30% to 60% of funds in typical LBO transactions. Banks normally obtain up-front fees anywhere from .5% to 4% of the loans.

Banks have the advantage of holding collateral in an LBO. Moreover, banks diversify by industry and geographic area through the use of participation agreements with other banks. Even though banks are collateralized and diversified, the Federal Reserve monitors the overall LBO exposure at banks.

2. ***Mezzanine Debt.*** Mezzanine debt is more commonly known as the junk bond layer. Generally 20% to 45% of the funds provided in a typical LBO are through use of these types of instruments. Interest rates vary from 2% to 10% above the rate charged on senior funds. Moreover, underwriting fees tend to run from 2% to 3% of the funds raised.

Mezzanine debt is unsecured and, in almost all cases, is subordinated to the senior bank lender. Historically, investors have been adequately compensated with interest rates that have been high enough to offset the high level of default risk. However, the collapse in the junk bond market in late 1989 and 1990 far exceeded prior default rates. The LBO marketplace is quite cyclical. The marketplace thrived again until 2008 and 2009, when the default rate began to escalate again during the credit crunch.

3. ***Equity Investors.*** The total equity in an LBO is generally between 10% and 20% of the funding. However, the trend is for new transactions to include a higher proportion of equity. For creditors, the increased equity cushion is a welcome trend. Noting the level of equity in an individual transaction is important.

There are usually two types of equity in an LBO. First, the management team may contribute to the total funding. The management commitment is important to creditors since it signals confidence in the project. *Ceteris paribus*: the more management equity, the safer the account for the creditor. Usually the management team will receive additional incentives in the form of stock options.

The second type of equity investment is usually contributed by either an LBO fund or by venture capitalists. Blackstone Capital Partners and Apollo Investment Fund are two of the best-known LBO funds. There are several other funds run by smaller companies. The equity fund will generally place significant restrictions on the management team to maximize its control. The equity fund may have an ultimate goal of taking the LBO public, which is sometimes called a reverse LBO.

Assessing LBO Credit Quality

The funding mix that can be used to create an LBO impacts upon the credit quality. Credit analysts need to be aware that a particular funding source will try to protect its own interests first. As business conditions change, the overall risk associated with a particular LBO needs to be assessed. Some important focal points to monitor the riskiness of an LBO include:

- *The Business Plan.* If profit margins were tight before the LBO, they will probably remain tight after the LBO. Management should be willing to explain where the company is going after the LBO. How will the target be run differently? Another question to be addressed is: Will assets be carved out in order to retire debt?
- *The Growth Rate.* Post-LBO sales growth factored into the pro forma is often very difficult to achieve. Companies with a strong market position obviously have an advantage. If the company is cyclical, then a recession could erode potential growth. Also, products that are not susceptible to a rapid technological change provide more predictable cash flows.
- *The Expenses.* Companies with strong unions may not be in a position to gain anticipated wage concessions after an LBO. Companies that use commodity products, such as oil in the manufacturing process, may have too much volatility in their Cost of Goods Sold to justify extending trade credit after an LBO.
- *Debt Load.* The Times Interest Earned (TIE) and EBITDA coverage ratios are useful to determine the ability to service the debt load under alternative scenarios. If sales go down and costs go up, will the business have an escape mechanism to survive? The higher the interest expense, the greater the potential problems if the numbers in the pro forma do not materialize.
- *Overestimating the Price of the LBO Candidate.* Major LBO failures have occurred because the price paid for a target was too high. The average American company has a price-earnings ratio of about 17 to 1. Sometimes a simple process such as multiplying earnings by 17 to arrive at a price can be compared to the results used with a sophisticated model. Basic intuition can often help the credit manager recognize that the price paid in an LBO was far too high. When the price is too high, the LBO invariably has a greater likelihood of failure.

- ***Industry Factors.*** Credit managers should focus on industry concerns for the core business. If the LBO candidate is a low-cost producer, the LBO has a better chance of surviving. On the other hand, if the competition initiates a price war, the business might not survive.
- ***Changes in the Economy.*** A sound LBO should have limited sensitivity to changes in the business cycle. If a core business is cyclical, such as the housing industry, an LBO is usually not appropriate. If the LBO has debt that is tied to an interest rate index, then a quick increase in interest rates could take the LBO into bankruptcy.

When these qualitative factors are considered together with the quantitative pro forma cash flow analysis, credit managers can gain meaningful insight. The ultimate decision to extend credit into an LBO is always based upon judgment. Cash flow analysis combined with qualitative analysis is the superior approach to making the most informed business credit decision.

STOCK AND REAL ESTATE VALUATION ESSENTIALS

Sometimes major bankruptcies can be closely related to the potential for fraud or major changes in economic conditions. The dire straits experienced during a bankruptcy impact investors as well as creditors. Therefore, credit managers should understand the basics pertaining to how assets are valued.

The financial community can be lulled into missing important signals. The growing list of bankruptcies at Lehman Brothers, Washington Mutual, CIT Group, IndyMac Bancorp, General Motors and Chrysler can be traced to the credit crunch. However, many bankruptcies such as Enron, Global Crossing and WorldCom can be traced to accounting gimmicks.

Common Stock Valuation. There are a number of ways in which common stock can be valued. The most common approach is to use good fundamentals. Good fundamentals seemed to go out of vogue during the latter half of the 1990s in the stock market and in the later part of the next decade in the real estate market. An examination that uses fundamental analysis for valuation can be a valuable resource for credit analysts.

Bubbles can occur in any market. When markets deviate from traditional valuations, there is a market correction that will be coming. Creditors can monitor traditional valuations in a marketplace to help to prepare for the corrections. In other words, history can teach us valuable lessons.

Warren Buffet is probably the most widely recognized fundamental analyst. Buffet is the chairman of Berkshire Hathaway Inc. He does not receive any stock options, and his annual salary is only $100,000. Although Buffet's principles seemed out of vogue during the 1990s, Buffet is now once again considered one of the most highly regarded stock pickers in the world.

Buffet subscribes to the principles of his mentor, Benjamin Graham. Graham is the co-author of *Security Analysis*, which is sometimes referred to as the bible of fundamental analysis. Graham is also the author of *The Intelligent Investor*. These books are very highly recommended resources for those readers who are interested in Buffet's approach to stock valuation techniques.

Corporate officers are often under pressure to generate an improvement in earnings. Stockholders simply want to see the value of their investments go up. The pressures can lead to numbers games that can potentially compromise the quality of the financial information reported.

The website for the Electronic Data Gathering, Analysis and Retrieval system (EDGAR), an online resource provided by the Securities and Exchange Commission, is www.sec.gov/edgar.shtml. This site has a number of free resources that are potentially useful, both to credit managers and to investors. Some of the information available includes:

The **8-K** report includes any material events that are occurring or significant corporate changes.

The **10-K** report is more inclusive than a typical company annual report.

The **10-Q** quarterly report is more abbreviated than an annual 10-K report.

A **Proxy Statement**, also called a Schedule 14-A, reflects all issues for which the stockholders will be voting on.

A **Prospectus** is a thorough disclosure of financial information that is made available prior to issuing any new debt or equity to the public.

Fundamental analysts use public information to employ several stock valuation techniques. They consider the economy, industry and individual stock; this is called a **top-down approach**. Fundamental analysts often use the following techniques: (1) price-earnings ratio, (2) market-to-book value ratio, (3) market-to-EBITDA ratio, (4) market-to-sales,

(5) dividend models, (6) cash flow models and (7) multiples of unique visitors to websites.

Price-Earnings (PE) Ratio. The market price per share compared to the earnings per share is used. If the market price is $20 and the earnings per share is $1, the price-earnings ratio is 20x. Ethics could be compromised by increasing the recognition of revenue or by not recognizing certain expenses; either situation could increase profit and the implied price if the price is based upon a price-earning ratio. If officers are rewarded through stock options, they could purchase the stock at the option price and then turn around and sell the stock at the artificially high price that was pumped up by using accounting gimmicks. Market participants rely upon timely and accurate information from accountants.

Also, when the PE for the overall stock market is around 18x earnings, the market is close to a historical norm. When the overall price-earnings ratio shoots to 50x earnings, then the market may be in for a correction. A top-down approach would look at the PE multiple for the overall market, then the PE multiple for an industry, and finally the PE multiple for individual companies within an industry. Overvalued or undervalued stocks may be identifiable by using good fundamentals.

Market-to-Book Value. Book value is the difference between assets and liabilities; it is commonly referred to as owner's equity. The basis for using a market-to-book approach is a comparison of the market price per share to the book value per share. This is another multiplier approach similar to the price-earnings ratio. If assets are not properly reported, investors can be deceived. Creditors can also be led astray because the equity may not be there as a cushion for them to rely upon.

Market-to-EBITDA. Using a multiple of earnings before interest, taxes, depreciation and amortization is a focus on excluding unusual items found in the income statement from the multiple used in the PE valuation. This approach is also subject to manipulation. However, when a division is spun off or a company buys another company, the market-to-EBITDA is commonly used.

Market-to-Sales. Using a multiple of sales is often deemed to be crude because expenses are not part of the analysis process. Yet in industries where there are no profits, a security analyst stretches to find some way to value stock. If revenue is not being properly recognized, the technique could be very misleading.

Dividend Models. The most popular dividend model assumes a constant growth rate in future dividends; it is sometimes called the Gordon Growth Model or dividend discount model (DDM). By projecting future dividends and then discounting dividends at the investor's required rate of return less the growth rate in future dividends, an implied price can be obtained. There are several dividend models, and each is based upon a different growth rate in future dividends. If management is not honest about reporting profits, the results using the model will be off target.

Cash Flow Models. The model used to illustrate LBO cash flow analysis in the previous section of this chapter can also be used to value common stock. The models rely upon accurate accounting information.

Unique Visitors to Websites. During the 1990s, e-commerce companies were being valued based upon the number of unique visitors to their websites. There were reports of fraudulent information concerning visitors to websites as management tried to pump up the price of certain stocks. The blow-up in e-commerce stocks has discredited this approach.

Each of the stock valuation models has a focus upon return, timing and risk. At least in theory, if the inputs were accurate, the models would all lead to the same implied stock valuation. The models suggest what the stock is worth intrinsically—not what the stock is actually selling for in the marketplace. For example, if the implied stock price is $20 and the actual market price is only $15, the stock would be perceived as a good buy.

Stock valuation techniques are subject to considerable manipulation. Keep in mind that the market price is the collective evaluation of the stock price by all market participants. Confidence in management and accounting data is central to each approach using fundamentals. Remember that accounting gimmicks can be used to manipulate the stock price and also deceive creditors.

Market expectations may tempt managers to manipulate data to mask problems. Credit managers should be aware of the pitfalls and then not be bashful about questioning the numbers. The skills employed in stock valuation can be beneficial because they demonstrate the focal points used in the investment community. These focal points should be examined closely when considering where to look for accounting gimmicks.

The Residential Real Estate Marketplace. Good fundamentals can also be applied to the real estate marketplace. For example, a 20% downpayment, which had been a longstanding tradition, protects the creditor. The borrower is less likely to go underwater if property values fall. When the borrower is underwater, the loan balance exceeds market value; the borrower may just walk away from the obligation.

Specific traditional focal points for the real estate borrower had been used in the residential real estate marketplace. For example, cash flow-driven affordability ratios were used to gauge whether or not someone could afford a home. Affordability for a home loan might suggest that the home loan payment of principal, interest and taxes should not exceed either 25% to 30% of the borrower's gross income or 33% to 38% of the total installment debt including the real estate mortgage.

During the buildup to the sub-prime real estate market blowout, *NINJA loans* became popular. A NINJA loan simply suggests that the borrower has *no income, no job and no assets*. Loans had been set up with a negative amortization schedule, which meant that the loan balance owing would increase over time. Moreover, short-term teaser interest rates were used that had resets leading toward a much higher and likely unaffordable payment. Cash flow was too often ignored. Traditional fundamental lending focal points had been tossed to the wayside. The easy money for loans had to dry up at some point. When the real estate market spiraled downward, many lenders were left holding the losses because they had aggressively deviated from good fundamentals.

There are very important lessons to be learned from the tech bubble of the late 1990s, the accounting scandals from the early part of the first decade of the 21st century and the real estate bubble later in the decade. Markets are interdependent. Credit managers need to pay attention to good fundamentals. When any market deviates from traditional fundamental valuations, there will often be a harsh correction.

CASH FLOW-BASED CREDIT TOOLS

Academia has developed a number of financial analysis tools that are based upon cash flow analysis. The final section of this chapter will delve into two models that rely upon cash flow analysis. First, Emery's Lambda Index will be used to examine liquidity. Next, Altman's Z-score will be presented as a measure of financial solvency. Both tools have particular relevance to credit management applications.

Emery's Lambda Index

The Lambda Index was developed by Gary Emery, a professor of finance at the University of Oklahoma. The index is useful as a measure of a firm's liquidity. The value of the Lambda Index is that it incorporates cash flow uncertainty into consideration. Traditional measures of liquidity, such as the current ratio and the quick ratio, fail to consider the uncertainty of cash flow.

All of the information used to calculate Emery's Lambda can be culled from financial statements. Variations on Emery's formula exist; however, the focus here is limited to Emery's formula. There are three factors that are used in the equation, which is shown below:

$$\text{Lambda} = \frac{\text{Initial liquid reserve} + \begin{array}{c} \text{Total anticipated net cash flow} \\ \text{during the analysis horizon} \end{array}}{\text{Uncertainty about net cash flow during the analysis horizon}}$$

The first term is the *initial liquid reserve*. Cash, marketable securities and any unused bank lines are included in this term. The unused bank lines can be found in the footnotes to the financial statement. These are funds that can be quickly converted into cash.

The second term in the numerator represents an arithmetic average of the *cash flow from operations* during the prior four years. This number is found in the statement of cash flows; it is the cash flow generated from operating activities. The number is positive if the average during the past four years has been positive; however, if the average has been negative, it is subtracted from the first term.

The third term, which is in the denominator, represents the standard deviation of the cash flow from operations during the past four-year period. The standard deviation is calculated by using the cash flow from operations during the prior four-year period. In finance, the *standard deviation* is used to measure total risk using the variability of returns. The higher the standard deviation, the greater the risk.

Standard deviation is a bit tricky to calculate, so an example will be used. Many financial calculators are programmed to perform the standard deviation calculation. The data in Table 10-6 show the calculation of the standard deviation for the cash flow from operations for the Jones Co., which is $40,311. This number will be used in the denominator of Emery's Lambda Index.

Emery's Lambda Index for a hypothetical company called Jones Co. will be demonstrated. Assume that the cash plus marketable securities plus bank line availability total $17,000. This is the first term in the index calculation. The second term is the average cash flow from operations or $425,000, which is found in Table 10-6 (Step A). The

10: Cash Flow Analysis and Valuation Essentials 247

TABLE 10-6 Illustration of the Standard Deviation Calculation Operating Cash Flows for the Jones Co.

An illustration of the calculation for the standard deviation of cash flow from operations for the Jones Co.:

Year	Cash Flow from Operations
2015	$450,000
2016	370,000
2017	420,000
2018	460,000

Step A. Calculate the average, which is also called the mean:

(450,000 + 370,000 + 420,000 + 460,000) divided by 4 = $425,000

Step B. Calculate the deviation from the mean.

450,000 – 425,000 = 25,000
370,000 – 425,000 = -55,000
420,000 – 425,000 = -5,000
460,000 – 425,000 = 35,000

Step C. Square the deviations from the mean calculated in Step B.

25,000 × 25,000 = 625,000,000
-55,000 × -55,000 = 3,025,000,000
-5,000 × -5,000 = 25,000
35,000 × 35,000 = 1,225,000,000

Step D. Sum the squares calculated in Step C.

625,000,000 + 3,025,000,000 + 25,000 + 1,225,000,000 = 4,875,025,000

Step E. Divide by n – 1: there are four years used, so 4 – 1 = 3

4,875,025,000 divided by 3 = 1,625,008,333
(This number is called the variance by statisticians.)

Step F. Calculate the standard deviation. Simply take the square root of the variance in Step E

Square Root of 1,625,008,333 = **$40,311 = Standard Deviation**

---

denominator is the standard deviation of the cash flows from operations, which is $40,311 and also found in Table 10-6 (Step F).

$$\textbf{Lambda Index for Jones Co.} = \frac{17,000 + 425,000}{40,311} = 11$$

The Lambda Index for the Jones Co. suggests that the company has liquid resources that are equal to 11 times its typical operating cash flow needs. The higher the index, the more likely a company will have the available liquidity to meet the needs of creditors. The denominator is a key driver in the index. If the uncertainty of cash flow from operations is high, the index drops and a danger signal should be recognized. Also, if a company experiences a severe drain on cash flow from operations due to poor accounts receivable collection and an inability to turn inventory, the index will drop quickly.

Lambda can become a useful gauge for credit managers. The index is an excellent way to measure liquidity for new account analysis and for monitoring existing customers.

Altman's Z-score

Altman's Z-score was developed by Edward I. Altman, a professor of finance at New York University. The model was developed in 1968 to measure financial distress and predict bankruptcy. There are several other bankruptcy prediction models in existence, but the Altman Z-score seems to have stood well over the test of time. The Altman Z-score seems to be the model that most other models are compared to when evaluating bankruptcy prediction models.

The early efforts to predict bankruptcy were based upon univariate models. Such models used one variable, such as a financial ratio, to predict a bankruptcy. The results would be compared against an industry. Needless to say, several variables can have an interactive effect, which was not taken into consideration with a univariate model. Balance sheet decomposition models then became a focus. These models would focus upon the changing mix of assets such as long term or short term and the corresponding mix of short-term debt, long-term debt and equity.

Altman designed a multivariate model that was based upon the use of multiple discriminant analysis. Altman's model was designed so that several key variables would be examined simultaneously. The model has its limitations. For example, industry variables are not the same, so the model should be modified to fit a particular industry; many companies are diversified, which makes it difficult to categorize them into any one industry; and the Z-score might be more useful in predicting distress than it is for predicting bankruptcy.

There is considerable experimentation being done with the use of neural network topology models to predict bankruptcy. A neural network

10: Cash Flow Analysis and Valuation Essentials

integrates computer-based techniques that draw behavior patterns from simulations. Neural network models are potentially useful for credit scoring, the prediction of financial distress, the prediction of slow payments and the prediction of bankruptcy.

Altman's Z-score is designed to be compared against the data from a particular company. The multivariate model uses five variables. The Altman's Z-score function uses the following equation:

$$Z = .012X1 + .014X2 + .033X3 + .006X4 + .999X5$$

The numbers that appear before each X represent a weight assigned to the variable. Each X is numbered consecutively with the number that appears after the X. The first four variables are expressed as percentages; the final variable is a decimal. The five X variables are explained below:

X1 = Net working capital divided by total assets.

X2 = Retained earnings divided by total assets.

X3 = Earnings before interest and taxes divided by total assets.

X4 = Market value of the common and preferred stock divided by book value of debt.

X5 = Sales divided by total assets.

An application for the Altman Z-score will be made. The data in Table 10-7 are for the Arrow Company. The numbers used for the necessary financial data would be culled from the company's financial statements.

Table 10-7 shows the Altman Z-score calculation for the Arrow company. A Z-score above 2.99 is favorable. Since the Arrow Company has a Z-score of 3.0066, it is not a candidate for bankruptcy. A score

---

TABLE 10-7	Altman's Z-score Illustration The Arrow Company	
X1 = $500 ÷ $5,000 = 10%	10.0 × .012 =	.12
X2 = $750 ÷ $5,000 = 15%	15.0 × .014 =	.21
X3 = $800 ÷ $5,000 = 16%	16.0 × .033 =	.528
X4 = $2,500 ÷ $2,000 = 125%	125.0 × .006 =	.75
X5 = $7,000 ÷ $5,000 = 1.4%	1.4 × .999 =	<u>1.3986</u>
		Z-score = 3.0066

below 1.81 is a likely bankruptcy candidate. Altman refers to a Z-score between 1.81 and 2.99 as falling into the zone of ignorance, which means that the bankruptcy prediction is not as definite.

The Altman Z-score is an example of a financial tool derived through in-depth statistical analysis. The potential to use various tools to analyze financial data can be of significant benefit. There are computer software packages that furnish a detailed analysis that include both a Lambda Index and a Z-score. However, financial data are not substitutes for good judgment. Credit managers should continue to place a high priority on staying in touch with changes as they are occurring.

CHAPTER 10: FOLLOW-UP

Recap of Important Concepts

1. Cash flow analysis is an essential skill for credit analysis. The tools useful to complete a thorough cash flow analysis draw heavily from the accounting and finance functional areas of business.
2. Cash flow has several definitions. Moreover, there are numerous ways to perform a cash flow analysis. This chapter has provided several definitions of cash flow and numerous tools that can be used to perform a cash flow analysis.
3. When performing a cash flow analysis of a balance sheet, the two key focal points should be: (a) the sources and uses of funds concept and (b) the cash conversion cycle.
4. The statement of cash flows contains three sections that are divided by type of activity: operating, investing and financing. Credit analysis of this statement involves breaking down activities to focus upon the pertinent changes that have occurred.
5. Discounted cash flow models are often used to analyze projected income statements in order to establish a value for a firm. Sensitivity analysis and scenario analysis are performed on key variables in order to identify the risk associated with the valuation. Valuing an LBO, an IPO, a division spinoff or merger is not an exact science. An error in the valuation can lead to serious financial consequences.
6. There are a number of focal points for credit analysts to use to distinguish a sound LBO from a likely LBO disaster. The qualitative analysis needs to be combined with cash flow analysis on an ongoing basis. The financial position of an LBO can change quickly.
7. The valuation of common stock can be a concern because corporate managers may be compromised in attempts to push up stock values so that they can cash in on options. Credit managers should have a foundation in stock valuation to gain insights into potential pitfalls in accounting information.
8. Emery's Lambda Index provides a unique measure of customer liquidity. The index is based upon the riskiness of cash flows.
9. Altman's Z-score is a multivariate model that can be used to forecast financial distress. While there are other bankruptcy prediction models, the Altman Z-score has stood up well to the test of time.

Review/Discussion Questions

1. Distinguish between the following terms: "cash flow" and "free cash flow." Which cash flow measure is more important to credit analysis? Why?
2. How are balance sheet accounts categorized as a source or use?
3. The Walker Company has an average accounts payable of 60 days. The company holds inventory for an average of 75 days while the average accounts receivable collection period is 45 days. What is the Cash Conversion Cycle for the Walker Company?
4. Does the statement of cash flows always follow the same format? If so, explain the format. If not, how can the format vary?
5. Explain how each of the following terms is important to pro forma analysis of an income statement when valuing an LBO:
   a. Projected Post LBO Income Statements
   b. Free Cash Flow
   c. Terminal Value
   d. Discounting the Net Cash Flows
   e. Sensitivity Analysis
6. Provide an overview of the funding layers that are often tiered in an LBO. Try to identify the type of risk taken by each layer that provides funds in an LBO.
7. How does Emery's Lambda Index differ from other traditional measures of liquidity?
8. Examine the five variables that the Altman Z-score uses to predict bankruptcy. Identify an industry where the variables used would not be appropriate.
9. Common stock is valued using several different techniques. How can financial information used to value stock be misused by corporate executives who are paid through incentive based stock options?
10. Does the blowout in the residential real estate market bear any similarity to the market correction that occurred in the Internet marketplace during the late 1990s? If so, how? If not, why not?

Test Your Knowledge

1. What is an LBO?
2. What is the purpose of the statement of cash flows?
3. Identify each of the three sections in the statement of cash flows. What should a credit manager look for when analyzing this statement?

10: Cash Flow Analysis and Valuation Essentials

253

4. The consolidated balance sheet for Thomas Roofing Co. at the beginning and end of 2016 is shown below. Identify the changes as a source or a use in the appropriate column.

	Jan. 1	Dec. 31	Source	Use
Cash	3	4	___	___
Accounts Receivable	40	37	___	___
Inventory	35	39	___	___
Total Current Assets	78	80	___	___
Gross Fixed Assets	46	50	___	___
Accumulated Depreciation	9	11	___	___
Total Assets	115	119	___	___
Accounts Payable	46	41	___	___
Notes Payable	30	29	___	___
Total Current Liabilities	76	70	___	___
Bonds	10	10	___	___
Common Stock	12	15	___	___
Retained Earnings	17	24	___	___
Total Liabilities & Equity	$115	$119	___	___

5. What factors can be used to distinguish a sound LBO from a weak LBO? Be complete and be specific in your response.

6. Calculate the Lambda Index for the Stevens Company based upon the following information:

   Cash flow for operating activities: 2015 = $200,000
      2016 = $210,000
      2017 = $170,000
      2018 = $175,000

   Cash plus marketable securities plus bank line availability are equal to $40,000.

7. The Altman Z-score has been around for several years. What are the strengths and weaknesses of using a bankruptcy prediction model such as the Altman Z-score?

8. Accounting information is particularly important to the investment community. Zero in on at least two valuation techniques used by a fundamental stock analyst that could be influenced by management pressures to keep the stock price at a high level. In other words, if numbers are fudged, which numbers would be likely to benefit top-level managers who are willing to compromise on accounting rules? How did this situation occur at Enron, Global Crossing and WorldCom?

Credit Management Online

www.businessweek.com/—The *Bloomberg Businessweek* website provides fresh news concerning hot business topics on a weekly basis. Practical concerns for at least one accounting-related issue appear in almost every issue. There are several links to current business subjects.

ww2.cfo.com/cash-management/2015/06/barely-working-capital/—*CFO* is a periodical aimed at corporate treasurers. This link will take you to their annual working capital study. To view the results that show the cash conversion cycle both by company and by industry simply click on the link to "complete results." This is excellent research that is available on an annual basis.

www.forbes.com/—*Forbes* does a nice job of stirring up contemporary business issues. There are numerous links to related business topics.

www.fortune.com/—Several different *Fortune* directories provide a fresh look at a wide range of companies. There also are several useful links to business topics.

www.icpas.org/—Hosted by the Illinois CPA Society, this site tackles tough accounting issues. There are links to career services, accounting education and accounting legislation.

www.nasdaq.com/—Information concerning NASDAQ stocks can be obtained on this website. There are also links to global markets, investor tools and personal finance.

www.nyse.com/—Hosted by the New York Stock Exchange, this website provides free, dowloadable information for listed companies. There are links to regulation, the trading floor and the pressroom.

www.valueline.com/—Value Line supports an excellent website for investors. Its company and industry reports include a long-term track record and a short-term forecast. Click on "education" to gain useful knowledge about stock valuation analysis.

References Useful for Further Reading

Alfaro, Esteban, et al. "Bankruptcy Forecasting: An Empirical Comparison of AdaBoost and Neural Networks." *Decision Support Systems* (April 2008): 110-122.

Altman, Edward I., and Edith Hotchkiss. *Corporate Financial Distress and Bankruptcy.* Hoboken, NJ: Wiley, 2006.

Altman, Edward I. "A Further Empirical Investigation of the Bankruptcy Cost Question." *Journal of Finance* (September 1984): 1067-1089.

Al-Sulaiti, Khalid I., and Omar Almwajeh. "Applying Altman Z-score Model of Bankruptcy on Service Organizations and Its Implications on Marketing Concepts and Strategies." *Journal of International Marketing & Marketing Research* (June 2007): 59-74.

Barron, Jacob, and Tom Diana. "NACM Tackles Issues Before Congress During Advocacy Day 2007." *Business Credit* (May 2007): 28-30.

Board of Governors of the Federal Reserve Board. *Federal Reserve System Monthly Report on Credit and Liquidity Programs and the Balance Sheet.* (August 2009): 1-24.

Brigham, Eugene F., and Joel F. Houston. *Fundamentals of Financial Management.* 12th Ed. npi: South-Western/Cengage Learning, 2009.

Calandro Jr., Joseph. "Considering the Utility of Altman's Z-score As a Strategic Assessment and Performance Management Tool." *Strategy & Leadership* (September 2007): 37-43.

Carr, Matthew. "Briefcase Full of Blues." *Business Credit* (November/December 2008): 26-29.

Emory, Gary, and Ronald G. Lyons. "The Lambda Index: Beyond the Current Ratio." *Business Credit* (November/December 1991): 22-23.

Fisher, Daniel. "Cash Doesn't Lie." *Forbes* (April 12, 2010): 52-55.

Graham, Benjamin, and David L. Dodd. *Security Analysis.* 4th Ed. New York: McGraw-Hill, 1962.

Graham, Benjamin, and Warren E. Buffet. *The Intelligent Investor.* 4th Ed. New York: Harper Business, 1973.

Griffin, Paul A., David H. Lont, and Yuan Sun. "Agency Problems and Audit Fees: Further Tests of the Free Cash Flow Hypothesis." *Accounting & Finance* (June 2010): 321-350.

Katz, David K. "Free Cash Flow: At the Brink?" *CFO* (June 21, 2010): www.cfo.com/printable/article.cfm/14506018.

Katz, David K. "Working It Out." *CFO* (June 1, 2010): www.cfo.com/printable/article.cfm/14499542.

Leone, Marie. "Study Predicts 50% Cut in Free Cash Flow." *CFO* (March 27, 2009): www.cfo.com/printable/article.cfm/13396210.

McCafferty, Joseph. "Going with the (Free-cash) Flow." *CFO* (September 10, 2004): www.cfo.com/printable/article.cfm/3147058.

Mills, John, Lynn Bible, and Richard Mason. "Defining Free Cash Flow." *CPA Journal* (January 2002): 36-41.

Mota, Diana. "Nontraditional Analysis Tools Can Help Eliminate a Metrics 'False Positive'." *Business Credit* (September/October 2016): 38-39.

Ohlson, James A., and Jagadison K. Aier. "On the Analysis of Firms' Cash Flows." *Contemporary Accounting Research* (Winter 2009): 1091-1114.

Ozbayrak, M., and M. Akgün. "The Effects of Manufacturing Control Strategies on the Cash Conversion Cycle in Manufacturing Systems." *International Journal of Production Economics* (October 2006): 535-550.

Rosplock, Michael F. "Advanced Analytical Techniques for Performing Forensic Financial Analysis." *Business Credit* (June 2001): 26-31.

Rosplock, Michael F. "Forensic Financial Tools." *Business Credit* (April 2000): 48-51.

"S&P to Give Preliminary Ratings to LBO and High Yield Deals." *Euroweek* (May 14, 2010): 43.

Sheahan, Matthew. "Common Stock Becoming Familiar in HY Deals." *Bank Loan Report* (May 3, 2010): 1-5.

Smith, Shelley. "Z-Score Creator Says Junk Rally 'Too Furious,' Likes Distressed Debt." *Bloomberg Businessweek* (May 4, 2010): Businessweek.com.

Stuart, Alix. "Bankruptcy's Buoyant Crystal Ball." *CFO* (October 22, 2008): www.cfo.com/printable/article.cfm/12459738.

Swanson, Christopher J., and Shayne C. Kavanagh. "Identifying Shortfalls: The Importance of Cash Flow Analysis in Times of Fiscal Stress." *Government Finance Review* (April 2009): 34-38.

Truitt, Phyllis. "Limiting and Monitoring Risk without Decreasing Sales in Economic Downturns." *Business Credit* (February 2009): 18-19.

Trunzo, Giuseppe, CICP. "The Credit Management Revolution." *Business Credit* (June 2017): 14-15.

Tsang, Michael, and Hwang Inyoung. "Beware of Buyout Firms Bearing IPOs." *Bloomberg Businessweek* (May 24, 2010): 41-42.

"What Venture Capitalists Need to Know About Interpreting and Analyzing Cash Flow Statements of Their Portfolio Companies." *ProQuest Newsstand Business Wire* (June 24, 2010): Document ID 2065572861.

Wimley, C.J. "How Companies Are Improving Cash Flow and Reducing Costs with Credit and Collections Automation." *Business Credit* (October 2008): 66-69.

Part IV
Secured Credit
and Bankruptcy

Chapter 11

SECURED CREDIT ARRANGEMENTS AND LETTERS OF CREDIT

"When are unconfirmed letters of credit appropriate? What is forfaiting? What are the risks of taking bank guarantees? These are all tools, and no single one is appropriate for every situation. What you need is a complete toolkit and an instruction manual that helps you identify when and how to use the hammer, the screwdriver or the power drill."[1]

Walter (Buddy) Baker
Vice President/Manager, Trade Services Sales, Fifth Third Bank

Integrating secured credit arrangements into a credit manager's toolkit provides legal challenges. Additionally, identifying the requirements that meet the legal mandates of secured credit can become complex. A credit manager should be able to establish criteria to select the most appropriate outside support when using secured credit arrangements and letters of credit. This chapter will provide a foundation to use when secured credit arrangements become the appropriate mechanism to mitigate risk.

A *secured credit arrangement* is one in which a debtor provides collateral to a creditor. There are psychological and financial incentives for credit managers to seek to secure specific accounts. Psychologically, a debtor is more inclined to service an obligation with a secured creditor. Financial incentives are centered upon the ability to generate proceeds from the disposal of assets used as collateral.

The role of the credit manager in utilizing technical skills is contributing to an improved status for the profession. A credit manager can contribute to corporate profitability by recognizing an opportunity to increase sales at an acceptable risk level. The technical skills used to properly secure an account demonstrate the potential for a credit manager to enhance profitability.

---

[1] Walter (Buddy) Baker, "Confirmed Irrevocable Letters of Credit Are Not Always the Answer," *Business Credit* (March 2008): 64.

The **Key Learning Objectives** contained in Chapter 11 are:

1. Identify the types of situations in which credit managers should consider taking a security interest position.
2. Focus on the usefulness of several modes of reducing risk through the use of various credit arrangements.
3. Understand an overview of the Uniform Commercial Code (UCC), the law that governs business transactions in the United States.
4. Analyze the pitfalls in perfecting liens under Article 9 of the UCC.
5. Examine ways in which credit managers can use letters of credit effectively.

In this chapter, the focus is being placed on providing the technical skills essential to work with various sophisticated types of credit arrangements. When secured credit arrangements are properly utilized, creditors reduce risk and contribute to profitability. These arrangements can become complicated by a bankruptcy; the specific concerns of creditors during a bankruptcy will become a focal point in Chapter 12 of this book.

SITUATIONS IN WHICH TO CONSIDER THE USE OF SECURED FINANCING

A typical business creditor who sells on open account terms is relying specifically upon the full faith and credit of a purchaser. In the event of nonpayment per terms, the creditor then follows legal procedures to obtain payment. There are not any specific assets that support the unsecured creditor's claim.

Trade creditors are often asked to extend credit into high-risk situations. By obtaining some form of security or mechanism to reduce risk, a creditor can reduce the likelihood of not being repaid. In the event of nonpayment, a creditor can exercise certain legal rights available to repossess property in order to satisfy a debt.

Examples of situations where a secured credit arrangement may become useful include:

- *Conversion of an Open Account.* A slow-paying unsecured account receivable can be converted to a secured interest-bearing note receivable.
- *Marginal Accounts.* A start-up business or an undercapitalized business may be too risky to extend credit to without some type of security.

- *A Large One-Shot Deal.* An opportunity to sell an account that cannot justify a high credit exposure can become a situation where security can be used to reduce risk.
- *A Key Account.* A customer who represents a high percentage of total receivables exposure on an ongoing basis may be an ideal candidate to consider for security arrangements.
- *An Export Sale.* International transactions can often entail special types of risk that can be reduced through the use of a letter of credit.
- *A Long-Term Credit Arrangement.* When a debtor finances a long-term asset, the asset being financed is often secured.

The business credit grantor who obtains security on an occasional basis needs to be able to identify specific situations when security can be useful. There are certain creditors who will use security for most of their customers. For example, an automobile manufacturer who floor-plans inventory for car dealers may secure all open accounts through a floor-plan inventory financing arrangement. On the other hand, a distributor of metal alloys may only occasionally secure an account. In either case, precise procedures should be established so that the creditor is in a strong legal position in the event of a default by the debtor.

The internal controls that are formulated depend upon the nature of the security. In order to properly use security, a credit analyst should have a complete understanding of the various types of security available. The rest of this chapter will provide a foundation of the pertinent laws and then identify specific opportunities that are available to secure an account.

MODES TO CREATIVELY REDUCE RISK

The one common attribute for any type of security is that it should be of value to the creditor in the event of default. As a general rule, if a business transaction does not make sense without the security, the creditor needs to use extreme control when relying upon security. The cardinal rule for securing a transaction is to recognize the probable quick-sale value of collateral and then limit exposure accordingly.

One way of classifying security is to group the collateral by type of agreement. For example, assets could be grouped as real property or personal property. Guarantees could be grouped as personal or corporate. Each classification of security requires specific concerns for the credit analyst to consider. Six commonly used modes of protection for creditors are: real property, personal property, guarantees, letters of credit, mechanic's liens and trade acceptances.

1. ***Real Property.*** Real property consists of land, buildings and anything deemed attached to the land or building. If a creditor accepts real property as security, a public filing is made in the county office. Creditors usually require a title search and can obtain title insurance to protect the creditor against claims not found in a title search.

   Creditors who use real property for collateral should consider obtaining an appraisal to estimate the value of the collateral. Sometimes creditors who believe that they have personal property as collateral can find out that the property is deemed to be real property. If in doubt concerning the status of property, a creditor who relies on personal property should obtain a Landlord Waiver or a Mortgagee Waiver to protect the creditor against claims on assets by a landlord or mortgage lender.

2. ***Personal Property.*** Personal property refers to movable assets. All property that is not classified as real property is deemed to be personal property. Personal property can be divided into two categories of goods: (a) those goods kept in the possession of the creditor and (b) those goods that are in the possession of the debtor.

   A. *A Pledge.* When a debtor places personal property in the possession of a creditor, a pledge occurs. Stocks and bonds can be pledged as collateral. Other assets that are sometimes pledged include the cash surrender value of insurance, a certificate of deposit or a savings account.

   The creditor should obtain a separate pledge agreement. This agreement authorizes a creditor to sell items pledged in the event of nonpayment. The creditor should take physical possession of items pledged. For example, there have been instances when a debtor has pledged the same shares of stock to many different creditors; needless to say, the collateral could not support the debt from the various creditors who relied upon the collateral. Grabill Industries of Oak Forest, IL was affected by such an incident. It's owner, William Stoecker, engineered the largest bank fraud con in Illinois history.

   Finally, creditors who rely upon the cash value of an insurance policy should consider notifying an insurance company or bank to block any potential withdrawal of funds by the debtor until the credit commitment is fulfilled.

B. ***Collateral Held by the Debtor.*** Typical assets held by the debtor include accounts receivable, inventory, machinery and equipment. A creditor can perfect a security interest by following the requirements of Article 9 of the UCC. This type of arrangement is commonly used by suppliers.

Since the topic is somewhat complex, a separate major section of this chapter will be used to develop the subject of perfecting liens under the UCC.

3. ***Guarantees.*** In general, a business transaction should not hinge solely upon obtaining a guarantee. However, a guarantee does represent a commitment from a third party that can strengthen the position of a creditor. Guarantees may be set up in either of two ways: (1) a *Guarantee of Payment*, which allows the creditor to present an obligation to the guarantor immediately upon default by the debtor; or (2) a *Guarantee of Collection*, which requires the creditor to first attempt to collect from a debtor, and if unsuccessful, the creditor may seek payment from the guarantor.

A. A ***personal guarantee*** should be signed by the obligor as an individual, not as someone acting in the capacity of an officer of a company. By using a personal guarantee, a creditor can pierce a corporate shield to hold the guarantor responsible for the debt.

- The guarantor should provide a signed personal financial statement.
- The credit manager should be careful because personal assets are often inflated on the financial statement.
- The creditor can gain a psychological advantage from a guarantor by using a personal guarantee.
- Credit managers have suggested that the envelope in which a personal financial statement is mailed should be saved along with the guarantee; if the financial statement is bogus, then there may be a potential for mail fraud.

Exhibit 11-1 provides an example of an Individual Personal Guarantee form. The executed guarantee should be maintained for safekeeping. There are creditors who have collected on guarantees years after writing off indebtedness to bad debts.

B. ***Corporate guarantees*** can be difficult to enforce. When a guarantee is obtained from a corporate entity, creditors should consider obtaining a *board of directors' resolution* that authorizes

EXHIBIT 11-1   Personal Guarantee Form

Date _____ 20 __

I, _____, residing at _____,
for and in consideration of your extending credit at my request to _(Name of
Company)_ (hereinafter referred to as the "Company"), of which I am _____,
hereby personally guarantee to you the payment at _____ in the
State of _____ of any obligation of the Company. I hereby agree to bind
myself to pay you on demand any sum which may become due to you by the
Company whenever the Company shall fail to pay the same. It is understood that this
guarantee shall be a continuing and irrevocable guarantee and indemnity for such
indebtedness of the Company. I do hereby waive notice of default, nonpayment, and
notice thereof and consent to any modification or renewal of the credit agreement
hereby guaranteed.

Signature: _____

Witness: _____
Address: _____

the corporation to guarantee the obligation. When intercompany transactions are involved, a corporate guarantee can be useful. Also, when a subsidiary is not strong enough to justify open-account terms, a parent company could furnish a corporate guarantee. Selling a joint venture may also provide an opportunity to sell on open-account terms if there are other companies willing to guarantee the obligation of the joint venture.

4. ***Letters of Credit.*** A letter of credit is a negotiable instrument that is backed by a bank, in which the bank agrees to pay a vendor upon presentation and compliance with the terms and conditions specified in the letter of credit. The letter of credit essentially allows a creditor to substitute a debtor's creditworthiness for a bank's creditworthiness. When the documents specified in the letter of credit are accepted by the bank, a *banker's acceptance* is created. Due to the potential complications of working with letters of credit, the final major section of this chapter will expand the focus upon using letters of credit.

5. ***Mechanic's Liens.*** Mechanic's liens are commonly used in the construction industry. This type of lien is placed upon a building, improvements in realty and, in most jurisdictions, on land on which the building is situated. The purpose of a mechanic's lien is to ensure compensation for labor or material furnished for construction purposes. The lien is filed by a contractor, subcontractor or party

supplying labor or materials in the county where the property is located. State laws govern the details that pertain to mechanic's liens.

6. ***Trade Acceptances.*** A trade acceptance is a form of a time draft. When a creditor ships goods to a customer, the creditor draws a draft on the customer's bank that orders the customer to pay for the goods at a specified time. The creditor can endorse and then discount the draft or collect from the customer on the date that the draft matures. There are no liens filed. The customer accepts the responsibility to pay, and the draft is not subject to a customer stop payment or a customer claim of nonperformance. Trade acceptances have been popular in Europe for many years; they tend to be used only occasionally in the United States. Trade acceptances usually are not secured by any assets. They provide an alternative way in which to set up a payment arrangement.

Six commonly used modes of protection for creditors have been introduced: real property, personal property, guarantees, letters of credit, mechanic's liens and trade acceptances. Each of the six modes has its usefulness by reducing certain types of risk. Two of the most complex yet widely used ways to protect trade creditors will be developed more fully: perfecting liens under Article 9 of the UCC and utilizing letters of credit.

THE UNIFORM COMMERCIAL CODE

The legal system that governs business transactions in the United States has been built around state laws. Business laws had been patterned after the English common law legal system, but the state laws varied. The Uniform Commercial Code (UCC) was developed during the early 1950s and has been adopted by all 50 states in order to make state laws uniform in nature.

The UCC consists of the following nine articles:

- Article 1: General Provisions
- Article 2: Sales
- Article 2A: Leases
- Article 3: Negotiable Instruments
- Article 4: Bank Deposits and Collections
- Article 4A: Funds Transfers
- Article 5: Letters of Credit
- Article 6: Bulk Sales

- Article 7: Documents of Title
- Article 8: Investment Securities
- Article 9: Secured Transactions

The UCC is now more than 60 years old. There have been a number of revolutionary changes in business practices that could not have been envisioned when the UCC was first adopted. Computer technology and enhancements in communication have mandated change. The legal system has a mechanism to keep up with the changes.

There are two main legal groups that are involved in developing business law: the *American Law Institute (ALI)* and the *National Conference of Commissioners on Uniform State Laws (NCCUSL)*. Both ALI and NCCUSL have been involved in jointly sponsoring laws to unify business laws.

ALI was formed in 1923. It consists of a voluntary group of judges, lawyers and academics. ALI strives to address uncertainty in the legal system by updating laws so that the laws keep in touch with changes in business practices.

NCCUSL was formed in 1892. It consists of commissioners from each state who are appointed by their state legislature or governor. NCCUSL examines the laws in a state to determine if certain business practices might be worthwhile to develop uniformly across all states.

ALI and NCCUSL have collaborated in updating the UCC. Each state then ultimately decides whether or not to adopt the recommended changes. In 1995, both ALI and NCCUSL recommended changes to the Letters of Credit provisions in Article 5 of the UCC. The changes to Article 5 bring the UCC into conformity with the Uniform Customs and Practices for Documentary Credits, commonly referred to as UPC 500. The revisions to Article 5 of the UCC are generally consistent with UPC 500.

In 1998, both ALI and NCCUSL completed revisions to Article 9 of the UCC. By July 31, 2001, all 50 states had approved the revisions. These revisions are now in effect. Some of the key changes will be discussed in the next section.

Article 9 of the UCC

The purpose of the UCC is to allow the laws that govern business transactions to exist in a uniform manner in all states. The prior section showed how the UCC is divided into nine articles. Article 9 of the UCC pertains to secured transactions involving personal property. In general, personal property includes all property except real estate.

The changes effective under Article 9 of the Code are the first wholesale revisions in almost 30 years. The basic framework remains intact. However, Article 9 now has broader applications. For example, consignment sales now fall under this article. Article 9 now contains specific rules for consumer transactions. Deposit accounts are also included in Article 9.

Documentation deficiencies make Article 9 one of the most frequently litigated sections of the UCC. For the most part, credit managers have become adept at handling the intricacies of the UCC. An attorney could, however, be quite helpful in examining documentation and formalizing procedural concerns.

The two basic documents used to secure personal property are the Security Agreement and the UCC Financing Statement. There are also a number of other documents that can be useful to a credit manager in connection with the basic documents such as a lien search, a subordination agreement, a board of directors' resolution, or a landlord or mortgagee waiver agreement. The following is an overview of the two basic documents and a discussion of other aspects:

The Security Agreement. Under this agreement, the customer and debtor agree to certain specific points that govern the lien in the security. Factors such as the specific collateral and the nature of the debt obligation that the collateral secures are included in the security agreement.

The UCC Financing Statement. By properly perfecting a lien on property (properly filing required documents), the Financing Statement becomes a public record acknowledging that a lien exists.

Under changes in the UCC, the debtor no longer must sign the financing statement. The form has been standardized. A creditor may file a lien but needs the authorization of the debtor to be legally eligible to file the lien. The exact legal name of the debtor must be used. Trade names are not acceptable. To be effective, a lien search that is conducted using the proper name of the debtor should turn up the lien. If a search fails to show up the filing, the filing is not valid.

Another key change under the revised UCC is the location of the filing. For personal property, only one filing is necessary. Liens should be filed with the Secretary of State of the debtor's place of filing registration statements. For example, if a company has filed its corporate charter in the state of Delaware, the lien should be filed with the Secretary of State in Delaware. For a non-registered business, the filing should be made at the executive office if the business has more than one location. For individuals, the filing should be made in the state of the individual's principal residence.

The description of the collateral should be specific in the security agreement; however, the financing statement can include generic descriptions such as blanket liens. Banks sometimes file blanket liens that include all assets now owned or hereafter acquired. It is always preferable to include model numbers and serial numbers of equipment or other complete descriptions of collateral.

If there is any doubt concerning the potential of the security to become a fixture, most attorneys recommend another filing. The second filing should be made in the debtor's county office, or at the place where real estate liens are filed in the jurisdiction.

Exhibit 11-2 provides the standard UCC Financing Statement. The financing statement can be filed electronically in all jurisdictions. The document must be completed carefully with a particular focus on the exact legal name of the obligor and a careful description of the precise collateral. Since state laws for filing can vary, some creditors like to use a private company to record liens.

Documentation Concerns. Creditors should perform a lien search when dealing with secured transactions. The search is used to determine whether any other conflicting liens exist against the debtor. It is always a good idea to search through your own filing to make sure that the lien has been properly recorded.

In general, the first lien filed has a first claim on the collateral. A subordination must be obtained from any creditor that has a prior lien on an asset in order to assure first claim on any collateral. For example, a bank may have a blanket lien on all assets now owned or hereafter acquired for a company. A creditor can move into a first lien position only after obtaining a subordination from the bank on specific assets. Any leverage to obtain the subordination should be used prior to shipping goods. The bank has a vested interest in making certain the company receives new goods and continues operations, so it will be more apt to furnish a subordination. One exception to the first filing being in a first lien position is the case of a purchase money security interest, which will be discussed later.

A board of directors' resolution should be obtained when there is a question concerning the authority of the person signing the security agreement for the debtor. The board of directors' resolution specifically

EXHIBIT 11-2   UCC Financing Statement Form

UCC FINANCING STATEMENT
FOLLOW INSTRUCTIONS

A. NAME & PHONE OF CONTACT AT FILER (optional)

B. E-MAIL CONTACT AT FILER (optional)

C. SEND ACKNOWLEDGMENT TO: (Name and Address)

Print   **Reset**

THE ABOVE SPACE IS FOR FILING OFFICE USE ONLY

1. DEBTOR'S NAME: Provide only one Debtor name (1a or 1b) (use exact, full name; do not omit, modify, or abbreviate any part of the Debtor's name); if any part of the Individual Debtor's name will not fit in line 1b, leave all of item 1 blank; check here ☐ and provide the Individual Debtor information in item 10 of the Financing Statement Addendum (Form UCC1Ad)

1a. ORGANIZATION'S NAME				
OR 1b. INDIVIDUAL'S SURNAME	FIRST PERSONAL NAME		ADDITIONAL NAME(S)/INITIAL(S)	SUFFIX
1c. MAILING ADDRESS	CITY	STATE	POSTAL CODE	COUNTRY

2. DEBTOR'S NAME Provide only one Debtor name (2a or 2b) (use exact, full name; do not omit, modify, or abbreviate any part of the Debtor's name); if any part of the Individual Debtor's name will not fit in line 2b, leave all of item 2 blank; check here ☐ and provide the Individual Debtor information in item 10 of the Financing Statement Addendum (Form UCC1Ad)

2a. ORGANIZATION'S NAME				
OR 2b. INDIVIDUAL'S SURNAME	FIRST PERSONAL NAME		ADDITIONAL NAME(S)/INITIAL(S)	SUFFIX
2c. MAILING ADDRESS	CITY	STATE	POSTAL CODE	COUNTRY

3. SECURED PARTY'S NAME (or NAME of ASSIGNEE of ASSIGNOR SECURED PARTY) Provide only one Secured Party name (3a or 3b)

3a. ORGANIZATION'S NAME				
OR 3b. INDIVIDUAL'S SURNAME	FIRST PERSONAL NAME		ADDITIONAL NAME(S)/INITIAL(S)	SUFFIX
3c. MAILING ADDRESS	CITY	STATE	POSTAL CODE	COUNTRY

4. COLLATERAL: This financing statement covers the following collateral

5. Check only if applicable and check only one box: Collateral is ☐ held in a Trust (see UCC1Ad, item 17 and Instructions) ☐ being administered by a Decedent's Personal Representative

6a. Check only if applicable and check only one box
☐ Public-Finance Transaction   ☐ Manufactured-Home Transaction   ☐ A Debtor is a Transmitting Utility

6b. Check only if applicable and check only one box
☐ Agricultural Lien   ☐ Non-UCC Filing

7. ALTERNATIVE DESIGNATION (if applicable):   ☐ Lessee/Lessor   ☐ Consignee/Consignor   ☐ Seller/Buyer   ☐ Bailee/Bailor   ☐ Licensee/Licensor

8. OPTIONAL FILER REFERENCE DATA:

FILING OFFICE COPY — UCC FINANCING STATEMENT (Form UCC1) (Rev. 04/20/11)

International Association of Commercial Administrators (IACA) authorizes a particular individual to expressly enter into a secured financing arrangement. Otherwise, a debtor can to try to void a security arrangement because the signor was acting *ultra vires* (beyond the scope of legal authority).

A waiver from a landlord (if the debtor rents the premises) or a waiver from a mortgagee (if the debtor owns the premises through a mortgage) could be useful. This type of waiver protects the creditor in the event that the debtor fails to pay rent to the landlord or fails to make mortgage payments to the mortgagee. The waiver by the landlord or mortgagee prevents the landlord or mortgagee from holding a possible prior claim on the creditor's collateral.

When a debtor's name changes, an amended financing statement should be filed to ensure that the lien is properly filed. It is possible to lose a secured status in a bankruptcy proceeding if the filing is seriously misleading. Others parties could be seriously misled. Filing the amended UCC Financing Statement reflecting the name change protects the creditor's interest.

The documentation requirements can be summarized as technical and cumbersome. However, the payoff from a properly perfected lien readily demonstrates the credit manager's utilization of technical skills that can make a significant contribution to an employer.

Remedies for Creditors. In the event of a default, a secured creditor has a right to collateral. If a debtor voluntarily surrenders collateral, the secured creditor may use the proceeds of the collateral to offset debt. When a debtor does not peacefully surrender collateral, the creditor files a lawsuit, obtains a judgment and then gets a court order to obtain collateral.

The quick-sale value of collateral often does not coincide with the book value of the debt. In the event of a deficiency, creditors become unsecured creditors for the amount of the deficiency. On the other hand, any excess received from the sale of collateral belongs to the debtor.

As a general rule, the creditors who use Article 9 of the UCC rely on collateral based upon the estimated quick-sale value. The following guidelines may prove useful for a rough estimate of quick-sale value.

- *Accounts Receivable.* A credit manager should rely on only 70% to 80% of accounts receivable that are now aged as current.

- ***Inventory.*** Work in process is often not of any value as collateral. Raw materials and finished goods may justify relying on 50% of book value, depending upon the secondary market.
- ***Equipment.*** Delivery and installation of equipment are not of any value. About 80% of the book value may be a justifiable base for equipment. However, the secondary market for the specific type of equipment should be considered.
- ***Land and Building.*** As a general rule, 80% to 90% of appraised value is used. Location is critically important to the collateral value for real estate.

A few of the common problems that credit managers often associate with perfecting liens under Article 9 of the UCC include:

- Customers are often reluctant to agree to give collateral to a supplier. Negotiation skills are key to overcoming customer reluctance. Knowing when the creditor has leverage to gain the customer's cooperation is crucial to such negotiations. The credit manager needs to know the customer and be ready to demonstrate a willingness to achieve a mutually agreeable position regarding supply and security.
- Time requirements for filing the UCC form often preclude establishing a properly secured credit arrangement. In a liquidation, it must be remembered that the proceeds from a properly perfected lien are distributed in order of priority claimants. A lien should be perfected over a 90-day period or the lien may be construed to be a preference by a trustee in a bankruptcy liquidation.
- Reliance upon the proceeds generated by the collateral can leave the credit manager with a deficiency. Collateral is not a substitute for sound credit principles and decisions. Caution concerning possible quick-sale market value of collateral after a repossession should be emphasized. A field audit of collateral can help to determine the presence of worthy collateral.
- Under a lease transaction, it is highly recommended that the creditor file a UCC Financing Statement to perfect a lien in the leased equipment. A bank with a blanket lien on assets may claim the leased equipment as its collateral. A properly perfected lien can potentially protect the creditor's claim to the leased equipment.

The Case of the Purchase Money Security Interest (PMSI)

There is one particularly troublesome subject that relates to Article 9 and perfecting liens: the *purchase money security interest (PMSI)*. A PMSI is unique because of the "purchase money" aspect of the specific transaction. Two situations provide opportunities whereby a security interest becomes a purchase money security interest. In both situations, a creditor obtains a priority lien in newly acquired assets.

The first situation occurs when the seller of goods takes a security interest to secure all or part of the sale, using the goods being sold as collateral. For example, a manufacturer or wholesaler selling a product could reduce the credit risk for the vendor by taking a PMSI in the assets sold.

The second situation in which a PMSI can be created is when a third party provides funds to enable a debtor to acquire assets. For example, a bank or finance company could provide the funds for a debtor to purchase assets; these assets are used as collateral by the lending bank or finance company.

Both types of PMSI transactions entail the need for the lien holder to take precautions. Normally, the conflicting security interests rank in priority according to the time and date the filing is recorded. However, a properly perfected PMSI can have priority over a previously recorded lien. The essential aspect of PMSI transactions is the proper perfection of the security interest.

The credit manager should be concerned with classifying collateral into different categories of goods. For PMSI purposes, goods may be categorized as consumer goods, equipment or inventory. As remarkable as it may seem, the same item could fall into any of the three categories of goods depending upon the situation. For example, if a doctor bought a microwave oven for use at home, it would be classified as a consumer good. If used by the doctor in the office, the microwave oven would be classified as equipment. Finally, if held in inventory by an appliance dealer, the microwave oven would be classified as inventory.

In general, the revisions to Article 9 make it more difficult to attack a PMSI for competing claims. PMSI transactions require the filing of liens with the Secretary of State. Specific filing requirements are influenced by the classification of goods as consumer goods, equipment or inventory. In order to eliminate uncertainty, the security agreement should specify the manner in which the goods will be used.

Consumer Goods. A credit manager entering into a PMSI transaction in consumer goods is not required to file a financing statement. However, the credit manager's interest in the collateral would not be weakened if a lien is filed.

Equipment. A credit manager taking a PMSI in equipment must perfect a lien on the equipment before or within 10 days after the debtor receives possession of the equipment. By filing before or within 20 days of delivery, the PMSI creditor moves into a first lien position ahead of a previously filed blanket lien that may have covered all equipment. The PMSI lien holder must give new value that enables the debtor to acquire the equipment. Banks or finance companies may want to use a paid proceeds letter when disbursing the funds to an equipment vendor in order to clarify their PMSI position.

Inventory. A PMSI in inventory can be very complex. However, if a credit manager follows the requirements of the UCC and appropriate state laws, a PMSI creditor will receive priority over other blanket security interests in the same collateral.

A PMSI in inventory should be perfected before or at the time the debtor receives possession of the inventory. The PMSI creditor should give written notice via a certified letter to all other creditors who claim a security interest in the inventory of the debtor. The written notice given to the other creditors should state that the PMSI creditor has, or expects to acquire, a purchase money security interest in inventory of the debtor. The letter also should describe the inventory by items or type of product.

There are a few somewhat complex concerns that credit managers could occasionally encounter with PMSI transactions. These concerns include goods that are further processed, commingled funds, inventory proceeds accounts and the protection of the PMSI stature. These concerns are not often encountered but can become crucial in certain situations.

Article 9 of the UCC requires the use of considerable legal expertise. The law has been updated to meet the needs of the changing business community. There are Business Law courses available at most colleges to gain additional depth in this topic. Perhaps the best way to update skills is through NACM-sponsored online courses and NACM Affiliate-led classes, which provide useful opportunities to become proficient at properly perfecting liens.

LETTERS OF CREDIT

Letters of credit originated in Venice centuries ago as a mechanism for vendors to get paid more quickly. In a letter of credit transaction in contemporary times, a bank promises to pay the beneficiary (creditor) a specified sum upon presentation of the specific documentation. The letter of credit is simply a mode of payment. What is special about a letter of credit is that the credit risk is transferred from the purchaser of goods to the purchaser's bank.

Circumstances in which letters of credit are used can vary dramatically. Moreover, there are specific laws that govern letters of credit. Since more than half of the letters of credit issued have discrepancies, credit analysts need to carefully consider the complexities of working with letters of credit.

Standby Letters of Credit

A Standby Letter of Credit is useful when selling to a marginal domestic customer. This type of arrangement is basically a bank guarantee. In the event that a purchaser fails to honor a credit obligation, the creditor may look to the bank for payment. There has been a trend toward an increased use of Standby Letters of Credit and away from the use of documentary letters of credit.

Article 5 of the UCC applies to any letter of credit that is issued or confirmed in the United States. When Article 5 of the Uniform Commercial Code was revised in 1995, it was designed so that it was largely in compliance with UCP 500. Banks may elect to incorporate the use of the International Standby Practices, often referred to as ISP98, which went into effect on January 1, 1999, as the rules for letters of credit that pertain to international trade. Banks may elect to incorporate ISP98 or the Uniform Customs and Practice for Documentary Credits (UCP), which then become the operative rules pertaining to international letters of credit.

The International Chamber of Commerce (ICC) has established rules for documentary letters of credit, which are called the ***Uniform Customs and Practice for Documentary Credits (UCP)***. First published in 1933, the UCP has been revised in 1951, 1962, 1974, 1983, 1994 and 2007. UCP 600 is the sixth time ICC rules have been revised; this process seems to happen about every 10 years.

Exhibit 11-3 shows an example of a Standby Letter of Credit. In this example, the creditor is the beneficiary for an amount not to exceed $80,000. The invoices must be at least 30 days past due in order to draw on the bank for payment. If the customer pays for goods in a timely manner, the letter of credit is never drawn upon. The term "standby" suggests that the bank is standing by to pay in the event of a default.

11: Secured Credit Arrangements and Letters of Credit

275

EXHIBIT 11-3 Standby Letter of Credit

National Bank of Ohio
Columbus, OH

May 1, 20xx

The Ethical Creditor Co.
Chicago, IL

We hereby issue in your favor our Irrevocable Letter of Credit for an amount not to exceed $80,000.00 for the account of _____ and/or _____ available by your drafts drawn at sight on us and accompanied by the following documents: (1) commercial invoice, (2) copy of truck bill of lading and (3) your signed statement that the merchandise covered by the invoice has been shipped and a period of at least 30 days has elapsed since the date of the invoice.

This Irrevocable Letter of Credit will expire on December 1, 20xx, at our counters in Columbus, OH.

This credit is subject to the Uniform Customs and Practice for Documentary Credits, International Chamber of Commerce Publication Number 600, known as UCP 600.

We engage with you that drafts drawn under and in compliance with the terms of the credit will be duly honored upon presentation if presented on or before the expiring date of this credit.

BY _____
  President and Chief Executive Officer

Note that Exhibit 11-3 contains a paragraph concerning UCP 600. The UCP is written into most letters of credit in order to clarify the settlement of payments. The current rules are known as UCP 600, which went into effect on July 1, 2007. UCP 600 provides a set of rules used both for international and domestic transactions.

Export Letters of Credit

When the shipment of goods crosses national boundaries, export letters of credit are one method of settling payment. For many years, it was quite typical to fund exports through a letter of credit; as of 2015, about 41% of U.S. exports were funded through letters of credit.

A credit manager can reduce the risk of export payment problems by obtaining a letter of credit. If the creditor is not comfortable relying upon the credit risk of a foreign bank, the creditor may ask a domestic bank to confirm the letter of credit. By adding a confirmation to a letter of credit,

276 Credit Management: Principles and Practices

the creditor may look to the credit risk of the confirming bank for payment.

UCP 600 has updated the rules used for letters of credit. Standardized practices, used in various economies and cultures, provide for improved consistency under UCP 600. The export services departments of large U.S. banks often make available one-day seminars to help familiarize credit managers with UCP 600.

Under UCP 600, all letters of credit are deemed to be irrevocable unless a letter of credit specifically states that it is a revocable letter of credit. This is because the buyer holds the option to revoke or back out of a revocable letter of credit. UCP 600 does not eliminate revocable letters of credit; it simply means that creditors must watch for the term "revocable" and get it changed before accepting the letter of credit. UCP 600 also firms up the time period for a bank to examine documents. A bank now has five days to assert any document discrepancies rather than a "reasonable" time.

Problems Using Letters of Credit

For the creditor who only occasionally uses an export letter of credit, banks will facilitate letters of credit for a fee. Those creditors who work with letters of credit regularly face numerous types of problems. A few of the typical problems are briefly summarized:

- *Bogus Letters of Credit.* International fraud is not uncommon. When dealing with certain countries, payment arrangements are often difficult. Creditors who have an intuition concerning the validity of a letter of credit should ask their domestic bank to confirm the letter of credit.
- *Bank Fees.* Banks may charge a fee for opening, advising, confirming, amending, extending, accepting and discounting letters of credit. The fees are always negotiable between the buyer and seller. A seller in a strong position in terms of demand for product may request that the phrase "all fees for the account of opener" be added to the letter of credit.
- *Drafts.* Drafts represent an order to pay the creditor upon acceptance of the documentation in the letter of credit. A *sight draft* is payable when the drawee bank accepts the draft. A *time draft* is payable at a specified date after acceptance. Since funds can be tied up for a period of time, the terms specified in a time draft should be considered prior to entering the letter of credit transaction. When a

time draft is accepted by a bank, a banker's acceptance is created. Creditors often discount the banker's acceptance at their bank to gain immediate access to funds. The use of time drafts has been increasing; the mix is about 50% time drafts to 50% sight drafts.

- ***Documentation Deficiencies.*** Creditors should carefully inspect the terms and conditions in a letter of credit before accepting the letter of credit. An internal documentation checklist is often helpful in minimizing documentation problems, yet documentation problems occur often. In a majority of instances, the letter of credit documentation is not in complete compliance with the letter of credit. This means that document deficiencies often exist. Banks often look for reasons to avoid funding a letter of credit. Specific documentation deficiencies (discussed in Chapter 3 of this book) need to be anticipated. Creditors can request an amendment if the deficiency is detected early. However, UCP 600 is generally considered the operative set of rules to guide credit managers through a documentation deficiency when the UCP is included as governing language on the letter of credit.

There is certainly considerable risk borne through problems associated with the use of letters of credit. Yet letters of credit alleviate credit risk when they are used properly. The skills essential for credit managers to master letters of credit remain at the pinnacle of importance.

CONCLUSIONS

Secured credit arrangements can become one of the most complex topics in credit management. They afford an opportunity to employ skills that demand considerable legal expertise. They also require considerable time to document properly. Moreover, since laws are updated regularly, credit analysts need to keep in touch with changes on an ongoing basis. The benefits derived from reducing risk and contributing to profit are well worth the effort. The final chapter of this book will address bankruptcy issues. Bankruptcy can be closely related to the secured credit arrangements developed in this chapter.

CHAPTER 11: FOLLOW-UP

Recap of Important Concepts

1. A secured credit arrangement is one in which credit managers obtain collateral from a debtor. Several situations create opportunities for credit analysts to reduce risk by obtaining security.

2. Real property consists of land, buildings and anything deemed attached to the land or building. Real property is not often available as collateral to trade creditors; when it is available, there are unique concerns to be addressed.

3. A pledge is created when personal property is placed in the hands of a creditor. Stocks, bonds, certificates of deposit, savings accounts and the cash surrender value of life insurance are typical types of assets that are pledged.

4. Both personal and corporate guarantees can be used to protect a creditor's interest. Personal guarantees allow a creditor to pierce a corporate shield; they can also provide a psychological incentive. Corporate guarantees are useful when a number of intercompany transactions exist with a debtor and related companies.

5. Mechanic's liens are placed upon real property to make sure that a contractor or subcontractor is compensated for providing labor or material. These liens are commonly used in the construction industry.

6. Trade creditors can use a trade acceptance to potentially strengthen their position when selling marginal customers. The trade acceptance can be discounted at a bank. It is not subject to a customer claim for nonperformance.

7. Article 9 of the UCC is used to perfect liens on personal property held by a debtor. There have been a number of changes made to Article 9 to bring it up to date with current business practices. Accounts receivable, inventory, machinery and equipment are assets that are often used as collateral.

8. Normally the first filing of a lien prevails in terms of recording a lien on assets under Article 9 of the UCC. There are two exceptions: (a) when a creditor obtains a subordination from another creditor who has filed a prior lien and (b) when a creditor properly perfects a purchase money security interest.

9. A letter of credit is a mode of payment where the creditworthiness of a debtor is substituted with the creditworthiness of a bank. A standby letter of credit is particularly useful when selling a marginal domestic

account. As long as a debtor pays a creditor per agreed-upon terms, the standby letter of credit need not be drawn upon.

10. Documentary letters of credit are the most common method of settling payment on export sales. Credit managers often seek a confirmation from their domestic bank when a creditor is not comfortable with the bank that issued the letter of credit. Credit analysts should anticipate document deficiencies that occur on more than half of the letters of credit used. UCP 600 is particularly important to a credit manager who uses letters of credit for export sales.

Review/Discussion Questions

1. What types of customers are suitable candidates for a trade creditor to consider in the establishment of a secured credit arrangement?
2. What is the difference between a pledge and a secured credit arrangement under Article 9 of the UCC? What type of assets are typically used in a pledge arrangement?
3. How can personal guarantees be useful to protect the interests of a creditor? What factors should a credit analyst review when considering a personal guarantee?
4. What is the purpose of filing a mechanic's lien? Who has a right to file a mechanic's lien? Where is the lien filed?
5. The following questions relate to Article 9 of the UCC.
   a. Where is a UCC filing recorded?
   b. Does the debtor have to sign a UCC filing?
   c. Why would a credit manager perform a search of UCC filings?
   d. Who should sign the security agreement? If a creditor is unsure of the validity of authority, what safeguards can be taken?
   e. Does the balance owed to a creditor usually coincide with the quick-sale value of an asset? If not, what general guidelines can be used to recognize the potential quick-sale value for assets?
6. Identify three reasons for document deficiencies on a letter of credit. What should a creditor do if a document deficiency is discovered?
7. For a trade creditor, what attributes should a bank possess to represent the interests of the trade creditor who uses letters of credit?

Test Your Knowledge

1. What is a letter of credit?
2. What is the purpose of UCP 600 as it relates to letters of credit?
3. When would a credit manager use a subordination from a bank?

280

4. Compare and contrast a standby letter of credit with an export letter of credit.
5. Why would a credit manager obtain a confirmation on an export letter of credit?
6. Under what circumstances is a purchase money security interest created? How should a creditor protect a first lien position when obtaining the purchase money security interest?
7. What is the difference between a guarantee of payment and a guarantee of collection?
8. How can a banker's acceptance be created when using an export letter of credit?
9. Compare and contrast a trade acceptance with a banker's acceptance.
10. Explain the different types of documents that support a secured creditor who intends to perfect a lien in specific equipment.

Credit Management Online

www.ali.org/—The American Law Institute (ALI) is an independent organization that works on revising and drafting business laws.

https://iccwbo.org/—The International Chamber of Commerce (ICC) established rules for documentary letters of credit including UCP 600.

https://iccwbo.org/?s=ucp+600—Articles and books on UCP 600.

http://www1.internetlc.com/?kw=internet%20services—The complete text for UCP 600 can be downloaded from this link.

www.law.cornell.edu/uniform/ucc.html—The Cornell University Law School has a considerable amount of material available online concerning the Uniform Commercial Code. Some of the information is free, and other pieces can be downloaded for a fee.

www.lexisnexis.com/—This is a commercial site hosted by Lexis-Nexis Document Solutions, which offers a considerable amount of free, downloadable information about revisions to Article 9 of the Uniform Commercial Code. The site offers a newsletter as well as online filings and searches.

https://nacmsts.com/services/ucc-filing.html—NACM provides UCC filing services and notice, lien, bond and waiver filings.

www.nccusl.org/Update/—This link will take you to the website for the National Conference of Commissioners on Uniform State Laws (NCCUSL). The site is geared toward attorneys who draft legislation intended to monitor and amend legal business practices that impact upon state laws.

References Useful for Further Reading

"American Exporters Discover Forfaiting: Old Techniques, New Opportunities." *World Trade* (September 2007): 22-24.

Baker, Walter (Buddy). "10 Things for Exporters to Keep in Mind When Arranging Standby Letters of Credit." *Business Credit* (May 2008): 26-28.

Baker, Walter (Buddy). "Confirmed, Irrevocable Letters of Credit Are Not Always the Answer." *Business Credit* (March 2008): 64-69.

Cassling, Donald R. "The Issuer of a Letter of Credit Has No Duty to a Third Party Not Named as a Beneficiary in the Letter of Credit." *Banking Law Journal* (April 2010): 382-384.

Cowan, Stephen. "Email Guarantees: When is a Guarantee Not a Guarantee?" *Credit Management* (August 2006): 48-50.

Debattista, Charles. "The New UCP 600: Changes to the Tender of the Seller's Shipping Documents under Letters of Credit." *Journal of Business Law* (June 2007): 329-354.

Diana, Tom. "Navigating Lien Laws Requires a Different Roadmap for Each State." *Business Credit* (May 2007): 66-67.

Diana, Tom. "New Rules Ahead for Letters of Credit." *Business Credit* (March 2007): 56-58.

Davidson, Teresa D., et al. "Leases." *Business Lawyer* (August 2009): 1187-1197.

Frangos, Alex. "Deutsche Bank Sues Trump." *The Wall Street Journal–Eastern Edition* (December 2008): B2.

Ghadimi, Rene. "Common Mistakes under the UCC." *Secured Lender* (May 2009): 34-38.

Horowitz, Deborah. "Banco Santander and the UCP 600." *Journal of Business Law* 6 (October 2008): 508-525.

Levy, Eyal. "Shining a Light on a Niche Area of Financing in the Current Credit Market." *Secured Lender* (November 2007): 50-62.

Meyer, Keith G. "A Primer on Purchase Money Security Interests Under Revised Article 9 of the Uniform Commercial Code." *The University of Kansas Law Review* (November 2001): 143-194.

Moran, Gwen. "The Cost of Found Money." *Entrepreneur* (May 2010): 64.

Nathan, Bruce. "The Limits of Consignment Rights When Consigned Goods Are Manufactured Into Finished Product." *Business Credit* (July/August 2009): 22-25.

Nathan, Bruce, Esq. and Eric Chafetz, Esq. "The Strict Compliance Requirement for Letters of Credit is Really Strict." *Business Credit* (February 2017): 20-23.

"New Standards for Letters of Credit Go Into Effect." *Secured Lender* (July 2007): 12.

"Personal Guarantees." *Accountancy* (December 2008): 69-70.

Scranton, David F. "New Letter of Credit Rules Call for Careful Review." *Banking Law Journal* (February 2007): 126-130.

Shaw, Martin. "UCP 500." *Business Credit* (November/December 2001 through June 2002). (This was a seven-part monthly series of articles that appeared in *Business Credit*.)

Spiwak, Lisa E. "The Most Commonly Used Defenses by Personal Guarantors, And the Way to Beat Them." *Business Credit* (April 2006): 28.

Spriggs, Curtis. "Making Promissory Notes Work." *Business Credit* (April 2010): 22-23.

Stern, Nicholas. "Letter of Credit Basics: Some Expert Tips to Avoid Common Mistakes." *Business Credit* (April 2017): 36-37.

Taneja, Pradeep. "UCP 600: A Document Restoring the Credibility of LCs." *Business Credit* (February 2007): 56-57.

Thorne, Deborah. "Navigating Turbulent Waters: A Checklist of the Tools Provided by the Uniform Commercial Code." *Business Credit* (April 2009): 30-33.

Ulph, Janet. "The UCP600: Documentary Credits in the Twenty-first Century." *Journal of Business Law* (June 2007): 355-377.

Wood, Jeffrey S. "Drafting Letters of Credit: Basic Issues under Article 5 of the Uniform Commercial Code, UCP 600, and ISP98." *Banking Law Journal* (February 2008): 103-149.

Zellmer, Jill A.G., Theodore E. Francis, and Edwin E. Smith. "Legal Guidance for Compliance with Revised Article 9 of the UCC: Part 1." *Secured Lender* (November 2001): 90.

Zellmer, Jill A.G., Theodore E. Francis, and Edwin E. Smith. "Legal Guidance for Compliance with Revised Article 9 of the UCC: Part 2." *Secured Lender* (January 2002): 8.

Chapter 12

BANKRUPTCY AND REORGANIZATION

"Many today would argue that if lenders and debtors want to obtain the advantage of Section 363 to sell the debtor's assets, the lenders must 'pay the price.' Without active participation of unsecured creditors and objections to allowing bankruptcy courts to become federal foreclosure forums, Chapter 11 will increasingly be used as a vehicle for foreclosure by the secured creditors without any benefit to unsecured creditors."[1]

Deborah Thorne, Esq.
Bankruptcy Attorney

The quote from bankruptcy attorney Deborah Thorne emphasizes the need for credit managers to develop a legal understanding of bankruptcy law with a particular focus upon credit management applications. The surge in bankruptcy filings places the skill-set essential to work through bankruptcy cases into a high level of demand. Sometimes it may seem to be comparatively easy to extend credit, but some credit managers believe that a higher level of expertise lies in the area of working out of problems after the credit has been extended. This chapter will develop a foundation of bankruptcy-related legal concepts that can be used to support credit decisions.

The term *bankruptcy* is sometimes said to have a "broken bench" tradition known as *banca rotta*. In medieval times in Venice, Italy, when a merchant would fail to repay suppliers in a timely manner, the suppliers would break the benches that displayed the goods for sale. Not only would the merchants have their benches broken, but the common practice included stripping the clothes from the merchant and then tying the merchant to a stake and placing him or her on display in the town square.

In the era when the United States had achieved its independence from England, debtors who were unable to service their indebtedness were subject to being tossed into debtors' prison. The first federal bankruptcy legislation was sponsored by the initial U.S. Secretary of the Treasury,

---

[1] Deborah Thorne, "Pay to Play: Liquidation of Assets Using Chapter 11 Should Provide Unsecured Creditors with a Share of the Proceeds," *Business Credit* (June 2009): 38-41.

Alexander Hamilton, so that a colleague who had fled to France could stay out of prison. The first bankruptcy law helped Hamilton's colleague return to the U.S. to face his creditors; the colleague was Robert Morris, who had accumulated much of his debt to help finance George Washington's army. The bank trade association was later named after Robert Morris as the Robert Morris Associates, now called Risk Management Association or RMA.

Today, the bankruptcy laws are more debtor oriented. Using readily available legal assistance, many debtors will develop a workout plan prior to actually filing a bankruptcy petition. For the credit professional, there is a need to understand the bankruptcy process. The tactics to consider, in light of the alternatives available, make bankruptcy one of the most complex topics essential to sound credit practices.

Bankruptcy is an integrative subject. In order to master the learning objectives established for this chapter, several of the topics from prior chapters will be useful. Topics such as extending credit, setting up payment arrangements, utilizing cash flow models, appreciating Altman's Z-score model and arranging security each become an important focal point for bankruptcy analysis.

The **Key Learning Objectives** in Chapter 12 include:

1. Review the current bankruptcy data.
2. Understand the various chapters of the Bankruptcy Code.
3. Analyze the priority of claims in a Chapter 7 bankruptcy liquidation.
4. Examine a Chapter 11 bankruptcy with a focus placed upon resurrecting viable debtors and the key credit management concerns during the reorganization process.
5. Identify some of the issues, trends and problems that are bankruptcy-related from a credit professional's perspective.

CURRENT BANKRUPTCY LAW AND TRENDS

The purpose of bankruptcy is twofold: (1) to provide creditors with an orderly mechanism to assess the risk-reward tradeoff inherent when extending credit and (2) to furnish honest debtors with a way in which they can move toward a fresh start. One key goal is for the legal system to be operationally efficient; this means holding down the legal and other professional expenses of the bankruptcy while expediting the process.

The current bankruptcy law was enacted in 1978 and has been amended several times; the most substantive changes were made in

2005. The latest legislative change added the Bankruptcy Abuse Prevention and Consumer Protection Act of 2005 (***BAPCPA***).

According to statistics taken directly from the Administrative Office of the U.S. Courts, the number of bankruptcies nationally during 2016 was 794,960. Of the filings, the most were under Chapter 7 and the least were under Chapter 12. In 2016, by Chapter:

Chapter 7   490,365 total filing (15,033 were business filings)
Chapter 11   7,292 total filings (6,174 were business filings)
Chapter 12   461 total filings (461 were business filings)
Chapter 13   296,655 total filings (2,259 were business filings)

Bankruptcy is a lagging indicator; the trend in the number of filings tends to change after a change in economic conditions. Bankruptcies declined from 1,261,140 in 2012 to 794,960 in 2016. The 2016 total can be further broken down to 770,846 for nonbusiness and 24,114 for business. For additional updates, check the website for the Administrative Office of the U.S. Courts. http://www.uscourts.gov/sites/default/files/data_tables/bf_f2_1231.2016.pdf.

While the decline in bankruptcies may seem counterintuitive, given that the country's economic position was still precarious throughout 2016, one of the strategies used by policymakers to mitigate the effects of slow growth was to keep interest rates low. This allowed companies that were overleveraged to continue operating, since their financing costs were so low. Interestingly enough, analysts predicted that bankruptcies would only begin to increase after the economy had recovered, interest rates started to rise and banks began to feel more comfortable shedding parts of their lending portfolio.

The recession of 2007-2009, saw some of the biggest and most noteworthy bankruptcy filings in U.S. history. Table 12-1 shows the 20 largest public company bankruptcies from 1980 to 2016.

This chapter will provide an understanding of the basics of the Bankruptcy Code, then explore essentials of the two key chapters for business filings (Chapter 7 and Chapter 11) and, finally, review some key bankruptcy-related issues in credit management.

286 Credit Management: Principles and Practices

TABLE 12-1   The 20 Largest Public Company Bankruptcies in U.S. History 1980-2016

Company	Filing Date	Total Prebankruptcy Assets
Lehman Bros. Holdings, Inc.	September 15, 2008	$691,063,000,000
Washington Mutual, Inc.	September 26, 2008	327,913,000,000
WorldCom Inc.	July 21, 2002	103,914,000,000
General Motors Corporation	June 1, 2009	91,047,000,000
CIT Group	November 1, 2009	80,448,000,000
Enron Corporation	December 2, 2001	65,503,000,000
Conseco, Inc.	December 17, 2002	61,392,000,000
Energy Future Holdings Corp.	April 29, 2014	40,970,000,000
MF Global Holdings Ltd	October 31, 2011	40,541,000,000
Chrysler LLC	April 30, 2009	39,300,000,000
Thornburg Mortgage, Inc.	May 1, 2009	36,521,000,000
Pacific Gas and Electric Co.	April 6, 2001	36,152,000,000
Texaco, Inc.	April 12, 1987	34,940,000,000
Financial Corp. of America	September 9, 1988	33,864,000,000
Refco, Inc.	October 17, 2005	33,333,000,000
IndyMac Bancorp, Inc.	July 31, 2008	32,734,000,000
Global Crossing Ltd.	January 28, 2002	30,185,000,000
Bank of New England Corp.	January 7, 1991	29,773,000,000
General Growth Properties	April 16, 2009	29,557,000,000
Lyondell Chemical Company	January 6, 2009	27,392,000,000

Source: BankruptcyData.com

THE BANKRUPTCY CODE

The Bankruptcy Reform Act of 1978 went into effect on October 1, 1979. This was the first major revision of bankruptcy laws since the Chandler Act of 1938. The Bankruptcy Act of 1978 set the standards for our current bankruptcy system. There have been additional changes that include, most recently, BAPCPA.

When the Bankruptcy Act of 1978 was first passed, all even-numbered chapters were repealed. Since then, one even-numbered chapter has been added. The purpose of the 1978 Act was to streamline and expedite the bankruptcy process. The Bankruptcy Code consists of the following nine separate chapters:

Chapters 1, 3 and 5. These chapters pertain to general provisions that outline the administration and duties of the parties involved in the bankruptcy proceeding. Chapter 1 contains definitions of the many terms used in the Bankruptcy Code. Chapter 3 contains specific duties such as commencement of bankruptcy, the powers of trustees and the administration of the case. Chapter 5 sets the priorities for creditors, establishes guidelines for nondischargeable debts, identifies preference and other avoidance powers of the trustee, contains duties of the trustee, and contains provisions for creditors' proofs of claim.

Chapter 7. This chapter is sometimes referred to as a *straight bankruptcy*. Business liquidations occur under Chapter 7. Individuals may also file for bankruptcy under Chapter 7. As a matter of fact, a majority of personal bankruptcies are filed as a straight liquidation. Specific liquidation priorities will be developed more fully in a later section of this chapter of the book.

For most business credit grantors, Chapter 7 is one of two bankruptcy chapters with the highest degree of importance. Understanding the payments to claims under various levels of priority claims will be demonstrated with an example later in this chapter of the book. The process involves the mechanics of distributing a liquidating dividend to claimants under Chapter 7. The liquidation process is important to fully appreciate the ultimate risk of a business failure.

Chapter 9. Chapter 9 of the code pertains to municipalities and governmental units. The first legislation that allowed for a municipal filing was enacted during the Great Depression in 1937. Since then, fewer than 700 municipal filings have occurred. In addition to several municipal utilities, various cities, towns and counties have filed for Chapter 9 protection. Most notable are Detroit, MI (the largest at $18.5 billion, in 2013), Jefferson County, AL (the second largest at $4 billion, 2011), Hillview, KY (2015) Central Falls, RI (2011) and several cities in CA. Surpassing Detroit, in 2017, Puerto Rico filed for Chapter 9 protection with over $70 billion in public-sector debt.

A Chapter 9 can only be filed voluntarily. There is no provision for the liquidation of assets in a Chapter 9. The bankruptcy process involves filing the petition, negotiating between the creditors and the municipality, confirming the plan and making sure that the plan is properly implemented. The Governmental Accounting Standards Board (GASB) provides details for the mechanics involving the guidelines for local governments to use when they are considering filing under Chapter 9.

Other cities are considering bankruptcy as a means to restructure debt. Cuts in sales tax revenue caused by the recession, an inability to easily pass tax increases due to falling real estate prices accompanied by rising unemployment, and significant increases in unfunded pension obligations for municipal employees have resulted in serious financial problems, causing many municipalities to consider filing for Chapter 9 bankruptcy protection.

Chapter 11. Chapter 11 pertains to a business reorganization although certain individuals may also file under Chapter 11. Most Chapter 11s involve a ***debtor-in-possession (DIP)***; the DIP typically attempts to rehabilitate a business, sell a business as a going concern or conduct an orderly liquidation. According to the Administrative Office of the U.S. Courts, there were 7,292 total filings in 2016 of which 6,174 represented business filings. The Chapter 11 process is of considerable importance to creditors. Chapter 11 will be developed more fully in a later section.

Along with Chapter 7 of the Bankruptcy Code, Chapter 11 is vitally important to business creditors. The Chapter 11 process resurrects several concerns that are often encountered by business credit grantors. Many of these concerns will be discussed in the coming pages.

Chapter 12. A Chapter 12 filing is available to family farmers or family fishermen. Chapter 12 was first enacted in 1986; it can only be commenced through a voluntary petition. A family farmer must have total debt of less than $4,153,150 (subject to increases for inflation) and a family fisherman who runs a commercial fishing operation must have total debt of less than $1,924,550 (subject to increases for inflation) to be eligible. These debt levels are adjusted periodically to reflect changes in the consumer price index.

The purpose of filing a Chapter 12 is to provide small farmers or commercial fishermen with a chance to reorganize debt and retain their land or fishing operation. The family farmer or family fisherman must have regular annual income; the debt is usually set up to be repaid in full over a three to five-year plan unless the court approves a longer period of time. There were 461 Chapter 12 filings during the year 2016.

Chapter 13. Sometimes Chapter 13 is called the ***Wage Earner Plan***. Individuals with wages or income are eligible to file under Chapter 13. A sole proprietor who runs a small business is also eligible to file a Chapter 13. A Chapter 13 filing has become a mechanism useful to individuals who are attempting to prevent a home mortgage foreclosure. To be eligible for Chapter 13, the debtor must have secured debt of less than $1,184,200 (subject to increases for inflation) and unsecured debt of less than 394,725 (subject to increases for inflation).

For the debtor, the advantages of using Chapter 13 are the "*cramdown*" and "*extension*" possibilities. A cramdown allows for a repayment plan to be established by the trustee and debtor; it does not require creditor concurrence. In a Chapter 13, a debtor is permitted to cramdown the debt owed to a secured party (generally a mortgage holder on real estate) so that the amount paid to the secured party is equal to the value of the property itself. The extension of time for repayment in a Chapter 13 proceeding means the debtor is permitted to repay to its unsecured creditors a sum of money equal to the sum of the debtor's disposable income over that three-year period of time with a trustee concurrence. In certain instances (e.g., hardship), a debtor may be permitted to extend the payback period to five years. In 2016, there were 296,655 Chapter 13 filings, of which 2,259 were business filings.

Chapter 15. In 2005, BAPCPA added a new Chapter 15 to the Bankruptcy Code. The purpose of Chapter 15 is to address situations involving debtors located in more than one country. Chapter 15 represents the U.S. adoption of the Model Law on Cross-Border Insolvency put forth by the United Nations Commission on International Trade Law (UNCITRAL), adopted in 1997. UNCITRAL has been adopted, with modifications, by 60 member states.

The five principle objectives for Chapter 15 are specified below:[2]

1. To promote cooperation between foreign courts and the United States;
2. To establish greater legal certainty for investments and trade;
3. To provide for an efficient administration that pertains to cross-border insolvencies to protect the interests of creditors and other stakeholders;
4. To afford protection and maximization of the debtor's assets; and
5. To facilitate the rescue of a business that is experiencing financial problems to protect both investors and employees.

A Chapter 15 proceeding in the U.S. is often ancillary to an insolvency proceeding held in another country. Chapter 15 allows foreign creditors an opportunity to participate in a U.S. bankruptcy. The representative from a foreign insolvency proceeding files a petition seeking recognition of the foreign proceeding. If the motion is granted, the U.S. Bankruptcy Court would recognize and defer to the rulings in the foreign proceeding. The bankruptcy court would look to factors such as the location of the operations and the economic activity of the debtor to decide whether to recognize the foreign proceeding.

There are a number of reasons for a business to file a Chapter 15. The petition may be filed by a foreign company to protect its assets located

---

[2] www.uscourts.gov/FederalCourts/Bankruptcy/BankruptcyBasics/Chapter15.aspx

in the U.S. Cases have also been commenced to make it easier to sell off assets during the bankruptcy. Another motive for a Chapter 15 might be to bind all creditors to the restructuring terms that had been approved in a proceeding conducted in another country. The procedures involved with a Chapter 15 are different from the other Chapters of U.S. bankruptcy law, so creditors need to understand the practices used in the governing foreign jurisdiction.

In 1978, a pilot for the *U.S. Trustee Program* was set up; in 1986, the U.S. Trustee Program was fully established. The Department of Justice administers the U.S. Trustee Program, which operates in all states except Alabama and North Carolina. There are 21 regions that service the bankruptcy courts. Trustees will review cases for debtor fraud and serve as a "watch dog" over the bankruptcy process. The most typical types of fraud include hidden assets and furnishing creditors with false financial statements. The review of bust-outs also falls under the purview of the U.S. Trustee system. A *bust-out* can occur through various types of deliberate schemes, often to purchase large quantities of assets and then declare bankruptcy.

Effective in 2005, BAPCPA expanded the responsibilities for the U.S. Trustee Program, which include additional oversight of Chapter 11 small business proceedings and means testing to determine the eligibility of individuals to file Chapter 7 petitions. To learn more about the U.S. Trustee Program, visit www.justice.gov/ust/about-program.

Sometimes creditors may refer to a *Chapter 22* bankruptcy filing. There is no Chapter 22 contained in the Bankruptcy Code; the tongue-in-cheek reference to Chapter 22 is used when a company files a Chapter 11 petition twice. Companies such as Trans World Airlines, Montgomery Ward, Crown Books, Converse Shoes and LTV Steel, in addition to many in the oil and gas industry, all went through so-called Chapter 22s. A *Chapter 33* proceeding simply infers that a debtor has visited Chapter 11 in bankruptcy three times; this too is a slang term because there really is no Chapter 33 in the Bankruptcy Code.

CHAPTER 7: LIQUIDATION

Historically, business schools have emphasized entrepreneurial drive and the success stories in American business. Yet failure is a fact of life in a capitalistic economy. Certain lessons need to be remembered. In particular, a liquidation can be analyzed to better understand certain legal concerns and the financial payoffs to creditors demonstrated through the use of cash flow models by using various parameters.

Once the Chapter 7 case begins, the case creates an estate and a Chapter 7 trustee is appointed by the U.S. Trustee's office. The role of the trustee is to equitably distribute any proceeds derived by maximizing the sale of assets. In a Chapter 7 liquidation, the trustee gathers the assets for the insolvent firm. The assets are sold off with the proceeds distributed according to the creditors' legal priority of claims allowed under the Bankruptcy Code. A Chapter 7 bankruptcy is intended to provide an equitable distribution of assets to the claimants.

Claims priority rules establish the liquidating dividends to claimants in accordance with the specific priority of their claims. Generally, higher priority claims are paid in full before any distribution is made to lower priority claims. Pre-petition unsecured claims are near the bottom of the priority scheme; these claims are sometimes referred to as the claims of general unsecured creditors. However, it is possible for a trustee to negotiate with secured creditors and improve upon a liquidating dividend to general creditors.

For example, in the majority of liquidations, unsecured creditors do not receive a dividend; these are referred to as no-asset cases. However, a secured creditor may be inclined to negotiate with the trustee and carve out a portion of the secured creditor's claim for the benefit of lower priority claims. For example, a bank that is secured by assets might receive more for collateral by the trustee selling off the assets in an orderly fashion, perhaps even running the debtor's business for a short time, instead of forcing a fire sale liquidation. In this instance, a trustee overseeing the proceeding might insist that the secured creditor provide a dividend to lower priority creditors, thus deviating from the usual claims priority rules.

Although the claims priority rules are sometimes circumvented, they do provide essential structure. The process of working through a liquidation can be used as a vehicle to provide a foundation for a more complete understanding of bankruptcy. Creditors are better able to negotiate with distressed debtors in a Chapter 11 if they understand how much they might be paid if the case were to be converted into a Chapter 7 liquidation proceeding.

Claims Priority Rules

A Chapter 7 liquidation is subject to a prioritization of claims upon assets. The distribution is governed by rules that go beyond the scope of this book. While priorities have been established, they are often difficult to work through. In general, the distribution of the proceeds derived from selling off the assets satisfies claimants in the following sequence:

1. ***Secured Creditors.*** Secured creditor claims are first in the order of priority of the liens filed against any of the debtor's assets if the lien is properly perfected. Each secured claim is specific to the liened property. For example, a debtor may own a piece of real estate and there are secured liens on that real estate. In addition, that same debtor may own inventory that is secured by a lien held by a bank. Each of those creditors is entitled to a secured claim equal to the value of the asset against which it has a lien. But, the lien and thus secured claim of the real property mortgage holder does not cross over to the inventory and the lien and thus secured claim of the inventory lender does not cross over to the real estate. After the lien amount is established and paid, any excess amount received from security remains in the bankruptcy estate. Any deficiency in funds resulting from the sale of collateral makes the secured creditor an unsecured creditor for the amount of the deficiency. For example, if the secured claim is $25,000 and the secured creditor receives only $15,000 from the sale of the collateral, then the secured creditor will be left with an unsecured claim in the amount of $10,000.

   There is a push in lending for secured creditors to fully understand collateral values. The quick sale value during a liquidation may bring in fewer dollars than the book value for the outstanding loan balance. For example, in the real estate marketplace many lenders are in a position where market prices have fallen drastically; consequently, these lenders find themselves in a deficiency position after selling off the assets that had been used as collateral.

2A. ***Chapter 7 Administrative Priority Claims.*** These expenses represent the cost of winding down the debtor and/or preserving the business during the Chapter 7 bankruptcy proceeding. Included here are expenses for professionals used during the bankruptcy, such as the trustee, accountants, realtors and attorneys. Their fees are often referred to as the expenses of the estate. These administrative claims of the estate have a priority over certain other types of administrative claims made by creditors.

2B. ***Chapter 11 Administrative Priority Claims.*** In the Chapter 11 context, certain claims have an administrative priority. Claims are also made available to the above professionals, as well as to vendors providing goods and services for the benefit of the debtor. The purpose of this level in the prioritization of claims is to encourage creditors to extend new credit to a Chapter 11 debtor that is operating during a Chapter 11 proceeding. The theory is that the debtor needs fresh inventory to generate new sales and to continue its ongoing operations. Only credit extended after the Chapter 11 proceeding is filed receives this priority. If the Chapter 11 proceeding is converted to a Chapter 7 liquidation, then the shipments made to the DIP (debtor-in-possession) receive this level in the prioritization of claims, though they remain subordinate to the Chapter 7 administrative expenses previously discussed.

Companies making shipments to a DIP while operating in a Chapter 11 should consider notations on their invoices that clearly spell out the fact that these shipments are being made to a debtor-in-possession operating in a Chapter 11. Creditors need to ascertain that there is a sufficient asset base to cover this level of priority claim before extending credit to a debtor. In a no-asset case or in cases with insufficient assets to pay these claims, the prioritization at this level will not benefit the creditor. Some companies have a policy of requiring payments on a cash-in-advance basis for any DIP shipments because of the risk that there will not be enough money generated from the proceeds to fund these claims.

2C. ***Administrative Claims under Section 503(b)(9).*** In 2005, BAPCPA created an opportunity, in certain situations, for the unpaid seller of goods (but not for services) to potentially move up to an administrative priority claim. Under Section 503(b)(9) of the Bankruptcy Code, a creditor is granted an administrative priority claim for the value of the goods sold to and received by the buyer in the ordinary course of business within 20 days of the buyer's bankruptcy filing.

Note that a secured creditor always has a first priority lien position on the asset against which it has a perfected lien. A creditor who has sold and delivered goods to a debtor within the 20-day period immediately preceding a buyer's filing is entitled to a Section 503(b)(9) claim for the value of those goods. That administrative claim is an absolute priority claim and must be paid *pari passu* (equally) with all other administrative claims. If a debtor's estate happens to be administratively insolvent, then all administrative claims will share equally in whatever diminished assets there might be.

Any creditor seeking to assert Section 503(b)(9) claims needs to keep current with bankruptcy procedures and practices in local district courts. The *Manual of Credit and Commercial Laws* and *Business Credit* magazine are two excellent ways to keep current with the procedures to follow to assert a Section 503(b)(9) administrative claim.

Please note that claims under 2B and 2C are a focus for the trustee. They are both administrative claims that are paid after only the Chapter 7 administrative claims of the estate are paid in full. Then the Chapter 11 claims will be paid in the order of priorities set by the statute. The distribution of proceeds from the asset liquidation is governed by the allowance of the claims and an equitable distribution on account of the claims. Under Section 503(b)(9) claims and also for administrative claims for sales made to a Chapter 11 DIP, the trustee will look to see what each claimant is entitled to receive.

3. ***Involuntary Case Claims.*** In an involuntary case, a claim arising in the ordinary course of debtor's business or financial affairs after the commencement of the case but before the earlier of the appointment of a trustee and the order for relief.

4. ***Wages and Compensation Claims.*** Wages earned within 180 days prior to a bankruptcy filing receive a priority claim limited to a certain amount per wage earner cap (subject to increase for inflation).

5. ***Employee Benefit Plans.*** Unsecured claims for contributions to an employee benefit plan arising from services rendered within 180 days prior to a bankruptcy filing to the extent of $10,950 multiplied by the number of employees covered by the pension plan less any amounts paid to the wage and compensation claims and less any amounts paid on behalf of the estate to any other benefit plan.

6. ***Grain Producers or Fisherman Claims.*** Allowed unsecured claims of persons engaged in the production or raising of grain where the debtor owns or operates a grain storage facility, or a

fisherman who has sold to a debtor who is engaged in operating a fish produce storage or processing facility.

7. ***Customer Deposits.*** A deposit that is limited to a certain amount per claimant (subject to increases for inflation) is next in the order for priority claims. This priority is available to individuals who place a deposit on property or services for personal, family or household use.

8. ***Taxes.*** Certain federal, state, county or other types of government agencies receive the next level in the ordering of the priority of claims.

9. ***Unsecured Claims of a Federal Depository Institutions Regulatory Agency.*** These are claims based upon any commitment by the debtor to a Federal depository institutions regulatory agency to maintain the capital of an insured depository institution.

10. ***Claims Arising from the Unlawful Operation of a Motor Vehicle or Vessel.*** Allowed claims for death or personal injury resulting from the operation of a motor vehicle or vessel if such operation was unlawful because the debtor was intoxicated from using alcohol, a drug or another substance.

11. ***Unsecured Creditors.*** These claims are often referred to as general unsecured creditors' claims. They include trade creditors, landlord claims, and deficiency claims of secured creditors and debenture holders, among others. When there are assets available for general unsecured creditors, they usually participate in a *pro rata* liquidation dividend. This simply means that general unsecured creditors are paid proportionately on their claims from the funds that remain available after the other claimants holding a higher priority are paid in full.

A subordinated debenture also holds a claim as an unsecured creditor. However, any *pro rata* funds allocated to subordinated debentures because they are an unsecured creditor must be turned over as proceeds to the party to whom the creditor is subordinated, unless that party holding the subordination has already been paid in full. The subordinated debenture is often the junk bondholder who normally receives nothing in a liquidation.

12. ***Preferred Stockholders.*** Preferred stockholders are paid after all creditors are paid in full. Since there is seldom enough available to fund creditors, preferred stockholders usually receive nothing from the proceeds in the liquidation, and the stock is deemed valueless.

13. ***Common Stockholders.*** Last in line are the common shareholders who bear what accountants often refer to as the "residual risk." Any remaining funds in the liquidation are allocated to common stockholders after all other claimants are paid in full. There is usually nothing remaining for common stockholders in liquidation.

One might ask: Why would a firm go bankrupt if it could pay all of its creditors in full?

A ***superpriority claim*** can be authorized by a bankruptcy court during a Chapter 11 proceeding. The superpriority claimant has priority over all administrative expenses and other types of pre-petition unsecured claims. Superpriority status is what is given to a secured lender under the following scenario. A lender is owed money pre-petition and is secured. Subsequent to the bankruptcy filing, the lender is willing to lend additional sums of money but only if it is assured that it will be first in line to be repaid above all other creditors. There may be pre-petition creditors which are also secured. A superpriority position will grant that lender secured status above any and all creditors whether or not those creditors are pre-petition or post-petition creditors and no matter what they may have as secured collateral.

The bankruptcy court may authorize a superpriority claim when a debtor in a Chapter 11 is unable to obtain new financing during the Chapter 11. If the Chapter 11 proceeding is converted to a Chapter 7 liquidation, the superpriority claimant, typically in addition to its secured claim, has a first priority claim on all unencumbered assets. Superpriority claims will normally fall in line behind a Chapter 7 trustee's fees and the expenses of the estate.

Liquidation Case Study

In order to provide a more complete explanation of the liquidation process, a hypothetical case study will be used. A balance sheet that lists all obligations (claims) at the time of liquidation is furnished in Table 12-2 for the KPT Manufacturing Company. This balance sheet is used to illustrate the allocation of proceeds in the liquidation.

There is $2,000,000 in liabilities on the books, but only $1,000,000 is derived from the sale of the assets to serve as the liquidating dividends. At issue is the appropriate allocation of $1,000,000 to be paid out to the claimants.

The following six steps are illustrated in Table 12-2 and discussed below:

12: Bankruptcy and Reorganization

TABLE 12-2 **KPT Manufacturing Company**
Balance Sheet – June 20, 2016

Cash	$ 25,000	Accounts Payable	$ 750,000
Accounts Receivable	825,000	Accrued Taxes	100,000
Inventory	750,000	Notes Payable to Bank	250,000
Total Current Assets	1,600,000	Total Current Liabilities	1,100,000
Fixed Assets (Net)	400,000	First Mortgage Bonds	400,000
		Subordinated Debentures	300,000
		Total Debt	1,800,000
		Preferred Stock	50,000
		Common Equity	150,000
Total Assets	**$2,000,000**	Total Liabilities and Equity	**$2,000,000**

Assumptions:
1. First mortgage bonds are secured only by fixed assets.
2. The Bank holds the subordination from the debentures.
3. The Proceeds in the liquidation include:
   a. $700,000 from the liquidation of the current assets.
   b. $300,000 from the liquidation of fixed assets.
4. Administrative expenses incurred to the estate are 20% of the total liquidation proceeds.
5. In this case, there were no claims made under 503(b)(9), nor accrued wages, nor unfunded pension obligations, nor sales made to debtor-in-possession.

Task: **Determine distribution of the $1,000,000 liquidation proceeds working through priorities.**

Step 1. First Mortgage Bonds receive $300,000 from the sales of the fixed assets. The bonds are unsecured for the $100,000 deficiency. (*See* Assumptions 1 and 3.)

Step 2. Administrative expenses receive $200,000. (*See* Assumption 4.)

Step 3. Accrued taxes receive $100,000 as a priority creditor. (For simplicity, assume no other priority claimants.)

Step 4. Determine the payout percentage for unsecured creditors. The $600,000 paid out so far indicates that $400,000 remained to be paid. The remaining unsecured debt totaling $1,400,000 consisting of: accounts payable $750,000, bank debt $250,000, first mortgage bonds $100,000, and subordinated debentures $300,000.

Step 5. The remaining proceeds are $400,000 ÷ remaining creditors' claims of $1,400,000 = .285714 on the dollar, as a *pro rata* distribution allocated to general creditors as follows:

Accounts Payable	.285714 × $750,000 = $214,286
Bank Debt	.285714 × $250,000 = $ 71,429
First Mortgage	.285714 × $100,000 = $ 28,571
Subordinated Debt	.285714 × $300,000 = $ 85,714

Step 6. Funds that would have been allocated to the subordinated debentures go to the bank. (*See* Assumption 2.) The $1,000,000 liquidation proceeds are distributed as follows:

	Payout	Book Claim	% of Book Claim
Accounts Payable	$ 214,286	$ 750,000	29 %
Accrued Taxes	100,000	100,000	100
Notes Payable Bank	157,143	250,000	63
First Mortgage Bonds	328,571	400,000	82
Subordinated Debt	0	300,000	0
Preferred Stock	0	50,000	0
Common Equity	0	150,000	0
Administrative Expenses	200,000	Not on org. books	NA
Total Paid Out	**$ 1,000,000**	**$ 2,000,000**	**50 %**

- **Step 1.** The first funds to be paid out are allocated to the first mortgage holder, who is owed $400,000 in the liabilities section of the Balance Sheet. *See Assumption 3*, which identifies the collateral as only the fixed assets. If only $300,000 is received when this specific collateral is sold off, then the first mortgage holder will receive $300,000 and have a deficiency for $100,000. The deficiency falls to the level of an unsecured claim. Only the first mortgage holder is entitled to a secured claim from the specific collateral, which happens to be fixed assets in this case.
- **Step 2.** Next in line are the administrative expenses, which represent 20% of the total liquidation proceeds. This comes out to $200,000; this number was given in *Assumption 4*. Administrative expenses can vary widely, but they are often quite substantial.
- **Step 3.** For simplicity's sake, the only priority claim is the accrued taxes, which show up in the Balance Sheet as $100,000. In most liquidations, there are other types of priority claims.
- **Step 4.** A proportionate distribution (*pro rata*) needs to be calculated. A fraction is used to allocate funds on a *pro rata* basis to the general unsecured creditors. The numerator is the funds available that have not yet been paid out to prior claimants. The denominator is the sum of the remaining liabilities.

  The numerator is derived by identifying any funds remaining after paying out the priority claims. There was originally $1,000,000 available for distribution, of which secured creditors were paid $300,000, administrative expenses were paid $200,000 and accrued taxes were paid $100,000. The remaining funds to distribute to general creditors are $400,000.

  The denominator is derived by adding accounts payable ($750,000), unsecured bank debt ($250,000), the remaining unsecured portion of the first mortgage ($100,000) beyond the liquidation value of the collateral and subordinated debt ($300,000), which total $1,400,000.

  The *pro rata* distribution is calculated by dividing $400,000 by $1,400,000 for a recovery percentage of 28.714%, expressed in decimal form as .28714.
- **Step 5.** The funds that are owed to each respective general unsecured creditor are multiplied by the *pro rata* distribution obtained in Step 4.
- **Step 6.** The funds that would have gone to the subordinated debt are shifted over to the Notes Payable to the bank because of

Assumption 2 in the directions. Banks often hold subordinations when junk bonds are used. The final payout percentages that have been used in Step 6 are derived by dividing each dollar paid to each claimant by the original Balance Sheet book claim for each claimant.

The numbers used in the KPT Manufacturing Company liquidation can be revealing. Note that the stockholders and subordinated debt holders were completely excluded from receiving any dividend. Also note that the First Mortgage holders realized a substantial dividend that includes $300,000 from the collateral and $28,571 from the unsecured claimholders' *pro rata* distribution. Finally, note that unsecured creditors were hurt because of a forced sale of assets and the high cost of administrative expenses; they received only approximately 29% of their original claim.

Computer models are available to help credit managers work through various liquidation scenarios. By understanding the implications of a liquidation, credit managers are better able to evaluate the risk-reward tradeoff in a bankruptcy.

The KPT case study is an example of a liquidation using the priority rules. By understanding the sequence of the payout for the proceeds, negotiations in a Chapter 11 proceeding can be conducted with a clearer understanding of the potential results. In lieu of a cash payout, a Chapter 11 debtor could offer creditors a stake in the equity of the reorganized firm as an alternative to a liquidation.

The "what if" scenarios can make liquidation one of the most complex topics in finance. As a matter of fact, in most liquidations the unsecured creditors can expect to receive only a small fraction (if anything) of their total claims.

CHAPTER 11: REORGANIZATION

In a Chapter 11 proceeding, businesses often attempt to reorganize. The primary focal points include initiating a case and examining the proceeding to include responsibilities for both the debtor and the creditor. In this section of the book, the focus is placed upon the process of a Chapter 11. The final section of this book will delve into some of the complex legal concerns relevant to creditors during a bankruptcy.

Initiating a Chapter 11 Proceeding

A bankruptcy petition is filed in a U.S. Bankruptcy Court. The petition may be filed by a debtor or by creditors that meet certain criteria. A bankruptcy petition may be commenced where the domicile, residence, principal place of business or principal assets of the debtor have been located for the past 180 days or the longer portion of the past 180 days than any other location. Alternatively, the petition may be filed in the state of incorporation of the debtor. Note that a corporation's "residence" may be in the state of incorporation. However, the venue may be transferred to another district court in the interest of justice or for convenience. The jurisdiction can be important to a case. U.S. Bankruptcy Courts do not have the same track records for expediting cases or for successfully rehabilitating debtors.

Most bankruptcy petitions are initiated by the debtor. The filing of a *voluntary petition*, once accepted by the bankruptcy court, creates an order of relief. The order for relief triggers an automatic stay, which generally enjoins all collection activity for debt incurred prior to the filing.

An *involuntary petition* may be filed by creditors under either Chapter 7 or Chapter 11, but typically it is filed under Chapter 7. Such creditors are called "petitioning creditors." There are two circumstances in which creditors may file an involuntary petition: (1) When the debtor has 12 or more total creditors, at least three of the creditors whose claims aggregate more than $14,425 (subject to increases for inflation) that are not subject to *bona fide* dispute in dollar amount or liability may join together to file a petition; (2) when the debtor has fewer than 12 total creditors, any one creditor with a claim of at least $14,425 (subject to increases for inflation) that is not subject to *bona fide* dispute in dollar amount or liability can file the involuntary petition. Creditors should be careful to seek legal counsel prior to filing an involuntary petition, because an improperly filed involuntary petition could potentially subject the petitioning creditors to costs and/or sanctions.

Normally a debtor has 20 days to contest an involuntary petition. The court could order a trial to determine whether or not the involuntary petition is acceptable to grant relief to the petitioners. Relief on an involuntary petition is conditional on proving the debtor's inability to pay debts as they mature. Assuming the bankruptcy court approves the involuntary petition and grants an order for relief, it is common for the debtor to request the case be converted to Chapter 11; this is an absolute right. Often, assuming there is concern that a debtor is squandering its assets, a petitioning creditor not only will file an involuntary petition, but will also move for the bankruptcy court to appoint a trustee to step into the debtor's shoes and preserve its assets.

Regardless of the voluntary or involuntary nature of the petition, once a bankruptcy case is initiated, an automatic stay is created. The stay protects the debtor from both collection and judicial activities that originated before the commencement of the bankruptcy proceeding. Creditors should stop collection activity on antecedent debt and work through the bankruptcy court. Failure to stop collection activities after the bankruptcy filing is considered a violation of the automatic stay and may result in the bankruptcy court penalizing the creditor.

Chapter 11 Time Frame

A large, complex Chapter 11 case could easily take two years to complete. However, the LTV Corp. bankruptcy case spanned a seven-year period. The size of the business filing, the complexity of the issues that relate to the case and the jurisdiction overseeing the case each can play an important role. The costs of administering the case increase in a protracted proceeding. BAPCPA in some ways attempted to speed up the process by imposing certain time deadlines. In many cases, a quicker Chapter 11 process provides a debtor an increased likelihood of surviving.

The duration of a Chapter 11 can be reduced significantly through a *prepackaged Chapter 11*. The main purpose of a prepackaged Chapter 11 is to speed up the time spent in Chapter 11 and cut costs. For example, the fees during the Revco bankruptcy exceeded $40 million. Moreover, the stigma of being involved in a protracted bankruptcy case is detrimental to being able to hold on to key employees. By formulating a plan and soliciting the creditors' votes before a filing, a prepackaged bankruptcy can significantly reduce the time frame for the proceeding.

Prepackaged bankruptcy proceedings have been around for almost 30 years. USG Corp. was able to file a prepackaged Chapter 11 in March 1993 and then emerge from bankruptcy 38 days later. Chrysler Corporation took 40 days to emerge from bankruptcy in 2009. More recently, in 2016, Southcross Holdings LP was able to emerge from bankruptcy in only 15 days, the shortest prepackaged Chapter 11 ever, while shedding $700 million in funded debt and preferred equity obligations.

A ***prearranged bankruptcy*** is similar to a prepackaged bankruptcy. The distinction between a prearranged bankruptcy and a prepackaged bankruptcy is that in a prearranged bankruptcy the negotiations between the debtor and creditors have not been agreed upon by all necessary parties. For example, in a prepackaged bankruptcy the bondholders may have formally agreed to modification of their debt; in a prearranged bankruptcy some creditors may agree to a modification while others only express an interest, but the requisite votes needed to approve the plan have not been fully agreed upon when the filing occurs. Therefore, a prearranged bankruptcy proceeding may not progress as quickly as a prepackaged bankruptcy.

One key focal point during the bankruptcy process has been to shed debt through the use of a Chapter 11 proceeding. For example, Penn Virginia Corporation was able to emerge from a bankruptcy in August 2016 after four months. It was able to shed $1.1 billion in debt through the restructuring process. The point is that the faster process in using a prepackaged bankruptcy should not be the only criteria to focus upon.

The DIP during Chapter 11

The debtor in a Chapter 11 is commonly referred to as a ***debtor-in-possession*** (DIP). The DIP continues to operate a business as a going concern during the Chapter 11 proceeding. Under BAPCPA, the Bankruptcy Code grants the DIP an exclusive right to file a plan of reorganization for the first 120 days of the case. The bankruptcy court can use its authority to extend the debtor's period of exclusivity beyond the initial 120-day period. The DIP is required to furnish the court with certain documentation, including (1) a schedule of assets and liabilities, (2) a schedule of current income and expenses, (3) a schedule of executory contracts and leases and (4) a statement of financial affairs. This publicly filed information may assist creditors in determining the continued viability of the business.

The debtor often experiences a liquidity crisis at the time of the Chapter 11 filing. A motion is sometimes made by the DIP to the court to allow for the debtor to obtain ***DIP financing***. Banks often obtain a security interest in the debtor's assets when DIP financing is approved. The fresh infusion of funds can alleviate the liquidity crisis. However, in order to entice a bank to provide DIP financing, the bank normally gains a superpriority claim which has priority over other administrative expenses.

Another motion sometimes made by the DIP is for the authorization to use ***cash collateral***. Cash collateral represents the proceeds obtained from the sale of a creditor's collateral. One example for the use of cash collateral would be a DIP in a commercial business which buys inventory from trade creditors and sells that inventory to end users. There is generally a bank that has financed the debtor's business operations and that bank generally has a secured lien on all the inventory. When the debtor sells the inventory to an end user, the money which the debtor gets for that inventory becomes cash collateral. It is necessary for the debtor to use its cash to continue its business operations and therefore, the debtor may apply to the court for permission to use its cash collateral. The court will usually authorize a debtor's use of cash collateral provided the secured creditor is given adequate protection such as replacement liens or monthly interest payments. The application for cash collateral will be on notice to creditors and other parties who have appeared in the case. When the debtor makes such a request to the court, they will also commonly serve notice to the debtor's 20 largest unsecured creditors.

The DIP is required to submit a complete set of schedules of all liabilities (creditors) and all assets. The bankruptcy court requires the DIP to submit monthly operating reports, demonstrating its monthly performance during the Chapter 11 proceeding. With court approval, the DIP may elect either to assume or reject executory contracts. Executory contracts are contracts where each party has material obligations remaining to perform. Supply agreements are often executory contracts. The process of assumption and rejection is discussed in greater detail below.

The Creditors during a Chapter 11

Creditors often face a number of difficult decisions during a Chapter 11 proceeding. Once a petition is filed with the bankruptcy court, the creditor should stop direct collection activity with the debtor. Usually the debtor continues to operate the business as a DIP. However, creditors can make a motion to have the court appoint a trustee to run the business. This might occur if there is gross mismanagement or fraud by management.

Section 341 of the Bankruptcy Code is the reference used for a 341 meeting of creditors, which is the first meeting of creditors at which the debtor must be present to answer questions from the U.S. Trustee and creditors about its assets and liabilities. The ***Public Access to Court Electronic Records (PACER)*** system provides free access to bankruptcy court dockets throughout the United States. Any member of the public can sign up for PACER access. A $0.10 per page fee is charged for obtaining information or documents. PACER provides information about the timing and location of the 341 meeting. In addition, all creditors should receive written notice of the meeting. There are many small bankruptcy cases where none of the creditors appear at the 341 meeting. However, if there is any suspicion of fraud, it is important to attend the 341 hearing and alert the U.S. Trustee. Creditors are often actively engaged in the 341 meetings in larger cases.

During a Chapter 11 proceeding in large cases, the 20 largest unsecured creditors are usually invited by the U.S. Trustee to sit on the ***unsecured creditors' committee***, which acts as a fiduciary to represent the interests of all unsecured creditors Sometimes the committee invitation can be extended to the 50 largest unsecured creditors in a larger case. Committee composition is meant to be a diverse cross-section of the creditor body, such as trade vendors, landlords and bondholders. The committee is entitled to retain counsel, whose fees are paid by the debtor. Although a creditor may have to invest considerable time to serve on a creditors' committee, the potential rewards can be substantial. The creditors examine possible signs of fraud. Interrelated company transactions or the removal of major assets by the debtor can create a need to monitor the bankruptcy to protect the interest of creditors. Creditors may be in a position to look for additional assets that were not included on the debtor's schedule. Unsecured creditors may look at liens to ensure that the liens have been properly perfected. The creditors' committee also plays an important role in negotiating a debtor's reorganization plan or sometimes presents its own reorganization plan.

Upon a customer's bankruptcy filing, one of the first actions taken by a creditor should be to investigate the potential to exercise ***reclamation rights***. Although BAPCPA has worked toward remedying the problems that historically were associated with a creditor's right of reclaiming goods sold to the debtor under the Uniform Commercial Code (UCC), by expanding the reclamation clawback period from 10 days to 45 days, reclamation has infirmities that have limited its effectiveness. This includes that *reclamation claims are typically deemed valueless to the extent that the debtor's secured lender has a prior floating lien in the inventory sought to be reclaimed.* Creditors, however, have been afforded another avenue for recovery in the form of the Section 503(b)(9) administrative priority claim.

As discussed above, under Section 503(b)(9), a creditor is afforded an administrative priority claim for goods sold to and received by the debtor in the ordinary course within 20 days of the debtor's bankruptcy filing. Section 503(b)(9) does not afford creditors the right to reclaim goods, only the right to receive an administrative priority claim. The full recovery of administrative claims under the Bankruptcy Code is not a sure thing. It is highly recommended that creditors seek legal counsel when exercising reclamation and Section 503(b)(9) rights.

Creditors are required to file a *proof of claim* with a bankruptcy court in a Chapter 7, 12 or 13 case. In a Chapter 11, if the debtor properly lists the creditor on the schedule without indicating that the claim is disputed, contingent or unliquidated, then the creditor is not required to file a proof of claim. However, if the amount is incorrect or the claim is listed as disputed, contingent or unliquidated, then the creditor must timely and properly file a proof of claim. It is recommended that the proof of claim be sent to the correct bankruptcy court clerk or claims agent, depending on the case, via certified mail and/or overnight courier, so that there is evidence that the proof of claim was, in fact, timely received. When filing the proof of claim, a creditor may also include an extra copy of its proof of claim along with a self-addressed stamped envelope and request that the extra copy be stamped "received" and returned to the creditor for its records. While a creditor may still hand print or type the proof of claim form, that form can now be generated, filled out and signed electronically. More importantly, most courts permit proofs of claim to be electronically filed by creditors enabling a creditor to get an immediate electronic receipt and claim number from the bankruptcy court. Creditors should follow up to ensure that they are on the schedule of creditors and/or that their proof of claim has been received.

Form 410 is the standard proof of claim form to use during a bankruptcy. Exhibit 12-3 shows Form 410, as most recently amended, which can be downloaded as a pdf fillable form at www.uscourts.gov/FederalCourts/Bankruptcy.aspx. Usually a ledger of unpaid invoices and copies of invoices are attached to the form to support the amount claimed.

306 Credit Management: Principles and Practices

EXHIBIT 12-3   FORM 410 - PROOF OF CLAIM

Fill in this information to identify the case:

Debtor 1 _____

Debtor 2
(Spouse, if filing) _____

United States Bankruptcy Court for the: _____ District of _____

Case number _____

Official Form 410

Proof of Claim

04/16

Read the instructions before filling out this form. This form is for making a claim for payment in a bankruptcy case. Do not use this form to make a request for payment of an administrative expense. Make such a request according to 11 U.S.C. § 503.

Filers must leave out or redact information that is entitled to privacy on this form or on any attached documents. Attach redacted copies of any documents that support the claim, such as promissory notes, purchase orders, invoices, itemized statements of running accounts, contracts, judgments, mortgages, and security agreements. **Do not send original documents;** they may be destroyed after scanning. If the documents are not available, explain in an attachment.

A person who files a fraudulent claim could be fined up to $500,000, imprisoned for up to 5 years, or both. 18 U.S.C. §§ 152, 157, and 3571.

Fill in all the information about the claim as of the date the case was filed. That date is on the notice of bankruptcy (Form 309) that you received.

Part 1:	**Identify the Claim**

1. Who is the current creditor?

Name of the current creditor (the person or entity to be paid for this claim) _____

Other names the creditor used with the debtor _____

2. Has this claim been acquired from someone else?

☐ No
☐ Yes. From whom? _____

3. Where should notices and payments to the creditor be sent?

Federal Rule of Bankruptcy Procedure (FRBP) 2002(g)

Where should notices to the creditor be sent?

Name _____

Number   Street _____

City   State   ZIP Code

Contact phone _____

Contact email _____

Where should payments to the creditor be sent? (if different)

Name _____

Number   Street _____

City   State   ZIP Code

Contact phone _____

Contact email _____

Uniform claim identifier for electronic payments in chapter 13 (if you use one):

_ _

4. Does this claim amend one already filed?

☐ No
☐ Yes. Claim number on court claims registry (if known) _____   Filed on _____
MM / DD / YYYY

5. Do you know if anyone else has filed a proof of claim for this claim?

☐ No
☐ Yes. Who made the earlier filing? _____

Official Form 410   Proof of Claim   page 1

12: Bankruptcy and Reorganization

307

Part 2: Give Information About the Claim as of the Date the Case Was Filed

6. Do you have any number you use to identify the debtor?

☐ No
☐ Yes. Last 4 digits of the debtor's account or any number you use to identify the debtor: ____ ____ ____ ____

7. How much is the claim?

$_____ **Does this amount include interest or other charges?**
☐ No
☐ Yes. Attach statement itemizing interest, fees, expenses, or other charges required by Bankruptcy Rule 3001(c)(2)(A).

8. What is the basis of the claim?

Examples: Goods sold, money loaned, lease, services performed, personal injury or wrongful death, or credit card.

Attach redacted copies of any documents supporting the claim required by Bankruptcy Rule 3001(c).

Limit disclosing information that is entitled to privacy, such as health care information.

_____

9. Is all or part of the claim secured?

☐ No
☐ Yes. The claim is secured by a lien on property.

Nature of property:
☐ Real estate. If the claim is secured by the debtor's principal residence, file a *Mortgage Proof of Claim Attachment* (Official Form 410-A) with this *Proof of Claim*.
☐ Motor vehicle
☐ Other. Describe: _____

Basis for perfection: _____
Attach redacted copies of documents, if any, that show evidence of perfection of a security interest (for example, a mortgage, lien, certificate of title, financing statement, or other document that shows the lien has been filed or recorded.)

Value of property: $_____
Amount of the claim that is secured: $_____

Amount of the claim that is unsecured: $_____ (The sum of the secured and unsecured amounts should match the amount in line 7.)

Amount necessary to cure any default as of the date of the petition: $_____

Annual Interest Rate (when case was filed)_____%
☐ Fixed
☐ Variable

10. Is this claim based on a lease?

☐ No
☐ Yes. Amount necessary to cure any default as of the date of the petition. $_____

11. Is this claim subject to a right of setoff?

☐ No
☐ Yes. Identify the property: _____

Official Form 410   Proof of Claim   page 2

Credit Management: Principles and Practices

12. **Is all or part of the claim entitled to priority under 11 U.S.C. § 507(a)?**

A claim may be partly priority and partly nonpriority. For example, in some categories, the law limits the amount entitled to priority.

☐ No

☐ Yes. *Check one:*

Amount entitled to priority

☐ Domestic support obligations (including alimony and child support) under 11 U.S.C. § 507(a)(1)(A) or (a)(1)(B).　$_____

☐ Up to $2,850* of deposits toward purchase, lease, or rental of property or services for personal, family, or household use. 11 U.S.C. § 507(a)(7).　$_____

☐ Wages, salaries, or commissions (up to $12,850*) earned within 180 days before the bankruptcy petition is filed or the debtor's business ends, whichever is earlier. 11 U.S.C. § 507(a)(4).　$_____

☐ Taxes or penalties owed to governmental units. 11 U.S.C. § 507(a)(8).　$_____

☐ Contributions to an employee benefit plan. 11 U.S.C. § 507(a)(5).　$_____

☐ Other. Specify subsection of 11 U.S.C. § 507(a)(___) that applies.　$_____

* Amounts are subject to adjustment on 4/01/19 and every 3 years after that for cases begun on or after the date of adjustment.

Part 3: Sign Below

The person completing this proof of claim must sign and date it. FRBP 9011(b).

If you file this claim electronically, FRBP 5005(a)(2) authorizes courts to establish local rules specifying what a signature is.

A person who files a fraudulent claim could be fined up to $500,000, imprisoned for up to 5 years, or both. 18 U.S.C. §§ 152, 157, and 3571.

Check the appropriate box:

☐ I am the creditor.

☐ I am the creditor's attorney or authorized agent.

☐ I am the trustee, or the debtor, or their authorized agent. Bankruptcy Rule 3004.

☐ I am a guarantor, surety, endorser, or other codebtor. Bankruptcy Rule 3005.

I understand that an authorized signature on this *Proof of Claim* serves as an acknowledgment that when calculating the amount of the claim, the creditor gave the debtor credit for any payments received toward the debt.

I have examined the information in this *Proof of Claim* and have a reasonable belief that the information is true and correct.

I declare under penalty of perjury that the foregoing is true and correct.

Executed on date _____
MM / DD / YYYY

_____
Signature

Print the name of the person who is completing and signing this claim:

Name _____
First name　　　　Middle name　　　　Last name

Title _____

Company _____
Identify the corporate servicer as the company if the authorized agent is a servicer.

Address _____
Number　　　Street

_____
City　　　　　　　　State　　ZIP Code

Contact phone _____　Email _____

Official Form 410　　　　　　Proof of Claim　　　　　　page 3

A creditor with a pre-petition supply contract may be asked to make post-petition shipments under the contract. In recent cases, debtors have taken the position that creditors that supply the debtor are required to ship to the debtor under the pre-petition terms, notwithstanding the debtor's unpaid pre-petition invoices. If the creditor refuses to ship or requests cash-in-advance terms, the debtor may take action and allege that the creditor violated the automatic stay. Creditors should consult with counsel regarding their state law rights, including those under UCC Section 2-609, to counter such attempts by the debtor, provided the creditor has a reasonable basis for insecurity about the debtor's ability to perform under the contract. It is also recommended that the creditor insist that the debtor assume the contract as discussed below.

A decision to make new shipments to a DIP is difficult. Some creditors insist on cash in advance. However, the DIP is often in a position of very limited working capital. Any fresh credit extended on an open account basis should reflect on the invoices that shipments are being made to a DIP. In the event that the Chapter 11 is converted into a liquidation, the shipments made to a DIP have a priority claim. However, there is a possibility that funds will not be available to cover this priority claim in a liquidation.

The intent of most Chapter 11 proceedings is to file a plan of reorganization. Although a plan of liquidation may also be filed. When a plan is filed by a DIP, that DIP must also file a *disclosure statement*. The disclosure statement is a document which is meant to explain to all creditors what each class of creditors will receive under the plan and how the plan will be implemented (financed and carried out).

Creditors vote on the plan of reorganization or the plan of liquidation. In order to achieve confirmation of a plan, over one-half of the voting creditors in each class holding at least two-thirds of the amount of claims must vote in favor of the plan. At least one "impaired" class (a class that is not being paid 100%) must vote in favor of the plan. Creditors may present their own plan after a debtor's period of exclusivity ends.

The *cramdown* provision (as in cram the plan down the creditors' throats) allows a bankruptcy court to confirm a plan without the approval of each class of creditors. However, at least one impaired class must vote to accept the plan. The threat of a cramdown can be used if a class of creditors is not negotiating in good faith; another class of creditors could become impaired if one class of creditors tries to wield excessive power during the negotiation process. Once approved, the plan is said to be "confirmed." Sometimes a reorganization plan can be difficult for creditors to evaluate. The debtor must prove that the creditors under the proposed plan will be treated no worse than in a hypothetical Chapter 7 liquidation. For example, if creditors are offered equity in a swap arrangement, how would it compare to a cash bid? The liquidation value can be estimated through the use of a cash flow model. Creditors ultimately vote on the plan to preserve their own best interests. The effective date of a plan can depend on many different factors. Sometimes a plan specifically states a date or occurrence upon which the plan will become effective. Sometimes a plan is effective upon the first payment under the plan. The DIP either will emerge as a reorganized business, or its assets will be sold and the business will be liquidated.

The Small Business Chapter 11 Proceeding

A small business that meets the definition of a small business is urged to proceed as a *small business Chapter 11 bankruptcy proceeding*. For the purposes of qualifying as a small business, a business has to have aggregate secured and unsecured debt not exceeding $2,566,000 (subject to increases for inflation). The small business Chapter 11 proceeding is considered to be a fast track case. This type of bankruptcy moves along more quickly, which can reduce administrative costs and increase the likelihood of emerging successfully from the bankruptcy proceeding.

In a case which is a small business, on request of a party in interest and for cause, the court may order that a committee of creditors not be appointed. Ordinarily, the U.S. Trustee will try to convene a committee in every Chapter 11 proceeding and it is up to the debtor or creditor or some other party in interest to specifically ask the court not to appoint a committee in a small business case. There is currently no mandate that a small business MUST proceed as a small business Chapter 11 bankruptcy proceeding. While that certainly was the intent of creating the small business procedure, some debtors and/or their counsel simply do not elect to be treated as a small business and creditors need to watch out for the debtor who qualifies as a small business but chooses not to act as one. More and more courts are mandating that a DIP who is a small business must use a special form disclosure statement.

BANKRUPTCY: PROBLEMS AND ISSUES

The one constant in a capitalistic system is change. As laws are applied and case decisions establish precedents, certain unexpected outcomes occur. Myriad problems and issues can be attributed to bankruptcy law.

For creditors, some of the most relevant problems, issues and trends include: (1) preferences, (2) fraudulent conveyances, (3) executory contracts, (4) bankruptcy prediction models, (5) alternatives to bankruptcy and (6) automation of bankruptcy courts. Each of these topics will be examined in this section of the chapter.

Preferences

Under common law, nothing barred a merchant from preferring one creditor over another in the payment of debts. Thus, a debtor facing the threat of insolvency would simply pay off relatives and selected creditors, leaving nothing for the bulk of the creditors. Almost from the beginning of the bankruptcy laws in England, a trustee in bankruptcy could recover payments to unsecured creditors deemed preferential. 11 U.S.C. §547 is the bankruptcy provision authorizing the trustee to recover preferential transfers.

From the point of view of an unsecured trade creditor, the preference provisions cut both ways. The creditor may receive preferential treatment and, if challenged, may be required to repay those monies. In other cases, however, others have received preferential treatment and the creditor might want to encourage the trustee to recover those payments from other creditors.

Members of the creditors' committee, should be alert to any sign that the debtor made payments to creditors. Since virtually any payment on account of an antecedent debt made within 90 days of the filing of bankruptcy is at least suspect, and further, since the burden of proof is on the recipient to prove the applicability of a preference defense, the creditor should scrutinize all payments very carefully for possible challenge.

Proving a Preference. In order to fall within the definition of a preferential transfer under 11 U.S.C. §547, the trustee or the debtor in possession must prove: (1) that a transfer of the debtor's assets was made to or for the benefit of a creditor; (2) for or on account of an antecedent debt; (3) while the debtor was insolvent; (4) within 90 days of the petition for relief or within one year if the transfer was to an insider; and (5) the effect of which is to give the creditor more than the creditor would otherwise receive in a Chapter 7 liquidation.

Legal defenses exist for creditors that pertain to preferences. One such defense is called the ***ordinary course of business defense***. A creditor defending a preference lawsuit must prove all of the following to take advantage of the ordinary course of business defense: (1) the debt paid by the alleged preference was incurred in the ordinary course of business of the debtor and creditor; (2) the payment or the transfer was made in the ordinary course of business of the debtor and creditor; and (3) the payment or the transfer was made according to ordinary business terms.

Another preference-related defense is called the ***new value defense***. The new value defense reduces preference exposure by the amount of new credit the creditor had extended to or for the debtor's benefit subsequent to the preference. The new value cannot be secured by an otherwise unavoidable security interest and cannot be paid by an otherwise unavoidable transfer to or for the creditor's benefit.

There is also a ***contemporaneous exchange for new value defense*** that may be used by creditors. A transfer to a creditor, which was intended to be contemporaneous with the extension of credit or the delivery of goods by the creditor and was a substantially contemporaneous exchange, is an exception to the preference rule. In its simplest form, the contemporaneous exchange exception is illustrated by a COD delivery where the debtor pays for goods delivered COD with a check tendered upon receipt of the goods. Technically, of course, the check is not paid until the check has cleared. While this situation is, in the most technical fashion, a potential preference, the provisions of the Code specifically except it.

Creditors should seek legal counsel when dealing with preference demands and/or lawsuits.

Fraudulent Conveyances

The basic premise that underlies a *fraudulent conveyance* is a transfer of assets, for less than reasonably equivalent value, to a third party, at the time when the debtor is insolvent or which transfer renders the debtor insolvent. Both state laws and the Bankruptcy Code contain statutes that pertain to fraudulent conveyances. The fraudulent conveyance laws can be traced back more than 400 years to English common law.

There have been leveraged buyout transactions (LBO) where the issue of fraudulent conveyances has been used by unsecured creditors to obtain a judgment against LBO participants forcing them to return assets to the estate, where there otherwise would not have been sufficient funds for creditors. If a bank has provided funds as a secured lender to underwrite an LBO and the debtor is rendered insolvent or with unreasonably little capital, the bank's lien could be at risk. Unsecured creditors have used the fraudulent conveyance chip during the Chapter 11 negotiation process. Dividends to unsecured creditors can be substantially increased as a result.

Creditors should seek legal counsel when dealing with a fraudulent conveyance case. Applicable laws may ultimately decide the potential application to the transaction at issue. Under the Bankruptcy Code, a trustee can reach back over a two-year period from the petition date to recover funds. This period may be longer if the trustee uses state fraudulent transfer law, as is permitted by the Bankruptcy Code.

In the LBO of *Wieboldt Stores, Inc. (Raleigh, Chapter 11 Trustee v. Schottenstein)*, the bankruptcy court found that a fraudulent conveyance had occurred. Also, in the *O'Day Corporation* case, a bank lost its security interest based on an LBO fraudulent conveyance ruling. However, in *Jeannette Corporation (Moody, Chapter 7 Trustee v. Security Pacific Business Credit, Inc.)*, the court ruled that the secured lenders' rights should not be voided. Sometimes the issue can come down to a test for solvency of the business at the time of the transfer. Should the Balance Sheet test or Liquidation Value of Assets test be used? The issue remains unresolved.

Executory Contracts

An *executory contract* is an agreement where each party still has material obligations remaining to perform. For example, a supply agreement, a conditional sales contract or a lease agreement would often be categorized as an executory contract. When a Chapter 11 occurs, the debtor must either assume or reject an executory contract either during the case or in connection with confirmation. Assumption and rejection require bankruptcy court approval.

If the contract is assumed, then the debtor is required to "cure all" payments under the contract (as well as any non-monetary defaults), including any pre-petition obligations, and also provide assurance that future obligations under the contract will be fulfilled. In connection with a motion to assume an executory contract, the debtor will specify what it believes to be the correct "cure amount." If this amount is less than the full amount the creditor believes it is owed, the creditor should object to the proposed assumption and/or negotiate with the debtor to obtain the correct cure amount. Bankruptcy allows a debtor to get out of unattractive executory contracts. If the debtor rejects the contract, then the debtor is relieved of future obligation under the contract. Since the debtor is deemed to have breached the contract if the contract is rejected, the creditor is entitled to pursue damages incurred as a result of the breach of contract by way of filing a rejection damages proof of claim. The creditor is also relieved of future obligations under the contract.

Bankruptcy Prediction Models

The ability to predict bankruptcy prior to the actual filing would furnish a tremendous edge to a creditor. Academics have conducted a number of studies that use financial ratios to predict bankruptcy. Most of these studies isolate specific financial ratios or combinations of financial ratios in an attempt to detect observable trends. Current research suggests that industry-specific ratios may provide more accurate results.

Edward I. Altman, a professor of finance at New York University, is perhaps the most renowned academic to work on bankruptcy prediction models. Altman has used a multivariate model that includes five weighted financial ratios to predict bankruptcy. The results are presented in a statistic called a Z-score. Altman's model was illustrated in Chapter 10 of this book.

The crux of the issue concerning bankruptcy prediction models is somewhat similar to the credit scoring models discussed in Chapter 6 of this book. One problem often expressed by credit practitioners is that the release of the financial data comes too late to be useful in making effective credit decisions. Yet there have been significant inroads made that allow for technology to contribute to a wider use of models to predict bankruptcy. There are computer programs that furnish credit managers with a Z-score. This information can be useful when making credit decisions.

Alternatives to Bankruptcy

The high costs associated with bankruptcy proceedings encourage both the debtor and creditor to seek ways to address financial distress in a forum outside federal bankruptcy court. Two specific alternatives to bankruptcy are (1) an assignment for the benefit of creditors and (2) an out-of-court workout.

Assignment for the Benefit of Creditors

An *assignment for the benefit of creditors*, often called an assignment, is a way to liquidate a business outside of bankruptcy. The assignment is a voluntary transfer of all of the debtor's property to an assignee who acts as a trustee. The assignee sells off the debtor's assets and distributes the proceeds to creditors in accordance with the order of priority under state law. Any excess proceeds are returned to the debtor. Any deficiencies become a bad debt write-off for creditors.

State laws govern the use of an assignment. The administrative costs can be lower than those in a Chapter 7 liquidation. The results of an assignment are the orderly liquidation of assets and a *pro rata* distribution of cash to creditors based upon their claims. Rarely are there enough funds available to pay creditors in full. An assignment has the advantage of being speedier and less costly than a bankruptcy. However, the assignment simply is not appropriate in many cases due to complexities of debtor-creditor relationships. Situations in which a business is deteriorating quickly can afford an opportunity to use an assignment.

Out-of-Court Workout

An *out-of-court workout* is an informal reorganization of a business. The debtor continues to operate a business as a going concern. The goal of the out-of-court workout is to gain a moratorium on debt payments and/or to get creditors to agree to a reduced and/or *pro rata* settlement. Sometimes creditors are offered additional debt or stock in a business in order to gain acceptance for the out-of-court workout. State laws also govern out-of-court workouts.

There are situations when a business can avoid bankruptcy in order to get back on its feet. A *composition* is an agreement outside of bankruptcy where creditors agree to a reduction in the total debt owed. An *extension* is an agreement allowing a debtor more time to make payments owed to creditors. Sometimes a combination of a composition and an extension can be useful.

An out-of-court workout is done on a voluntary basis. The agreement does not require the consent of all creditors. However, creditors that do not agree are forced, at times, to sue the debtor and collect on any judgment. Creditors face the issue of whether the proposed composition is superior to a formal bankruptcy proceeding. In an out-of-court workout, there is usually a creditors' committee that will impose a number of covenants upon the debtor.

There can be circumstances that make a formal bankruptcy preferable to either an assignment or an out-of-court workout. A formal bankruptcy provides a mechanism that includes a statement of the affairs of a business that is made under oath. A bankruptcy can bind dissenting creditors to a negotiated deal among a substantial portion of creditors. Moreover, a bankruptcy can allow for the rejection of executory contracts, the recapturing of preferential payments and the prevention of fraudulent conveyances.

Even assuming the above options are a better alternative to bankruptcy, dissenting creditors have the power to commence an involuntary bankruptcy proceeding, thwarting such non-bankruptcy attempts. On rare occasions, such as when an involuntary case is filed while an assignment for benefit of creditors is already pending, the bankruptcy court may dismiss an involuntary petition.

Automation of Bankruptcy Courts

The wide use of the Internet makes electronic modes of working with bankruptcy quite efficient. Developed and maintained by the Administrative Office of the U.S. Courts, the Public Access to Court Electronic Records (PACER) resource provides information for the federal judiciary including U.S. Bankruptcy Courts. Now widely used, PACER makes available official case information online to anyone who registers for an account. Direct links to all courts that offer PACER can be accessed at www.pacer.gov/.

Another website that is useful for bankruptcies pending in Canada is located at www.bankruptcycanada.com/. Here information pertaining to specific provinces can be reviewed. Proposals and trustees' comments can also be downloaded.

Enhancements in technology will continue to make improvements in information availability. The feeling of being overwhelmed with paper is being replaced with improved access to and the use of meaningful electronic information. For credit managers, an understanding of the essential aspects of bankruptcy is more important than ever. The expectation of becoming more productive by making better use of valuable information can be realized.

CHAPTER 12: FOLLOW-UP

Recap of Important Concepts

1. The financial meltdown and resulting credit crunch during the period from 2007 to 2009 have led to a surge in the number of bankruptcies filed. Not only have more individuals filed but also half of the largest 18 bankruptcies for publicly traded companies in U.S. history have occurred during the 2007-2009 period.
2. Chapter 7 of the Bankruptcy Code is used for straight liquidations by both businesses and individuals. Credit analysts should be aware of the priority of claims used to distribute the proceeds in a liquidation.
3. A business reorganization is conducted under Chapter 11 of the Bankruptcy Code. The bankruptcy process can be initiated through either a voluntary or an involuntary petition filed in a U.S. District Court.
4. The debtor-in-possession (DIP) has certain responsibilities during a Chapter 11 case. The DIP must present a disclosure statement and monthly financial statements, affirm or reject executory contracts, and strive to ultimately emerge from the Chapter 11 case by working through a viable reorganization plan.
5. Creditors often face a number of difficult decisions during a Chapter 11 case. Creditors should consider exercising a right of reclamation. The decision to extend fresh credit to a DIP can vary by circumstances. Creditors often can benefit by serving on a creditors' committee. The ultimate vote on a reorganization plan addresses the decision of whether the debtor is more valuable as a going concern or in a liquidation.
6. A municipality would file a bankruptcy petition under Chapter 9 of the Bankruptcy Code. Chapter 12 is used by family farmers and family fishermen to reorganize debt. Chapter 13 of the Bankruptcy Code is used by individuals with regular income and by small businesses.
7. The Bankruptcy Abuse Prevention and Consumer Prevention Act of 2005 (BAPCPA) changed the focus of Chapter 15 to cross-border cases. The purpose of Chapter 15 is now placed upon remedying situations for debtors and creditors who are involved in cases located in more than one country.

8. Noteworthy trends in Chapter 11 include the use of prepackaged and prearranged bankruptcy, debtor petitions to use DIP financing through a bank and the use of cash collateral by a debtor.
9. BAPCPA has streamlined the small business Chapter 11 bankruptcy process, leading to expedited proceedings.
10. The treatment of a creditor in a preferential manner can create a need to return payments received within a 90-day period of a bankruptcy. There are several legal defenses that exist to protect payments from being classified as preferential.
11. A fraudulent conveyance is the transfer of a debtor's assets to a third party so that the debtor is left judgment proof. There have been leveraged buyout (LBO) transactions where fraudulent conveyance law has benefited unsecured creditors at the expense of secured lenders.
12. Bankruptcy prediction models examine financial ratios to predict bankruptcy. Credit practitioners can access Z-score information by using software packages that provide financial statement analysis. The ability to forecast bankruptcy is intuitively appealing.
13. An assignment for the benefit of creditors or an out-of-court workout can be used as an alternative to bankruptcy. The focus is often placed upon an extension or a composition to modify debt obligations.
14. With the PACER system, U.S. Bankruptcy Courts are now automated. There have been significant enhancements made concerning the availability of relevant information through the use of the Internet.

Review/Discussion Questions

1. Under which chapter(s) of the Bankruptcy Code would each of the following debtors file a bankruptcy petition?
   a. An individual or business seeking to liquidate
   b. A family farmer
   c. A municipality
   d. An individual or business seeking to reorganize
   e. A company in Mexico concerned with inventory stored in the United States and a creditor in the U.S.
2. In what order of priority are the distribution of assets made in a Chapter 7 proceeding?
3. What is a superpriority claim in a Chapter 11 proceeding?
4. What is a prepackaged bankruptcy under Chapter 11?

12: Bankruptcy and Reorganization

5. Must a creditor file a Proof of Claim in order to receive a liquidating dividend? Explain your response.
6. What is a preference in a bankruptcy proceeding?
7. How can the principles of fraudulent conveyance be of use to unsecured creditors after an LBO files for bankruptcy?
8. Who is asked to serve on a creditors' committee? What do members of the creditors' committee do?

Test Your Knowledge

1. Under what circumstances can a creditor or creditors file an involuntary bankruptcy petition? Be specific.
2. What is a Chapter 11 bankruptcy? What is a small business Chapter 11 proceeding?
3. What is an assignment for the benefit of creditors?
4. What is the voting requirement needed for creditors to approve a Chapter 11 reorganization?
5. What factors should a credit manager take into consideration when asked to ship to a debtor-in-possession?
6. Under what circumstances may a creditor exercise a right of reclamation? Describe the process to be used by a creditor who is exercising the right of reclamation.
7. How far back does the period for a preference normally extend? If a preference is given to an insider, how far back does a preference extend? Identify two defenses that can be used by a creditor in order to defend against clawing back funds in a preference situation.
8. Compare and contrast an out-of-court workout and an assignment for the benefit of creditors.
9. Use the Absolute Priority Rule to perform a liquidation. The cash received in the liquidation is $1,500,000 of which $400,000 is received from the sale of fixed assets and $1,100,000 from the sale of current assets. Your task is to allocate the $1,500,000 in proceeds from the liquidation to the appropriate claimant.

   - Assume administrative expenses are $300,000.
   - Assume that Debentures are subordinated to the bank.
   - Assume that Accounts Payable are not related to DIP sales.

○ Assume the First Mortgage Bond is secured by the fixed assets.

Accounts Receivable	1,000,000	Accrued Taxes	100,000
Inventory	1,100,000	Short-term Bank Debt	1,300,000
Current Assets	2,100,000	Accounts Payable	800,000
Fixed Assets	2,000,000	Current Liabilities	2,200,000
Total Assets	**4,100,000**	Subordinated Debentures	1,100,000
		First Mortgage Bond	300,000
		Common Equity	500,000
		Total Liabilities and Equity	**4,100,000**

Online Assignment

Select a recent bankruptcy of your choice. Find out the docket number for the case. What information is contained in the docket? When is the first meeting of creditors? What activities are on the agenda at the first meeting of creditors? What other useful information can you find online about the bankruptcy proceeding? (Note to instructors: You may want to use one particular bankruptcy to assign to the entire class. This can lead to enriching discussion in class.)

Credit Management Online

www.abiworld.org/—The American Bankruptcy Institute is dedicated to research and education. This website provides numerous education-related activities. There are articles concerning legislation, international bankruptcy laws and specific U.S. court opinions. Although much of the material is free, ABI members have access to additional resources.

www.bankruptcycanada.com/—This site contains information concerning most aspects of business and personal bankruptcy in Canada.

www.bankruptcydata.com/—This is a commercial site; however, there is a considerable amount of information that is available for free. Subscribers can access premium services for a fee. There are links to specific cases and courts.

www.financiallit.org/—The Institute for Financial Literacy website offers articles and resources that are of particular use in consumer finance and personal bankruptcy.

www.justice.gov/ust/—The U.S. Department of Justice Trustee Program website contains information pertaining to the U.S. Trustee Program. There are 21 regions that cover all district courts except those for Alabama and North Carolina. Fraud prevention is one key goal of the program. Information about the Bankruptcy Abuse Prevention and Consumer Protection Act of 2005 (BAPCPA) is also available.

www.nbkrc.com/—The National Bankruptcy Research Center (NBKRC) holds a national database for bankruptcy filings. Information for particular cases may be accessed on a subscription basis. Statistical data pertaining to bankruptcy is also available.

online.wsj.com/mdc/public/page/2_3024-indicatehtml? mod=djemRTEh—The link will take you directly to the *Wall Street Journal's* Economic Indicator Archive. There is a wealth of current and historical macroeconomic information available.

www.pacer.gov/—This link will take you directly to the Public Access to Court Electronic Records (PACER). The free site is operated by the Administrative Office of the U.S. Courts. Each court maintains its own database of cases.

topics.law.cornell.edu/wex/bankruptcy—Hosted by the Legal Information Institute (LII) at Cornell Law School, this site offers numerous resources including the entire U.S. Bankruptcy Code.

www.uscourts.gov/FederalCourts/Bankruptcy.aspx—Maintained by the federal government, this site provides bankruptcy information that is available directly from the U.S. Bankruptcy Courts. Forms, rules, resources and an overview of all bankruptcy chapters are available. There are also links to a glossary of bankruptcy-related terms and websites for each of the U.S. Bankruptcy Courts.

www.uscourts.gov/Statistics/BankruptcyStatistics.aspx—This link will take you directly to the Administrative Office of the U.S. Courts where you can obtain current macroeconomic statistical data concerning bankruptcy.

References Useful for Further Reading

Barron, Jacob. "Business Bankruptcies Hit Pre-BAPCPA Numbers: Could Reform Send Them Even Higher?" *Business Credit* (June 2010): 40-41.

Barron, Jacob. "Liquidate or Rehabilitate?" *Business Credit* (May 2009): 6-8.

Binford, Jason B., Scott Everett, and Hon Harlin Hale. "The Top Ten Cases That Every Bankruptcy Practitioner Should Know." *The Federal Lawyer* (February 2010): 40-46.

Bishara, Fahad A. "History of Insolvency and Bankruptcy from an International Perspective." *Business History Review* 83.4 (Winter 2009): 872-875.Blakeley, Scott. "Bad Check and Bankruptcy: Can Your Debtor Discharge Your 'NSF' Debt?" *Business Credit* (November/December 2006): 54-55.

Bodoff, Joseph. "Why You Should Participate on Creditors' Committees." *Business Credit* (September 2007): 24-26.

Carr, Matthew. "Avoid Unwanted Exposure: Creating a Defense Against Preference Payments." *Business Credit* (November/December 2007): 54-55.

Chen, Shirley. "Multinational Insolvency: Chapter 15 and a Foreign Representative's Rights to Administrate Debtor's Assets in the United States." *Business Credit* (May 2008): 34-35.

Cowie, Norman. "The Great and Wonderful § 341 Hearing." *Business Credit* (November/December 2006): 59-60.

Fitzpatrick, Laura. "A Brief History of: Bankruptcy." *Time* (June 15, 2009): 17.

Franklin, David. "The New Face of Canadian Bankruptcy and Insolvency Laws." *Debt Cubed* (March 2010): 11.

Futterman, Matthew. "Texas Rangers Make Bankruptcy Play." *The Wall Street Journal* (May 25, 2010): C1-C2.

Gauthier, Stephen J. "GASB Issues Final Statement on Bankruptcies." *Government Finance Review* (April 2010): 77-78.

Grzeskowiak, Jennifer. "Bankruptcy for Cities." *American City & County* (April 2010): 14.

Helyar, John, and Jonathan Keehner. "Tom Hicks Says Goodbye to Sports." *Bloomberg Businessweek* (May 31, 2010): 42-43.

Holman, Kelly. "Six Flags Rides Out of Bankruptcy." *High Yield Report* (May 10, 2010): 29.

Ingrassia, Paul. "The Lessons of the GM Bankruptcy." *The Wall Street Journal* (June 2010): A19.

"Judge Clears CIT to Use Some Financing." *American Banker* (November 4, 2009): 16.

Korybut, Michael. "How Preferences Are Treated Under the New Bankruptcy Law." *Secured Lender* (January 2007): 20-26.

Larson, Stuart. "What Every Commercial Landlord Should Know About the Treatment of Leases in Chapter 11 Reorganizations." *Business Credit* (April 2008): 20-22.

Lemerle, Maxime. "The Insolvency U-Turn: Business Insolvency Decline Will Stop in Midstream." *Business Credit* (March 2016): 22-24.

McCabe, Phil. "Lack of Lending Behind the Surge in Company Closures." *International Journal of Bank Marketing* (November 2009): 547-551.Madris, Howard, and Michael Joncich. "Preference Defense Checklist." *Business Credit* (June 2010): 42-44.

Mota, Diana. "Resolving Bankruptcy: Laws That Govern the Restructuring or Dissolution of Insolvent Companies Continue to Evolve Worldwide." *Business Credit* (May 2015): 18-21.

Nathan, Bruce. "Compelling Bankruptcy Trade Credit: The Great Unknown." *Business Credit* (September/October 2009): 12-17.

Nathan, Bruce. "Creditors' Committee Disclosure Obligations Updated: The Use of Internet Websites." *Business Credit* (April 2010): 42-45.

Nathan, Bruce. "The Critical Vendor Roller Coaster." *Business Credit* (February 2008): 20-23.

Nathan, Bruce, and Eric Horn. "Demystifying Chapter 15 of the Bankruptcy Code." *Business Credit* (June 2009): 14-19.

Nathan, Bruce. "Effective Seller Remedies When Confronting a Financially Distressed Buyer Prior to Bankruptcy." *Business Credit* (February 2009): 30-33.

Nathan, Bruce. "The Interplay Between Section 503(b)(9) Priority Claims and Preference Claims." *Business Credit* (March 2010): 6-10.

Nathan, Bruce. "Recent Case Law Developments Concerning 503(b)(9) 20-Day Goods Priority Claims." *Business Credit* (November/December 2009): 20-23.

Nathan, Bruce. "The Risks of a Single Creditor Involuntary Bankruptcy Petition; Tread Extra Carefully!" *Business Credit* (October 2007): 24-28.

Nathan, Bruce. "Section 503(b)(9) Goods Supplier Priority—Beware of the Debtor's Setoff Rights." *Business Credit* (February 2010): 48-51.

National Association of Credit Management. *Manual of Credit and Commercial Laws*, Current edition. Columbia, Md.

O'Brien, Elizabeth. "Ten Things That Bankruptcy Court Won't Tell You." *SmartMoney* (October 2009): 82-84.

Pickerill, Carl N. "Executory Contracts Re-Revisited." *American Bankruptcy Law Journal* 83.1 (Winter 2009): 63-110.

Rozens, Aleksandrs. "Moody's Says Half of Defaults Came from Private Equity." *Mergers & Acquisitions Report* (March 29, 2010): 9.

Ryan, Vincent. "Breezing Through Bankruptcy." *CFO* (1 June 2010): www.cfo.com/printable/article.cfm/14499487.

Schirmang, Sandra, Deborah Thorne and Valerie Venable. "Creditors' Committees: What You Should Know Before Deciding to Serve." *Business Credit* (May 2009): 38-42.

Shappell, Brian. "The Need for Speed: Is the Rapid Pace of Filings in the New Era of Bankruptcies Setting the Stage for More Failures?" *Business Credit* (May 2010): 12-14.

Stearn Jr., Robert J. "Proving Solvency: Defending Preference and Fraudulent Transfer Litigation." *Business Lawyer* 62.2 (February 2007): 359-395.

Stern, Nicholas. "Look Beyond Payment History for Signs of Potential Bankruptcy." *Business Credit* (June 2016): 8-9.

Tarbous, Ken. "Finished with Bankruptcy, CIT Lending Again." *High Yield Report* (December 21, 2009): 24.

Thorne, Deborah. "Alternatives to Bankruptcy: What Credit Professionals Should Know About Liquidation and Restructuring Outside of Court." *Business Credit* (September/October 2009): 26-28.

Thorne, Deborah. "Assignments for the Benefit of Creditors: Creditor Considerations." *Business Credit* (November/December 2007): 43-45.

Thorne, Deborah. "Cash Collateral and DIP Financing Orders." *Business Credit* (November/December 2009): 40-42.

Thorne, Deborah. "Leave No Stone Unturned: Fraudulent Transfer Recovery in a Liquidating Chapter 11." *Business Credit* (April 2010): 14-16.

Thorne, Deborah. "Out-of-Court Liquidations Pose Questions for Credit Professionals." *Business Credit* (June 2009): 22-24.

Thorne, Deborah. "Pay to Play: Liquidation of Assets Using Chapter 11 Should Provide Unsecured Creditors with a Share of the Proceeds." *Business Credit* (June 2009): 38-41.

Turner, Karen Lee. "Prepackaged and Pre-arranged Bankruptcies." *Business Credit* (July/August 2008): 8-10.

Williams, David. "10 Tips for Selling Your Bankruptcy Claims." *Business Credit* (November/December 2008): 50-54.

Yamauchi, Rei. "How the New DIP Model Works." *International Financial Law Review* (September 2009): 51-53.

Index

absolute priority rule, 292-296, 296-299

accountant's opinion, 196-199. *See also* auditor's opinion

accounting
issues/problems, 215-217
rules, 203, 214-215, 216. *See also* Generally Accepted Accounting Rules (GAAP)

accumulated depreciation, 230

adverse opinion, 197

aging schedules, 27

Altman, Edward I., 137, 245, 248-250, 284, 314

American Institute of Certified Public Accountants (AICPA),196-197, 217

American International Group (AIG), 11, 96, 98

American Law Institute (ALI), 266

annual percentage rate (APR), 96, 108, 109-112

anti-dumping regulations, 52

antitrust laws/regulations, 52, 96, 99-101
Clayton Act, 99
Federal Trade Commission Act, 100
guidelines, 101
Robinson-Patman Act, 100-101
Sherman Act, 99

application, credit, 20, 25, 85, 102, 145, 181
ECOA and Regulation B, 104-106
processing, 125-129
sample, 149-150

Arthur Andersen, 198, 217

Article 9 of the UCC, 260, 263, 265, 266-273

asset management ratios, 203, 204-206, 209

assignment for the benefit of creditors, 22, 315

Association of Credit Executives (ACE), 10-11

auditor's opinion, 196-199

automated clearing house (ACH), 179, 180

automating credit, 11, 38-40, 172-173, 179-180

automation, bankruptcy, 316

bad debt, 6, 25, 76, 81, 82
expenses, 26, 27-28, 30, 40
losses/write-offs, 22, 78-79, 80, 87, 88-89, 185, 263, 315
predicting, 138-139, 186-187
reserves, 88-89

balance sheet, 12, 57, 89, 199-203, 204, 206, 208, 211, 212, 213, 215, 216, 217, 229-231, 296-299
cash conversion cycle, 230-231
method, 89
sources/uses of funds, 229-230, 234

Bank of New England Corp., 286

bank references, 57-58, 86, 130-132, 161

banker's acceptance, 112-113, 264, 276-277

banking services, 65

bankruptcy (Chapter 12), 22, 87, 88, 98, 157, 159, 185, 210, 215
alternatives, 314-316
automation of, 316
BAPCPA, 286
Chapter 7 (liquidation), 285, 287, 290-299
Chapter 9 (municipal), 287-288
Chapter 11 (reorganization), 86, 98, 216, 285, 288, 290, 291, 293-294, 296, 299-310, 313
Chapter 12 (family farmer), 285, 288
Chapter 13 (individual), 285, 288-289
Chapter 15 (cross-border), 289-290
claims priority rules, 292-296

Code, 286-290
executory contracts, 302-303, 311, 313-314, 316
Form 410, 306-308
fraudulent conveyances, 312-313
history, 215, 283-286
law, 284-286
PACER, 303-304, 316
prearranged bankruptcy, 302
prediction models, 314
preferences, 271, 287, 311-312
prepackaged bankruptcy, 301-302
problems and issues, 310-316
proof of claim, 305-308
secured creditors, 260, 270, 292
small business, 310
trends, 284-286
trustee(s), 271, 287, 288-289, 290, 291, 292, 294, 296, 301, 303-304, 313, 315
unsecured creditors, 291, 295, 303, 304, 311, 312-313
Bankruptcy Abuse Prevention and Consumer Protection Act of 2005 (BAPCPA), 285, 286, 289-290, 293, 301, 302, 304
bankruptcy alternatives, 314-316
assignment for the benefit of creditors, 22, 315
out-of-court workout, 315-316
bankruptcy problems and issues, alternatives, 314-316
automation of the courts, 316
fraudulent conveyances, 312-313, 316
prediction models, 136, 248-250, 314
preferences, 271, 311-312
barter arrangement, 178
Basel Accord agreements (Basel I, Basel II, Basel III), 54
Bear Stearns, 11, 96
benchmarking, 25, 26-30, 39, 40, 82, 88

book value, 216, 243, 249, 270-271, 292
Buffet, Warren, 242
business credit reporting. *See* credit reports
business process outsourcing (BPO), 26, 37-38, 39
bust-outs, 143, 290

"C" corporation, 127
Canons of Business Credit Ethics, 4, 5
capacity, 124-125
capital, 83, 97, 98, 113-114, 124, 208, 313
bank, 53-54
cost of, 78, 83-84, 175, 210, 235, 236
working, 82, 209-210, 249, 313
Cash Conversion Cycle, 230-231
cash flow, 112, 114, 124, 156, 178-179, 217, 228, 241
from operations, 245-248
cash flow analysis (Chapter 10)
balance sheet, 229-231
income statement, 234-241
model applied to an LBO, 235-241
pro forma, 234-241
stock and real estate valuation, 241-245
tools, 245-250
cash flow statement, 230, 231-234
activities, 232
Altman Z-score, 248-250
direct method, 232
indirect method, 233
Lambda Index, 245-248
cash terms, 174-175
cash in advance, 175
cash on delivery, 174
cash with order, 174
cashier's check, 174
certified check, 174
wire transfer and ACH, 174
certification in credit, 6, 15

Certified Credit and Risk
    Analyst (CCRA), 6, 15
Certified Credit Executive (CCE),
    6, 15, 35
Certified International Credit
    Professional (CICP),
    6, 15, 48
certified public accountants (CPAs),
    198
Chapter 7, 285, 287, 290-299
  absolute priority rule, 290-296
  claims priority rules, 292-296
  liquidation case study, 296-299
Chapter 9, 287-288
Chapter 11, 86, 98, 216, 285, 288
    290, 291, 293-294, 296, 299-
    310, 313
  creditors, 303-305
  DIP, 302-303
  expedited small business
    proceeding, 310
  initiating a proceeding in, 300-301
  proof of claim, 305-308
  time frame, 301-302
Chapter 12, 285, 288
Chapter 13, 285, 288-289
Chapter 15, 289-290
character, 124
CHIPS, Clearing House Interbank
  Payment System, 180
Chrysler, 96, 241, 286, 301
CIT Group, 241, 286
claims, 292-296
  absolute priority, 294
  administrative, 292-294, 305
  proof of, 305, 306-308
  secured, 292, 298
  superpriority, 296, 302
  unsecured, 291, 294-295, 296, 298
Clayton Act, 99
Clearing House Interbank Payment
  System (CHIPS), 180
collateral, 6, 21, 22, 86, 87, 108,
    125, 128, 131, 178, 239, 259,

    261, 262, 263, 267, 268, 270-
    271, 272-273, 291, 292, 296,
    298, 299, 302-303
collection (Chapter 8)
  activity, 37, 182-185
  as a credit function, 8, 10, 40,
    87, 88
  availability, 180-182
  compensation, 37, 187-188
  costs, 40
  Credit Managers' Index (CMI),
    185-186
  deductions, 87
  escheatment, 189
  FDCPA, 107
  filings, 160
  integrating technology, 172-173
  methods of, 182-185
  outsourcing, 37-38, 188
  reviewing the system, 186-187
  trade credit terms, 173-180
common-size analysis, 40, 199-203
compensation
  claims, 294
  credit and collection, 36
  labor and material, 264-265
  risk, 50
conditions, 125
Conseco, Inc., 286
consignment terms, 60, 86, 178, 267
consumer credit
  legislation. *See* legislation
  reports, 152, 158, 60, 161-162
  scoring, 162-163
consumer goods, 272-273
contra account terms, 178
cost of capital, 78, 83-84, 175,
    210, 235, 236
country risk, 55-56
Countrywide Financial, 96
credere, 123
credit
  as a profession, 3-7
  automation of activity, 39-40

availability, 55, 181-182
business information, analyzing,
  129-135
centralized, 32-33
criteria, 4-8
decentralized, 33-34, 152
disclosure of terms, 107
job specifications, 31-34
limits, 20, 55, 80, 85, 87, 180-182
scoring, 135-143
Credit and Financial Development
  Division (CFDD), 15
credit application, 20, 25, 85, 102,
  145, 181
  ECOA and Regulation B, 104-106
  processing, 125-129
  sample, 149-150
Credit Business Associate (CBA),
  6, 15
Credit Business Fellow (CBF), 6, 15
credit cards, 77, 80, 108, 139, 162,
  179, 180
credit controls, 81-82
  existing customers, 182
  internal, 125-126
credit department
  costs/expenses, 27-28, 79-80,
    127-128
  objectives, 77-80
credit insurance, export, 48, 60-61
credit investigation (Chapter 6)
  analyzing information, 129-135
  credit scoring analysis, 135-143
  credit scoring problems, 141-143
  Five Cs of Credit, 124-125
  limiting extent, 127-128
  monitoring existing accounts, 143
  processing applications, 125-129
  sources of information, 128-129
  tasks, 20
Credit Managers' Index (CMI),
  185-186
credit policy/procedures (Chapter 4),
  9, 20, 21, 22, 28, 33, 75-89,
  112, 128, 138, 141, 179, 181,

183, 186-187
audit, checklist, 85-88
bad debt reserves, 88-89
compliance with law, 95
criticisms of, 80-81
defined, 80
development of, 128
economic value added, 83-84
establishing, 80-81
objectives of, 77-80
receivables portfolio analysis,
  82-83
review, need to, 80-81
role of the credit function, 76-77
signs to review, 81-82
strategic planning, 76-77
write-offs, 88-89
credit reports (Chapter 7)
  business, 129, 133-134, 151-163
  consumer, 106-107, 129, 161-162
Credit Research Foundation (CRF),
  30, 88, 179
credit scoring
  analysis, 135-143
  benefits, 140-141
  corporation (sample), 140
  development and mechanics,
    136-137
  examples, 138-139
  individual (sample), 139
  models, 136-137
  problems, 141-143
credit tasks, 37-38, 79, 85, 181-182
  essential for advancement, 10-13
  essential for employment,
    7-10, 20-23
CreditNet.com, 129, 160
creditors
  assignment for the benefit of,
    315
  Chapter 7, 291-296
  Chapter 11, 303-305
creditors' committee,
    87, 304, 310, 311, 314, 315
cultural risk, 51-52

Index 331

currency
  convertibility, 63
  market forces, 64
current ratio, 203-204, 209
customs, 52

days sales outstanding (DSO), 28-30,
    77-78, 81, 210, 231
  period ratio, 204-205, 209
debit cards, 179, 180
debt management ratios, 206-207,
    209
debt to equity ratio, 206, 209
debtor-in-possession (DIP), 86, 288,
    293-294, 302-303, 309, 310
deductions, 21, 87, 134, 173,
    185, 187-188
demographic shifts, 134
deposits, 295
disclaimer, 197
disclosure
  of personal financial information,
    113
discount, 20, 34, 87, 100, 101, 114,
    140, 175-177, 179
  interest, 109, 111-112
  model, 244
  rate, 236, 237
dividend, 208, 234, 238, 244
dividend model, 244
documentary letters of credit, 58
documentation
  concerns, 268, 270
  discrepancies and deficiencies
    (LC), 58-60, 277
Dodd-Frank Wall Street Reform
    and Consumer Protection Act,
    96-98
Duff & Phelps, 129
Dun & Bradstreet, 129, 153
  Business Information Report,
    156-157
  business report categories, 156
  other products, 158
  PAYDEX Score, 156, 157

ratings, 137, 153-155
DuPont analysis, 210-211

earnings
  before interest, taxes, depreciation
    and amoritization (EBITDA),
    228, 240, 243
  retention rate, 213
economic risk, 56
economic value added (EVA), 83-84
Electronic Data Gathering, Analysis
    and Retrevial system
    (EDGAR), 242
electronic funds transfers,
    87, 134, 179-180
electronic payment arrangements,
    179-180
embargoes, 52
Emery, Gary, 245-248
Energy Future Holdings Corp., 286
Enron, 11, 101, 198, 215, 216, 217,
    241, 286
enterprise resource planning (ERP),
    23, 134, 172-173
Equal Credit Opportunity Act
    (ECOA), 104-106, 141, 150
Equifax, 129, 160, 161-162
equipment, PMSI, 272-273
equity
  capital, 83-84, 208
  investors, 236, 239
escheatment, 189
ethics, 4, 5, 11, 34, 130, 243
executory contracts, 302-303, 311,
    313-314, 316
expenses, 27-28, 30, 40, 88, 127, 200
    203-204, 240
  bad debt, 89
  bankruptcy, 292-293
  improperly capitalizing, 216
  interest, 83, 84, 199, 200, 206, 207,
    209, 237, 240
  operating, 83, 84, 199, 200, 209,
    212, 228, 232, 237
  percentage bad debt, 28

Experian, 129, 158-160, 161-162, 163
  Business Credit Advantage Report, 158-160
export credit insurance, 48, 60-61
Export-Import Bank, 60, 66, 129
export letters of credit, 58-61, 135, 178, 275-276

Fair Credit Billing Act, 108
Fair Credit Reporting Act (FCRA), 106-107, 161
Fair Debt Collection Practices Act (FDCPA), 107
Fair Isaac Corporation (FICO) score, 162-163
family farmer, 288
Federal Trade Commission (FTC), 96, 100, 105, 106, 107
  Red Flags Rules, 102-103
Federal Trade Commission Act, 100
Fedwire, 180
FICO score, 162-163
finance charge. *See* interest rate calculations
Finance, Credit and International Business (FCIB), 6, 15, 48, 55, 56-57, 129, 160
Financial Accounting Standards Board (FASB), 216, 231
Financial Corp. of America, 286
financial ratios, 203-214, 245-250, 314
financial statement analysis (Chapter 9)
  accounting issues/problems, 215-217
  basic defensive interval (BDI), 211-212
  common-size analysis, 199-203
  DuPont analysis, 210-211
  international standards (IFRS), 214-215
  problems, 215-217
  ratio analysis, 203-208, 209

source of, 196-199
sources/uses funds, 229-230, 234
sustainable growth, 212-214
tools, 208-214
zero working capital, 209-210
financial statements, 199, 302
  footnotes, 215
  personal, 198
financing statement, UCC, 267-268
  UCC-1 (sample), 269
Fitch's Investors Service, 129
Five Cs of Credit, 124-125
fixed asset turnover ratio, 205-206, 209
fixed charge coverage ratio, 206-207, 209
foreign company analysis, 56-58
Foreign Corrupt Practices Act, 51-52
Foreign Credit Insurance Association (FCIA), 60, 66
foreign exchange risk, 49-50, 54-55, 61-62
  banking services, 65
  currency convertibility, 63
  hedging a transaction, 64, 65
  market forces, 64
  spot vs. forward rates, 62-63
forfaiting, 50
Form 410, 305
  sample, 306-308
forward rate, 62-63
fraud, 143
  prevention, 6, 14, 100, 102-103, 126, 143, 199, 241, 244, 262, 263, 276, 290, 303, 304
  Red Flags Rules (FTC), 102-103
fraudulent conveyances, 312-313
futures contracts/hedge, 63, 64, 65

General Agreement on Tariffs and Trade (GATT), 47, 52-53
General Agreement on Trade in Services (GATS), 53
General Growth Properties, 286

Index
333

General Motors Corp., 96, 98, 216, 241, 286
Generally Accepted Accounting Principles (GAAP), 195, 196-199, 203, 214-215
Global Crossing, 11, 101, 198, 215, 216, 241, 286
Gramm-Leach-Bliley Act (GLB), 113-114
Graydon International, 161
guarantees
  corporate, 86, 125, 126-127, 261, 263-264
  personal, 86, 106, 107, 125, 126, 127, 132, 198, 261, 263
  personal, as part of credit application (sample), 150
  personal (sample), 264

hedge, 64, 65

income statement, 83, 84, 89, 199-202, 204, 206, 207, 216, 228, 229, 232-233
  pro forma analysis, 234-241
industry credit groups, 5, 14, 20, 27, 38, 129, 133-135
IndyMac Bancorp, 96, 241, 286
initial liquid reserve, 246
insurance, export, 48, 60-61
interest rate
  calculations, 109-112
  related concerns, 112-113
International Accounting Standards Board (IASB), 214
International Certified Credit Executive (ICCE), 6, 15, 48
International Chamber of Commerce (ICC), 274
International Financial Reporting Standards (IFRS), 57, 195, 214-215
international risk, 48, 49-50, 56-57
  bank liquidity and bank capital adequacy, 50, 53-54

country, 49-50, 55-56, 57
cultural, 50, 51-52, 55
economic, 56
foreign exchange, 54-55, 61-65
language, 50, 51-52, 55
legal, 50, 52-53, 55
political, 50, 55, 56, 57, 60
social, 50, 53, 55, 56
international trade
  export credit insurance, 48, 60-61
  export letters of credit, 58-60
  foreign company analysis, 56-58
  foreign exchange risk, 54-55, 61-65
  risk, 49-56
Internet, 20, 88, 134, 151, 156, 179, 316
inventory, 81, 105, 178, 203-204, 204-205, 228, 230, 271, 273, 292, 293, 303-304
  carrying period ratio, 205, 209, 210, 231
  floor-plan, 261
  valuation, 215
investigation. *See* credit investigation
invoices, 40, 59, 112, 114, 175, 179, 183, 184, 187, 188, 274, 275, 293, 305, 309

job specifications, 7-13, 31-34

Lambda Index, 245-248
language risk, 50, 51-52, 55
legal entity/name, 126-127
legal risk (international), 50, 52-53, 55
legislation (Chapter 5),
  Clayton Act, 99
  consumer credit, 103-104
  ECOA and Regulation B, 104-106, 141, 150
  Fair Credit Billing Act, 108
  FCRA, 106-107, 161
  FDCPA, 107

Federal Trade Commission Act, 100
GLB, 113-114
Law of Usury, 108-113
Prompt Payment Act, 114-115
Red Flags Rules, 102-103
Robinson-Patman Act, 100-101
Sherman Act, 99
SOX, 12, 23, 89, 101-102, 198
Truth in Lending Act
    and Regulation Z, 107-108
Lehman Brothers, 11, 96, 241, 286
letters of credit (Chapter 11), 21, 37,
    76, 86, 125, 178, 259, 264,
    265, 273-277
documentary, 58
documentation discrepancies,
    58-60
export, 58-61, 135, 178, 275-276
problems, 59, 276-277
standby, 132, 178, 274-275
standby (sample), 275
leveraged buyouts (LBOs)
    (Chapter 10), 228, 312
analysis, 234-241
application of cash flow model,
    235-236
assessing credit quality, 240-241
calculating present value, 236-238
qualitative concerns, 238-239
leveraged cash out (LCO), 238
liens, 76, 86, 109, 125, 129, 157,
    159, 160, 161, 178, 261, 263,
    264-265, 267-268, 271, 272-
    273, 292, 303, 304
searches, 37, 86, 267
limited liability corporation (LLC),
    127
liquidation, 216, 271, 287
case study, 296-299
in Chapter 7, 287, 290-299
in Chapter 11, 288
priorities of claims, 292-296

liquidity
bank, 53-54
problem, 210, 212
ratios, 203-204, 209, 245-248
litigation, 52-53, 87, 131, 161,
    185, 197-199
lockbox system, 36, 65, 173-174, 183
Lyondell Chemical Company, 286

macroeconomic forces, 135
market forces, 64
market value, 96, 215-217, 245,
    249, 271
ratios, 243
Maslow's hierarchy of needs, 35
mechanic's liens, 86, 261, 264-265
MF Global Holdings Ltd., 286
monthly statements, 87, 183
Moody's, 83, 129, 143, 153, 203
Morris, Robert, 130, 284
motivation, 34-37

National Association of Credit
    Management (NACM),
    4, 13-15, 57, 130
affiliates, 14-16, 27, 38, 129, 217,
    273
Business Credit Reports, 129
Canons of Business Credit Ethics,
    4, 5
certification/designation, 6, 14,
    15, 35, 48
code of ethics, 5
Credit Managers' Index (CMI), 185
education, 14-15, 217, 273
goals of, 14
National Trade Credit Report
    (NTCR), 161
National Conference of
    Commissioners on Uniform
    State Laws (NCCUSL), 266
NINJA loan, 245
North Atlantic Free Trade Agree-
    ment (NAFTA), 47, 52-53

Index

notes, 87, 109, 112

off-balance sheet financing, 215
online payment systems, 180
open account terms, 20, 58, 87, 111,
112, 174, 175-177, 260-261,
309
oral account discussion, 105, 134, 135
organization chart, 31-32
functional, 31
product, 32
out-of-court workout, 315-316
outsourcing, 26, 36, 37-38, 188

PACER, 303-304, 316
Pacific Gas and Electric Co., 286
payables deferral period ratio,
204, 209
payment history, 132-133, 134, 137,
140, 155, 156, 157, 158-159,
161, 163
pension liabilities, 287, 294
percentage bad debt, 28, 30
personal property,
261, 262-263, 265, 266, 267
personal visits, 20, 87, 127, 184
pledge, 22, 86, 125, 262
political risk, 50, 55, 56, 57, 60
Popham, Estelle, 4, 7
prearranged bankruptcy, 302
prediction models, bankruptcy, 314
preferences, 271, 287, 311-312
prepackaged bankruptcy, 301-302
price discrimination. *See* antitrust
regulation
prime rate, 113
principles for the exchange of
credit information, 130, 131
priorities of liquidation, 292-296
process-related focal points, 39-40
processing credit applications
establishing controls, 125-126
legal form of debtor entity,
126-127
limiting the investigation, 127-128

sources of information, 128-129
professional certification, 6, 15
profit margin ratio, 207, 209
profitability ratios, 207-208, 209
Prompt Payment Act, 114-115
proof of claim, 305
sample, 306-308
Public Access to Court Electronic
Records (PACER), 303-304,
316
purchase money security interest
(PMSI), 272-273

qualified opinion, 197
quick ratio, 204, 209
quotes, 63

ratios (Chapter 9, Chapter 10),
analysis, 40, 157, 203-208, 209
asset management, 204-206, 209
cash flow statement, 233-234
debt management, 206-207, 209
financial, 314
influences on (DuPont Analysis),
210-211
liquidity, 203-204, 209, 245-248
market value, 243
price earnings, 240, 243
profitability, 207-208, 209
summary, 208, 209
real estate valuation, 241, 244-245
real property, 262
receivables portfolio analysis, 82-83
reciprocal trade companies (RTCs),
178
reclamation, 304
Red Flags Rules (FTC), 102-103
reengineering credit, 39-40
Refco, Inc., 286
references
bank, 57-58, 86, 130-132, 161
trade, 132-133
Regulation B (ECOA), 104-106,
141, 150

Regulation Z, 107-108
regulations (Chapter 5)
   antitrust, 99-101
   federal, 101-108, 113-115, 141,
      150, 161, 198
   international, 52-53
remedies for creditors, 270-271
reorganization, Chapter 11, 299-310
restructuring (corporate), 135
return on assets (ROA) ratio,
   208, 209
return on equity (ROE) ratio,
   208, 209
   DuPont equations, 210-211
revenue recognition, 216
risk, 261-265, 273-277, 313
   See also international risk
Risk Management Associates
   (RMA), 130, 203, 284
   general figure ranges, 131
Robinson-Patman Act, 100-101

"S" corporation, 127
salaries in credit, 35, 36-37, 88
sales department, 33, 77, 184,
   186, 187
Sarbanes-Oxley Act of 2002 (SOX),
   12, 23, 89, 101-102, 198
seasonal datings, 179
secured credit arrangements
   (Chapter 11), 259
   Article 9 of the UCC, 266-273
   financing situations, 260-261
   guarantees, 263-264
   letters of credit, 264, 273-277
   mechanic's liens, 264-265
   personal property, 262-263
   real property, 262
   risk reduction, 261-265
   trade acceptances, 265
   Uniform Commercial Code,
      265-273
Securities and Exchange
   Commission (SEC),
      101-102, 129, 198, 242

security agreement, 267, 268,
   270, 272
September 11, 2001, 217
Sherman Act, 99
short payments, 40, 187-188
social risk, 50, 53, 55, 56
sources/uses of funds, 229-230, 234
Southcross Holdings LP, 301
special terms, 177-179
spot rate, 62-63, 65
Standard & Poor's, 55, 83, 129, 143,
   203
standard deviation, 246-247
standard industrial classification
   (SIC), 137, 157, 159
standby letter of credit, 132, 178,
   274-275
Statement of Principles for the
   Exchange of Credit
   Information, 131
stock valuation, 241-244
   based on unique visitors
      to websites, 244
stockholders, 53, 126, 127,
   242, 295-296, 299
stored value cards, 179, 180
strategic planning, 76-77, 78, 80, 85
Strong, Edward, 7-8
Sunbeam, 101, 198
superpriority claim, 296, 302
sustainable growth, 212-214

tariffs, 52, 64
tax, 295
   returns, 199
technology, 136, 172-173, 183, 316
   focal points, 38-40
   issues, 217
telephone collections, 184
terms of sale(s) (Chapter 8),
   30, 58, 61, 86, 173-181, 205
Texaco, Inc., 286
Thornberg Mortgage, Inc., 286
times interest earned ratio, 206, 209

Index

total quality management (TQM), 39-40
trade acceptances, 265
trade concerns (international), 135
trade credit terms, 173-181
  cash, 174-175
  electronic payment arrangements, 179-181
  open account, 175-177
  special, 177-179
trade references, 132-133
TransUnion, 129, 161, 162, 163
Troubled Asset Relief Program (TARP), 96
Truth in Lending Act, 107-108

Uniform Commercial Code (UCC), 21, 76, 157, 160, 161, 178, 260, 263, 265-273
  Article 9 (Secured Transactions), 266-273
  UCC-1 Financing Statement (sample), 269
Uniform Customs and Practice for Documentary Credits (UCP 500/UCP 600), 58, 274-277
unqualified opinion, 197
unsecured claims, 291, 294-295, 296, 298
U.S. Bankruptcy Courts, 129, 289, 300, 316
U.S. Department of Commerce, 52, 129
U.S. Trustee Program, 290
usury, 108-113

VantageScore, 163

Wage Earner Plan, 288-289
wages, 294
Washington Mutual, 96, 241, 286
wire transfers, 174, 179, 180

working capital, 82, 209-210, 231, 249, 309
World Trade Organization (WTO), 53
WorldCom, 11, 101, 198, 215, 216, 241, 286
written industry credit reports, 133-134

Xerox Corporation, 216

Z-score, 248-250, 284, 314
zero working capital, 209-210

CPSIA information can be obtained
at www.ICGtesting.com
Printed in the USA
FFOW01n1927160418
46265433-47716FF